Walker & Boutall ph. sc.

William Shakespeare

from the "Droeshout" painting now in the
Shakespeare Memorial Gallery at Stratford-on-Avon.

A LIFE

OF

WILLIAM SHAKESPEARE

BY

SIDNEY LEE

WITH PORTRAITS AND FACSIMILES

New York

THE MACMILLAN COMPANY

LONDON: MACMILLAN & CO., Ltd.

1901

Norwood Press
J. S. Cushing & Co. — Berwick & Smith
Norwood Mass. U.S.A.

PREFACE

————◆◆————

THIS work is based on the article on Shakespeare which I contributed last year to the fifty-first volume of the 'Dictionary of National Biography.' But the changes and additions which the article has undergone during my revision of it for separate publication are so numerous as to give the book a title to be regarded as an independent venture. In its general aims, however, the present life of Shakespeare endeavours loyally to adhere to the principles that are inherent in the scheme of the 'Dictionary of National Biography.' I have endeavoured to set before my readers a plain and practical narrative of the great dramatist's personal history as concisely as the needs of clearness and completeness would permit. I have sought to provide students of Shakespeare with a full record of the duly attested facts and dates of their master's career. I have avoided merely æsthetic criticism. My estimates of the value of Shakespeare's plays and poems are intended solely to fulfil the obligation that lies on the biographer of indicating succinctly the character of the successive labours, which were woven into the texture of his hero's life. Æsthetic studies of Shakespeare abound, and to increase their number is a work of supererogation. But Shakespearean literature, as far as it is known to me, still lacks a book that shall supply within a brief compass an exhaustive and well-arranged statement of the facts of Shakespeare's career, achievement, and reputation, that shall reduce conjecture to the smallest dimensions consistent with coherence, ɩ   shall give verifiable references to all the origina sources of information. After studying Elizabethan literature, history, and bibliography for more than eighteen years, I believed that I might, without exposing myself to a charge of presumption, attempt something in the way of filling this gap, and that I might be able to supply, at least tentatively, a guide-book to Shakespeare's life and work that should be, within its limits, complete and trustworthy. How far my belief was justified the readers of this volume will decide.

I cannot promise my readers any startling revelations. But my researches have enabled me to remove some ambiguities which puzzled my predecessors, and to throw light on one or two topics that have hitherto obscured the course of Shakespeare's career. Particulars that have not been before incorporated in Shakespeare's biography will be found in my treatment of the following subjects: the conditions under which 'Love's Labour's Lost' and the 'Merchant of Venice' were written; the references in Shakespeare's plays to his native town and county; his father's applications to the Heralds' College for coat-armour; his relations with Ben Jonson and the boy actors in 1601 ; the favour extended to his work by James I and his Court; the circumstances which led to the publication of the First Folio, and the history of the dramatist's portraits. I have somewhat expanded the notices of Shakespeare's financial affairs which have already appeared in the article in the 'Dictionary of National Biography,' and a few new facts will be found in my revised estimate of the poet's pecuniary position.

In my treatment of the sonnets I have pursued what I believe to be an original line of investigation. The strictly autobiographical interpretation that critics have of late placed on these poems compelled me, as Shakespeare's biographer, to submit them to a very narrow scrutiny. My conclusion is adverse to the claim of the sonnets to rank as autobiographical documents, but I have felt bound, out of respect to writers from whose views I dissent, to give in detail the evidence on which I base my judgment. Matthew Arnold sagaciously laid down the maxim that 'the criticism which alone can much help us for the future is a criticism which regards Europe as being for intellectual and artistic [1] purposes one great con-

---

[1] Arnold wrote 'spiritual,' but the change of epithet is needful to render the dictum thoroughly pertinent to the topic under consideration.

federation, bound to a joint action and working to a common result.' It is criticism inspired by this liberalising principle that is especially applicable to the vast sonnet-literature which was produced by Shakespeare and his contemporaries. It is criticism of the type that Arnold recommended that can alone lead to any accurate and profitable conclusion respecting the intention of the vast sonnet-literature of the Elizabethan era. In accordance with Arnold's suggestion, I have studied Shakespeare's sonnets comparatively with those in vogue in England, France, and Italy at the time he wrote. I have endeavoured to learn the view that was taken of such literary endeavours by contemporary critics and readers throughout Europe. My researches have covered a very small portion of the wide field. But I have gone far enough, I think, to justify the conviction that Shakespeare's collection of sonnets has no reasonable title to be regarded as a personal or autobiographical narrative.

In the Appendix (Sections III. and IV.) I have supplied a memoir of Shakespeare's patron, the Earl of Southampton, and an account of the Earl's relations with the contemporary world of letters. Apart from Southampton's association with the sonnets, he promoted Shakespeare's welfare at an early stage of the dramatist's career, and I can quote the authority of Malone, who appended a sketch of Southampton's history to his biography of Shakespeare (in the

'Variorum' edition of 1821), for treating a knowledge of Southampton's life as essential to a full
knowledge of Shakespeare's. I have also printed in
the Appendix a detailed statement of the precise circumstances under which Shakespeare's sonnets were
published by Thomas Thorpe in 1609 (Section v.),
and a review of the facts that seem to me to confute
the popular theory that Shakespeare was a friend and
protégé of William Herbert, third Earl of Pembroke,
who has been put forward quite unwarrantably as the
hero of the sonnets (Sections vi., vii., viii.).[1] I have
also included in the Appendix (Sections ix. and x.)
a survey of the voluminous sonnet-literature of the
Elizabethan poets between 1591 and 1597, with which
Shakespeare's sonnetteering efforts were very closely
allied, as well as a bibliographical note on a corresponding feature of French and Italian literature
between 1550 and 1600.

Since the publication of the article on Shakespeare in the 'Dictionary of National Biography,' I
have received from correspondents many criticisms
and suggestions which have enabled me to correct
some errors. But a few of my correspondents have
exhibited so ingenuous a faith in those forged docu-

[1] I have already published portions of the papers on Shakespeare's
relations with the Earls of Pembroke and Southampton in the *Fort-
nightly Review* (for February of this year) and in the *Cornhill Magazine*
(for April of this year), and I have to thank the proprietors of those
periodicals for permission to reproduce my material in this volume.

ments relating to Shakespeare and forged references to his works, which were promulgated chiefly by John Payne Collier more than half a century ago, that I have attached a list of the misleading records to my chapter on 'The Sources of Biographical Information' in the Appendix (Section I.). I believe the list to be fuller than any to be met with elsewhere.

The six illustrations which appear in this volume have been chosen on grounds of practical utility rather than of artistic merit. My reasons for selecting as the frontispiece the newly discovered 'Droeshout' painting of Shakespeare (now in the Shakespeare Memorial Gallery at Stratford-on-Avon) can be gathered from the history of the painting and of its discovery which I give on pages 288–90. I have to thank Mr. Edgar Flower and the other members of the Council of the Shakespeare Memorial at Stratford for permission to reproduce the picture. The portrait of Southampton in early life is now at Welbeck Abbey, and the Duke of Portland not only permitted the portrait to be engraved for this volume, but lent me the negative from which the plate has been prepared. The Committee of the Garrick Club gave permission to photograph the interesting bust of Shakespeare in their possession,[1] but, owing to the fact that it is moulded in black terra-cotta, no satisfactory negative could be obtained; the

---

[1] For an account of its history see p. 295.

engraving I have used is from a photograph of a
white plaster cast of the original bust, now in the
Memorial Gallery at Stratford. The five autographs
of Shakespeare's signature — all that exist of unquestioned authenticity — appear in the three remaining plates. The three signatures on the will have
been photographed from the original document at
Somerset House, by permission of Sir Francis Jeune,
President of the Probate Court; the autograph on
the deed of purchase by Shakespeare in 1613 of
the house in Blackfriars has been photographed
from the original document in the Guildhall Library,
by permission of the Library Committee of the City
of London; and the autograph on the deed of
mortgage relating to the same property, also dated
in 1613, has been photographed from the original
document in the British Museum, by permission of
the Trustees. Shakespeare's coat-of-arms and motto,
which are stamped on the cover of this volume, are
copied from the trickings in the margin of the draft-
grants of arms now in the Heralds' College.

The Baroness Burdett-Coutts has kindly given me
ample opportunities of examining the two peculiarly
interesting and valuable copies of the First Folio [1] in
her possession. Mr. Richard Savage, of Stratford-on-
Avon, the Secretary of the Birthplace Trustees, and
Mr. W. Salt Brassington, the Librarian of the Shakespeare Memorial at Stratford, have courteously re-

[1] See pp. 309, 311.

plied to the many inquiries that I have addressed to them verbally or by letter. Mr. Lionel Cust, the Director of the National Portrait Gallery, has helped me to estimate the authenticity of Shakespeare's portraits. I have also benefited, while the work has been passing through the press, by the valuable suggestions of my friends the Rev. H. C. Beeching and Mr. W. J. Craig, and I have to thank Mr. Thomas Seccombe for the zealous aid he has rendered me while correcting the final proofs.

October 12, 1898.

CONTENTS

I

PARENTAGE AND BIRTH

II

CHILDHOOD, EDUCATION, AND MARRIAGE

III

THE FAREWELL TO STRATFORD

IV

ON THE LONDON STAGE

V

EARLY DRAMATIC WORK

VI

THE FIRST APPEAL TO THE READING PUBLIC

VII

THE SONNETS AND THEIR LITERARY HISTORY

VIII

THE BORROWED CONCEITS OF THE SONNETS

IX

THE PATRONAGE OF THE EARL OF SOUTHAMPTON

X

THE SUPPOSED STORY OF INTRIGUE IN THE SONNETS

XI

THE DEVELOPMENT OF DRAMATIC POWER

XII

THE PRACTICAL AFFAIRS OF LIFE

XIII

MATURITY OF GENIUS

XIV

THE HIGHEST THEMES OF TRAGEDY

XV

THE LATEST PLAYS

XVI

THE CLOSE OF LIFE

XVII

SURVIVORS AND DESCENDANTS

XVIII

AUTOGRAPHS, PORTRAITS, AND MEMORIALS

XIX

BIBLIOGRAPHY

XX

POSTHUMOUS REPUTATION

XXI

GENERAL ESTIMATE

APPENDIX

I

THE SOURCES OF BIOGRAPHICAL KNOWLEDGE

II

THE BACON-SHAKESPEARE CONTROVERSY

III

THE YOUTHFUL CAREER OF THE EARL OF SOUTHAMPTON

IV

THE EARL OF SOUTHAMPTON AS A LITERARY PATRON

V

THE TRUE HISTORY OF THOMAS THORPE AND 'MR. W. H.'

X

BIBLIOGRAPHICAL NOTE ON THE SONNET IN FRANCE, 1550–1600

LIST OF ILLUSTRATIONS

WILLIAM SHAKESPEARE

—◆—

I

PARENTAGE AND BIRTH

SHAKESPEARE came of a family whose surname was
borne through the middle ages by residents in very
Distribu-
tion of the
name.   many parts of England — at Penrith in
Cumberland, at Kirkland and Doncaster in
Yorkshire, as well as in nearly all the
midland counties. The surname had originally a
martial significance, implying capacity in the wield-
ing of the spear.[1] Its first recorded holder is John
Shakespeare, who in 1279 was living at 'Freyndon,'
perhaps Frittenden, Kent.[2] The great mediæval
guild of St. Anne at Knowle, whose members included the leading inhabitants of Warwickshire, was
joined by many Shakespeares in the fifteenth century.[3]

---

[1] Camden, *Remains*, ed. 1605, p. 111; Verstegan, *Restitution*, 1605.
[2] *Plac. Cor.* 7 Edw. I, Kanc.; cf. *Notes and Queries*, 1st ser. xi. 122.
[3] Cf. the *Register of the Guild of St. Anne at Knowle*, ed. Bickley,
1894.

In the sixteenth and seventeenth centuries the surname is found far more frequently in Warwickshire
than elsewhere.   The archives of no less than twenty-
four towns and villages there contain notices of
Shakespeare families in the sixteenth century, and
as many as thirty-four Warwickshire towns or villages
were inhabited by Shakespeare families in the seventeenth century.   Among them all William was a
common Christian name.   At Rowington, twelve
miles to the north of Stratford, and in the same
hundred of Barlichway, one of the most prolific
Shakespeare families of Warwickshire resided in the
sixteenth century, and no less than three Richard
Shakespeares of Rowington, whose extant wills were
proved respectively in 1560, 1591, and 1614, were
fathers of sons called William.   At least one other
William Shakespeare was during the period a resident in Rowington.   As a consequence, the poet has
been more than once credited with achievements
which rightly belong to one or other of his numerous
contemporaries who were identically named.

The poet's ancestry cannot be defined with absolute certainty.   The poet's father, when applying for
The poet's a grant of arms in 1596, claimed that his
ancestry.   grandfather (the poet's great-grandfather)
received for services rendered in war a grant of land
in Warwickshire from Henry VII.[1]   No precise confirmation of this pretension has been discovered, and
it may be, after the manner of heraldic genealogy,
fictitious.   But there is a probability that the poet

[1] See p. 189.

came of good yeoman stock, and that his ancestors to the fourth or fifth generation were fairly substantial landowners.[1]   Adam Shakespeare, a tenant by military service of land at Baddesley Clinton in 1389, seems to have been great-grandfather of one Richard Shakespeare who held land at Wroxhall in Warwickshire during the first thirty-four years (at least) of the sixteenth century.   Another Richard Shakespeare who is conjectured to have been nearly akin to the Wroxhall family was settled as a farmer at Snitterfield, a village four miles to the north of Stratford-on-Avon, in 1528.[2]   It is probable that he was the poet's grandfather.   In 1550 he was renting a messuage and land at Snitterfield of Robert Arden; he died at the close of 1560, and on February 10 of the next year letters of administration of his goods, chattels, and debts were issued to his son John by the Probate Court at Worcester.   His goods were valued at 35l. 17s.[3]   Besides the son John, Richard of Snitterfield certainly had a son Henry; while a Thomas Shakespeare, a considerable landholder at

[1] Cf. *Times*, October 14, 1895; *Notes and Queries*, 8th ser. viii. 501; articles by Mrs. Stopes in *Genealogical Magazine*, 1897.

[2] Cf. Halliwell-Phillipps, *Outlines of the Life of Shakespeare*, 1887, ii. 207.

[3] The purchasing power of money was then eight times what it is now, and this and other sums mentioned should be multiplied by eight to compare them with modern currency (see p. 197 *n*).   The letters of administration in regard to Richard Shakespeare's estate are in the district registry of the Probate Court at Worcester, and were printed in full by Mr. Halliwell-Phillipps in his *Shakespeare's Tours* (privately issued 1887), pp. 44–5.   They do not appear in any edition of Mr. Halliwell-Phillipps's *Outlines*.   Certified extracts appeared in *Notes and Queries*, 8th ser. xii. 463–4.

Snitterfield between 1563 and 1583, whose parentage
is undetermined, may have been a third son. The son
Henry remained all his life at Snitterfield, where he
engaged in farming with gradually diminishing success ; he died in embarrassed circumstances in December 1596. John, the son who administered Richard's
estate, was in all likelihood the poet's father.

About 1551 John Shakespeare left Snitterfield,
which was his birthplace, to seek a career in the
The poet's   neighbouring borough of Stratford-on-Avon.
father.   There he soon set up as a trader in all
manner of agricultural produce. Corn, wool, malt,
meat, skins, and leather were among the commodities
in which he dealt. Documents of a somewhat later
date often describe him as a glover. Aubrey, Shakespeare's first biographer, reported the tradition that he
was a butcher. But though both designations doubtless indicated important branches of his business,
neither can be regarded as disclosing its full extent.
The land which his family farmed at Snitterfield
supplied him with his varied stock-in-trade. As long
as his father lived he seems to have been a frequent
visitor to Snitterfield, and, like his father and brothers,
he was until the date of his father's death occasionally
designated a farmer or 'husbandman' of that place.
But it was with Stratford-on-Avon that his life was
mainly identified.

In April 1552 he was living there in Henley Street,
a thoroughfare leading to the market town of Henley-
in-Arden, and he is first mentioned in the borough
records as paying in that month a fine of twelve-

pence for having a dirt-heap in front of his house. His frequent appearances in the years that follow as either plaintiff or defendant in suits heard in the local court of record for the recovery of small debts suggest that he was a keen man of business. In early life he prospered in trade, and in October 1556 purchased two freehold tenements at Stratford — one, with a garden, in Henley Street (it adjoins that now known as the poet's birthplace), and the other in Greenhill Street with a garden and croft. Thenceforth he played a prominent part in municipal affairs. In 1557 he was elected an ale-taster, whose duty it was to test the quality of malt liquors and bread. About the same time he was elected a burgess or town councillor, and in September 1558, and again on October 6, 1559, he was appointed one of the four petty constables by a vote of the jury of the court-leet. Twice — in 1559 and 1561 — he was chosen one of the affeerors — officers appointed to determine the fines for those offences which were punishable arbitrarily, and for which no express penalties were prescribed by statute. In 1561 he was elected one of the two chamberlains of the borough, an office of responsibility which he held for two years. He delivered his second statement of account to the corporation in January 1564. When attesting documents he occasionally made his mark, but there is evidence in the Stratford archives that he could write with facility; and he was credited with financial aptitude. The municipal accounts, which were checked by tallies and counters, were audited by him after he

His settlement at Stratford.

ceased to be chamberlain, and he more than once advanced small sums of money to the corporation.

With characteristic shrewdness he chose a wife of assured fortune — Mary, youngest daughter of Robert Arden, a wealthy farmer of Wilmcote in the parish of Aston Cantlowe, near Stratford. The Arden family

The poet's mother. in its chief branch, which was settled at Parkhall, Warwickshire, ranked with the most influential of the county. Robert Arden, a progenitor of that branch, was sheriff of Warwickshire and Leicestershire in 1438 (16 Hen. VI), and this sheriff's direct descendant, Edward Arden, who was himself high sheriff of Warwickshire in 1575, was executed in 1583 for alleged complicity in a Roman Catholic plot against the life of Queen Elizabeth.[1] John Shakespeare's wife belonged to a humbler branch of the family, and there is no trustworthy evidence to determine the exact degree of kinship between the two branches. Her grandfather, Thomas Arden, purchased in 1501 an estate at Snitterfield, which passed, with other property, to her father Robert; John Shakespeare's father, Richard, was one of this Robert Arden's Snitterfield tenants. By his first wife, whose name is not known, Robert Arden had seven daughters, of whom all but two married; John Shakespeare's wife seems to have been the youngest. Robert Arden's second wife, Agnes or Anne, widow of John Hill (*d.* 1545), a substantial farmer of Bearley, survived him; but by her he had no issue. When he died at the end of 1556, he owned a farmhouse at Wilmcote

---

[1] French, *Genealogica Shakespeareana*, pp. 458 seq.; cf. p. 191 *infra.*

and many acres, besides some hundred acres at Snitterfield, with two farmhouses which he let out to tenants. The post-mortem inventory of his goods, which was made on December 9, 1556, shows that he had lived in comfort; his house was adorned by as many as eleven 'painted cloths,' which then did duty for tapestries among the middle class. The exordium of his will, which was drawn up on November 24, 1556, and proved on December 16 following, indicates that he was an observant Catholic. For his two youngest daughters, Alice and Mary, he showed especial affection by nominating them his executors. Mary received not only 6l. 13s. 4d. in money, but the fee-simple of Asbies, his chief property at Wilmcote, consisting of a house with some fifty acres of land. She also acquired, under an earlier settlement, an interest in two messuages at Snitterfield.[1] But, although she was well provided with worldly goods, she was apparently without education; several extant documents bear her mark, and there is no proof that she could sign her name.

John Shakespeare's marriage with Mary Arden doubtless took place at Aston Cantlowe, the parish church of Wilmcote, in the autumn of 1557 (the church registers begin at a later date). On September 15, 1558, his first child, a daughter, Joan, was baptised in the church of Stratford. A second child, another daughter, Margaret, was baptised on December 2, 1562; but both these children died in infancy. The poet William, the first son and third child, was

---

[1] Halliwell-Phillipps, ii. 179.

born on April 22 or 23, 1564. The latter date is
generally accepted as his birthday, mainly (it would
appear) on the ground that it was the day
of his death. There is no positive evidence
on the subject, but the Stratford parish
registers attest that he was baptised on April 26.

The poet's birth and baptism.

Some doubt is justifiable as to the ordinarily
accepted scene of his birth. Of two adjoining houses
forming a detached building on the north
side of Henley Street, that to the east was
purchased by John Shakespeare in 1556, but there is
no evidence that he owned or occupied the house to
the west before 1575. Yet this western house has
been known since 1759 as the poet's birthplace, and
a room on the first floor is claimed as that in which
he was born.[1] The two houses subsequently came
by bequest of the poet's granddaughter to the family
of the poet's sister, Joan Hart, and while the eastern
tenement was let out to strangers for more than
two centuries, and by them converted into an inn,
the 'birthplace' was until 1806 occupied by the
Harts, who latterly carried on there the trade of
butcher. The fact of its long occupancy by
poet's collateral descendants accounts for the
fication of the western rather than the east
ment with his birthplace. Both houses
chased in behalf of subscribers to a pu
1846, and, after extensive restoration,
into a single domicile for the purp
museum. They were presente

Alleged birthplace.

[1] Cf. Halliwell-Phillipps.

alderman, a post which he retained till September 30 the following year.   In 1573 Alexander Webbe, the husband of his wife's sister Agnes, made him overseer of his will; in 1575 he bought two houses in Stratford, one of them doubtless the alleged birthplace in Henley Street; in 1576 he contributed twelvepence to the beadle's salary.   But after Michaelmas 1572 he took a less active part in municipal affairs; he grew irregular in his attendance at the council meetings, and signs were soon apparent that his luck had turned.   In 1578 he was unable to pay, with his colleagues, either the sum of fourpence for the relief of the poor or his contribution 'towards the furniture of three pikemen, two bellmen, and one archer' who were sent by the corporation to attend a muster of the trained bands of the county.

Meanwhile his family was increasing.   Four children besides the poet — three sons, Gilbert (baptised Oc...... 13, 1566), Richard (baptised March 11, 1574), and Edmund (baptised May 3, 1580), with a daughter Joan (baptised April 15, 1569) — reached maturity.   A daughter Ann was baptised September 28, 1571, and was buried on April 4, 1579. To meet his growing liabilities, the father borrowed money from his wife's kinsfolk, and he and his wife

Brothers and si-

visit Stratford is, on the other hand, conclusive proof that his religion was not that of the contemporary puritan, whose hostility to all forms of dramatic representations was one of his most persistent characteristics. The Elizabethan puritans, too, according to Guillim's *Display of Heraldrie* (1610), regarded coat-armour with abhorrence, yet John Shakespeare with his son made persistent application for a grant of arms to the College of Arms.   (Cf. *infra*, pp. 186 seq.)

mortgaged, on November 14, 1578, Asbies, her
valuable property at Wilmcote, for 40*l.* to Edmund
Lambert of Barton-on-the-Heath, who had married
her sister, Joan Arden. Lambert was to receive no
interest on his loan, but was to take the ' rents and
profits' of the estate. Asbies was thereby alienated
for ever. Next year, on October 15, 1579, John and
his wife made over to Robert Webbe, doubtless a
relative of Alexander Webbe, for the sum apparently
of 40*l.*, his wife's property at Snitterfield.[1]

John Shakespeare obviously chafed under the
humiliation of having parted, although as he hoped
The only temporarily, with his wife's property of
father's
financial Asbies, and in the autumn of 1580 he offered
difficulties. to pay off the mortgage; but his brother-in-
law, Lambert, retorted that other sums were owing,
and he would accept all or none. The negotiation,
which was the beginning of much litigation, thus
proved abortive. Through 1585 and 1586 a creditor,
John Brown, was embarrassingly importunate, and,
after obtaining a writ of distraint, Brown informed
the local court that the debtor had no goods on which
distraint could be levied.[2] On September 6, 1586,
John was deprived of his alderman's gown, on the
ground of his long absence from the council meetings.[3]

---

[1] The sum is stated to be 4*l.* in one document (Halliwell-Phillipps,
ii. 176) and 40*l.* in another (*ib.* p. 179); the latter is more likely to be
correct.   [2] *Ib.* ii. 238.

[3] Efforts recently made to assign the embarrassments of Shakespeare's father to another John Shakespeare of Stratford deserve little
attention. The second John Shakespeare or Shakspere (as his name is
usually spelt) came to Stratford as a young man in 1584, and was for ten
years a well-to-do shoemaker in Bridge Street, filling the office of Master

Happily John Shakespeare was at no expense for the education of his four sons. They were entitled to free tuition at the grammar school of Stratford, which was reconstituted on a mediæval foundation by Edward VI. The eldest son, William, probably entered the school in 1571, when Walter Roche was master, and perhaps he knew something of Thomas Hunt, who succeeded Roche in 1577. The instruction that he received was mainly confined to the Latin language and literature. From the Latin accidence, boys of the period, at schools of the type of that at Stratford, were led, through conversation books like the 'Sententiæ Pueriles' and Lily's grammar, to the perusal of such authors as Seneca, Terence, Cicero, Virgil, Plautus, Ovid, and Horace. The eclogues of the popular renaissance poet, Mantuanus, were often preferred to Virgil's for beginners. The rudiments of Greek were occasionally taught in Elizabethan grammar schools to very promising pupils; but such coincidences as have been detected between expressions in Greek plays and in Shakespeare seem due to accident, and not to any study, either at school or elsewhere, of the Athenian drama.[1]

Education.

of the Shoemakers' Company in 1592 — a certain sign of pecuniary stability. He left Stratford in 1594 (cf. Halliwell-Phillipps, ii. 137–40).

[1] James Russell Lowell, who noticed some close parallels between expressions of Shakespeare and those of the Greek tragedians, hazarded the suggestion that Shakespeare may have studied the ancient drama in a *Græcè et Latinè* edition. I believe Lowell's parallelisms to be no more than curious accidents — proofs of consanguinity of spirit, not of any indebtedness on Shakespeare's part. In the *Electra* of Sophocles, which is akin in its leading motive to *Hamlet*, the Chorus consoles Electra for the supposed death of Orestes with the same com-

Dr. Farmer enunciated in his 'Essay on Shakespeare's Learning' (1767) the theory that Shakespeare knew no language but his own, and owed whatever knowledge he displayed of the classics and of Italian and French literature to English translations. But several of the books in French and Italian whence Shakespeare derived the plots of his dramas — Belleforest's 'Histoires Tragiques,' Ser Giovanni's 'Il Pecorone,' and Cinthio's 'Hecatommithi,' for example

monplace argument as that with which Hamlet's mother and uncle seek to console him. In *Electra* are the lines 1171-3:

Θνητοῦ πέφυκας πατρός, Ἠλέκτρα, φρόνει·
Θνητὸς δ' Ὀρέστης· ὥστε μὴ λίαν στένε.
Πᾶσιν γὰρ ἡμῖν τοῦτ' ὀφείλεται παθεῖν

(*i.e.* 'Remember, Electra, your father whence you sprang is dead. Dead, too, is Orestes. Wherefore grieve not overmuch, for by all of us has this debt of suffering to be paid'). In *Hamlet* (I. ii. 72 seq.) are the familiar sentences:

> Thou know'st 'tis common ; all that live must die. . . .
> But you must know, your father lost a father;
> That father lost, lost his . . . But to persèver
> In obstinate condolement is a course
> Of impious stubbornness.

Cf. Sophocles's *Œdipus Coloneus*, 880 : Τοις τοι δικαίοις χα' βραχὺς νικᾷ μέγαν ('In a just cause the weak vanquishes the strong,' Jebb), and 2 *Henry VI*, iii. 233, 'Thrice is he armed that hath his quarrel just.' Shakespeare's 'prophetic soul' in *Hamlet* (I. v. 40) and the *Sonnets* (cvii. 1) may be matched by the πρόμαντις θυμός of Euripides's *Andromache*, 1075; and Hamlet's 'sea of troubles' (III. i. 59) by the κακῶν πέλαγος of Æschylus's *Persæ*, 443. Among all the creations of Shakespearean and Greek drama, Lady Macbeth and Æschylus's Clytemnestra, who 'in man's counsels bore no woman's heart' (γυναικὸς ἀνδρόβουλον ἐλπίζον κέαρ, *Agamemnon*, 11), most closely resemble each other. But a study of the points of resemblance attests no knowledge of Æschylus on Shakespeare's part, but merely the close community of tragic genius that subsisted between the two poets.

— were not accessible to him in English translations; and on more general grounds the theory of his ignorance is adequately confuted. A boy with Shakespeare's exceptional alertness of intellect, during whose schooldays a training in Latin classics lay within reach, could hardly lack in future years all means of access to the literature of France and Italy.

With the Latin and French languages, indeed, and with many Latin poets of the school curriculum, Shakespeare in his writings openly acknowledged his acquaintance. In 'Henry V' the dialogue in many scenes is carried on in French, which is grammatically accurate if not idiomatic. In the mouth of his schoolmasters, Holofernes in 'Love's Labour's Lost' and The poet's Sir Hugh Evans in 'Merry Wives of classical Windsor,' Shakespeare placed Latin phrases equipment. drawn directly from Lily's grammar, from the 'Sententiæ Pueriles,' and from 'the good old Mantuan.' The influence of Ovid, especially the 'Metamorphoses,' was apparent throughout his earliest literary work, both poetic and dramatic, and is discernible in the 'Tempest,' his latest play (v. i. 33 seq.). In the Bodleian Library there is a copy of the Aldine edition of Ovid's 'Metamorphoses' (1502) and on the title is the signature 'W^m. Sh^e.,' which experts have declared — not quite conclusively — to be a genuine autograph of the poet.[1] Ovid's Latin text was certainly not unfamiliar to him, but his closest adaptations of Ovid's 'Metamorphoses' often reflect the phraseology of the popular English version by

[1] Macray, *Annals of the Bodleian Library*, 1890, pp. 379 seq.

Arthur Golding, of which some seven editions were issued between 1565 and 1597. From Plautus Shakespeare drew the plot of the 'Comedy of Errors,' but it is just possible that Plautus's comedies, too, were accessible in English. Shakespeare had no title to rank as a classical scholar, and he did not disdain a liberal use of translations. His lack of exact scholarship fully accounts for the 'small Latin and less Greek' with which he was credited by his scholarly friend, Ben Jonson. But Aubrey's report that 'he understood Latin pretty well' need not be contested, and his knowledge of French may be estimated to have equalled his knowledge of Latin, while he doubtless possessed just sufficient acquaintance with Italian to enable him to discern the drift of an Italian poem or novel.[1]

Of the few English books accessible to him in his schooldays, the chief was the English Bible, either in the popular Genevan version, first issued in a complete form in 1560, or in the bishops' revision of 1568, which the Authorised Version of 1611 closely followed. References to scriptural characters and incidents are not conspicuous in Shakespeare's plays, but such as they are, they are drawn from all parts of the Bible, and indicate that general acquaintance with the narrative of both Old and New Testaments which a clever boy would be certain to acquire either in the schoolroom or at church on Sundays. Shakespeare quotes or adapts

Shake-
speare and
the Bible.

[1] Cf. Spencer Baynes, 'What Shakespeare learnt at School,' in *Shakespeare Studies*, 1894, pp. 147 seq.

biblical phrases with far greater frequency than he makes allusion to episodes in biblical history. But many such phrases enjoyed proverbial currency, and others which were more recondite were borrowed from Holinshed's 'Chronicles' and secular works whence he drew his plots. As a rule his use of scriptural phraseology, as of scriptural history, suggests youthful reminiscence and the assimilative tendency of the mind in a stage of early development rather than close and continuous study of the Bible in adult life.[1]

Shakespeare was a schoolboy in July 1575, when Queen Elizabeth made a progress through Warwickshire on a visit to her favourite, the Earl of Leicester, at his castle of Kenilworth. References have been detected in Oberon's vision in Shakespeare's 'Midsummer Night's Dream' (II. ii. 148–68) to the fantastic pageants and masques with which the Queen during her stay was entertained in Kenilworth Park. Leicester's residence was only fifteen miles from Stratford, and it is possible that Shakespeare went thither with his father to witness some of the open-air festivities; but two full descriptions which were published in 1576, in pamphlet form, gave Shakespeare knowledge of all that took place.[2] Shakespeare's opportunities of recreation outside Stratford were in any case restricted during his schooldays. His father's financial difficul-

---

[1] Bishop Charles Wordsworth, in his *Shakespeare's Knowledge and Use of the Bible* (4th ed. 1892), gives a long list of passages for which Shakespeare may have been indebted to the Bible. But the Bishop's deductions as to the strength of Shakespeare's piety are strained.

[2] See p. 160 *infra*.

ties grew steadily, and they caused his removal from
school at an unusually early age.   Probably in 1577,

With-   when he was thirteen, he was enlisted by his
drawal
from   father in an effort to restore his decaying for-
school.   tunes.   'I have been told heretofore,' wrote
Aubrey, 'by some of the neighbours that when he was a
boy he exercised his father's trade,' which, according to
the writer, was that of a butcher.   It is possible that
John's ill-luck at the period compelled him to confine
himself to this occupation, which in happier days
formed only one branch of his business.   His son may
have been formally apprenticed to him.   An early Stratford tradition describes him as 'a butcher's apprentice.' [1]
'When he kill'd a calf,' Aubrey proceeds less convincingly, ' he would doe it in a high style and make a
speech.   There was at that time another butcher's
son in this towne, that was held not at all inferior to
him for a naturall witt, his acquaintance, and coeta-
nean, but dyed young.'

At the end of 1582 Shakespeare, when little more
than eighteen and a half years old, took a step which

The poet's was little calculated to lighten his father's
marriage.   anxieties.   He married.   His wife, according to the inscription on her tombstone, was his
senior by eight years.   Rowe states that she ' was the
daughter of one Hathaway, said to have been a substantial yeoman in the neighbourhood of Stratford.'

On September 1, 1581, Richard Hathaway, 'husbandman ' of Shottery, a hamlet in the parish of Old

---

[1] Notes of John Dowdall, a tourist in Warwickshire in 1693
(published in 1838).

Stratford, made his will, which was proved on July 9, 1582, and is now preserved at Somerset House.

Richard Hathaway of Shottery. His house and land, 'two and a half virgates,' had been long held in copyhold by his family, and he died in fairly prosperous circumstances. His wife Joan, the chief legatee, was directed to carry on the farm with the aid of her eldest son, Bartholomew, to whom a share in its proceeds was assigned. Six other children — three sons and three daughters — received sums of money; Agnes, the eldest daughter, and Catherine, the second daughter, were each allotted 6l. 13s. 4d., 'to be paid at the day of her marriage,' a phrase common in wills

Anne Hathaway. of the period. Anne and Agnes were in the sixteenth century alternative spellings of the same Christian name; and there is little doubt that the daughter 'Agnes' of Richard Hathaway's will became, within a few months of Richard Hathaway's death, Shakespeare's wife.

Anne Hathaway's cottage. The house at Shottery, now known as Anne Hathaway's cottage, and reached from Stratford by field-paths, undoubtedly once formed part of Richard Hathaway's farmhouse, and, despite numerous alterations and renovations, still preserves many features of a thatched farmhouse of the Elizabethan period. The house remained in the Hathaway family till 1838, although the male line became extinct in 1746. It was purchased in behalf of the public by the Birthplace trustees in 1892.

No record of the solemnisation of Shakespeare's marriage survives. Although the parish of Stratford

included Shottery, and thus both bride and bridegroom were parishioners, the Stratford parish register
is silent on the subject. A local tradition, which
seems to have come into being during the present
century, assigns the ceremony to the neighbouring
hamlet or chapelry of Luddington, of which neither
the chapel nor parish registers now exist. But one
important piece of documentary evidence directly
bearing on the poet's matrimonial venture is accessible.
In the registry of the bishop of the diocese (Worcester)
a deed is extant wherein Fulk Sandells and John
Richardson, 'husbandmen of Stratford,' bound themselves in the bishop's consistory court, on November
28, 1582, in a surety of 40*l.*, to free the bishop of all
liability should a lawful impediment — 'by reason of
The bond   any precontract' [*i.e.* with a third party] or
against
impedi-   consanguinity — be subsequently disclosed to
ments.   imperil the validity of the marriage, then in
contemplation, of William Shakespeare with Anne
Hathaway. On the assumption that no such impediment was known to exist, and provided that Anne
obtained the consent of her 'friends,' the marriage
might proceed 'with once asking of the bannes of
matrimony betwene them.'

Bonds of similar purport, although differing in
significant details, are extant in all diocesan registries
of the sixteenth century. They were obtainable on
the payment of a fee to the bishop's commissary, and
had the effect of expediting the marriage ceremony
while protecting the clergy from the consequences of
any possible breach of canonical law. But they were not

common, and it was rare for persons in the comparatively humble position in life of Anne Hathaway and
young Shakespeare to adopt such cumbrous formalities
when there was always available the simpler, less expensive, and more leisurely method of marriage by
'thrice asking of the banns.' Moreover, the wording
of the bond which was drawn before Shakespeare's
marriage differs in important respects from that
adopted in all other known examples.[1] In the latter
it is invariably provided that the marriage shall not
take place without the consent of the parents or
governors of both bride and bridegroom. In the case
of the marriage of an 'infant' bridegroom the formal
consent of his parents was absolutely essential to
strictly regular procedure, although clergymen might
be found who were ready to shut their eyes to the
facts of the situation and to run the risk of solemnis-
ing the marriage of an 'infant' without inquiry as to
the parents' consent. The clergyman who united
Shakespeare in wedlock to Anne Hathaway was
obviously of this easy temper. Despite the circumstance that Shakespeare's bride was of full age and he
himself was by nearly three years a minor, the Shakespeare bond stipulated merely for the consent of the
bride's 'friends,' and ignored the bridegroom's parents altogether. Nor was this the only irregularity
in the document. In other pre-matrimonial covenants

---

[1] These conclusions are drawn from an examination of like documents in the Worcester diocesan registry. Many formal declarations
of consent on the part of parents to their children's marriages are also
extant there among the sixteenth-century archives.

of the kind the name either of the bridegroom himself or of the bridegroom's father figures as one of the
two sureties, and is mentioned first of the two. Had the
usual form been followed, Shakespeare's father would
have been the chief party to the transaction in behalf
of his 'infant' son. But in the Shakespeare bond
the sole sureties, Sandells and Richardson, were farmers of Shottery, the bride's native place. Sandells
was a 'supervisor' of the will of the bride's father,
who there describes him as 'my trustie friende and
neighbour.'

The prominence of the Shottery husbandmen in
the negotiations preceding Shakespeare's marriage
suggests the true position of affairs. Sandells and
Richardson, representing the lady's family, doubtless
secured the deed on their own initiative, so that
Shakespeare might have small opportunity of evad-
ing a step which his intimacy with their friend's
daughter had rendered essential to her reputation.
The wedding probably took place, without the consent of the bridegroom's parents, — it may be without
their knowledge, — soon after the signing of the
deed. Within six months — in May 1583 — a daugh-
Birth of a   ter was born to the poet, and was baptised
daughter.   in the name of Susanna at Stratford parish
church on the 26th.

Shakespeare's apologists have endeavoured to
show that the public betrothal or formal 'troth-plight'
which was at the time a common prelude to a wedding carried with it all the privileges of marriage.
But neither Shakespeare's detailed description of a

betrothal[1] nor of the solemn verbal contract that ordinarily preceded marriage lends the contention

Formal
betrothal
probably
dispensed
with. much support.   Moreover, the whole circumstances of the case render it highly improbable that Shakespeare and his bride submitted to the formal preliminaries of a betrothal.   In that ceremony the parents of both contracting parties invariably played foremost parts, but the wording of the bond precludes the assumption that the bridegroom's parents were actors in any scene of the hurriedly planned drama of his marriage.

A difficulty has been imported into the narration of the poet's matrimonial affairs by the assumption of his identity with one 'William Shakespeare,' to whom, according to an entry in the Bishop of Worcester's register, a license was issued on November 27, 1582 (the day *before* the signing of the Hathaway bond), authorising his marriage with Anne Whateley of Temple Grafton.   The theory that the maiden name of Shakespeare's wife was Whateley is quite untenable, and it is unsafe to assume that the bishop's clerk, when making a note of the grant of the license in his register, erred so extensively as to write 'Anne

---

[1] *Twelfth Night*, act v. sc. i. ll. 160–4 :

> A contract of eternal bond of love,
> Confirm'd by mutual joinder of your hands,
> Attested by the holy close of lips,
> Strengthen'd by interchangement of your rings ;
> And all the ceremony of this compact
> Seal'd in my [*i.e.* the priest's] function by my testimony.

In *Measure for Measure* Claudio's offence is intimacy with the Lady Julia after the contract of betrothal and before the formality of marriage (cf. act i. sc. ii. l. 155, act iv. sc. i. l. 73).

Whateley of Temple Grafton' for 'Anne Hathaway of Shottery.' The husband of Anne Whateley cannot reasonably be identified with the poet. He was doubtless another of the numerous William Shakespeares who abounded in the diocese of Worcester. Had a license for the poet's marriage been secured on November 27,[1] it is unlikely that the Shottery husbandmen would have entered next day into a bond 'against impediments,' the execution of which might well have been demanded as a preliminary to the grant of a license but was wholly supererogatory after the grant was made.

[1] No marriage registers of the period are extant at Temple Grafton to inform us whether Anne Whateley actually married *her* William Shakespeare or who precisely the parties were. A Whateley family resided in Stratford, but there is nothing to show that Anne of Temple Grafton was connected with it. The chief argument against the conclusion that the marriage license and the marriage bond concerned different couples lies in the apparent improbability that two persons, both named William Shakespeare, should on two successive days not only be arranging with the Bishop of Worcester's official to marry, but should be involving themselves, whether on their own initiative or on that of their friends, in more elaborate and expensive forms of procedure than were habitual to the humbler ranks of contemporary society. But the Worcester diocese covered a very wide area, and was honeycombed with Shakespeare families of all degrees of gentility. The William Shakespeare whom Anne Whateley was licensed to marry may have been of a superior station, to which marriage by license was deemed appropriate. On the unwarranted assumption of the identity of the William Shakespeare of the marriage bond with the William Shakespeare of the marriage license, a romantic theory has been based to the effect that 'Anne Whateley of Temple Grafton,' believing herself to have a just claim to the poet's hand, secured the license on hearing of the proposed action of Anne Hathaway's friends, and hoped, by moving in the matter a day before the Shottery husbandmen, to insure Shakespeare's fidelity to his alleged pledges.

III

THE FAREWELL TO STRATFORD

ANNE HATHAWAY'S greater burden of years and the likelihood that the poet was forced into marrying her by her friends were not circumstances of happy augury. Although it is dangerous to read into Shakespeare's dramatic utterances allusions to his personal experience, the emphasis with which he insists that a woman should take in marriage an 'elder than herself,'[1] and that prenuptial intimacy is productive of 'barren hate, sour-ey'd disdain, and discord,' suggest a personal interpretation.[2]   To both these unpromising features was added, in the poet's case, the absence of a means of livelihood, and his course of life in the

---

[1] *Twelfth Night*, act ii. sc. iv. l. 29:

> Let still the woman take
> An elder than herself; so wears she to him,
> So sways she level in her husband's heart. . .

[2] *Tempest*, act iv. sc. i. ll. 15–22:

> If thou dost break her virgin knot before
> All sanctimonious ceremonies may
> With full and holy rite be minister'd,
> No sweet aspersion shall the heavens let fall
> To make this contract grow; but barren hate,
> Sour-ey'd disdain, and discord, shall bestrew
> The union of your bed with weeds so loathly
> That you shall hate it both.

years that immediately followed implies that he bore his domestic ties with impatience. Early in 1585 twins were born to him, a son (Hamnet) and a daughter (Judith); both were baptised on February 2. All the evidence points to the conclusion, which the fact that he had no more children confirms, that in the later months of the year (1585) he left Stratford, and that, although he was never wholly estranged from his family, he saw little of wife or children for eleven years. Between the winter of 1585 and the autumn of 1596 — an interval which synchronises with his first literary triumphs — there is only one shadowy mention of his name in Stratford records. In April 1587 there died Edmund Lambert, who held Asbies under the mortgage of 1578, and a few months later Shakespeare's name, as owner of a contingent interest, was joined to that of his father and mother in a formal assent given to an abortive proposal to confer on Edmund's son and heir, John Lambert, an absolute title to the estate on condition of his cancelling the mortgage and paying 20*l.* But the deed does not indicate that Shakespeare personally assisted at the transaction.[1]

Shakespeare's early literary work proves that while in the country he eagerly studied birds, flowers, and trees, and gained a detailed knowledge of horses and dogs. All his kinsfolk were farmers, and with them he doubtless as a youth practised many field sports. Sympathetic references to hawking, hunting, coursing, and angling abound in his early plays and

1 Halliwell-Phillipps, ii. 11–13.

poëms.[1] And his sporting experiences passed at times
beyond orthodox limits. A poaching adventure, according to a credible tradition, was the immediate
cause of his long severance from his native place. 'He
had,' wrote Rowe in 1709, 'by a misfortune common
enough to young fellows, fallen into ill company, and,
among them, some, that made a frequent practice of
deer-stealing, engaged him with them more than
once in robbing a park that belonged to Sir
Thomas Lucy of Charlecote near Stratford.
For this he was prosecuted by that gentleman, as he thought, somewhat too severely ; and, in
order to revenge that ill-usage, he made a ballad upon
him, and though this, probably the first essay of his
poetry, be lost, yet it is said to have been so very
bitter that it redoubled the prosecution against him
to that degree that he was obliged to leave his
business and family in Warwickshire and shelter
himself in London.' The independent testimony of
Archdeacon Davies, who was vicar of Saperton,
Gloucestershire, late in the seventeenth century, is to
the effect that Shakespeare 'was much given to all
unluckiness in stealing venison and rabbits, particularly from Sir Thomas Lucy, who had him oft
whipt, and sometimes imprisoned, and at last made
him fly his native county to his great advancement.'
The law of Shakespeare's day (5 Eliz. cap. 21)

Poaching at Charlecote.

[1] Cf. Ellacombe, *Shakespeare as an Angler*, 1883; J. E. Harting,
Ornithology of Shakespeare, 1872. The best account of Shakespeare's
knowledge of sport is given by the Right Hon. D. H. Madden in his
entertaining and at the same time scholarly *Diary of Master William
Silence : a Study of Shakespeare and Elizabethan Sport*, 1897.

punished deer-stealers with three months' imprisonment and the payment of thrice the amount of the
damage done.

The tradition has been challenged on the ground
that the Charlecote deer-park was of later date than
Unwar-   the sixteenth century. But Sir Thomas
ranted   Lucy was an extensive game-preserver,
doubts of
the tradi- and owned at Charlecote a warren in which
tion.   a few harts or does doubtless found an
occasional home. Samuel Ireland was informed
in 1794 that Shakespeare stole the deer, not from
Charlecote, but from Fulbroke Park, a few miles
off, and Ireland supplied in his 'Views on the
Warwickshire Avon,' 1795, an engraving of an old
farmhouse in the hamlet of Fulbroke, where he asserted that Shakespeare was temporarily imprisoned
after his arrest. An adjoining hovel was locally
known for some years as Shakespeare's 'deer-barn,'
but no portion of Fulbroke Park, which included the
site of these buildings (now removed), was Lucy's
property in Elizabeth's reign, and the amended
legend, which was solemnly confided to Sir Walter
Scott in 1828 by the owner of Charlecote, seems pure
invention.[1]

The ballad which Shakespeare is reported to have
fastened on the park gates of Charlecote does not, as
Rowe acknowledged, survive. No authenticity can
be allowed the worthless lines beginning 'A parliament member, a justice of peace,' which were repre-

[1] Cf. C. Holte Bracebridge, *Shakespeare no Poacher*, 1862; Lock-
hart, *Life of Scott*, vii. 123.

sented to be Shakespeare's on the authority of an old
man who lived near Stratford and died in 1703. But
such an incident as the tradition reveals has left a
distinct impress on Shakespearean drama. Justice
Justice   Shallow is beyond doubt a reminiscence of
Shallow.   the owner of Charlecote. According to
Archdeacon Davies of Saperton, Shakespeare's 'revenge was so great that' he caricatured Lucy as
'Justice Clodpate,' who was (Davies adds) represented
on the stage as 'a great man,' and as bearing, in
allusion to Lucy's name, 'three louses rampant for
his arms.' Justice Shallow, Davies's 'Justice Clodpate,' came to birth in the 'Second Part of Henry IV'
(1598), and he is represented in the opening scene of
the 'Merry Wives of Windsor' as having come from
Gloucestershire to Windsor to make a Star-Chamber
matter of a poaching raid on his estate. The 'three
luces hauriant argent' were the arms borne by the
Charlecote Lucys, and the dramatist's prolonged
reference in this scene to the 'dozen white luces'
on Justice Shallow's 'old coat' fully establishes
Shallow's identity with Lucy.

The poaching episode is best assigned to 1585,
but it may be questioned whether Shakespeare, on
The flight   fleeing from Lucy's persecution, at once
from Strat-   sought an asylum in London. William Bees-
ford.
              ton, a seventeenth-century actor, remem-
bered hearing that he had been for a time a country
schoolmaster 'in his younger years,' and it seems
possible that on first leaving Stratford he found some
such employment in a neighbouring village. The

suggestion that he joined, at the end of 1585, a band of youths of the district in serving in the Low Countries under the Earl of Leicester, whose castle of Kenilworth was within easy reach of Stratford, is based on an obvious confusion between him and others of his name.[1] The knowledge of a soldier's life which Shakespeare exhibited in his plays is no greater and no less than that which he displayed of almost all other spheres of human activity, and to assume that he wrote of all or of any from practical experience, unless the evidence be conclusive, is to underrate his intuitive power of realising life under almost every aspect by force of his imagination.

[1] Cf. W. J. Thoms, *Three Notelets on Shakespeare*, 1865, pp. 16 seq.

IV

ON THE LONDON STAGE

To London Shakespeare naturally drifted, doubtless trudging thither on foot during 1586, by way
of Oxford and High Wycombe.[1] Tradition

The jour-
ney to
London.

points to that as Shakespeare's favoured
route, rather than to the road by Banbury
and Aylesbury. Aubrey asserts that at Grendon
near Oxford, 'he happened to take the humour of
the constable in " Midsummer Night's Dream "'— by
which he meant, we may suppose, ' Much Ado about
Nothing ' — but there were watchmen of the Dogberry
type all over England, and probably at Stratford
itself. The Crown Inn (formerly 3 Cornmarket
Street) near Carfax, at Oxford, was long pointed out
as one of his resting-places.

To only one resident in London is Shakespeare
likely to have been known previously.[2] Richard

---

[1] Cf. Hales, *Notes on Shakespeare*, 1884, pp. 1–24.

[2] The common assumption that Richard Burbage, the chief actor with
whom Shakespeare was associated, was a native of Stratford is wholly
erroneous. Richard was born in Shoreditch, and his father came from
Hertfordshire. John Heming, another of Shakespeare's actor-friends
who has also been claimed as a native of Stratford, was beyond reason
able doubt born at Droitwich in Worcestershire. Thomas Greene, a

Field, a native of Stratford, and son of a friend of Shakespeare's father, had left Stratford in 1579 to serve an apprenticeship with Thomas Vautrollier, the London printer. Shakespeare and Field, who was made free of the Stationers' Company in 1587, were soon associated as author and publisher; but the theory that Field found work for Shakespeare in Vautrollier's printing-office is fanciful.[1] No more can be said for the attempt to prove that he obtained employment as a lawyer's clerk. In view of his general quickness of apprehension, Shakespeare's accurate use of legal terms, which deserves all the attention that has been paid it, may be attributable in part to his observation of the many legal processes in which his father was involved, and in part to early intercourse with members of the Inns of Court.[2]

Richard Field, his townsman.

Tradition and common-sense alike point to one of the only two theatres (The Theatre or The Curtain) that existed in London at the date of his arrival as an early scene of his regular occupation. The compiler of 'Lives of the Poets' (1753)[3] was the first to relate the story that

Theatrical employment.

popular comic actor at the Red Bull Theatre early in the seventeenth century, is conjectured to have belonged to Stratford on no grounds that deserve attention ; Shakespeare was in no way associated with him.

[1] Blades, *Shakspere and Typography*, 1872.

[2] Cf. Lord Campbell, *Shakespeare's Legal Acquirements*, 1859. Legal terminology abounded in all plays and poems of the period, *e.g.* Barnabe Barnes's *Sonnets*, 1593, and *Zepheria*, 1594 (see Appendix IX).

[3] Commonly assigned to Theophilus Cibber, but written by Robert Shiels and other hack-writers under Cibber's editorship.

his original connection with the playhouse was as holder of the horses of visitors outside the doors. According to the same compiler, the story was related by D'Avenant to Betterton; but Rowe, to whom Betterton communicated it, made no use of it. The two regular theatres of the time were both reached on horseback by men of fashion, and the owner of The Theatre, James Burbage, kept a livery stable at Smithfield. There is no inherent improbability in the tale. Dr. Johnson's amplified version, in which Shakespeare was represented as organising a service of boys for the purpose of tending visitors' horses, sounds apocryphal.

There is every indication that Shakespeare was speedily offered employment inside the playhouse. In 1587 the two chief companies of actors, claiming respectively the nominal patronage of the Queen and Lord Leicester, returned to London from a provincial tour, during which they visited Stratford. Two subordinate companies, one of which claimed the patronage of the Earl of Essex and the other that of Lord Stafford, also performed in the town during the same year. Shakespeare's friends may have called the attention of the strolling players to the homeless lad, rumours of whose search for employment about the London theatres had doubtless reached Stratford. A playhouse servitor. From such incidents seems to have sprung the opportunity which offered Shakespeare fame and fortune. According to Rowe's vague statement, 'he was received into the company then in being at first in a very mean rank.'

D

William Castle, the parish clerk of Stratford at the
end of the seventeenth century, was in the habit of
telling visitors that he entered the playhouse as a
servitor.   Malone recorded in 1780 a stage tradition
'that his first office in the theatre was that of
prompter's attendant,' or call-boy.   His intellectual
capacity and the amiability with which he turned
to account his versatile powers were probably soon
recognised, and thenceforth his promotion was
assured.

Shakespeare's earliest reputation was made as an
actor, and, although his work as a dramatist soon
The acting eclipsed his histrionic fame, he remained a
companies. prominent member of the actor's profession
till near the end of his life.   By an Act of Parliament of 1571 (14 Eliz. cap. 2), which was re-enacted
in 1596 (39 Eliz. cap. 4), players were under the
necessity of procuring a license to pursue their
calling from a peer of the realm or 'personage of
higher degree'; otherwise they were adjudged to be
of the status of rogues and vagabonds.   The Queen
herself and many Elizabethan peers were liberal in
the exercise of their licensing powers, and few actors
failed to secure a statutory license, which gave them a
rank of respectability, and relieved them of all risk
of identification with vagrants or 'sturdy beggars.'
From an early period in Elizabeth's reign licensed
actors were organised into permanent companies.   In
1587 and following years, besides three companies
of duly licensed boy-actors that were formed from
the choristers of St. Paul's Cathedral and the Chapel

Royal and from Westminster scholars, there were
in London at least six companies of fully licensed
adult actors; five of these were called after the noblemen to whom their members respectively owed their
licenses (viz. the Earls of Leicester, Oxford, Sussex,
and Worcester, and the Lord Admiral, Charles, lord
Howard of Effingham), and one of them whose actors
derived their license from the Queen was called the
Queen's Company.

The patron's functions in relation to the companies
seem to have been mainly confined to the grant
or renewal of the actors' licenses. Constant alterations of name, owing to the death or change from
other causes of the patrons, render it difficult to
trace with certainty each company's history. But
there seems no doubt that the most influential of
the companies named — that under the nominal
patronage of the Earl of Leicester — passed on his
death in September 1588 to the patronage of
Ferdinando Stanley, lord Strange, who became Earl
of Derby on September 25, 1592. When the Earl of
Derby died on April 16, 1594, his place as patron and
licenser was successively filled by Henry Carey, first
The Lord
Chamber-
lain's
company. lord Hunsdon, Lord Chamberlain (*d.* July 23,
1596), and by his son and heir, George
Carey, second lord Hunsdon, who himself
became Lord Chamberlain in March 1597. After
King James's succession in May 1603 the company
was promoted to be the King's players, and, thus advanced in dignity, it fully maintained the supremacy

which, under its successive titles, it had already long enjoyed.

It is fair to infer that this was the company that Shakespeare originally joined and adhered to through life. Documentary evidence proves that he was a member of it in December 1594; in May A member of the Lord Chamberlain's. 1603 he was one of its leaders. Four of its chief members — Richard Burbage, the greatest tragic actor of the day, John Heming, Henry Condell, and Augustine Phillips — were among Shakespeare's lifelong friends. Under this company's auspices, moreover, Shakespeare's plays first saw the light. Only two of the plays claimed for him — 'Titus Andronicus' and '3 Henry VI' — seem to have been performed by other companies (the Earl of Sussex's men in the one case, and the Earl of Pembroke's in the other).

When Shakespeare became a member of the company it was doubtless performing at The Theatre, the playhouse in Shoreditch which James Burbage, the father of the great actor, Richard Burbage, had constructed in 1576; it abutted on the Finsbury Fields, and stood outside the City's boundaries. The only other London playhouse then in existence — the Curtain in Moorfields — was near at hand; its name survives in Curtain Road, Shoreditch. But at an early date The London theatres. in his acting career Shakespeare's company sought and found new quarters. While known as Lord Strange's men, they opened on February 19, 1592, a third London theatre, called the Rose, which Philip Henslowe, the speculative theatrical manager, had erected on the Bankside, Southwark. At the date of the inauguration of the Rose Theatre Shakespeare's company was temporarily allied with another company, the Admiral's men, who numbered the great actor Edward Alleyn among them. Alleyn for a few months undertook the direction of the amalgamated companies, but they quickly parted, and no further opportunity was offered Shakespeare of enjoying professional relations with Alleyn. The Rose Theatre was doubtless the earliest scene of Shakespeare's pronounced successes alike as actor and dramatist. Subsequently for a short time in 1594 he frequented the stage of another new theatre at Newington Butts, and between 1595 and 1599 the older stages of the Curtain and of The Theatre in Shoreditch. The Curtain remained open till the Civil Wars, although its vogue after 1600 was eclipsed by that of younger rivals. In 1599 Richard Burbage and his brother Cuthbert demolished the old building of The Theatre and built, mainly out of the materials of the dismantled fabric, the famous theatre called the Globe on the Bankside. It was octagonal in shape, and built of wood, and doubtless Shakespeare described it (rather than the Curtain) as 'this wooden O' in the opening chorus of 'Henry V' (l. 13). After 1599 the Globe was mainly occupied by Shakespeare's company, and in its profits he acquired an important share. From the date of its inauguration until the poet's retirement, the Globe — which quickly won the first place among London theatres — seems to have been the sole playhouse with

which Shakespeare was professionally associated. The
equally familiar Blackfriars Theatre, which was created
out of a dwelling-house by James Burbage, the actor's
father, at the end of 1596, was for many years afterwards leased out to the company of boy-actors known
as 'the Queen's Children of the Chapel'; it was not
occupied by Shakespeare's company until December
1609 or January 1610, when his acting days were
nearing their end.[1]

In London Shakespeare resided near the theatres.
According to a memorandum by Alleyn (which
Malone quoted), he lodged in 1596 near
'the Bear Garden in Southwark.' In 1598
one William Shakespeare, who was assessed
by the collectors of a subsidy in the sum of 13s. 4d.
upon goods valued at 5l., was a resident in St. Helen's
parish, Bishopsgate, but it is not certain that this tax-
payer was the dramatist.[2]

Place of
residence
in London.

The chief differences between the methods of
theatrical representation in Shakespeare's day and
our own lay in the facts that neither scenery nor
scenic costume nor women-actors were known to
the Elizabethan stage. All female *rôles* were, until
the Restoration in 1660, assumed in the public
theatres by men or boys.[3] Consequently the skill
needed to rouse in the audience the requisite illusions

---

[1] The site of the Blackfriars Theatre is now occupied by the offices
of the *Times* newspaper in Victoria Street, London, E.C.

[2] Cf. *Exchequer Lay Subsidies City of London*, 146/369, Public
Record Office ; *Notes and Queries*, 8th ser. viii. 418.

[3] Shakespeare alludes to the appearance of men or boys in women's
parts when he makes Rosalind say laughingly to the men of the audience
in the epilogue to *As You Like It*, '*If I were a woman*, I would kiss

was far greater then than at later periods. But the professional customs of Elizabethan actors approximated in other respects more closely to those of their modern successors than is usually recognised. The practice of touring in the provinces was followed with even greater regularity then than now. Few companies

as many,' &c. Similarly, Cleopatra on her downfall in *Antony and Cleopatra*, v. ii. 220 seq., laments:

> the quick comedians
> Extemporally will stage us . . . and I shall see
> Some squeaking Cleopatra boy my greatness.

Men taking women's parts seem to have worn masks. Flute is bidden by Quince play Thisbe 'in a mask' in *Midsummer Night's Dream* (i. ii. 53). In French and Italian theatres of the time women seem to have acted publicly, but until the Restoration public opinion in England deemed the appearance of a woman on a public stage to be an act of shamelessness on which the most disreputable of her sex would hardly venture. With a curious inconsistency ladies of rank were encouraged at Queen Elizabeth's Court, and still more frequently at the Courts of James I and Charles I, to take part in private and amateur representations of masques and short dramatic pageants. During the reign of James I scenic decoration, usually designed by Inigo Jones, accompanied the production of masques in the royal palaces, but until the Restoration the public stages were bare of any scenic contrivance except a front curtain opening in the middle and a balcony or upper platform resting on pillars at the back of the stage, from which portions of the dialogue were sometimes spoken, although occasionally the balcony seems to have been occupied by spectators (cf. a sketch made by a Dutch visitor to London in 1596 of the stage of the Swan Theatre in *Zur Kenntniss der altenglischen Bühne von Karl Theodor Gaedertz. Mit der ersten authentischen innern Ansicht der Schwans Theatre in London*, Bremen 1888). Sir Philip Sidney humorously described the spectator's difficulties in an Elizabethan playhouse, where, owing to the absence of stage scenery, he had to imagine the bare boards to present in rapid succession a garden, a rocky coast, a cave, and a battlefield (*Apologie for Poetrie*, p. 52). Three flourishes on a trumpet announced the beginning of the performance, but a band of fiddlers played music between the acts. The scenes of each act were played without interruption.

remained in London during the summer or early
autumn, and every country town with two thousand
or more inhabitants could reckon on at least one visit
from travelling actors between May and October. A
rapid examination of the extant archives of some
seventy municipalities selected at random shows that
Shakespeare's company between 1594 and 1614 frequently performed in such towns as Barnstaple, Bath,
Bristol, Coventry, Dover, Faversham, Folkestone,
Hythe, Leicester, Maidstone, Marlborough, New
Romney, Oxford, Rye in Sussex, Saffron Walden,
Shake-   and Shrewsbury.[1] Shakespeare may be
speare's   credited with faithfully fulfilling all his pro-
alleged
travels.   fessional functions, and some of the references
to travel in his sonnets were doubtless reminiscences
of early acting tours. It has been repeatedly urged,
moreover, that Shakespeare's company visited Scotland, and that he went with it.[2] In November 1599

---

[1] Cf. Halliwell-Phillipps's *Visits of Shakespeare's Company of Actors to the Provincial Cities and Towns of England* (privately printed,
1887). From the information there given, occasionally supplemented
from other sources, the following imperfect itinerary is deduced:

1593.	Bristol and Shrewsbury.	1607.	Oxford.
1594.	Marlborough.	1608.	Coventry and Marlborough.
1597.	Faversham, Bath, Rye, Bristol, Dover, and Marlborough.	1609.	Hythe, New Romney, and Shrewsbury.
603.	Richmond (Surrey), Bath, Coventry, Shrewsbury, Mort-lake, Wilton House.	1610.	Dover, Oxford, and Shrews-bury.
1604.	Oxford.	1612.	New Romney.
1605.	Barnstaple and Oxford.	1613.	Folkestone, Oxford, and Shrews-bury.
1606.	Leicester, Saffron Walden, Marlborough, Oxford, Dover, and Maidstone.	1614.	Coventry.

[2] Cf. Knight's *Life of Shakespeare* (1843), p. 41; Fleay, *Stage*, pp.
135–6.

English actors arrived in Scotland under the leader-
In Scotland. ship of Lawrence Fletcher and one Martin,
and were welcomed with enthusiasm by
the king.[1] Fletcher was a colleague of Shakespeare in 1603, but is not known to have been one
earlier. Shakespeare's company never included an
actor named Martin. Fletcher repeated the visit in
October 1601.[2] There is nothing to indicate that any
of his companions belonged to Shakespeare's company.
In like manner, Shakespeare's accurate reference in
'Macbeth' to the 'nimble' but 'sweet' climate of
Inverness,[3] and the vivid impression he conveys of

---

[1] The favour bestowed by James VI on these English actors was
so marked as to excite the resentment of the leaders of the Kirk. The
English agent, George Nicolson, in a (hitherto unpublished) despatch
dated from Edinburgh on November 12, 1599, wrote : 'The four Sessions of this Town (without touch by name of our English players,
Fletcher and Mertyn [*i.e.* Martyn], with their company), and not
knowing the King's ordinances for them to play and be heard, enacted
[that] their flocks [were] to forbear and not to come to or haunt profane
games, sports, or plays.' Thereupon the King summoned the Sessions
before him in Council and threatened them with the full rigour of the
law. Obdurate at first, the ministers subsequently agreed to moderate
their hostile references to the actors. Finally, Nicolson adds, 'the
King this day by proclamation with sound of trumpet hath commanded
the players liberty to play, and forbidden their hinder or impeach-
ment therein.' *MS. State Papers*, Dom. Scotland, P. R. O. vol. lxv.
No. 64.

[2] Fleay, *Stage*, pp. 126–44.

[3] Cf. Duncan's speech (on arriving at Macbeth's castle of Inverness) :

> This castle hath a pleasant seat ; the air
> Nimbly and sweetly recommends itself
> Unto our gentle senses.
>   *Banquo.*   This guest of summer,
> The temple-haunting martlet, does approve,
> By his lov'd mansionry, that the heaven's breath
> Smells wooingly here.   (*Macbeth* I. vi. 1–6.)

the aspects of wild Highland heaths, have been judged
to be the certain fruits of a personal experience; but
the passages in question, into which a more definite
significance has possibly been read than Shakespeare
intended, can be satisfactorily accounted for by Shakespeare's inevitable intercourse with Scotsmen in
London and the theatres after James I's accession.

A few English actors in Shakespeare's day occasionally combined to make professional tours through
foreign lands, where Court society invariably gave
them an hospitable reception. In Denmark, Germany,
Austria, Holland, and in France, many dramatic
performances were given before royal audiences by
English actors between 1580 and 1630.[1] That Shakespeare joined any of these expeditions is highly improbable. Actors of small account at home mainly
took part in them, and Shakespeare's name appears in
no extant list of those who paid professional visits
abroad. It is, in fact, unlikely that Shakespeare ever
set foot on the continent of Europe in either a private
or professional capacity. He repeatedly ridicules
In Italy.   the craze for foreign travel.[2] To Italy, it
is true, and especially to cities of Northern
Italy, like Venice, Padua, Verona, Mantua, and
Milan, he makes frequent and familiar reference, and

[1] Cf. Cohn, *Shakespeare in Germany*, 1865; Meissner, *Die englis-
chen Comödianten zur Zeit Shakespeare in Oestereich*, Vienna, 1884;
Jon Stefansson on 'Shakespeare at Elsinore' in *Contemporary Review*,
January 1896; *Notes and Queries*, 5th ser. ix. 43, and xi. 520; and M.
Jusserand's article in the *Nineteenth Century*, April 1898, on English
actors in France.

[2] Cf. *As You Like It*, IV. i. 22–40.

he supplied many a realistic portrayal of Italian life and sentiment. But the fact that he represents Valentine in the 'Two Gentlemen of Verona' (i. i. 71) as travelling from Verona to Milan by sea, and Prospero in 'The Tempest' as embarking on a ship at the gates of Milan (i. ii. 129–44), renders it almost impossible that he could have gathered his knowledge of Northern Italy from personal observation.[1] He doubtless owed all to the verbal reports of travelled friends or to books, the contents of which he had a rare power of assimilating and vitalising.

The publisher Chettle wrote in 1592 that Shakespeare was 'exelent in the qualitie [2] he professes,' and the old actor William Beeston asserted in the next century that Shakespeare 'did act exceedingly well.' [3]

Shake-speare's rôles.

But the *rôles* in which he distinguished himself are imperfectly recorded. Few surviving documents refer directly to performances by him. At Christmas 1594 he joined the popular actors William Kemp, the chief comedian of the day, and Richard Burbage, the greatest tragic actor, in 'two several comedies or interludes' which were acted on St. Stephen's Day and on Innocents' Day (December 27 and 28) at Greenwich Palace before the Queen. The players received 'xiii*li.* vj*s.* viij*d.* and by waye of her Majesties rewarde vj*li.*

---

[1] Cf. Elze, *Essays*, 1874, pp. 254 seq.

[2] 'Quality' in Elizabethan English was the technical term for the 'actor's profession.'

[3] Aubrey's *Lives*, ed. Andrew Clark, ii. 226.

xiii*s*. iiij*d*., in all xx*li*.'[1] Neither plays nor parts are named. Shakespeare's name stands first on the list of those who took part in the original performances of Ben Jonson's 'Every Man in his Humour' (1598). In the original edition of Jonson's 'Sejanus' (1603) the actors' names are arranged in two columns, and Shakespeare's name heads the second column, standing parallel with Burbage's, which heads the first. But here again the character allotted to each actor is not stated. Rowe identified only one of Shakespeare's parts, 'the Ghost in his own "Hamlet,"' and Rowe asserted his assumption of that character to be 'the top of his performance.' John Davies of Hereford noted that he 'played some kingly parts in sport.'[2] One of Shakespeare's younger brothers, presumably Gilbert, often came, wrote Oldys, to London in his younger days to see his brother act in his own plays; and in his old age, when his memory was failing, he recalled his brother's performance of Adam in 'As You Like It.' In the 1623 folio edition of Shakespeare's 'Works' his name heads the prefatory list 'of the principall actors in all these playes.'

That Shakespeare chafed under some of the conditions of the actor's calling is commonly inferred
Alleged scorn of an actor's calling. from the 'Sonnets.' There he reproaches himself with becoming 'a motley to the view' (cx. 2), and chides fortune for having provided for his livelihood nothing better than 'public

---

[1] Halliwell-Phillipps, i. 121 ; Mrs. Stopes in *Jahrbuch der deutschen Shakespeare-Gesellschaft*, 1896, xxxii. 182 seq.

[2] *Scourge of Folly*, 1610, epigr. 159.

means that public manners breed,' whence his name received a brand (cxi. 4–5). If such self-pity is to be literally interpreted, it only reflected an evanescent mood. His interest in all that touched the efficiency of his profession was permanently active. He was a keen critic of actors' elocution, and in 'Hamlet' shrewdly denounced their common failings, but clearly and hopefully pointed out the road to improvement. His highest ambitions lay, it is true, elsewhere than in acting, and at an early period of his theatrical career he undertook, with triumphant success, the labours of a playwright. But he pursued the profession of an actor loyally and uninterruptedly until he resigned all connection with the theatre within a few years of his death.

V

EARLY DRAMATIC EFFORTS

THE whole of Shakespeare's dramatic work was probably begun and ended within two decades (1591–
Dramatic   1611), between his twenty-seventh and forty-
work.   seventh year.   If the works traditionally
assigned to him include some contributions from
other pens, he was perhaps responsible, on the other
hand, for portions of a few plays that are traditionally
claimed for others.   When the account is balanced,
Shakespeare must be credited with the production
during these twenty years, of a yearly average of
two plays, nearly all of which belong to the supreme
rank of literature.   Three volumes of poems must be
added to the total.   Ben Jonson was often told by the
players that 'whatsoever he penned he never blotted
out (*i.e.* erased) a line.'   The editors of the First Folio
attested that 'what he thought he uttered with that
easinesse that we have scarce received from him a
blot in his papers.'   Signs of hasty workmanship are
not lacking, but they are few when it is considered
how rapidly his numerous compositions came from
his pen, and they are in the aggregate unimportant.

By borrowing his plots he to some extent econo-
mised his energy, but he transformed most of them,

and it was not probably with the object of conserv-
ing his strength that he systematically
levied loans on popular current literature like
Holinshed's 'Chronicles,' North's translation
of 'Plutarch,' widely read romances, and successful
plays.   In this regard he betrayed something of the
practical temperament which is traceable in the
conduct of the affairs of his later life.   It was doubtless with the calculated aim of ministering to the
public taste that he unceasingly adapted, as his
genius dictated, themes which had already, in the
hands of inferior writers or dramatists, proved capable of arresting public attention.

His bor-rowed plots.

The professional playwrights sold their plays out-
right to one or other of the acting companies, and they
retained no legal interest in them after the
manuscript had passed into the hands of the
theatrical manager.[1]   It was not unusual for
the manager to invite extensive revision of a play at
the hands of others than its author before it was produced on the stage, and again whenever it was revived.
Shakespeare gained his earliest experience as a dramatist by revising or rewriting behind the scenes plays
that had become the property of his manager.   It is
possible that some of his labours in this direction

The revi-sion of plays.

---

[1] One of the many crimes laid to the charge of the dramatist
Robert Greene was that of fraudulently disposing of the same play to
two companies. 'Ask the Queen's players,' his accuser bade him in
Cuthbert Cony-Catcher's *Defence of Cony-Catching,* 1592, 'if you
sold them not *Orlando Furioso* for twenty nobles [*i.e.* about 7*l.*],
and when they were in the country sold the same play to the Lord
Admiral's men for as many more.'

remain unidentified. In a few cases his alterations were slight, but as a rule his fund of originality was too abundant to restrict him, when working as an adapter, to mere recension, and the results of most of his labours in that capacity are entitled to rank among original compositions.

The determination of the exact order in which Shakespeare's plays were written depends largely on conjecture. External evidence is accessible in only a few cases, and, although always worthy of the utmost consideration, is not invariably conclusive. The date of publication rarely indicates the date of composition. Only sixteen of the thirty-seven plays commonly assigned to Shakespeare were published in his lifetime, and it is questionable whether any were published under his supervision.[1] But subject-matter and metre both afford rough clues to the period in his career to which each

Chrono-
logy of the
plays.

---

[1] The playhouse authorities deprecated the publishing of plays in the belief that their dissemination in print was injurious to the receipts of the theatre. A very small proportion of plays acted in Elizabeth's and James I's reign consequently reached the printing press, and most of them are now lost. But in the absence of any law of copyright publishers often defied the wishes of the owner of manuscripts. Many copies of a popular play were made for the actors, and if one of these copies chanced to fall into a publisher's hands, it was habitually issued without any endeavour to obtain either author's or manager's sanction. In March 1599 the theatrical manager Philip Henslowe endeavoured to induce a publisher who had secured a playhouse copy of the comedy of *Patient Grissell* by Dekker, Chettle, and Haughton to abandon the publication of it by offering him a bribe of 2*l*. The publication was suspended till 1603 (cf. Henslowe's *Diary*, p. 167). As late as 1633 Thomas Heywood wrote of 'some actors who think it against their peculiar profit to have them [*i.e.* plays] come into print.' (*English Traveller*, pref.)

play may be referred. In his early plays the spirit of comedy or tragedy appears in its simplicity; as his powers gradually matured he depicted life in its most complex involutions, and portrayed with masterly insight the subtle gradations of human sentiment and the mysterious workings of human passion. Comedy and tragedy are gradually blended; and his work finally developed a pathos such as could only come of ripe experience. Similarly the metre undergoes emancipation from the hampering restraints of fixed rule and becomes flexible enough to respond to every phase of human feeling. In Metrical the blank verse of the early plays a pause tests. is strictly observed at the close of each line, and rhyming couplets are frequent. Gradually the poet overrides such artificial restrictions; rhyme largely disappears; recourse is more frequently made to prose; the pause is varied indefinitely; extra syllables are, contrary to strict metrical law, introduced at the end of lines, and at times in the middle; the last word of the line is often a weak and unemphatic conjunction or preposition.[1] To the latest plays fantastic and punning conceits which abound in early work are rarely accorded admission. But, while Shakespeare's

[1] W. S. Walker in his *Shakespeare's Versification*, 1854, and Charles Bathurst in his *Difference in Shakespeare's Versification at Different Periods of his Life*, 1857, were the first to point out the general facts. Dr. Ingram's paper on 'The Weak Endings' in *New Shakspere Society's Transactions* (1874), vol. i., is of great value. Mr. Fleay's metrical tables, which first appeared in the same society's *Transactions* (1874), and have been reissued by Dr. Furnivall in a somewhat revised form in his introduction to Gervinus's *Commentaries* and in his *Leopold Shakspere*, give all the information possible.

E

achievement from the beginning to the end of his
career offers clearer evidence than that of any other
writer of genius of the steady and orderly growth
of his poetic faculty, some allowance must be made
for ebb and flow in the current of his artistic progress.
Early work occasionally anticipates features that become habitual to late work, and late work at times
embodies traits that are mainly identified with early
work.   No exclusive reliance in determining the precise chronology can be placed on the merely mechanical tests afforded by tables of metrical statistics.   The
chronological order can only be deduced with any
confidence from a consideration of all the internal
characteristics as well as the known external history
of each play.   The premisses are often vague and
conflicting, and no chronology hitherto suggested receives at all points universal assent.

There is no external evidence to prove that any
piece in which Shakespeare had a hand was produced
before the spring of 1592.   No play by him was published before 1597, and none bore his name on the title-
page till 1598.   But his first essays have been with confidence allotted to 1591.   To 'Love's Labour's Lost'
'Love's   may reasonably be assigned priority in point
Labour's   of time of all Shakespeare's dramatic produc-
Lost.'   tions.   Internal evidence alone indicates the
date of composition, and proves that it was an early
effort; but the subject-matter suggests that its author
had already enjoyed extended opportunities of survey-
ing London life and manners, such as were hardly open
to him in the very first years of his settlement in the

metropolis. 'Love's Labour's Lost' embodies keen observation of contemporary life in many ranks of society, both in town and country, while the speeches of the hero Biron clothe much sound philosophy in masterly rhetoric. Its slender plot stands almost alone among Shakespeare's plots in that it is not known to have been borrowed, and stands quite alone in openly travestying known traits and incidents of current social and political life. The names of the chief characters are drawn from the leaders in the civil war in France, which was in progress between 1589 and 1594, and was anxiously watched by the English public.[1] Contemporary projects of academies for dis-

---

[1] The hero is the King of Navarre, in whose dominions the scene is laid. The two chief lords in attendance on him in the play, Biron and Longaville, bear the actual names of the two most strenuous supporters of the real King of Navarre (Biron's later career subsequently formed the subject of two plays by Chapman, *The Conspiracie of Duke Biron* and *The Tragedy of Biron*, which were both produced in 1605). The name of the Lord Dumain in *Love's Labour's Lost* is a common Anglicised version of that Duc de Maine or Mayenne whose name was so frequently mentioned in popular accounts of French affairs in connection with Navarre's movements that Shakespeare was led to number him also among his supporters. Mothe or La Mothe, the name of the pretty, ingenious page, was that of a French ambassador who was long popular in London; and, though he left England in 1583, he lived in the memory of playgoers and playwrights long after *Love's Labour's Lost* was written. In Chapman's *An Humourous Day's Mirth*, 1599, M. Le Mot, a sprightly courtier in attendance on the King of France, is drawn from the same original, and his name, as in Shakespeare's play, suggests much punning on the word 'mote.' As late as 1602 Middleton, in his *Blurt, Master Constable*, act ii. sc. ii. l. 215, wrote:

Ho God! Ho God! thus did I revel it
When Monsieur Motte lay here ambassador.

Armado, 'the fantastical Spaniard' who haunts Navarre's Court, and is dubbed by another courtier 'a phantasm, a Monarcho,' is a caricature

ciplining young men; fashions of speech and dress current in fashionable circles; recent attempts on the part of Elizabeth's government to negotiate with the Tsar of Russia; the inefficiency of rural constables and the pedantry of village schoolmasters and curates are all satirised with good humour. The play was revised in 1597, probably for a performance at Court. It was first published next year, and on the title-page, which described the piece as 'newly corrected and augmented,' Shakespeare's name first appeared in print as that of author of a play.

Less gaiety characterised another comedy of the same date, 'The Two Gentlemen of Verona,' which
'Two Gentlemen of Verona.' dramatises a romantic story of love and friendship. There is every likelihood that it was an adaptation — amounting to a re-

of a half-crazed Spaniard known as 'fantastical Monarcho' who for many years hung about Elizabeth's Court, and was under the delusion that he owned the ships arriving in the port of London. On his death Thomas Churchyard wrote a poem called *Fantasticall Monarcho's Epitaph*, and mention is made of him in Reginald Scott's *Discoverie of Witchcraft*, 1584, p. 54. The name Armado was doubtless suggested by the expedition of 1588. Braggardino in Chapman's *Blind Beggar of Alexandria*, 1598, is drawn on the same lines. The scene (*Love's Labour's Lost*, v. ii. 158 seq.) in which the princess's lovers press their suit in the disguise of Russians follows a description of the reception by ladies of Elizabeth's Court in 1584 of Russian ambassadors who came to London to seek a wife among the ladies of the English nobility for the Tsar (cf. Horsey's *Travels*, ed. E. A. Bond, Hakluyt Soc.). For further indications of topics of the day treated in the play, see 'A New Study of "Love's Labour's Lost,"' by the present writer in *Gent. Mag.*, Oct. 1880; and *Transactions of the New Shakspere Society*, pt. iii. p. 80*. The attempt to detect in the schoolmaster Holofernes a caricature of the Italian teacher and lexicographer, John Florio, seems unjustified (see p. 85 *n.*).

formation — of a lost 'History of Felix and Philo-
mena,' which had been acted at Court in 1584. The
story is the same as that of 'The Shepardess Felis-
mena' in the Spanish pastoral romance of 'Diana' by
George de Montemayor, which long enjoyed popularity in England. No complete English translation of
'Diana' was published before that of Bartholomew
Yonge in 1598, but a manuscript version by Thomas
Wilson, which was dedicated to the Earl of Southampton in 1596, was possibly circulated far earlier. Some
verses from 'Diana' were translated by Sir Philip Sidney and were printed with his poems as early as 1591.
Barnabe Rich's story of 'Apollonius and Silla' (from
Cinthio's 'Hecatommithi'), which Shakespeare employed again in 'Twelfth Night,' also gave him some
hints. Trifling and irritating conceits abound in the
'Two Gentlemen,' but passages of high poetic spirit
are not wanting, and the speeches of the clowns,
Launce and Speed, — the precursors of a long line of
whimsical serving-men, — overflow with farcical drol-
lery. The 'Two Gentlemen' was not published in
Shakespeare's lifetime; it first appeared in the folio
of 1623, after having, in all probability, undergone
some revision.[1]

Shakespeare next tried his hand, in the 'Comedy
of Errors' (commonly known at the time as 'Errors'),
'Comedy at boisterous farce. It also was first pub-
of Errors.' lished in 1623. Again, as in 'Love's Labour's
Lost,' allusion was made to the civil war in France.
France was described as making war against her heir

[1] Cf. Fleay, *Life*, pp. 188 seq.

(act v. sc. ii. l. 125). Shakespeare's farcical comedy may have been founded on a play, no longer extant, called 'The Historie of Error,' which was acted in 1576 at Hampton Court. In subject-matter it resembles the 'Menæchmi' of Plautus, and treats of mistakes of identity arising from the likeness of twin-born children. The scene (act iii. sc. i.) in which Antipholus of Ephesus is shut out from his own house, while his brother and wife are at dinner within, recalls one in the 'Amphitruo' of Plautus. Shakespeare doubtless had direct recourse to Plautus as well as to the old play, and he may have read Plautus in English. The earliest translation of the 'Menæchmi' was not licensed for publication before June 10, 1594, and was not published until the following year. No translation of any other play of Plautus appeared before. But it was stated in the preface to this first published translation of the 'Menæchmi' that the translator, W.W., doubtless William Warner, a veteran of the Elizabethan world of letters, had some time previously 'Englished' that and 'divers' others of Plautus's comedies, and had circulated them in manuscript 'for the use of and delight of his private friends, who, in Plautus's own words, are not able to understand them.'

Such plays as these, although each gave promise of a dramatic capacity out of the common way, cannot be with certainty pronounced to be beyond the ability of other men. It was in 'Romeo and Juliet,' Shakespeare's first tragedy, that he proved himself the possessor of a poetic and dramatic instinct of

unprecedented quality. In 'Romeo and Juliet' he turned to account a tragic romance of Italian origin,[1] 'Romeo which was already popular in English ver-
and Juliet.' sions. Arthur Broke rendered it into English verse from the Italian of Bandello in 1562, and William Painter had published it in prose in his 'Palace of Pleasure' in 1567. Shakespeare made little change in the plot as drawn from Bandello by Broke, but he impregnated it with poetic fervour, and relieved the tragic intensity by developing the humour of Mercutio, and by grafting on the story the new comic character of the Nurse.[2] The ecstasy of youthful passion is portrayed by Shakespeare in language of the highest lyric beauty, and although a predilection for quibbles and conceits occasionally passes beyond the author's control, 'Romeo and Juliet,' as a tragic poem on the theme of love, has no rival in any literature. If the Nurse's remark, ''Tis since the earthquake now eleven years' (I. iii. 23), be taken literally, the composition of the play must be referred

[1] The story, which has been traced back to the Greek romance of *Anthia and Abrocomas* by Xenophon Ephesius, a writer of the second century, seems to have been first told in modern Europe about 1470 by Masuccio in his *Novellino* (No. xxxiii.: cf. Mr. Waters's translation, i. 155–65). It was adapted from Masuccio by Luigi da Porto in his novel, *La Giuletta*, 1535, and by Bandello in his *Novelle*, 1554, pt. ii. No. ix. Bandello's version became classical; Belleforest translated it in his *Histoires Tragiques*, Lyons, 1564. At the same time as Shakespeare was writing *Romeo and Juliet*, Lope de Vega was dramatising the tale in his Spanish play called *Casteliones y Montisis* (*i.e.* Capulets and Montagus). For analysis of Lope's play, which ends happily, see *Variorum Shakespeare*, 1821, xxi. 451–60.

[2] Cf. *Originals and Analogues*, pt. i. ed. P. A. Daniel, New Shakspere Society.

to 1591, for no earthquake in the sixteenth century was experienced in England after 1580. There are a few parallelisms with Daniel's 'Complainte of Rosamond,' published in 1592, and it is probable that Shakespeare completed the piece in that year. It was first printed anonymously and surreptitiously by John Danter in 1597 from an imperfect acting copy. A second quarto of 1599 (by T. Creede for Cuthbert Burbie) was printed from an authentic version, but the piece had probably undergone revision since its first production.[1]

Of the original representation on the stage of three other pieces of the period we have more explicit information. These reveal Shakespeare undisguisedly as an adapter of plays by other hands. Though they lack the interest attaching to his unaided work, they throw invaluable light on some of his early methods of composition and his early relations with other dramatists.

On March 3, 1592, a new piece, called 'Henry VI,' was acted at the Rose Theatre by Lord Strange's men. It was no doubt the play which was subsequently known as Shakespeare's 'The First Part of Henry VI.' On its first performance it won a popular triumph. 'How would it have joyed brave Talbot (the terror of the French),' wrote Nash in his 'Pierce Pennilesse' (1592, licensed August 8), in reference to the striking scenes of Talbot's death (act iv. sc. vi. and vii.), 'to thinke that after he had

'Henry VI.'

[1] Cf. *Parallel Texts*, ed. P. A. Daniel, New Shakspere Society; Fleay, *Life*, pp. 191 seq.

lyne two hundred yeares in his Tombe, hee should
triumphe againe on the Stage, and have his bones newe
embalmed with the teares of ten thousand spectators
at least (at severall times) who, in the Tragedian that
represents his person, imagine they behold him fresh
bleeding!' There is no categorical record of the
production of a second piece in continuation of the
theme, but such a play quickly followed; for a third
piece, treating of the concluding incidents of Henry
VI's reign, attracted much attention on the stage
early in the following autumn.

The applause attending the completion of this historical trilogy caused bewilderment in the theatrical
profession. The older dramatists awoke to the fact that
their popularity was endangered by the young stranger
who had set up his tent in their midst, and one veteran
uttered without delay a rancorous protest. Robert
Greene, who died on September 3, 1592, wrote on his
deathbed an ill-natured farewell to life, entitled 'A
Greene's   Groats-worth of Wit bought with a Million
attack.   of Repentance.' Addressing three brother
dramatists — Marlowe, Nash, and Peele or Lodge — he
bade them beware of puppets 'that speak from our
mouths,' and of 'antics garnished in our colours.'
'There is,' he continued, 'an upstart Crow, beautified
with our feathers, that with his *Tygers heart wrapt in
a players hide* supposes he is as well able to bumbast
out a blanke verse as the best of you; and being an
absolute *Johannes factotum* is, in his owne conceit, the
only Shake-scene in a countrie. . . . Never more
acquaint [those apes] with your admired inventions,

for it is pity men of such rare wits should be subject
to the pleasures of such rude groomes.' The 'only
Shake-scene' is a punning denunciation of Shakespeare. The tirade was probably inspired by an
established author's resentment at the energy of a
young actor — the theatre's factotum — in revising
the dramatic work of his seniors with such masterly
effect as to imperil their hold on the esteem of
manager and playgoer. The italicised quotation
travesties a line from the third piece in the trilogy of
Shakespeare's 'Henry VI':

> Oh Tiger's heart wrapt in a woman's hide.

But Shakespeare's amiability of character and versatile
ability had already won him admirers, and his successes excited the sympathetic regard of colleagues
more kindly than Greene. In December 1592 Greene's
publisher, Henry Chettle, prefixed an apology for
Chettle's   Greene's attack on the young actor to his
apology.   'Kind Hartes Dreame,' a tract reflecting on
phases of contemporary social life. 'I am as sory,'
Chettle wrote, 'as if the originall fault had beene my
fault, because myselfe have seene his [*i.e.* Shakespeare's] demeanour no lesse civill than he [is] exelent in the qualitie he professes, besides divers of
worship have reported his uprightnes of dealing,
which argues his honesty, and his facetious grace in
writing that aprooves his art.'

The first of the three plays dealing with the reign
of Henry VI was originally published in the collected
edition of Shakespeare's works; the second and third

plays were previously printed in a form very dif-
ferent from that which they subsequently assumed when they followed the first part in the folio. Criticism has proved beyond doubt that in these plays Shakespeare did no more than add, revise, and correct other men's work. In 'The First Part of Henry VI' the scene in the Temple Gardens, where white and red roses are plucked as emblems by the rival political parties (act ii. sc. iv.), the dying speech of Mortimer, and perhaps the wooing of Margaret by Suffolk, alone bear the impress of his style. A play dealing with the second part of Henry VI's reign was published anony- mously from a rough stage copy in 1594, with the title 'The first part of the Contention betwixt the two famous houses of Yorke and Lancaster.' A play dealing with the third part was published with greater care next year under the title 'The True Tragedie of Richard, Duke of Yorke, and the death of good King Henry the Sixt, as it was sundrie times acted by the Earl of Pembroke his servants.' In both these plays Shakespeare's revising hand can be traced. The humours of Jack Cade in 'The Contention' can owe their savour to him alone. After he had hastily revised the original drafts of the three pieces, perhaps with another's aid, they were put on the stage in 1592, the first two parts by his own company (Lord Strange's men), and the third, under some exceptional arrangement, by Lord Pembroke's men. But Shakespeare was not content to leave them thus. Within a brief interval,

possibly for a revival, he undertook a more thorough revision, still in conjunction with another writer. 'The First Part of the Contention' was thoroughly overhauled, and was converted into what was entitled in the folio 'The Second Part of Henry VI'; there more than half the lines are new. 'The True Tragedie,' which became 'The Third Part of Henry VI,' was less drastically handled; two-thirds of it was left practically untouched; only a third was thoroughly remodelled.[1]

Who Shakespeare's coadjutors were in the two successive revisions of 'Henry VI,' is matter for conjecture. The theory that Greene and Peele produced the original draft of the three parts of 'Henry VI,' which Shakespeare recast, may help to account for Greene's indignant denunciation of Shakespeare as 'an upstart crow, beautified with the feathers' of himself and his fellow-dramatists. Much can be said, too, in behalf of the suggestion that Shakespeare joined Marlowe, the greatest of his predecessors, in the first revision of which 'The Contention' and the 'True Tragedie' were the outcome. Most of the new passages in the second recension seem assignable to Shakespeare alone, but a few suggest a partnership resembling that of the first revision. It is probable that Marlowe began the final revision, but his task was interrupted by his death, and the lion's share of the work fell to his younger coadjutor.

Shake-speare's coadjutors.

[1] Cf. Fleay, *Life*, pp. 235 seq.; *Trans. New Shakspere Soc.*, 1876, pt. ii. by Miss Jane Lee; Swinburne, *Study*, pp. 51 seq.

Shakespeare shared with other men of genius that receptivity of mind which impels them to assimilate much of the intellectual effort of their contemporaries and to transmute it in the process from unvalued ore into pure gold. Had Shakespeare not been professionally employed in recasting old plays by contemporaries, he would doubtless have shown in his writings traces of a study of their work. The verses of Thomas Watson, Samuel Daniel, Michael Drayton,

Shake-speare's as-similative power.
Sir Philip Sidney, and Thomas Lodge were certainly among the rills which fed the mighty river of his poetic and lyric invention. Kyd and Greene, among rival writers of tragedy, left more or less definite impression on all Shakespeare's early efforts in tragedy. It was, however, only to two of his fellow-dramatists that his indebtedness as a writer of either comedy or tragedy was material or emphatically defined. Superior as Shakespeare's powers were to those of Marlowe, his coadjutor in 'Henry VI,' his early tragedies often reveal him in the character of a faithful disciple of that vehement delineator of tragic passion. Shakespeare's early comedies disclose a like relationship between him and Lyly.

Lyly is best known as the author of the affected romance of 'Euphues,' but between 1580 and 1592

Lyly's in-fluence in comedy.
he produced eight trivial and insubstantial comedies, of which six were written in prose, one was in blank verse, and one was in rhyme. Much of the dialogue in Shakespeare's comedies, from 'Love's Labour's Lost' to 'Much Ado about Nothing,'

consists in thrusting and parrying fantastic conceits, puns, or antitheses. This is the style of intercourse in which most of Lyly's characters exclusively indulge. Three-fourths of Lyly's comedies lightly revolve about topics of classical or fairy mythology — in the very manner which Shakespeare first brought to a triumphant issue in his 'Midsummer Night's Dream.' Shakespeare's treatment of eccentric character like Don Armado in 'Love's Labour's Lost' and his boy Moth reads like a reminiscence of Lyly's portrayal of Sir Thopas, a fat vainglorious knight, and his boy Epiton in the comedy of 'Endymion,' while the watchmen in the same play clearly adumbrate Shakespeare's Dogberry and Verges. The device of masculine disguise for love-sick maidens was characteristic of Lyly's method before Shakespeare ventured on it for the first of many times in 'Two Gentlemen of Verona,' and the dispersal through Lyly's comedies of songs possessing every lyrical charm is not the least interesting of the many striking features which Shakespeare's achievements in comedy seem to borrow from Lyly's comparatively insignificant experiments.[1]

Marlowe, who alone of Shakespeare's contemporaries can be credited with exerting on his efforts

[1] In later life Shakespeare, in *Hamlet*, borrows from Lyly's *Euphues* Polonius's advice to Laertes; but, however he may have regarded the moral sentiment of that didactic romance, he had no respect for the affectations of its prose style, which he ridiculed in a familiar passage in 1 *Henry IV*, II. iv. 445: 'For though the camomile, the more it is trodden on, the faster it grows, yet youth the more it is wasted, the sooner it wears.'

in tragedy a really substantial influence, was in
1592 and 1593 at the zenith of his fame.
Two of Shakespeare's earliest historical
tragedies, 'Richard III' and 'Richard II,'
with the story of Shylock in his somewhat later
comedy of the 'Merchant of Venice,' plainly disclose
a conscious resolve to follow in Marlowe's footsteps.
In 'Richard III' Shakespeare, working singlehanded,
takes up the history of England near the point at
which Marlowe and he, apparently working in partnership, left it in the third part of 'Henry VI.' The
subject was already familiar to dramatists, but
Shakespeare sought his materials in the 'Chronicle'
of Holinshed. A Latin piece, by Dr. Thomas Legge,
had been in favour with academic audiences since 1579,
and in 1594 the 'True Tragedie of Richard
III' from some other pen was published anonymously; but Shakespeare's piece bears little resemblance to either. Throughout Shakespeare's 'Richard
III' the effort to emulate Marlowe is undeniable. The
tragedy is, says Mr. Swinburne, 'as fiery in passion, as
single in purpose, as rhetorical often, though never so
inflated in expression, as Marlowe's "Tamburlaine"
itself.' The turbulent piece was naturally popular.
Burbage's impersonation of the hero was one of his
most effective performances, and his vigorous enunciation of 'A horse, a horse! my kingdom for a
horse!' gave the line proverbial currency.

'Richard II' seems to have followed 'Richard III'
without delay. Subsequently both were published
anonymously in the same year (1597) as they had

(marginalia:) Marlowe's influence in tragedy.

(marginalia:) Richard III.

'been publikely acted by the right Honorable the Lorde Chamberlaine his servants'; but the deposition scene in 'Richard II,' which dealt with a topic distasteful to the Queen, was omitted from the early impressions. Prose is avoided throughout the play, a certain sign of early work. The piece was probably composed very early in 1593. Marlowe's tempestuous vein is less apparent in 'Richard II' than in 'Richard III.' But if 'Richard II' be in style and treatment less deeply indebted to Marlowe than its predecessor, it was clearly suggested by Marlowe's 'Edward II.' Throughout its exposition of the leading theme — the development and collapse of the weak king's character — Shakespeare's historical tragedy closely imitates Marlowe's. Shakespeare drew the facts from Holinshed, but his embellishments are numerous, and include the magnificently eloquent eulogy of England which is set in the mouth of John of Gaunt.

'Richard II.'

In 'As You Like It' (III. v. 80) Shakespeare parenthetically commemorated his acquaintance with, and his general indebtedness to, the elder dramatist by apostrophising him in the lines :

Acknowledgments to Marlowe.

> Dead Shepherd! now I find thy saw of might:
> 'Who ever loved that loved not at first sight?'

The second line is a quotation from Marlowe's poem 'Hero and Leander' (line 76). In the 'Merry Wives of Windsor' (III. i. 17–21) Shakespeare places in the mouth of Sir Hugh Evans snatches of verse from

Marlowe's charming lyric, 'Come live with me and be my love.'

Between February 1593 and the end of the year the London theatres were closed, owing to the prevalence of the plague, and Shakespeare doubtless travelled with his company in the country. But his pen was busily employed, and before the close of 1594 he gave marvellous proofs of his rapid powers of production.

'Titus Andronicus' was in his own lifetime claimed for Shakespeare, but Edward Ravenscroft, 'Titus An- who prepared a new version in 1678, wrote dronicus.' of it: 'I have been told by some anciently conversant with the stage that it was not originally his, but brought by a private author to be acted, and he only gave some master-touches to one or two of the principal parts or characters.' Ravenscroft's assertion deserves acceptance. The tragedy, a sanguinary picture of the decadence of Imperial Rome, contains powerful lines and situations, but is far too repulsive in plot and treatment, and too ostentatious in classical allusions, to take rank with Shakespeare's acknowledged work. Ben Jonson credits 'Titus Andronicus' with a popularity equalling Kyd's 'Spanish Tragedy,' and internal evidence shows that Kyd was capable of writing much of 'Titus.' It was suggested by a piece called 'Titus and Vespasian,' which Lord Strange's men played on April 11, 1592;[1] this is only extant in a German version acted by English players in Germany, and published in

F ¹ Henslowe, p. 24.

1620.[1] 'Titus Andronicus' was obviously taken in hand soon after the production of 'Titus and Vespasian,' in order to exploit popular interest in the topic. It was acted by the Earl of Sussex's men on January 23, 1593-4, when it was described as a new piece; but that it was also acted subsequently by Shakespeare's company is shown by the title-page of the first extant edition of 1600, which describes it as having been performed by the Earl of Derby's and the Lord Chamberlain's servants (successive titles of Shakespeare's company), as well as by those of the Earls of Pembroke and Sussex. It was entered on the 'Stationers' Register' to John Danter on February 6, 1594.[2] Langbaine claims to have seen an edition of this date, but none earlier than that of 1600 is now known.

For part of the plot of 'The Merchant of Venice,' in which two romantic love stories are skilfully blended with a theme of tragic import, Shakespeare had recourse to 'Il Pecorone,' a fourteenth-century 'Merchant collection of Italian novels by Ser Giovanni of Venice.' Fiorentino.[3] There a Jewish creditor demands a pound of flesh of a defaulting Christian debtor, and the latter is rescued through the advocacy of 'the lady of Belmont,' who is wife of the debtor's friend. The management of the plot in the

[1] Cf. Cohn, *Shakespeare in Germany*, pp. 155 seq.

[2] Arber, ii. 644.

[3] Cf. W. G. Waters's translation of *Il Pecorone*, pp. 44–60 (fourth day, novel 1). The collection was not published till 1558, and the story followed by Shakespeare was not accessible in his day in any language but the original Italian.

Italian novel is closely followed by Shakespeare. A similar story is slenderly outlined in the popular mediæval collection of anecdotes called 'Gesta Romanorum,' while the tale of the caskets, which Shakespeare combined with it in the 'Merchant,' is told independently in another portion of the same work. But Shakespeare's 'Merchant' owes much to other sources, including more than one old play. Stephen Gosson describes in his 'Schoole of Abuse' (1579) a lost play called 'the Jew . . . showne at the Bull [inn] . . . representing the greedinesse of worldly chusers and bloody mindes of usurers.' This description suggests that the two stories of the pound of flesh and the caskets had been combined before for purposes of dramatic representation. The scenes in Shakespeare's play in which Antonio negotiates with Shylock are roughly anticipated, too, by dialogues between a Jewish creditor Gerontus and a Christian debtor in the extant play of 'The Three Ladies of London,' by R[obert] W[ilson], 1584. There the Jew opens the attack on his Christian debtor with the lines:

> Signor Mercatore, why do you not pay me ? Think you I will be mocked in this sort ?
> This three times you have flouted me — it seems you make thereat a sport.
> Truly pay me my money, and that even now presently,
> Or by mighty Mahomet, I swear I will forthwith arrest thee.

Subsequently, when the judge is passing judgment in favour of the debtor, the Jew interrupts:

> Stay, there, most puissant judge. Signor Mercatore, consider what you do.
> Pay me the principal, as for the interest I forgive it you.

Above all is it of interest to note that Shakespeare in ' The Merchant of Venice ' betrays the last definable traces of his discipleship to Marlowe. Although the delicate comedy which lightens the serious interest of Shakespeare's play sets it in a wholly different category from that of Marlowe's ' Jew of Malta,' the humanised portrait of the Jew Shylock embodies distinct reminiscences of Marlowe's caricature of the Jew Barabbas. But Shakespeare soon outpaced his master, and the inspiration that he drew from Marlowe in the ' Merchant ' touches only the general conception of the central figure. Doubtless the popular interest aroused by the trial in February 1594 and the execution in June of the Queen's Jewish physician, Roderigo Lopez, incited Shakespeare to a new and subtler study of Jewish character.[1]   For Shylock (not the merchant Antonio)

Shylock and Roderigo Lopez.

---

[1] Lopez was the Earl of Leicester's physician before 1586, and the Queen's chief physician from that date.   An accomplished linguist, with friends in all parts of Europe, he acted in 1590 at the request of the Earl of Essex as interpreter to Antonio Perez, a victim of Philip II's persecution, whom Essex and his associates brought to England in order to stimulate the hostility of the English public to Spain.   Don Antonio (as the refugee was popularly called) proved querulous and exacting.   A quarrel between Lopez and Essex followed.   Spanish agents in London offered Lopez a bribe to poison Antonio and the Queen.   The evidence that he assented to the murderous proposal is incomplete, but he was convicted of treason, and, although the Queen long delayed signing his death-warrant, he was hanged at Tyburn on June 7, 1594.   His trial and execution evoked a marked display of anti-Semitism on the part of the London populace.   Very few Jews were domiciled in England at the time.   That a Christian named Antonio should be the cause of the ruin alike of the greatest Jew in Elizabethan England and of the greatest Jew of the Elizabethan drama is a curious confirmation of the theory that Lopez was the begetter of Shylock.   Cf. the article on

is the hero of the play, and the main interest cul-
minates in the Jew's trial and discomfiture. The
bold transition from that solemn scene which
trembles on the brink of tragedy to the gently
poetic and humorous incidents of the concluding
act attests a mastery of stagecraft; but the interest, although it is sustained to the end, is, after
Shylock's final exit, pitched in a lower key. The
'Venesyon Comedy,' which Henslowe, the manager,
produced at the Rose on August 25, 1594, was probably the earliest version of 'The Merchant of Venice,'
and it was revised later. It was not published till
1600, when two editions appeared, each printed from
a different stage copy.

To 1594 must also be assigned 'King John,'
which, like the 'Comedy of Errors' and 'Richard II,'
altogether eschews prose. The piece, which was not
printed till 1623, was directly adapted from a worthless
'King   play called 'The Troublesome Raigne of
John.'   King John' (1591), which was fraudulently
reissued in 1611 as 'written by W. Sh.,' and in 1622 as
by 'W. Shakespeare.' There is very small ground for
associating Marlowe's name with the old play. Into
the adaptation Shakespeare flung all his energy, and
the theme grew under his hand into genuine tragedy.
The three chief characters—the mean and cruel king,

Roderigo Lopez in the *Dictionary of National Biography;* 'The
Original of Shylock,' by the present writer, in *Gent. Mag.,* February
1880 ; Dr. H. Graetz, *Shylock in den Sagen, in den Dramen und in
der Geschichte,* Krotoschin, 1880 ; *New Shakspere Soc. Trans.,* 1887-92,
pt. ii. 158–92 ; 'The Conspiracy of Dr. Lopez,' by the Rev. Arthur
Dimock, in *English Historical Review* (1894), ix. 440 seq.

the noblehearted and desperately wronged Constance, and the soldierly humourist, Faulconbridge — are in all essentials of his own invention, and are portrayed with the same sureness of touch that marked in Shylock his rapidly maturing strength. The scene, in which the gentle boy Arthur learns from Hubert that the king has ordered his eyes to be put out, is as affecting as any passage in tragic literature.

At the close of 1594 a performance of Shakespeare's early farce, 'The Comedy of Errors,' gave him a passing notoriety that he could well have spared. The piece was played on the evening of Innocents' Day (December 28), 1594, in the hall of Gray's Inn, before a crowded audience of benchers, students, and their friends. There was some disturbance during the evening on the part of guests from the Inner Temple, who, dissatisfied with the accommodation afforded them, retired in dudgeon. ' So that night,' the contemporary chronicler states, 'was begun and continued to the end in nothing but confusion and errors, whereupon it was ever afterwards called the " Night of Errors." '[1] Shakespeare was acting on the same day before the Queen at Greenwich, and it is doubtful if he were present. On the morrow a commission of oyer and terminer inquired into the causes of the tumult, which was attributed to a sorcerer having ' foisted a company of base and common fellows to

marginal note: 'Comedy of Errors' in Gray's Inn Hall.

---

[1] *Gesta Grayorum*, printed in 1688 from a contemporary manuscript. A second performance of the *Comedy of Errors* was given at Gray's Inn Hall by the Elizabethan Stage Society on Dec. 6, 1895.

make up our disorders with a play of errors and confusions.'

Two plays of uncertain authorship attracted public
attention during the period under review (1591–4) —
'Arden of Feversham' (licensed for publication April 3,
1592, and published in 1592) and 'Edward III' (licensed
for publication December 1, 1595, and published in
1596). Shakespeare's hand has been traced in both,
mainly on the ground that their dramatic energy is of
a quality not to be discerned in the work of any
contemporary whose writings are extant. There
is no external evidence in favour of Shakespeare's
authorship in either case. 'Arden of Feversham'

Early plays dramatises with intensity and insight a
doubtfully sordid murder of a husband by a wife which
assigned to
Shake- took place at Faversham in 1551, and was
speare. fully reported by Holinshed. The subject
is of a different type from any which Shakespeare is
known to have treated, and although the play may be,
as Mr. Swinburne insists, 'a young man's work,' it
bears no relation either in topic or style to the work
on which young Shakespeare was engaged at a period
so early as 1591 or 1592. 'Edward III' is a play in
Marlowe's vein, and has been assigned to Shakespeare
on even more shadowy grounds. Capell reprinted it
in his 'Prolusions' in 1760, and described it as
'thought to be writ by Shakespeare.' Many speeches
scattered through the drama, and one whole scene —
that in which the Countess of Salisbury repulses the
advances of Edward III — show the hand of a master
(act ii. sc. ii.). But there is even in the style of

these contributions much to dissociate them from
Shakespeare's acknowledged productions, and to
justify their ascription to some less gifted disciple of
Marlowe.[1]   A line in act ii. sc. i. ('Lilies that fester
smell far worse than weeds') reappears in Shakespeare's 'Sonnets' (xciv. 1. 14).[2]   It was contrary to
his practice to literally plagiarise himself.   The line
in the play was doubtless borrowed from a manuscript copy of the 'Sonnets.'

Two other popular plays of the period, 'Mucedorus,' and 'Faire Em,' have also been assigned to
'Muce-   Shakespeare on slighter provocation.   In
dorus.'   Charles II's library they were bound together in a volume labelled 'Shakespeare, Vol. I,' and
bold speculators have occasionally sought to justify
the misnomer.

'Mucedorus,' an elementary effort in romantic
comedy, dates from the early years of Elizabeth's
reign; it was first published, doubtless after under-
going revision, in 1595, and was reissued, 'amplified
with new additions,' in 1610.   Mr. Payne Collier, who
included it in his privately printed edition of Shakespeare in 1878, was confident that a scene interpolated
in the 1610 version (in which the King of Valentia
laments the supposed loss of his son) displayed
genius which Shakespeare alone could compass.
However readily critics may admit the superiority in
literary value of the interpolated scene to anything
else in the piece, few will accept Mr. Collier's extravagant estimate.   The scene was probably from

[1] Cf. Swinburne, *Study of Shakspere*, pp. 231–74.   [2] See p. 89.

he pen of an admiring but faltering imitator of
Shakespeare.[1]

'Faire Em,' although not published till 1631, was
acted by Shakespeare's company while Lord Strange
was its patron, and some lines from it are
quoted for purposes of ridicule by Robert
Greene in his 'Farewell to Folly' in 1592. It is
another rudimentary endeavour in romantic comedy,
and has not even the pretension of 'Mucedorus' to
one short scene of conspicuous literary merit.

*Faire
Em.'*

[1] Cf. Dodsley's *Old Plays*, ed. W. C. Hazlitt, 1874, ii. 236-8.

VI

THE FIRST APPEAL TO THE READING PUBLIC

DURING the busy years (1591–4) that witnessed
his first pronounced successes as a dramatist, Shakespeare came before the public in yet another literary
capacity. On April 18, 1593, Richard Field, the
printer, who was his fellow-townsman, obtained a
license for the publication of ' Venus and Adonis,' a
Publica- metrical version of a classical tale of love.
tion of
'Venus and It was published a month or two later, with-
Adonis.' out an author's name on the title-page, but
Shakespeare appended his full name to the dedication,
which he addressed in conventional style to Henry
Wriothesley, third earl of Southampton. The Earl,
who was in his twentieth year, was reckoned the
handsomest man at Court, with a pronounced disposition to gallantry. He had vast possessions, was
well educated, loved literature, and through life
extended to men of letters a generous patronage.[1]
' I know not how I shall offend,' Shakespeare now
wrote to him, ' in dedicating my unpolished lines
to your lordship, nor how the world will censure me
for choosing so strong a prop to support so weak
a burden. . . . But if the first heir of my invention
prove deformed, I shall be sorry it had so noble
a godfather.' ' The first heir of my invention '

[1] See Appendix, Sections III. and IV.

implies that the poem was written, or at least designed, before Shakespeare's dramatic work. It is affluent in beautiful imagery and metrical sweetness, but imbued with a tone of license which may be held either to justify the theory that it was a precocious product of the author's youth, or to show that Shakespeare was not unready in mature years to write with a view to gratifying a patron's somewhat lascivious tastes. The title-page bears a beautiful Latin motto from Ovid's 'Amores':[1]

> Vilia miretur vulgus; mihi flavus Apollo
> Pocula Castalia plena ministret aqua.

The influence of Ovid, who told the story in his 'Metamorphoses,' is apparent in many of the details. But the theme was doubtless first suggested to Shakespeare by a contemporary effort. Lodge's 'Scillas Metamorphosis,' which appeared in 1589, is not only written in the same metre (six-line stanzas rhyming *a b a b c c*), but narrates in the exordium the same incidents in the same spirit. There is little doubt that Shakespeare drew from Lodge some of his inspiration.[2]

---

[1] See Ovid's *Amores*, liber i. elegy xv. ll. 35-6. Ovid's *Amores*, or Elegies of Love, were translated by Marlowe about 1589, and were first printed without a date on the title-page, probably about 1597. Marlowe's version had probably been accessible in manuscript in the eight years' interval. Marlowe rendered the lines quoted by Shakespeare thus:

> Let base conceited wits admire vile things,
> Fair Phœbus lead me to the Muses' springs!

[2] *Shakespeare's Venus and Adonis and Lodge's Scillas Metamorphosis*, by James P. Reardon, in 'Shakespeare Society's Papers,' iii.

A year after the issue of 'Venus and Adonis,' in 1594, Shakespeare published another poem in like vein, but far more mature in temper and execution. The digression (ll. 939–59) on the destroying power of Time, especially, is in an exalted key of meditation which is not sounded in the earlier poem. The metre, too, is changed ; seven-line stanzas (Chaucer's rhyme royal, *a b a b b c c*) take the place of six-line stanzas. The second poem was entered in the 'Stationers' Registers' on May 9, 1594, under the title of 'A Booke intitled the Ravyshement of Lucrece,' and was published in the same year under the title 'Lucrece.' Richard Field printed it, and John Harrison published and sold it at the sign of the White Greyhound in St. Paul's Churchyard. The classical story of Lucretia's ravishment and suicide is briefly recorded in Ovid's 'Fasti,' but Chaucer had retold it in his 'Legend of Good Women,' and Shakespeare must have read it there. Again, in topic and metre, the poem reflected a contemporary poet's work. Samuel Daniel's 'Com-

'Lucrece.'

143–6. Cf. Lodge's description of Venus's discovery of the wounded Adonis :

> Her daintie hand addrest to dawe her deere,
> Her roseall lip alied to his pale cheeke,
> Her sighs and then her lookes and heavie cheere,
> Her bitter threates, and then her passions meeke;
> How on his senseless corpse she lay a-crying,
> As if the boy were then but new a-dying.

In the minute description in Shakespeare's poem of the chase of the hare (ll. 673–708) there are curious resemblances to the *Ode de la Chasse* (on a stag hunt) by the French dramatist, Estienne Jodelle, in his *Œuvres et Meslanges Poétiques*, 1574.

plaint of Rosamond,' with its seven-line stanza (1592), stood to 'Lucrece' in even closer relation than Lodge's 'Scilla,' with its six-line stanza, to 'Venus and Adonis.' The pathetic accents of Shakespeare's heroine are those of Daniel's heroine purified and glorified.[1] The passage of Time is elaborated from one in Watson's 'Passionate Centurie of Love' (No. lxxvii.).[2] Shakespeare dedicated his second volume of poetry to the Earl of Southampton, the patron of his first. He addressed him in terms of devoted friendship, which were not uncommon at the time in communications between patrons and poets, but suggest that Shakespeare's relations with the brilliant young nobleman had grown closer since

[1] Rosamond, in Daniel's poem, muses thus when King Henry challenges her honour:

> But what ? he is my King and may constraine me;
> Whether I yeeld or not, I live defamed.
> The World will thinke Authoritie did gaine me,
> I shall be judg'd his Love and so be shamed;
> We see the faire condemn'd that never gamed,
>   And if I yeeld, 'tis honourable shame.
>   If not, I live disgrac'd, yet thought the same.

[2] Watson makes this comment on his poem or passion on Time (No. lxxvii.) : 'The chiefe contentes of this Passion are taken out of Seraphine [*i.e.* Serafino], Sonnet 132:

> Col tempo passa gli anni, i mesi, e l'hore,
> Col tempo le richeze, imperio, e regno,
> Col tempo fama, honor, fortezza, e ingegno,
> Col tempo giouentù, con beltà more, &c.'

Watson adds that he has inverted Serafino's order for ' rimes sake,' or ' upon some other more allowable consideration.' Shakespeare was also doubtless acquainted with Giles Fletcher's similar handling of the theme in Sonnet xxviii. of his collection of sonnets called *Licia* (1593).

he dedicated 'Venus and Adonis' to him in colder
language a year before. 'The love I dedicate to
your lordship,' Shakespeare wrote in the opening
pages of 'Lucrece,' 'is without end, whereof this pamphlet without beginning is but a superfluous moiety.
. . . What I have done is yours; what I have to do
is yours; being part in all I have, devoted yours.'

In these poems Shakespeare made his earliest
appeal to the world of readers, and the reading
public welcomed his addresses with unqualified enthusiasm. The London playgoer
already knew Shakespeare's name as that of
a promising actor and playwright, but his dramatic
efforts had hitherto been consigned in manuscript,
as soon as the theatrical representation ceased, to the
coffers of their owner, the playhouse manager. His
early plays brought him at the outset little reputation as a man of letters. It was not as the myriad-
minded dramatist, but in the restricted *rôle* of adapter
for English readers of familiar Ovidian fables that he
first impressed a wide circle of his contemporaries with
the fact of his mighty genius. The perfect sweetness
of the verse, and the poetical imagery in 'Venus and
Adonis' and 'Lucrece' practically silenced censure
of the licentious treatment of the themes on the part
of the seriously minded. Critics vied with each
other in the exuberance of the eulogies in which
they proclaimed that the fortunate author had gained
a place in permanence on the summit of Parnassus.
'Lucrece,' wrote Michael Drayton in his 'Legend of
Matilda' (1594), was 'revived to live another age.' In

*Enthusias-
tic recep-
tion of the
poems.*

1595 William Clerke in his 'Polimanteia' gave 'all praise' to 'sweet Shakespeare' for his 'Lucrecia.' John Weever, in a sonnet addressed to 'honey-tongued Shakespeare' in his 'Epigramms' (1595), eulogised the two poems as an unmatchable achievement, although he mentioned the plays 'Romeo' and 'Richard' and 'more whose names I know not.'   Richard Carew at the same time classed him with Marlowe as deserving the praises of an English Catullus.[1]   Printers and publishers of the poems strained their resources to satisfy the demands of eager purchasers.   No fewer than seven editions of 'Venus' appeared between 1594 and 1602 ; an eighth followed in 1617.   'Lucrece' achieved a fifth edition in the year of Shakespeare's death.

There is a likelihood, too, that Spenser, the greatest of Shakespeare's poetic contemporaries, was first drawn Shake-   by the poems into the ranks of Shakespeare's speare and   admirers.   It is hardly doubtful that Spenser Spenser.   described Shakespeare in 'Colin Clouts come home againe' (completed in 1594), under the name of 'Aetion,' — a familiar Greek proper name derived from 'Αετός, an eagle :

> And there, though last not least is Aetion ;
>   A gentler shepheard may no where be found,
>   Whose muse, full of high thought's invention,
>   Doth, like himselfe, heroically sound.

The last line seems to allude to Shakespeare's surname.   We may assume that the admiration was

[1] 'Excellencie of the English Tongue' in Camden's *Remaines,* p. 43.

mutual.   At any rate Shakespeare acknowledged
acquaintance with Spenser's work in a plain reference
to his 'Teares of the Muses' (1591) in 'Midsummer
Night's Dream' (v. i. 52–3).

> The thrice three Muses, mourning for the death
> Of learning, late deceased in beggary,

is stated to be the theme of one of the dramatic
entertainments wherewith it is proposed to celebrate
Theseus's marriage.   In Spenser's 'Teares of the
Muses' each of the Nine laments in turn her declin-
ing influence on the literary and dramatic effort of
the age.   Theseus dismisses the suggestion with the
not inappropriate comment:

> That is some satire keen and critical,
> Not sorting with a nuptial ceremony.

But there is no ground for assuming that Spenser in
the same poem referred figuratively to Shakespeare
when he made Thalia deplore the recent death of
'our pleasant Willy.'[1]   The name Willy was frequently used in contemporary literature as a term of
familiarity without relation to the baptismal name of
the person referred to.   Sir Philip Sidney was ad-

---

[1] All these and all that els the Comick Stage,
  With seasoned wit and goodly pleasance graced,
  By which man's life in his likest image
  Was limned forth, are wholly now defaced . . .
  And he, the man whom Nature selfe had made
  To mock her selfe and Truth to imitate,
  With kindly counter under mimick shade
  Our pleasant Willy, ah! is dead of late;
  With whom all joy and jolly merriment
  Is also deaded or in dolour drent. — (ll. 198–210.)

dressed as 'Willy' by some of his elegists. A comic actor, 'dead of late' in a literal sense, was clearly intended by Spenser, and there is no reason to dispute the view of an early seventeenth-century commentator that Spenser was paying a tribute to the loss English comedy had lately sustained by the death of the comedian, Richard Tarleton.[1] Similarly the 'gentle spirit' who is described by Spenser in a later stanza as sitting 'in idle cell' rather than turn his pen to base uses cannot be reasonably identified with Shakespeare.[2]

Meanwhile Shakespeare was gaining personal esteem outside the circles of actors and men of letters. His genius and 'civil demeanour' of which Chettle wrote arrested the notice not only of Southampton's but of other noble patrons of literature and the drama. His summons to act at Court with the most famous actors of the day at the Christmas Patrons at of 1594 was possibly due in part to personal court. interest in himself. Elizabeth quickly showed him special favour. Until the end of her reign his plays were repeatedly acted in her presence. The revised version of 'Love's Labour's Lost' was given at Whitehall at Christmas 1597, and tradition

---

[1] A note to this effect, in a genuine early seventeenth-century hand, was discovered by Halliwell-Phillipps in a copy of the 1611 edition of Spenser's *Works* (cf. *Outlines*, ii. 394–5).

[2] But that same gentle spirit, from whose pen
    Large streams of honnie and sweete nectar flowe,
    Scorning the boldnes of such base-borne men
    Which dare their follies forth so rashlie throwe,
        Doth rather choose to sit in idle cell
        Than so himselfe to mockerie to sell. — (ll. 217-22.)

G

credits the Queen with unconcealed enthusiasm for Falstaff, who came into being a little later. Under Elizabeth's successor he greatly strengthened his hold on royal favour, but Ben Jonson claimed that the Queen's appreciation equalled that of James I.

> Those flights upon the banks of Thames,
> That so did take Eliza and our James, —

of which Jonson wrote in his elegy on Shakespeare — included many representations of Shakespeare's plays by himself and his fellow-actors at the palaces of Whitehall, Richmond, or Greenwich during the last decade of Elizabeth's reign.

VII

THE SONNETS AND THEIR LITERARY HISTORY

IT was doubtless to Shakespeare's personal relations with men and women of the Court that his
sonnets owe their existence.   In Italy and France the
practice of writing and circulating series of sonnets in-

The vogue of the Elizabethan sonnet. scribed to great men and women flourished
continuously throughout the sixteenth cen-
tury.   In England, until the last decade of
that century, the vogue was intermittent.   Wyatt and
Surrey inaugurated sonnetteering in the English
language under Henry VIII, and Thomas Watson
devoted much energy to the pursuit when Shakespeare was a boy.   But it was not until 1591, when
Sir Philip Sidney's collection of sonnets entitled
' Astrophel and Stella ' was first published, that the
sonnet enjoyed in England any conspicuous or continuous favour.   For the half-dozen years following
the appearance of Sir Philip Sidney's volume the
writing of sonnets, both singly and in connected sequences, engaged more literary activity in this country
than it engaged at any period here or elsewhere.[1]

---

[1] Section IX. of the Appendix to this volume gives a sketch of each
of the numerous collections of sonnets which bore witness to the un-
exampled vogue of the Elizabethan sonnet between 1591 and 1597.

Men and women of the cultivated Elizabethan nobility encouraged poets to celebrate in single sonnets their virtues and graces, and under the same patronage there were produced multitudes of sonnet-sequences which more or less fancifully narrated, after the manner of Petrarch and his successors, the pleasures and pains of love. Between 1591 and 1597 no aspirant to poetic fame in the country failed to seek a patron's ears by a trial of skill on the popular poetic instrument, and Shakespeare, who habitually kept abreast of the currents of contemporary literary taste, applied himself to sonnetteering with all the force of his poetic genius when the fashion was at its height.

Shakespeare had lightly experimented with the sonnet from the outset of his literary career. Three well-turned examples figure in 'Love's Labour's Lost,' probably his earliest play; two of the choruses in 'Romeo and Juliet' are couched in the sonnet form; and a letter of the heroine Helen, in 'All's Well that Ends Well,' which bears traces of very early composition, takes the same shape. It has, too, been argued ingeniously, if not convincingly, that he was author of the somewhat clumsy sonnet, 'Phaeton to his friend Florio,' which prefaced in 1591 Florio's 'Second Frutes,' a series of Italian-English dialogues for students.[1]

Shakespeare's first experiments.

---

[1] Minto, *Characteristics of English Poetry*, 1885, pp. 371, 382. The sonnet, headed 'Phaeton to his friend Florio,' runs:

> Sweet friend whose name agrees with thy increase,
> How fit arrival art thou of the Spring !
> For when each branch hath left his flourishing,
> And green-locked Summer's shady pleasure cease :

But these were sporadic efforts. It was not till the spring of 1593, after Shakespeare had secured a nobleman's patronage for his earliest publication, 'Venus and Adonis,' that he became a sonnetteer on an extended scale. Of the hundred and fifty-four sonnets that survive outside his plays, the greater *Majority of* number were in all likelihood composed *Shake-* between that date and the autumn of 1594, *speare's* during his thirtieth and thirty-first years. *sonnets* *composed* His occasional reference in the sonnets to his *in 1594.* growing age was a conventional device — traceable to Petrarch — of all sonnetteers of the day, and admits of

> She makes the Winter's storms repose in peace,
>   And spends her franchise on each living thing:
>   The daisies sprout, the little birds do sing,
>   Herbs, gums, and plants do vaunt of their release.
> So when that all our English Wits lay dead,
>   (Except the laurel that is ever green)
>   Thou with thy Fruit our barrenness o'erspread,
>   And set thy flowery pleasance to be seen.
> Such fruits, such flow'rets of morality,
>   Were ne'er before brought out of Italy.

Cf. Shakespeare's Sonnet xcviii. beginning:

> When proud-pied April, dress'd in all his trim
> Hath put a spirit of youth in everything.

But like descriptions of Spring and Summer formed a topic that was common to all the sonnets of the period. Much has been written of Shakespeare's alleged acquaintance with Florio. Farmer and Warburton argue that Shakespeare ridiculed Florio in Holofernes in *Love's Labour's Lost.* They chiefly rely on Florio's bombastic prefaces to his *Worlde of Wordes* and his translation of Montaigne's *Essays* (1603). There is nothing there to justify the suggestion. Florio writes more in the vein of Armado than of Holofernes, and, beyond the fact that he was a teacher of languages to noblemen, he bears no resemblance to Holofernes, a village schoolmaster. Shakespeare doubtless knew Florio as Southampton's *protégé*, and read his fine translation of Montaigne's *Essays* with delight. He quotes from it in *The Tempest:* see p. 253.

no literal interpretation.[1]   In matter and in manner
the bulk of the poems suggest that they came from
the pen of a man not much more than thirty. Doubtless he renewed his sonnetteering efforts occasionally

[1] Shakespeare writes in his Sonnets:

> My glass shall not persuade me I am old (xxii. 1).
> But when my glass shows me myself indeed,
> Beated and chopp'd with tann'd antiquity (lxii. 9–10).
> That time of year thou mayst in me behold
> When yellow leaves, or none, or few do hang (lxxiii. 1–2).
> My days are past the best (cxxxviii. 6).

Daniel in *Delia* (xxiii.) in 1591, when twenty-nine years old, exclaimed:

> My years draw on my everlasting night,
> . . .   My days are done.

Richard Barnfield, at the age of twenty, bade the boy Ganymede, to
whom he addressed his *Affectionate Shepherd* and a sequence of sonnets
in 1594 (ed. Arber, p. 23):

> Behold my gray head, full of silver hairs,
> My wrinkled skin, deep furrows in my face.

Similarly Drayton in a sonnet (*Idea*, xiv.) published in 1594, when he
was barely thirty-one, wrote:

> Looking into the glass of my youth's miseries,
> I see the ugly face of my deformed cares
> With withered brows all wrinkled with despairs;

and a little later (No. xliii. of the 1599 edition) he repeated how

> Age rules my lines with wrinkles in my face.

All these lines are echoes of Petrarch, and Shakespeare and Drayton
followed the Italian master's words more closely than their contemporaries. Cf. Petrarch's Sonnet cxliii. (to Laura alive), or Sonnet lxxxi. (to
Laura after death); the latter begins:

> Dicemi spesso il mio fidato speglio,
> L' animo stanco e la cangiata scorza
> E la scemata mia destrezza e forza:
> Non ti nasconder più; tu se' pur veglio.

(*i.e.* 'My faithful glass often shows me my weary spirit and my
wrinkled skin, and my decaying wit and strength: it cannot longer be
hidden from you, you are old.')

and at irregular intervals during the nine years which elapsed between 1594 and the accession of James I in 1603. But to very few of the extant examples can a date later than 1594 be allotted with confidence. Sonnet CVII., in which plain reference is made to Queen Elizabeth's death, may be fairly regarded as a belated and a final act of homage on Shakespeare's part to the importunate vogue of the Elizabethan sonnet. All the evidence, whether internal or external, points to the conclusion that the sonnet exhausted such fascination as it exerted on Shakespeare before his dramatic genius attained its full height.

In literary value Shakespeare's sonnets are notably unequal. Many reach levels of lyric melody and meditative energy that are hardly to be matched elsewhere in poetry. The best examples are charged with the mellowed sweetness of rhythm and metre, the depth of thought and feeling, the vividness of imagery and the stimulating fervour of expression which are the finest proofs of poetic power. On the other hand, many sink almost into inanity beneath the burden of quibbles and conceits. In both their excellences and their defects Shakespeare's sonnets betray near kinship to his early dramatic work, in which passages of the highest poetic temper at times alternate with unimpressive displays of verbal jugglery. In phraseology the sonnets often closely resemble such early dramatic efforts as 'Love's Labour's Lost' and 'Romeo and Juliet.' There is far more concentration in the sonnets than in 'Venus and Adonis' or in 'Lucrece,' although

Their literary value.

occasional utterances of Shakespeare's Roman heroine show traces of the intensity that characterises the best of them. The superior and more evenly sustained energy of the sonnets is to be attributed, not to the accession of power that comes with increase of years, but to the innate principles of the poetic form, and to metrical exigences, which impelled the sonneteer to aim at a uniform condensation of thought and language.

In accordance with a custom that was not uncommon, Shakespeare did not publish his sonnets; he circulated them in manuscript.[1] But their reputation grew, and public interest was aroused in them in spite of his unreadi-

Circulation in manuscript.

---

[1] The Sonnets of Sidney, Watson, Daniel, and Constable long circulated in manuscript, and suffered much the same fate as Shakespeare's at the hands of piratical publishers. After circulating many years in manuscript, Sidney's Sonnets were published in 1591 by an irresponsible trader, Thomas Newman, who in his self-advertising dedication wrote of the collection that it had been widely 'spread abroad in written copies,' and had 'gathered much corruption by ill writers' [*i.e.* copyists]. Constable produced in 1592 a collection of twenty sonnets in a volume which he entitled 'Diana.' This was an authorised publication. But in 1594 a printer and a publisher, without Constable's knowledge or sanction, reprinted these sonnets and scattered them through a volume of nearly eighty miscellaneous sonnets by Sidney and many other hands; the adventurous publishers bestowed on their medley the title of 'Diana,' which Constable had distinctively attached to his own collection. Daniel suffered in much the same way. See Appendix IX. for further notes on the subject. Proofs of the commonness of the habit of circulating literature in manuscript abound. Fulke Greville, writing to Sidney's father-in-law, Sir Francis Walsingham, in 1587, expressed regret that uncorrected manuscript copies of the then unprinted *Arcadia* were 'so common.' In 1591 Gabriel Cawood, the publisher of Robert Southwell's *Mary Magdalen's Funeral Tears*, wrote that manuscript copies of the work had long flown about 'fast and false.' Nash, in the preface to his

ness to give them publicity. A line from one of them:

Lilies that fester smell far worse than weeds (xciv. 14),[1]

was quoted in the play of 'Edward III,' which was probably written before 1595. Meres, writing in 1598, enthusiastically commends Shakespeare's 'sugred[2] sonnets among his private friends,' and mentions them in close conjunction with his two narrative poems. William Jaggard piratically inserted in 1599 two of the most mature of the series (Nos. cxxxviii. and cxliv.) in his 'Passionate Pilgrim.'

At length, in 1609, the sonnets were surreptitiously sent to press. Thomas Thorpe, the moving spirit in the design of their publication, was a camp-follower of the regular publishing army. He was professionally engaged in procuring for publication literary works which had been widely disseminated in written copies and had thus passed beyond their authors' control; for the law then recognised no natural right in an author to the creations of his brain, and the full owner of a manuscript copy of any literary composition was entitled to reproduce it, or to treat it as he pleased, without

Terrors of the Night, 1594, described how a copy of that essay, which a friend had 'wrested' from him, had 'progressed [without his authority] from one scrivener's shop to another, and at length grew so common that it was ready to be hung out for one of their figures [*i.e.* shop-signs], like a pair of indentures.'

[1] Cf. Sonnet lxix. 12:

To thy fair flower add the rank smell of weeds.

[2] For other instances of the application of this epithet to Shakespeare's work, see p. 179, note 1.

reference to the author's wishes. Thorpe's career as a procurer of neglected 'copy' had begun well. He made, in 1600, his earliest hit by bringing to light Marlowe's translation of the 'First Book of Lucan.' On May 20, 1609, he obtained a licence for the publication of 'Shakespeare's Sonnets,' and this tradesman-like form of title figured not only on the 'Stationers' Company's Registers,' but on the title-page. Thorpe employed George Eld to print the manuscript, and two booksellers, William Aspley and John Wright, to distribute it to the public. On half the edition Aspley's name figured as that of the seller, and on the other half that of Wright. The book was issued in June,[1] and the owner of the 'copy' left the public under no misapprehension as to his share in the production by printing above his initials a dedicatory preface from his own pen. The appearance in a book of a dedication from the publisher's (instead of from the author's) pen was, unless the substitution was specifically accounted for on other grounds, an accepted sign that the author had no hand in the publication. Except in the case of his two narrative poems, which were published in 1593 and 1594 respectively, Shakespeare made no effort to publish any of his works, and uncomplainingly submitted to the wholesale piracies of his plays and the ascription to him of books by other hands. Such practices were encouraged by his passive indifference and the contemporary condition of the law of copyright. He

[1] The actor Alleyn paid fivepence for a copy in that month (cf. Warner's *Dulwich MSS.*, p. 92).

cannot be credited with any responsibility for the publication of Thorpe's collection of his sonnets in 1609. With characteristic insolence Thorpe took the added liberty of appending a previously unprinted poem of forty-nine seven-line stanzas (the metre of 'Lucrece') entitled 'A Lover's Complaint,' in which a girl laments her betrayal by a deceitful youth. The poem, in a gentle Spenserian vein, has no connection with the 'Sonnets.' If, as is possible, it be by Shakespeare, it must have been written in very early days.

'A Lover's Complaint.'

A misunderstanding respecting Thorpe's preface and his part in the publication has led many critics into a serious misinterpretation of Shakespeare's poems.[1] Thorpe's dedication was couched in the bombastic language which was habitual to him. He advertised Shakespeare as ' our ever-living poet.' As the chief promoter of the undertaking, he called himself ' the well-wishing adventurer in setting forth,' and in resonant phrase designated as the patron of the venture

Thomas Thorpe and 'Mr. W. H.'

[1] The chief editions of the sonnets that have appeared, with critical apparatus, of late years are those of Professor Dowden (1875, reissued 1896), Mr. Thomas Tyler (1890), and Mr. George Wyndham, M.P. (1898). Mr. Gerald Massey's *Secret Drama of Shakespeare's Sonnets* — the text of the poems with a full discussion — appeared in a second revised edition in 1888. I regret to find myself in more or less complete disagreement with all these writers, although I am at one with Mr. Massey in identifying the young man to whom many of the sonnets were addressed with the Earl of Southampton. A short bibliography of the works advocating the theory that the sonnets were addressed to William, third Earl of Pembroke, is given in Appendix VI. ' Mr. William Herbert,' note 1.

a partner in the speculation, ' Mr. W. H.' In the conventional dedicatory formula of the day he wished 'Mr. W. H.' 'all happiness' and 'eternity,' such eternity as Shakespeare in the text of the sonnets conventionally foretold for his own verse. When Thorpe was organising the issue of Marlowe's ' First Book of Lucan' in 1600, he sought the patronage of Edward Blount, a friend in the trade. 'W. H.' was doubtless in a like position. He is best identified with a stationer's assistant, William Hall, who was professionally engaged, like Thorpe, in procuring 'copy.' In 1606 'W. H.' won a conspicuous success in that direction, and conducted his operations under cover of the familiar initials. In that year 'W. H.' announced that he had procured a neglected manuscript poem — ' A Foure-fold Meditation' — by the Jesuit Robert Southwell who had been executed in 1595, and he published it with a dedication (signed 'W. H.') vaunting his good fortune in meeting with such treasure-trove. When Thorpe dubbed ' Mr. W. H.,' with characteristic magniloquence, 'the onlie begetter [*i.e.* obtainer or procurer] of these ensuing sonnets,' he merely indicated that that personage was the first of the pirate-publisher fraternity to procure a manuscript of Shakespeare's sonnets and recommend its surreptitious issue. In accordance with custom, Thorpe gave Hall's initials only, because he was an intimate associate who was known by those initials to their common circle of friends. Hall was not a man of sufficiently wide public reputation to render it probable that the printing of his full name would excite additional interest in the book or attract buyers.

The common assumption that Thorpe in this boastful preface was covertly addressing, under the initials 'Mr. W. H.,' a young nobleman, to whom the sonnets were originally addressed by Shakespeare, ignores the elementary principles of publishing transactions of the day, and especially of those of the type to which Thorpe's efforts were confined.[1] There was nothing mysterious or fantastic, although from a modern point of view there was much that lacked principle, in Thorpe's methods of business. His choice of patron for this, like all his volumes, was dictated solely by his mercantile interests. He was under no inducement and in no position to take into consideration the affairs of Shakespeare's private life. Shakespeare, through all but the earliest stages of his career, belonged socially to a world that was cut off by im-

---

[1] It has been wrongly inferred that Shakespeare asserts in Sonnets cxxxv.–vi. and cxliii. that the young friend to whom he addressed some of the sonnets bore his own christian name of Will (see for a full examination of these sonnets Appendix VIII.). Further, it has been fantastically suggested that the line (xx. 7) describing the youth as ' A man in hue, all hues in his controlling' (*i.e.* a man in colour or complexion whose charms are so varied as to appear to give his countenance control of, or enable it to assume, all manner of fascinating hues or complexions), and other applications to the youth of the ordinary word 'hue,' imply that his surname was Hughes. There is no other pretence of argument for the conclusion, which a few critics have hazarded in all seriousness, that the friend's name was William Hughes. There was a contemporary musician called William Hughes, but no known contemporary of the name, either in age or position in life, bears any resemblance to the young man who is addressed by Shakespeare in his sonnets.

passable barriers from that in which Thorpe pursued his calling. It was wholly outside Thorpe's aims in life to seek to mystify his customers by investing a dedication with any cryptic significance.

No peer of the day, moreover, bore a name which could be represented by the initials 'Mr. W. H.' Shakespeare was never on terms of intimacy (although the contrary has often been recklessly assumed) with William, third Earl of Pembroke, when a youth.[1] But were complete proofs of the acquaintanceship forthcoming, they would throw no light on Thorpe's 'Mr. W. H.' The Earl of Pembroke was, from his birth to the date of his succession to the earldom in 1601, known by the courtesy title of Lord Herbert and by no other name, and he could not have been designated at any period of his life by the symbols 'Mr. W. H.' In 1609 Pembroke was a high officer of state, and numerous books were dedicated to him in all the splendour of his many titles. Star-Chamber penalties would have been exacted of any publisher or author who denied him in print his titular distinctions. Thorpe had occasion to dedicate two books to the earl in later years, and he there showed not merely that he was fully acquainted with the compulsory etiquette, but that his sycophantic temperament rendered him only eager to improve on the conventional formulas of servility. Any further considerations of Thorpe's address to 'Mr. W. H.' belongs to the

---

[1] See Appendix VI., 'Mr. William Herbert; and VII. 'Shakespeare and the Earl of Pembroke.'

biographies of Thorpe and his friend; it lies outside the scope of Shakespeare's biography.[1]

Shakespeare's 'Sonnets' ignore the somewhat complex scheme of rhyme adopted by Petrarch, whom the Elizabethan sonnetteers, like the French sonnetteers of the sixteenth century, recognised to be in most respects their master. Following the example originally set by Surrey and Wyatt, and generally pursued by Shakespeare's contemporaries, his sonnets aim at far greater metrical simplicity than the Italian or the French. They consist of three decasyllabic quatrains with a concluding couplet, and the quatrains rhyme alternately.[2]

The form of Shakespeare's Sonnets.

[1] The full results of my researches into Thorpe's history, his methods of business, and the significance of his dedicatory addresses, of which four are extant besides that prefixed to the volume of Shakespeare's Sonnets in 1609, are given in Appendix v., 'The True History of Thomas Thorpe and " Mr. W. H."'

[2] The form of fourteen-line stanza adopted by Shakespeare is in no way peculiar to himself. It is the type recognised by Elizabethan writers on metre as correct and customary in England long before he wrote. George Gascoigne, in his *Certayne Notes of Instruction concerning the making of Verse or Ryme in English* (published in Gascoigne's *Posies*, 1575), defined sonnets thus : 'Fouretene lynes, every lyne conteyning tenne syllables. The first twelve to ryme in staves of foure lynes by cross metre and the last two ryming togither, do conclude the whole.' In twenty-one of the 108 sonnets of which Sidney's collection entitled *Astrophel and Stella* consists, the rhymes are on the foreign model and the final couplet is avoided. But these are exceptional. As is not uncommon in Elizabethan sonnet-collections, one of Shakespeare's sonnets (xcix.) has fifteen lines ; another (cxxvi.) has only twelve lines, and those in rhymed couplets (cf. Lodge's *Phillis*, Nos. viii. and xxvi.) ; and a third (cxlv.) is in octosyllabics. But it is very doubtful whether the second and third of these sonnets rightly belong to Shakespeare's collection. They were probably written as independent lyrics ; see p. 97, note 1.

A single sonnet does not always form an independent poem. As in the French and Italian sonnets of the period, and in those of Spenser, Sidney, Daniel, and Drayton, the same train of thought is at times pursued continuously through two or more. The collection of Shakespeare's 154 sonnets thus presents the appearance of an extended series of independent poems, many in a varying number of fourteen-line stanzas. The longest sequence (i.–xvii.) numbers seventeen sonnets, and in Thorpe's edition opens the volume.

It is unlikely that the order in which the poems were printed follows the order in which they were Want of written. Fantastic endeavours have been continuity. made to detect in the original arrangement of the poems a closely connected narrative, but the thread is on any showing constantly interrupted.[1] The two It is usual to divide the sonnets into two 'groups.' groups, and to represent that all those numbered i.–cxxvi. by Thorpe were addressed to a young man, and all those numbered cxxvii.–cliv. were addressed to a woman. This division cannot be

[1] If the critical ingenuity which has detected a continuous thread of narrative in the order that Thorpe printed Shakespeare's sonnets were applied to the booksellers' miscellany of sonnets called *Diana* (1594), that volume, which rakes together sonnets on all kinds of amorous subjects from all quarters and numbers them consecutively, could be made to reveal the sequence of an individual lover's moods quite as readily, and, if no external evidence were admitted, quite as convincingly as Thorpe's collection of Shakespeare's sonnets. Almost all Elizabethan sonnets are not merely in the like metre, but are pitched in what sounds superficially to be the same key of pleading or yearning. Thus almost every collection gives at a first perusal a specious and delusive impression of homogeneity.

literally justified.   In the first group some eighty of the sonnets can be proved to be addressed to a man by the use of the masculine pronoun or some other unequivocal sign ; but among the remaining forty there is no clear indication of the kind.   Many of these forty are meditative soliloquies which address no person at all (cf. cv. cxvi. cxix. cxxi.).   A few invoke abstractions like Death (lxvi.) or Time (cxxiii.), or 'benefit of ill' (cxix.).   The twelve-lined poem (cxxvi.), the last of the first 'group,' does little more than sound a variation on the conventional poetic invocations of Cupid or Love personified as a boy.[1] And there is no valid objection to the assumption that the poet inscribed the rest of these forty sonnets to a woman (cf. xxi. xlvi. xlvii.).   Similarly, the sonnets in the second 'group' (cxxvii.–cliv.) have no uniform superscription.   Six invoke no person at all.   No. cxxviii. is an overstrained compliment on a lady playing on the virginals.   No. cxxix. is a metaphysical disquisition on lust.   No. cxlv. is a playful lyric in

---

[1] Shakespeare merely warns his 'lovely boy' that, though he be now the 'minion' of Nature's 'pleasure,' he will not succeed in defying Time's inexorable law. Sidney addresses in a lighter vein Cupid — 'blind-hitting boy,' he calls him — in his *Astrophel* (No. xlvi.). Cupid is similarly invoked in three of Drayton's sonnets (No. xxvi. in the edition of 1594, and Nos. xxxiii. and xxxiv. in that of 1605), and in six in Fulke Greville's collection entitled *Cælica* (cf. lxxxiv., beginning 'Farewell, sweet boy, complain not of my truth'). Lyly in his *Sapho and Phao*, 1584, and in his *Mother Bombie*, 1598, has songs of like temper addressed in the one case to 'O Cruel love!' and in the other to 'O Cupid! monarch over kings.' A similar theme to that of Shakespeare's Sonnet cxxvi. is treated by John Ford in the song, 'Love is ever dying,' in his tragedy of the *Broken Heart*, 1633.

H

octosyllabics, like Lyly's song of 'Cupid and Campaspe,' and its tone has close affinity to that and other of Lyly's songs. No. cxlvi. invokes the soul of man. Nos. cliii. and cliv. soliloquise on an ancient Greek apologue on the force of Cupid's fire.[1]

The choice and succession of topics in each 'group' give to neither genuine cohesion. In the first 'group' the long opening sequence (i.–xvii.) forms the poet's appeal to a young man to marry so that his youth and beauty may survive in children. There is almost a contradiction in terms between the poet's handling of that topic and his emphatic boast in the two following sonnets (xviii.–xix.) that his verse alone is fully equal to the task of immor-talising his friend's youth and accomplish-ments. The same asseveration is repeated in many later sonnets (cf. lv. lx. lxiii. lxxiv. lxxxi. ci. cvii.). These alternate with conven-tional adulation of the beauty of the object of the poet's affections (cf. xxi. liii. lxviii.) and descriptions of the effects of absence in intensifying devotion (cf. xlviii. l. cxiii.). There are many reflections on the nocturnal torments of a lover (cf. xxvii. xxviii. xliii. l. lxi.) and on his blindness to the beauty of spring or summer when he is separated from his love (cf. xcvii. xcviii.). At times a youth is rebuked for sensual indulgences; he has sought and won the favour of the poet's mistress in the poet's absence, but the poet is forgiving (xxxii.–xxxv. xl.–xlii. lxix. xcv.–xcvi.). In Sonnet lxx. the young man whom

Main topics of the first 'group.'

[1] See p. 113, note 2.

the poet addresses is credited with a different disposition and experience :

> And thou present'st a pure unstained prime.
> Thou hast pass'd by the ambush of young days,
> Either not assail'd, or victor being charg'd!

At times melancholy overwhelms the writer : he
despairs of the corruptions of the age (lxvi.), reproaches himself with carnal sin (cxix.), declares himself weary of his profession of acting (cxi. cxii.), and
foretells his approaching death (lxxi.–lxxiv.). Throughout are dispersed obsequious addresses to the youth in
his capacity of sole patron of the poet's verse (cf. xxiii.
xxxvii. c. ci. ciii. civ.). But in one sequence the friend
is sorrowfully reproved for bestowing his patronage
on rival poets (lxxviii.–lxxxvi.). In three sonnets
near the close of the first group in the original edition
the writer gives varied assurances of his constancy in
love or friendship which apply indifferently to man or
woman (cf. cxxii. cxxiv. cxxv.).

In two sonnets of the second 'group' (cxxvi.–
clii.) the poet compliments his mistress on her black
complexion and raven-black hair and eyes. In twelve
sonnets he hotly denounces his 'dark' mistress for
her proud disdain of his affection, and for her mani-
fold infidelities with other men. Apparently con-
Main tinuing a theme of the first 'group,' the poet
topics of
the second rebukes the woman, whom he addresses, for
'group.' having beguiled his friend to yield himself to
her seductions (cxxxiii.–cxxxvi.). Elsewhere he makes
satiric reflections on the extravagant compliments
paid to the fair sex by other sonnetteers (No. cxxx.),

or lightly quibbles on his name of 'Will' (cxxx.–vi.).
In tone and subject-matter numerous sonnets in the
second as in the first 'group' lack visible sign of
coherence with those they immediately precede or
follow.

It is not merely a close study of the text that
confutes the theory, for which recent writers have
fought hard, of a logical continuity in Thorpe's
arrangement of the poems in 1609. There remains
the historic fact that readers and publishers of the
seventeenth century acknowledged no sort of significance in the order in which the poems first saw the
light. When the sonnets were printed for a second
time in 1640 — thirty-one years after their first
appearance — they were presented in a completely
different order. The short descriptive titles which
were then supplied to single sonnets or to short
sequences proved that the collection was regarded as
a disconnected series of occasional poems in more
or less amorous vein.

In whatever order Shakespeare's sonnets be
studied, the claim that has been advanced in their
Lack of behalf to rank as autobiographical docu-
genuine ments can only be accepted with many
sentiment
in Eliza- qualifications. Elizabethan sonnets were
bethan commonly the artificial products of the poet's
sonnets.
fancy. A strain of personal emotion is occasionally
discernible in a detached effort, and is vaguely traceable in a few sequences ; but autobiographical confessions were very rarely the stuff of which the
Elizabethan sonnet was made. The typical collection

of Elizabethan sonnets was a mosaic of plagiarisms, a medley of imitative studies. Echoes of the French or of the Italian sonnetteers, with their Platonic idealism, are usually the dominant notes. The echoes often have a musical quality peculiar to themselves. Daniel's fine sonnet (xlix.) on 'Care-charmer, sleep,' although directly inspired by the French, breathes a finer melody than the sonnet of Pierre de Brach [1] apostrophising 'le sommeil chasse-soin' (in the collection entitled 'Les Amours d'Aymée'), or the sonnet of Philippe Desportes invoking 'Sommeil, paisible fils de la nuit solitaire' (in the collection entitled 'Amours d'Hippolyte').[2] But, throughout Elizabethan sonnet literature, the heavy debt to Italian and French effort is unmistakable.[3] Spenser, in 1569, at the outset of his literary career, avowedly translated numerous sonnets from Du Bellay and from Petrarch, and his friend Gabriel Harvey bestowed on him the title of 'an English Petrarch' — the highest praise that the critic conceived it possible to bestow on an English sonnetteer.[4] Thomas Watson in 1582, in his collec-

Their dependence on French and Italian models.

[1] 1547–1604. Cf. De Brach, *Œuvres Poétiques*, edited by Reinhold Dezeimeris, 1861, i. pp. 59–60.

[2] See Appendix IX.

[3] Section X. of the Appendix to this volume supplies a bibliographical note on the sonnet in France between 1550 and 1600, with a list of the sixteenth-century sonnetteers of Italy.

[4] Gabriel Harvey, in his *Pierces Supererogation* (1593, p. 61), after enthusiastic commendation of Petrarch's sonnets ('Petrarch's invention is pure love itself; Petrarch's elocution pure beauty itself'), justifies the common English practice of imitating them on the ground that 'all the noblest Italian, French, and Spanish poets have in their several veins

tion of metrically irregular sonnets which he entitled 'ΕΚΑΤΟΜΠΑΘΙΑ, or a Passionate Century of Love,' prefaced each poem, which he termed a ' passion,' with a prose note of its origin and intention. Watson frankly informed his readers that one ' passion' was ' wholly translated out of Petrarch;' that in another passion ' he did very busily imitate and augment a certain ode of Ronsard;' while ' the sense or matter of " a third " was taken out of Serafino in his " Strambotti." ' In every case Watson gave the exact reference to his

Petrarchised ; and it is no dishonour for the daintiest or divinest Muse to be his scholar, whom the amiablest invention and beautifullest elocution acknowledge their master.' Both French and English sonnetteers habitually admit that they are open to the charge of plagiarising Petrarch's sonnets to Laura (cf. Du Bellay's *Les Amours*, ed. Becq de Fouquières, 1876, p. 186, and Daniel's *Delia*, Sonnet xxxviii.). The dependent relations in which both English and French sonnetteers stood to Petrarch may be best realised by comparing such a popular sonnet of the Italian master as No. ciii. (or in some editions lxxxviii.) in *Sonetti in Vita di M. Laura*, beginning ' S' amor non è, che dunque è quel ch' i' sento ?' with a rendering of it into French like that of De Baif in his *Amours de Francine* (ed. Becq de Fouquières, p. 121), beginning, ' Si ce n'est pas Amour, que sent donques mon cœur; ' or with a rendering of the same sonnet into English like that by Watson in his *Passionate Century*, No. v., beginning, ' If 't bee not love I feele, what is it then ?' Imitation of Petrarch is a constant characteristic of the English sonnet throughout the sixteenth century from the date of the earliest efforts of Surrey and Wyatt. It is interesting to compare the skill in rendering the Italian master of the early and late sonnetteers. Petrarch's sonnet *In Vita di M. Laura* (No. lxxx. or lxxxi., beginning ' Cesare, poi che 'l traditor d' Egitto ') was independently translated both by Sir Thomas Wyatt, about 1530 (ed. Bell, p. 60), and by Francis Davison in his *Poetical Rhapsody* (1602, ed. Bullen, i. 90). Petrarch's sonnet (No. xcv. or cxiii.) was also rendered independently both by Wyatt (cf. Puttenham's *Arte of English Poesie*, ed. Arber, p. 23) and by Drummond of Hawthornden (ed. Ward, i. 100, 221).

foreign original, and frequently appended a quotation.[1] Drayton in 1594, in the dedicatory sonnet of his collection of sonnets entitled ' Idea,' declared that it was ' a fault too common in this latter time ' ' to filch from Desportes or from Petrarch's pen.'[2] Lodge did not acknowledge his borrowings more specifically than his colleagues, but he made a plain profession of indebtedness to Desportes when he wrote : ' Few men are able to second the sweet conceits of Philippe Desportes, whose poetical writings are ordinarily in everybody's hand.'[3] Giles Fletcher, who in his collection of

---

[1] Eight of Watson's sonnets are, according to his own account, renderings from Petrarch ; twelve are from Serafino dell' Aquila (1466–1500) ; four each come from Strozza, an Italian poet, and from Ronsard ; three from the Italian poet Agnolo Fiorenzuola (1493-1548) ; two each from the French poet, Etienne Forcadel, known as Forcatulus (1514?–1573), the Italian Girolamo Parabosco (*fl.* 1548), and Æneas Sylvius ; while many are based on passages from such authors as (among the Greeks) Sophocles, Theocritus, Apollonius of Rhodes (author of the epic ' Argonautica ') ; or (among the Latins) Virgil, Tibullus, Ovid, Horace, Propertius, Seneca, Pliny, Lucan, Martial, and Valerius Flaccus ; or (among other modern Italians) Politian (1454–94) and Baptista Mantuanus (1448–1516) ; or (among other modern Frenchmen) Gervasius Sepinus of Saumur, writer of eclogues after the manner of Virgil and Mantuanus.

[2] No importance can be attached to Drayton's pretensions to greater originality than his neighbours. The very line in which he makes the claim (' I am no pick-purse of another's wit') is a verbatim theft from a sonnet of Sir Philip Sidney.

[3] Lodge's *Margarite*, p. 79. See Appendix IX. for the text of Desportes's sonnet (*Diane*, livre ii. No. iii.) and Lodge's translation in *Phillis*. Lodge gave two other translations of the same sonnet of Desportes — in his romance of *Rosalind* (Hunterian Society's reprint, p. 74), and in his volume of poems called *Scillæs Metamorphosis* (p. 44). Sonnet xxxiii. of Lodge's *Phillis* is rendered with equal literalness from Ronsard. But Desportes was Lodge's special master.

sonnets called 'Licia' (1593) simulated the varying
moods of a lover under the sway of a great passion
as successfully as most of his rivals, stated on his
title-page that his poems were all written in 'imitation
of the best Latin poets and others.' Very many of
the love-sonnets in the series of sixty-eight penned
ten years later by William Drummond of Hawthornden have been traced to their sources in the Italian
sonnets not merely of Petrarch, but of the sixteenth-
century poets Guarini, Bembo, Giovanni Battista
Marino, Tasso, and Sannazzaro.[1] The Elizabethans
usually gave the fictitious mistresses after whom their
volumes of sonnets were called the names that had
recently served the like purpose in France. Daniel
followed Maurice Sève[2] in christening his collection
'Delia'; Constable followed Desportes in christening his collection 'Diana'; while Drayton not only
applied to his sonnets on his title-page in 1594 the
French term 'amours,' but bestowed on his imaginary heroine the title of Idea, which seems to have
been the invention of Claude de Pontoux,[3] although
it was employed by other French contemporaries.

With good reason Sir Philip Sidney warned the
public that 'no inward touch' was to be expected
from sonnetteers of this day, whom he describes as:

> [Men] that do dictionary's method bring
> Into their rhymes running in rattling rows;
> [Men] that poor Petrarch's long-deceasèd woes
> With newborn sighs and denizened wit do sing.

---

[1] See Drummond's *Poems*, ed. W. C. Ward, in Muses' Library,
1894, i. 207 seq.

[2] Sève's *Délie* was first published at Lyons in 1544.   [3] 1530-79.

Sidney unconvincingly claimed greater sincerity for his own experiments. But 'even amorous sonnets in Sonnet-teers' ad-missions of insincerity. the gallantest and sweetest civil vein,' wrote Gabriel Harvey in 'Pierces Supererogation' in 1593, 'are but dainties of a pleasurable wit.' Drayton's sonnets more nearly approached Shakespeare's in quality than those of any contemporary. Yet Drayton told the readers of his collection entitled 'Idea'[1] (after the French) that if any sought genuine passion in them, they had better go elsewhere. 'In all humours *sportively* he ranged,' he declared. Giles Fletcher, in 1593, introduced his collection of imitative sonnets entitled 'Licia, or Poems of Love,' with the warning, 'now in that I have written love sonnets, if any man measure my affection by my style, let him say I am in love. . . . Here, take this by the way, . . . a man may write of love and not be in love, as well as of

---

[1] In two of his century of sonnets (Nos. xiii. and xxiv. in 1594 edition, renumbered xxxii. and liii. in 1619 edition) Drayton hints that his 'fair Idea' embodied traits of an identifiable lady of his acquaintance, and he repeats the hint in two other short poems; but the fundamental principles of his sonnetteering exploits are defined explicitly in Sonnet xviii. in 1594 edition.

> Some, when in rhyme, they of their loves do tell, . . .
> Only I call [*i.e.* I call only] on my divine Idea.

Joachim du Bellay, one of the French poets who anticipated Drayton in addressing sonnets to ' L'Idée,' left the reader in no doubt of his intent by concluding one poem thus :

> Lá, ô mon âme, au plus hault ciel guidée,
> Tu y pourras recognoistre l'Idée
> De la beauté qu'en ce monde j'adore.

(Du Bellay's *Olive*, No. cxiii. published in 1568.)

husbandry and not go to the plough, or of witches and be none, or of holiness and be profane.' [1]

The dissemination of false sentiment by the sonnetteers, and their monotonous and mechanical treatment of 'the pangs of despised love' or the joys of requited affection, did not escape the censure of contemporary criticism. The air soon rang with sarcastic protests from the most respected writers of the day. In early life Gabriel Harvey wittily parodied the mingling of adulation and vituperation in the conventional sonnet-sequence in his 'Amorous Odious Sonnet intituled The Student's Loove or Hatrid.' [2] Chapman in 1595, in a series of sonnets entitled 'A Coronet for his mistress Philosophy,' appealed to his literary comrades to abandon 'the painted cabinet' of the love-sonnet for a coffer of genuine worth. But the most resolute of the censors of the sonnetteering vogue was the poet and lawyer, Sir John Davies. In a sonnet addressed about 1596 to his friend, Sir Anthony Cooke (the patron of Drayton's 'Idea'), he inveighed against the 'bastard sonnets' which 'base rhymers' 'daily' begot 'to their own shames and poetry's disgrace.' In his anxiety to stamp out the folly he wrote and circulated in manuscript a specimen series of nine 'gulling sonnets'

Contemporary censure of sonnetteers' false sentiment.

'Gulling Sonnets.'

---

[1] Ben Jonson pointedly noticed the artifice inherent in the metrical principles of the sonnet when he told Drummond of Hawthornden that 'he cursed Petrarch for redacting verses to sonnets which he said were like that tyrant's bed, where some who were too short were racked, others too long cut short' (Jonson's *Conversation*, p. 4).

[2] See p. 121 *infra*.

or parodies of the conventional efforts.[1]   Even Shakespeare does not seem to have escaped Davies's con-
demnation.   Sir John is especially severe on the
sonnetteers who handled conceits based on legal
technicalities, and his eighth 'gulling sonnet,' in
which he ridicules the application of law terms to
affairs of the heart, may well have been suggested
by Shakespeare's legal phraseology in his Sonnets
lxxxvii. and cxxiv.;[2] while Davies's Sonnet ix.,
beginning :

> To love, my lord, I do knight's service owe,

must have parodied Shakespeare's Sonnet xxvi., beginning :

> Lord of my love, to whom in vassalage, &c.[3]

Echoes of the critical hostility are heard, it is curious to note, in nearly all the references that Shake-

*Shake-
speare's
scornful
allusion to
sonnets in
his plays.*

speare himself makes to sonnetteering in his
plays.   'Tush, none but minstrels like of son-
netting,' exclaims Biron in 'Love's Labour's
Lost' (IV. iii. 158).   In the 'Two Gentlemen
of Verona' (III. ii. 68 seq.) there is a satiric touch in
the recipe for the conventional love-sonnet which
Proteus offers the amorous Duke :

> You must lay lime to tangle her desires
> By wailful sonnets whose composèd rime

---

[1] They were first printed by Dr. Grosart for the Chetham Society
in 1873 in his edition of 'the Dr. Farmer MS.,' a sixteenth and seventeenth century commonplace book preserved in the Chetham Library
at Manchester, pt. i. pp. 76–81.   Dr. Grosart also included the poems
in his edition of Sir John Davies's *Works*, 1876, ii. 53–62.

[2] Davies's Sonnet viii. is printed in Appendix IX.

[3] See p. 127 *infra*.

> Should be full fraught with serviceable vows . . .
> Say that upon the altar of her beauty
> You sacrifice your sighs, your tears, your heart.

Mercutio treats Elizabethan sonnetteers even less respectfully when alluding to them in his flouts at Romeo: 'Now is he for the numbers that Petrarch flowed in: Laura, to his lady, was but a kitchen-wench. Marry, she had a better love to be-rhyme her.'[1] In later plays Shakespeare's disdain of the sonnet is still more pronounced. In 'Henry V' (III. vii. 33 seq.) the Dauphin, after bestowing ridiculously magniloquent commendation on his charger, remarks, 'I once writ a sonnet in his praise, and begun thus: "Wonder of nature!"' The Duke of Orleans retorts: 'I have heard a sonnet begin so to one's mistress.' The Dauphin replies: 'Then did they imitate that which I composed to my courser; for my horse is my mistress.' In 'Much Ado About Nothing' (v. ii. 4-7) Margaret, Hero's waiting-woman, mockingly asks Benedick to 'write her a sonnet in praise of her beauty.' Benedick jestingly promises one so 'in high a style that no man living shall come over it.' Subsequently (v. iv. 87) Benedick is convicted, to the amusement of his friends, of penning 'a halting sonnet of his own pure brain' in praise of Beatrice.

---

[1] *Romeo and Juliet*, II. iv. 41-4.

VIII

THE BORROWED CONCEITS OF THE SONNETS

AT a first glance a far larger proportion of Shakespeare's sonnets give the reader the illusion of personal confessions than those of any contemporary, but when allowance has been made for the current conventions of Elizabethan sonnetteering, as well as for Shakespeare's unapproached affluence in dramatic instinct and invention — an affluence which enabled him to identify himself with every phase of human emotion—the autobiographic element in his sonnets, although it may not be dismissed altogether, is seen to shrink to slender proportions. As soon as the collection is studied comparatively with the many thousand sonnets that the printing presses of England, France, and Italy poured forth during the last years of the sixteenth century, a vast number of Shakespeare's performances prove to be little more than professional trials of skill, often of superlative merit, to which he deemed himself challenged by the efforts of contemporary practitioners. The thoughts and words of the sonnets of Daniel, Drayton, Watson, Barnabe Barnes, Constable, and Sidney were assimilated by Shakespeare in his poems as consciously and with as little compunction as the plays and novels of

Slender autobiographical element in Shakespeare's sonnets.

The imitative element.

contemporaries in his dramatic work.   To Drayton he was especially indebted.[1]   Such resemblances as are visible between Shakespeare's sonnets and those of Petrarch or Desportes seem due to his study of the English imitators of those sonnetteers.   Most of Ron-

[1] Mr. Fleay in his *Biographical Chronicle of the English Stage*, ii. 226 seq., gives a striking list of parallels between Shakespeare's and Drayton's sonnets which any reader of the two collections in conjunction could easily increase.   Mr. Wyndham in his valuable edition of Shakespeare's *Sonnets*, p. 255, argues that Drayton was the plagiarist of Shakespeare, chiefly on bibliographical grounds, which he does not state quite accurately.   One hundred sonnets belonging to Drayton's *Idea* series are extant, but they were not all published by him at one time.   Fifty-three were alone included in his first and only separate edition of 1594; six more appeared in a reprint of *Idea* appended to the *Heroical Epistles* in 1599; twenty-four of these were gradually dropped and thirty-four new ones substituted in reissues appended to volumes of his writings issued respectively in 1600, 1602, 1603, and 1605.   To the collection thus re-formed a further addition of twelve sonnets and a withdrawal of some twelve old sonnets were made in the final edition of Drayton's works in 1619.   There the sonnets number sixty-three.   Mr. Wyndham insists that Drayton's latest published sonnets have alone an obvious resemblance to Shakespeare's sonnets, and that they all more or less reflect Shakespeare's sonnets as printed by Thorpe in 1609.   But the whole of Drayton's century of sonnets except twelve were in print long before 1609, and it could easily be shown that the earliest fifty-three published in 1594 supply as close parallels with Shakespeare's sonnets as any of the forty-seven published subsequently.   Internal evidence suggests that all but one or two of Drayton's sonnets were written by him in 1594, in the full tide of the sonnetteering craze.   Almost all were doubtless in circulation in manuscript then, although only fifty-three were published in 1594. Shakespeare would have had ready means of access to Drayton's manuscript collection.   Mr. Collier reprinted all the sonnets that Drayton published between 1594 and 1619 in his edition of Drayton's poems for the Roxburghe Club, 1856.   Other editions of Drayton's sonnets of this and the last century reprint exclusively the collection of sixty-three appended to the edition of his works in 1619.

sard's nine hundred sonnets and many of his numerous odes were accessible to Shakespeare in English
adaptations, but there are a few signs that Shakespeare
had recourse to Ronsard direct.

Adapted or imitated conceits are scattered over
the whole of Shakespeare's collection. They are
usually manipulated with consummate skill, but
Shakespeare's indebtedness is not thereby obscured.
Shakespeare in many beautiful sonnets describes
spring and summer, night and sleep and their influence on amorous emotion. Such topics are common themes of the poetry of the Renaissance, and they
figure in Shakespeare's pages clad in the identical
livery that clothed them in the sonnets of Petrarch,
Ronsard, De Baif, and Desportes, or of English
disciples of the Italian and French masters.[1] In

---

[1] Almost all sixteenth-century sonnets on spring in the absence of
the poet's love (cf. Shakespeare's Sonnets xcviii. xcix.) are variations
on the sentiment and phraseology of Petrarch's well-known sonnet
xlii., ' In morte di M. Laura,' beginning:

> Zefiro torna e 'l bel tempo rimena,
> E i fiori e l'erbe, sua dolce famiglia,
> E garrir Progne e pianger Filomena,
> E primavera candida e vermiglia.
>   Ridono i prati, e 'l ciel si rasserena;
> Giove s' allegra di mirar sua figlia,
> L' aria e l' acqua e la terra è d' amor piena;
> Ogni animal d' amar si riconsiglia.
>   Ma per me, lasso, tornano i più gravi
> Sospiri, che del cor profondo tragge, &c.

See a translation by William Drummond of Hawthornden in Sonnets,
pt. ii. No. ix. Similar sonnets and odes on April, spring, and summer
abound in French and English (cf. Becq de Fouquière's *Œuvres choisies
de J.-A. De Baif,* passim, and *Œuvres choisies des Contemporains de
Ronsard,* p. 108 (by Remy Belleau); p. 129 (by Amadis Jamyn) et
passim). For descriptions of night and sleep see especially Ronsard's

Sonnet xxiv. Shakespeare develops Ronsard's conceit
that his love's portrait is painted on his heart; and in
Sonnet cxxii. he repeats something of Ronsard's phraseology in describing how his friend, who has just made
him a gift of 'tables,' is 'character'd' in his brain.[1] Sonnet xcix., which reproaches the flowers with stealing
their charms from the features of his love, is adapted
from Constable's sonnet to Diana (No. ix.), and may be
matched in other collections. Elsewhere Shakespeare
meditates on the theory that man is an amalgam of the
four elements, earth, water, air, and fire (xl.–v.).[2] In
all these he reproduces, with such embellishments as
his genius dictated, phrases and sentiments of Daniel,
Drayton, Barnes, and Watson, who imported them
direct from France and Italy. In two or three instances
Shakespeare showed his reader that he was engaged
in a mere literary exercise by offering him alternative
renderings of the same conventional conceit. In
Sonnets xlvi. and xlvii. he paraphrases twice over —
appropriating many of Watson's words — the unexhila-
rating notion that the eye and heart are in perpetual
dispute as to which has the greater influence on

Amours (livre i. clxxxvi., livre ii. xxii.; *Odes,* livre iv. No. iv., and
his *Odes Retranchées* in *Œuvres,* edited by Blanchemain, ii. 392–4).
Cf. Barnes's *Parthenophe and Parthenophil,* lxxxiii. cv.

[1] Cf. Ronsard's *Amours,* livre clxxviii.; *Amours pour Astrée,* vi.
The latter opens :

> Il ne falloit, mais tresse, autres tablettes
> Pour vous graver que celles de mon cœur
> Où de sa main Amour, nostre vainqueur,
> Vous a gravée et vos grâces parfaites.

[2] Cf. Spenser, lv.; Barnes's *Parthenophe and Parthenophil,* No.
lxxvii.; Fulke Greville's *Cælica,* No. vii.

lovers.[1] In the concluding sonnets, cliii. and cliv., he gives alternative versions of an apologue illustrating the potency of love which first figured in the Greek anthology, had been translated into Latin, and subsequently won the notice of English, French, and Italian sonnetteers.[2]

In the numerous sonnets in which Shakespeare boasted that his verse was so certain of immortality that it was capable of immortalising the person to whom it was addressed, he gave voice to no conviction that was peculiar to his mental constitution, to no involuntary exaltation of spirit, or spontaneous

Shakespeare's claims of immortality for his sonnets a borrowed conceit.

---

[1] A similar conceit is the topic of Shakespeare's Sonnet xxiv. Ronsard's Ode (livre iv. No. xx.) consists of a like dialogue between the heart and the eye. The conceit is traceable to Petrarch, whose Sonnet lv. or lxiii. ('Occhi, piangete, accompagnate il core') is a dialogue between the poet and his eyes, while his Sonnet xcix. or cxvii. is a companion dialogue between the poet and his heart. Cf. Watson's *Tears of Fancie*, xix. xx. (a pair of sonnets on the theme which closely resemble Shakespeare's pair); Drayton's *Idea*, xxxiii.; Barnes's *Parthenophe and Parthenophil*, xx., and Constable's *Diana*, vi. 7.

[2] The Greek epigram is in *Palatine Anthology*, ix. 627, and is translated into Latin in *Selecta Epigrammata*, Basel, 1529. The Greek lines relate, as in Shakespeare's sonnets, how a nymph who sought to quench love's torch in a fountain only succeeded in heating the water. An added detail Shakespeare borrowed from a very recent adaptation of the epigram in Giles Fletcher's *Licia*, 1593 (Sonnet xxvii.), where the poet's Love bathes in the fountain, with the result not only that 'she touched the water and it burnt with Love,' but also

> Now by her means it purchased hath that bliss
> Which all diseases quickly can remove.

Similarly Shakespeare in Sonnet cliv. not merely states that the 'cool well' into which Cupid's torch had fallen 'from Love's fire took heat perpetual,' but also that it grew 'a bath and healthful remedy for men diseased.'

I

ebullition of feeling.   He was merely proving that
he could at will, and with superior effect, handle a
theme that Ronsard and Desportes, emulating Pindar,
Horace, Ovid, and other classical poets, had lately
made a commonplace of the poetry of Europe.[1]   Sir
Philip Sidney, in his 'Apologie for Poetrie' (1595),
wrote that it was the common habit of poets 'to
tell you that they will make you immortal by their
verses.'[2]   'Men of great calling,' Nash wrote in his
'Pierce Pennilesse,' 1593, 'take it of merit to have their
names eternised by poets.'[3]   In the hands of Elizabethan sonnetteers the 'eternising' faculty of their

[1] In Greek poetry the topic is treated in Pindar's *Olympic Odes*, xi.,
and in a fragment by Sappho, No. 16 in Bergk's *Poetæ Lyrici Græci*.
In Latin poetry the topic is treated in Ennius as quoted in Cicero,
De Senectute c. 207; in Horace's *Odes* iii. 30; in Virgil's *Georgics*
iii. 9; in Propertius iii. 1; in Ovid's *Metamorphoses* xv. 871 seq. and
in Martial x. 27 seq.   Among French sonnetteers Ronsard attacked the
theme most boldly.   His odes and sonnets promise immortality to the
persons to whom they are addressed with an extravagant and a
monotonous liberality.   The following lines from Ronsard's Ode (livre
i. No. vii.), 'Au Seigneur Carnavalet,' illustrate his habitual treatment
of the theme :

C'est un travail de bon-heur	Les neuf divines pucelles
Chanter les hommes louables,	Gardent ta gloire chez elles;
Et leur bastir un honneur	Et mon luth, qu'ell'ont fait estre
Seul vainqueur des ans muables.	De leurs secrets le grand prestre,
Le marbre ou l'airain vestu	Par cest hymne solennel
D'un labeur vif par l'enclume	Respandra dessus ta race
N'animent tant la vertu	Je ne sçay quoy de sa grace
Que les Muses par la plume. . . .	Qui te doit faire eternel.

(*Œuvres de Ronsard*, ed. Blanchemain, ii. 58, 62.)
I quote two other instances from Ronsard on p. 116, note 1.
Desportes was also prone to indulge in the same conceit; cf. his
Cleonice, sonnet 62, which Daniel appropriated bodily in his *Delia*
(Sonnet xxvi.).   Desportes warns his mistress that she will live in his
verse like the phœnix in fire.

[2] Ed. Shuckburgh, p. 62.   [3] Shakespeare Soc. p. 93.

verse became a staple and indeed an inevitable topic. Spenser wrote in his 'Amoretti' (1595, Sonnet lxxv.):

> My verse your virtues rare shall eternise,
> And in the heavens write your glorious name.

Drayton and Daniel developed the conceit with unblushing iteration. Drayton, who spoke of his efforts as 'my immortal song' (*Idea*, vi. 14) and 'my world-out-wearing rhymes' (xliv. 7), embodied the vaunt in such lines as:

> While thus my pen strives to eternise thee (*Idea* xliv. 1).
> Ensuing ages yet my rhymes shall cherish (*ib.* xliv. 11).
> My name shall mount unto eternity (*ib.* xliv. 14).
> All that I seek is to eternise thee (*ib.* xlvii. 14).

Daniel was no less explicit:

> This [sc. verse] may remain thy lasting monument (*Delia* xxxvii. 9).
> Thou mayst in after ages live esteemed,
> Unburied in these lines (*ib.* xxxix. 9–10).
> These [sc. my verses] are the arks, the trophies I erect
> That fortify thy name against old age;
> And these [sc. verses] thy sacred virtues must protect
> Against the dark and time's consuming rage (*ib.* L. 9-12).

Shakespeare, in his references to his 'eternal lines' (xviii. 12) and in the assurances that he gives the subject of his addresses that the sonnets are, in Daniel's exact phrase, his 'monument' (lxxxi. 9, cvii. 13), was merely accommodating himself to the prevailing taste. Characteristically in Sonnet lv. he invested the topic with a splendour that was not approached by any other poet:[1]

---

[1] Other references to the topic appear in Sonnets xix. liv. lx. lxiii. lxv. lxxxi. and cvii.

Not marble, nor the gilded monuments
Of princes, shall outlive this powerful rhyme; [1]
But you shall shine more bright in these contents
Than unswept stone, besmear'd with sluttish time.
When wasteful war shall statues overturn,
And broils root out the work of masonry,
Nor Mars his sword nor war's quick fire shall burn
The living record of your memory.
'Gainst death and all-oblivious enmity
Shall you pace forth; your praise shall still find room,
Even in the eyes of all posterity
That wear this world out to the ending doom.
　　So, till the judgment that yourself arise,
　　You live in this, and dwell in lovers' eyes.

The imitative element is no less conspicuous in
the sonnets that Shakespeare distinctively addresses

---

[1] See the quotation from Ronsard on p. 114, note 1. This sonnet
is also very like Ronsard's Ode (livre v. No. xxxii.) 'A sa Muse,'
which opens:

> Plus dur que fer j'ay fini mon ouvrage,
> Que l'an, dispos à demener les pas,
> Que l'eau, le vent ou le brulant orage,
> L'injuriant, ne ru'ront point à bas.
> Quand ce viendra que le dernier trespas
> M'assoupira d'un somme dur, à l'heure,
> Sous le tombeau tout Ronsard n'ira pas
> Restant de luy la part meilleure. . . .
> Sus donque, Muse, emporte au ciel la gloire
> Que j'ay gaignee, annonçant la victoire
> Dont à bon droit je me voy jouissant. . . .

Cf. also Ronsard's Sonnet lxxii. in *Amours* (livre i.), where he declares
that his mistress's name

> Victorieux des peuples et des rois
> S'en voleroit sus l'aile de ma ryme.

But Shakespeare, like Ronsard, knew Horace's far-famed Ode (bk. iii.
30):

> Exegi monumentum aere perennius
> Regalique situ pyramidum altius,
> Quod non imber edax, non Aquilo impotens
> Possit diruere, aut innumerabilis
> Annorum series, et fuga temporum.

to a woman. In two of the latter (cxxxv.–vi.), where he quibbles over the fact of the identity of his own name of Will with a lady's 'will' (the synonym in Elizabethan English of both 'lust' and 'obstinacy'), he derisively challenges comparison with wire-drawn

Conceits in sonnets addressed to a woman. conceits of rival sonnetteers, especially of Barnabe Barnes, who had enlarged on his disdainful mistress's 'wills,' and had turned the word 'grace' to the same punning account as Shakespeare

Nor can there be any doubt that Shakespeare wrote with a direct reference to the concluding ten lines of Ovid's *Metamorphoses* (xv. 871–9):

> Jamque opus exegi, quod nec Jovis ira nec ignes,
> Nec poterit ferrum, nec edax abolere vetustas.
> Cum volet, illa dies, quæ nil nisi corporis hujus
> Jus habet, incerti spatium mihi finiat ævi;
> Parte tamen meliore mei super alta perennis
> Astra ferar nomenque erit indelebile nostrum.

This passage was familiar to Shakespeare in one of his favourite books — Golding's translation of the *Metamorphoses*. Golding's rendering opens:

> Now have I brought a worke to end which neither Jove's fierce wrath
> Nor sword nor fire nor fretting age, with all the force it hath
> Are able to abolish quite, &c.

Meres, after his mention of Shakespeare's sonnets in his *Palladis Tamia* (1598), quotes parts of both passages from Horace and Ovid, and gives a Latin paraphrase of his own, which, he says, would fit the lips of four contemporary poets besides Shakespeare. The introduction of the name Mars into Meres's paraphrase as well as into line 7 of Shakespeare's Sonnet lv. led Mr. Tyler (on what are in any case very trivial grounds) to the assumption that Shakespeare was borrowing from his admiring critic, and was therefore writing after 1598, when Meres's book was published. In Golding's translation reference is made to Mars by name (the Latin here calls the god Gradivus) a few lines above the passage already quoted, and the word caught Shakespeare's eye there. Shakespeare owed nothing to Meres's paraphrase, but Meres probably owed much to passages in Shakespeare's sonnets.

turned the word 'will.'[1] Similarly in Sonnet cxxx. beginning

> My mistress's eyes are nothing like the sun;
> Coral is far more red than her lips' red . . .
> If hairs be wires, black wires grow on her head.[2]

he satirises the conventional lists of precious stones, metals, and flowers, to which the sonnetteers likened their mistresses' features.

In two sonnets (cxxvii. and cxxxii.) Shakespeare amiably notices the black complexion, hair, and eyes of his mistress, and expresses a preference for features of that hue over those of the fair hue which was, he tells us, more often associated in poetry with beauty. He commends the 'dark lady' for refusing to practise those arts by which other women of the day gave their hair and faces colours denied them by Nature. Here Shakespeare repeats almost verbatim his own lines in 'Love's Labour's Lost' (iv. iii. 241–7), where the heroine Rosaline is described as 'black as ebony,' with 'brows decked in black,' and in 'mourning' for

The praise of 'blackness.'

---

[1] See Appendix VIII., 'The Will Sonnets,' for the interpretation of Shakespeare's conceit and like efforts of Barnes.

[2] Wires in the sense of hair was peculiarly distinctive of the sonnetteers' affected vocabulary. Cf. Daniel's *Delia*, 1591, No. xxvi., 'And golden hair may change to silver *wire;*' Lodge's *Phillis*, 1595, 'Made blush the beauties of her curléd *wire;*' Barnes's *Parthenophil*, sonnet xlviii., 'Her hairs no grace of golden *wires* want.' The comparison of lips with coral is not uncommon outside the Elizabethan sonnet, but it was universal there. Cf. 'Coral-coloured lips' (*Zepheria*, 1594, No. xxiii.); 'No coral is her lip' (Lodge's *Phillis*, 1595, No. viii.). 'Ce beau coral' are the opening words of Ronsard's *Amours*, livre i. No. xxiii., where a list is given of stones and metals comparable with women's features.

her fashionable sisters' indulgence in the disguising arts of the toilet. ' No face is fair that is not full so black,' exclaims Rosaline's lover.   But neither in the sonnets nor in the play can Shakespeare's praise of ' blackness' claim the merit of being his own invention. Sir Philip Sidney, in sonnet vii. of his ' Astrophel and Stella,' had anticipated it.   The ' beams' of the eyes of Sidney's mistress were ' wrapt in colour black ' and wore ' this mourning weed' so

> That whereas black seems beauty's contrary,
> She even in black doth make all beauties flow.[1]

To his praise of ' blackness' in ' Love's Labour's Lost' Shakespeare appends a playful but caustic comment on the paradox that he detects in the conceit.[2] Similarly, the sonnets, in which a dark complexion is pronounced to be a mark of beauty, are followed by others in which the poet argues in self-confutation that blackness of feature is hideous in a woman, and invariably indicates moral turpitude or blackness of heart.   Twice, in much the same language as had already served a like purpose in the play, does

[1] Shakespeare adopted this phraseology of Sidney literally in both the play and the sonnet; while Sidney's further conceit that the lady's eyes are in ' this mourning weed' in order ' to honour all their deaths who for her bleed' is reproduced in Shakespeare's Sonnet cxxxii. — one of the two under consideration — where he tells his mistress that her eyes ' have put on black' to become ' loving mourners' of him who is denied her love.

[2] O paradox!   Black is the badge of hell,
  The hue of dungeons and the scowl of night (*Love's Labour's Lost*, iv. iii. 254-5).
  To look like her are chimney-sweepers black,
  And since her time are colliers counted bright,
  And Ethiops of their sweet complexion crack.
  Dark needs no candle now, for dark is light (*ib.* 266-9).

he mock his 'dark lady' with this uncomplimentary interpretation of dark-coloured hair and eyes.

The two sonnets, in which this view of 'blackness' is developed, form part of a series of twelve, which belongs to a special category of sonnetteering effort. In them Shakespeare abandons the sugared sentiment which characterises most of his hundred and forty-two remaining sonnets. He grows vituperative and pours a volley of passionate abuse upon a woman whom he represents as disdaining his advances. The genuine anguish of a rejected lover often expresses itself in curses both loud and deep, but the mood of blinding wrath which the rejection of a lovesuit may rouse in a passionate nature does not seem from the internal evidence to be reflected genuinely in Shakespeare's sonnets of vituperation. It was inherent in Shakespeare's genius that he should import more dramatic intensity than any other poet into sonnets of a vituperative type; but there is also in his vituperative sonnets a declamatory parade of figurative extravagance which suggests that the emotion is feigned and that the poet is striking an attitude. He cannot have been in earnest in seeking to conciliate his disdainful mistress — a result at which the vituperative sonnets purport to aim — when he tells her that she is 'black as hell, as dark as night,' and with 'so foul a face' is 'the bay where all men ride.'

The sonnets of vituperation.

But external evidence is more conclusive as to the artificial construction of the vituperative sonnets. Again a comparison of this series with the efforts of the modish sonnetteers assigns to it its true character.

Every sonnetteer of the sixteenth century, at some point in his career, devoted his energies to vituperation of a cruel siren. Ronsard in his sonnets celebrated in language quite as furious as Shakespeare's a 'fierce tigress,' a 'murderess,' a 'Medusa.' Barnabe Barnes affected to contend in his sonnets with a female 'tyrant,' a 'Medusa,' a 'rock.' 'Women' (Barnes laments) 'are by nature proud as devils.' The monotonous and artificial regularity with which the sonneteers sounded the vituperative stop, whenever they had exhausted their notes of adulation, excited ridicule in both England and France. In Shakespeare's early life the convention was wittily parodied by Gabriel Harvey in 'An Amorous Odious sonnet intituled The Student's Loove or Hatrid, or both or neither, or what shall please the looving or hating reader, either in sport or earnest, to make of such contrary passions as are here discoursed.' [1] After extolling the beauty and virtue of his mistress above that of Aretino's Angelica, Petrarch's Laura, Catullus's Lesbia, and eight other far-famed objects of poetic adoration, Harvey suddenly denounces her in burlesque rhyme as 'a serpent in brood,' 'a poisonous toad,' 'a heart of marble,' and 'a stony mind as passionless as a block.' Finally he tells her,

Gabriel Harvey's 'Amorous Odious Sonnet.'

> If ever there were she-devils incarnate,
> They are altogether in thee incorporate.

In France Etienne Jodelle, a professional sonnet-

---

[1] The parody, which is not in sonnet form, is printed in Harvey's *Letter-book* (Camden Soc. pp. 101–43).

teer although he is best known as a dramatist, made

late in the second half of the sixteenth century an independent endeavour of like kind to stifle by means of parody the vogue of the vituperative sonnet. Jodelle designed a collection of three hundred sonnets which he inscribed to 'hate of a woman,' and he appropriately entitled them 'Contr' Amours' in distinction to 'Amours,' the term applied to sonnets in the honeyed vein. Only seven of Jodelle's 'Contr' Amours' are extant, but there is sufficient identity of tone between them and Shakespeare's vituperative efforts almost to discover in Shakespeare's invectives a spark of Jodelle's satiric fire.[1] The dark lady

[1] No. vii. of Jodelle's *Contr' Amours* runs thus:

> Combien de fois mes vers ont-ils doré
> Ces cheueux noirs dignes d'vne Meduse?
> Combien de fois ce teint noir qui m'amuse,
> Ay-ie de lis et roses coloré?
> Combien ce front de rides labouré
> Ay-ie applani? et quel a fait ma Muse
> Le gros sourcil, où folle elle s'abuse,
> Ayant sur luy l'arc d'Amour figuré?
> Quel ay-ie fait son œil se renfonçant?
> Quel ay-ie fait son grand nez rougissant?
> Quelle sa bouche et ses noires dents quelles?
> Quel ay-ie fait le reste de ce corps?
> Qui, me sentant endurer mille morts,
> Viuoit heureux de mes peines mortelles.
>
> (Jodelle's *Œuvres*, 1597, pp. 91–94.)

With this should be compared Shakespeare's sonnets cxxxvii., cxlviii., and cl. Jodelle's feigned remorse for having lauded the *black* hair and complexion of his mistress is one of the most singular of several strange coincidences. In No. vi. of Jodelle's *Contr' Amours*, Jodelle, after reproaching his 'traitres vers' with having untruthfully described his siren as a beauty, concludes:

> Ja si long temps faisant d'un Diable vn Ange
> Vous m'ouurez l'œil en l'iniuste louange,
> Et m'aueuglez en l'iniuste tourment.

of Shakespeare's 'sonnets' may therefore be relegated to the ranks of the creatures of his fancy. It is quite possible that he may have met in real life a dark-complexioned siren, and it is possible that he may have fared ill at her disdainful hands. But no such incident is needed to account for the presence of 'the dark lady' in the sonnets. It was the exacting conventions of the sonnetteering contagion, and not his personal experiences or emotions, that impelled Shakespeare to give 'the dark lady' of his sonnets a poetic being.[1] She has been compared, not very justly, with Shakespeare's splendid creation of Cleopatra in his play of

With this should be compared Shakespeare's Sonnet cxliv. lines 9–10:

> And whether that my angel be turn'd fiend
> Suspect I may, yet not directly tell.

A conventional sonnet of extravagant vituperation, which Drummond of Hawthornden translated from Marino (*Rime*, 1602, pt. i. p. 76) is introduced with grotesque inappropriateness into Drummond's collection of 'sugared' sonnets (see pt. i. No. xxxv.: Drummond's *Poems*, ed. W. C. Ward, i. 69, 217).

[1] The theories that all the sonnets addressed to a woman were addressed to the 'dark lady,' and that the 'dark lady' is identifiable with Mary Fitton, a mistress of the Earl of Pembroke, are baseless conjectures. The extant portraits of Mary Fitton prove her to be fair. The introduction of her name into the discussion is solely due to the mistaken notion that Shakespeare was the *protégé* of Pembroke, that most of the sonnets were addressed to him, and that the poet was probably acquainted with his patron's mistress. See Appendix VII. The expressions in two of the vituperative sonnets to the effect that the disdainful mistress had 'robb'd others' beds' revenues of their rents' (cxlii. 8) and 'in act her bed-vow broke' (clii. 37) have been held to imply that the woman denounced by Shakespeare was married. The first quotation can only mean that she was unfaithful with married men, but both quotations seem to be general phrases of abuse, the meaning of which should not be pressed closely.

' Antony and Cleopatra.'   From one point of view the same criticism may be passed on both.   There is no greater and no less ground for seeking in Shakespeare's personal environment the original of 'the dark lady' of his sonnets than for seeking there the original of his Queen of Egypt.

IX

THE PATRONAGE OF THE EARL OF SOUTHAMPTON

AMID the borrowed conceits and poetic figures of Shakespeare's sonnets there lurk suggestive references to the circumstances in his external life that attended their composition.   If few can be safely regarded as autobiographic revelations of sentiment, many of them offer evidence of the relations in which he stood to a patron, and to the position that he sought to fill in the circle of that patron's literary retainers.   Twenty

Biographic sonnets, which may for purposes of exposition
fact in the be entitled 'dedicatory' sonnets, are addressed
'dedica-
tory' to one who is declared without periphrasis
sonnets. and without disguise to be a patron of the poet's verse (Nos. xxiii., xxvi., xxxii., xxxvii., xxxviii., lxix., lxxvii.–lxxxvi., c., ci., ciii., cvi.).   In one of these — Sonnet lxxviii. — Shakespeare asserted :

> So oft have I invoked thee for my Muse
> And found such fair assistance in my verse
> As every alien pen hath got my use
> And under thee their poesy disperse.

Subsequently he regretfully pointed out how his patron's readiness to accept the homage of other poets seemed to be thrusting him from the enviable place of pre-eminence in his patron's esteem.

Shakespeare's biographer is under an obligation to attempt an identification of the persons whose relations with the poet are defined so explicitly. The problem presented by the patron is simple. Shakespeare states unequivocally that he has no patron but one.

The Earl of Southampton the poet's sole patron.

> Sing [sc. O Muse!] to the ear that doth thy lays esteem,
> And gives thy pen both skill and argument (c. 7–8).
> For to no other pass my verses tend
> Than of your graces and your gifts to tell (ciii. 11–12).

The Earl of Southampton, the patron of his narrative poems, is the only patron of Shakespeare that is known to biographical research. No contemporary document or tradition gives the faintest suggestion that Shakespeare was the friend or dependent of any other man of rank. A trustworthy tradition corroborates the testimony respecting Shakespeare's close intimacy with the Earl that is given in the dedicatory epistles of his 'Venus and Adonis' and 'Lucrece,' penned respectively in 1593 and 1594. According to Nicholas Rowe, Shakespeare's first adequate biographer, 'there is one instance so singular in its magnificence of this patron of Shakespeare's that if I had not been assured that the story was handed down by Sir William D'Avenant, who was probably very well acquainted with his affairs, I should not venture to have inserted; that my Lord Southampton at one time gave him a thousand pounds to enable him to go through with a purchase which he heard he had a mind to. A bounty very great and very rare at any time.'

There is no difficulty in detecting the lineaments of the Earl of Southampton in those of the man who is distinctively greeted in the sonnets as the poet's patron. Three of the twenty 'dedicatory' sonnets merely translate into the language of poetry the expressions of devotion which had already done duty in the dedicatory epistle in prose that prefaces 'Lucrece.' That epistle to Southampton runs:

> The love [1] I dedicate to your lordship is without end; whereof this pamphlet, without beginning, is but a superfluous moiety. The warrant I have of your honourable disposition, not the worth of my untutored lines, makes it assured of acceptance. What I have done is yours; what I have to do is yours; being part of all I have devoted yours. Were my worth greater, my duty would show greater; meanwhile, as it is, it is bound to your lordship, to whom I wish long life, still lengthened with all happiness.
>
> Your lordship's in all duty,
WILLIAM SHAKESPEARE.

Sonnet xxvi. is a gorgeous rendering of these sentences:

[1] 'Lover' and 'love' in Elizabethan English were ordinary synonyms for 'friend' and 'friendship.' Brutus opens his address to the citizens of Rome with the words, 'Romans, countrymen, and *lovers*,' and subsequently describes Julius Cæsar as 'my best *lover*' (*Julius Cæsar*, III. ii. 13–49). Portia, when referring to Antonio, the bosom friend of her husband Bassanio, calls him 'the bosom *lover* of my lord' (*Merchant of Venice*, III. iv. 17). Ben Jonson in his letters to Donne commonly described himself as his correspondent's 'ever true lover'; and Drayton, writing to William Drummond of Hawthornden, informed him that an admirer of his literary work was in love with him. The word 'love' was habitually applied to the sentiment subsisting between an author and his patron. Nash, when dedicating *Jack Wilton* in 1594 to Southampton, calls him 'a dear *lover* . . . of the *lovers* of poets as of the poets themselves.'

Lord of my love, to whom in vassalage
Thy merit hath my duty strongly knit,
To thee I send this written ambassage,
To witness duty, not to show my wit:
Duty so great, which wit so poor as mine
May make seem bare, in wanting words to show it,
But that I hope some good conceit of thine
In thy soul's thought, all naked, will bestow it;
Till whatsoever star that guides my moving,
Points on me graciously with fair aspect,
And puts apparel on my tatter'd loving
To show me worthy of thy sweet respect;
    Then may I dare to boast how I do love thee;
    Till then not show my head where thou may'st prove me.[1]

The 'Lucrece' epistle's intimation that the patron's love alone gives value to the poet's 'untutored lines' is repeated in Sonnet xxxii., which doubtless reflected a moment of depression:

If thou survive my well-contented day,
When that churl Death my bones with dust shall cover,
And shalt by fortune once more re-survey
These poor rude lines of thy deceased lover,
Compare them with the bettering of the time,
And though they be outstripp'd by every pen,
Reserve them for my love, not for their rhyme,
Exceeded by the height of happier men.

---

[1] There is little doubt that this sonnet was parodied by Sir John Davies in the ninth and last of his 'gulling' sonnets, in which he ridicules the notion that a man of wit should put his wit in vassalage to any one.

To love my lord I do knight's service owe,
And therefore now he hath my wit in ward ;
But while it [*i.e.* the poet's wit] is in his tuition so
Methinks he doth intreat [*i.e.* treat] it passing hard . . .
But why should love after minority
(When I have passed the one and twentieth year)
Preclude my wit of his sweet liberty,
And make it still the yoke of wardship bear ?
I fear he [*i.e.* my lord] hath another title [*i.e.* right to my wit] got
And holds my wit now for an idiot.

O, then vouchsafe me but this loving thought:
'Had my friend's Muse grown with this growing age
A dearer birth than this his love had brought,
To march in ranks of better equipage; [1]
  But since he died and poets better prove,
  Theirs for their style I'll read, his for his love.'

A like vein is pursued in greater exaltation of spirit in Sonnet xxxviii. :

How can my Muse want subject to invent,
While thou dost breathe, that pour'st into my verse
Thine own sweet argument, too excellent
For every vulgar paper to rehearse?
O give thyself the thanks, if aught in me
Worthy perusal stand against thy sight;
For who's so dumb that cannot write to thee,
When thou thyself dost give invention light?
Be thou the tenth Muse, ten times more in worth
Than those old nine which rhymers invocate;
And he that calls on thee, let him bring forth
Eternal numbers to outlive long date.
  If my slight Muse do please these curious days,
  The pain be mine, but thine shall be the praise.

The central conceit here so finely developed — that the patron may claim as his own handiwork the *protégé's* verse because he inspires it — belongs to the most conventional schemes of dedicatory adulation. When Daniel, in 1592, inscribed his volume of sonnets

[1] Mr. Tyler assigns this sonnet to the year 1598 or later, on the fallacious ground that this line was probably imitated from an expression in Marston's *Pigmalion's Image*, published in 1598, where 'stanzas' are said to 'march rich bedight in warlike equipage.' The suggestion of plagiarism is quite gratuitous. The phrase was common in Elizabethan literature long before Marston employed it. Nash, in his preface to Green's *Menaphon*, which was published in 1589, wrote that the works of the poet Watson 'march in equipage of honour with any of your ancient poets.'

K

entitled 'Delia' to the Countess of Pembroke, he
played in the prefatory sonnet on the same note, and
used in the concluding couplet almost the same words
as Shakespeare.   Daniel wrote:

> Great patroness of these my humble rhymes,
> Which thou from out thy greatness dost inspire . . . .
> O leave [*i.e.* cease] not still to grace thy work in me . . . .
> Whereof the travail I may challenge mine,
> But yet the glory, madam, must be thine.

Elsewhere in the Sonnets we hear fainter echoes
of the 'Lucrece' epistle. Repeatedly does the sonnetteer renew the assurance given there that his patron
is 'part of all' he has or is.   Frequently do we meet
in the Sonnets with such expressions as these:

> [I] by a *part of all* your glory live (xxxvii. 12);
> Thou art *all the better part of me* (xxxix. 2);
> My spirit is thine, *the better part of me* (lxxiv. 8);

while 'the love without end' which Shakespeare had
vowed to Southampton in the light of day reappears
in sonnets addressed to the youth as 'eternal love'
(cviii. 9), and a devotion 'what shall have no end'
(cx. 9).

The identification of the rival poets whose 'richly
compiled' 'comments' of his patron's 'praise' excited Shakespeare's jealousy is a more difficult
inquiry than the identification of the patron. The
rival poets with 'their precious phrase of all the
Muses filed' (lxxxv. 4) must be sought among
Rivals in   the writers who eulogised Southampton and
Southamp-   are known to have shared his patronage.
ton's
favour.   The field of choice is not small. Southampton
from boyhood cultivated literature and the society of

literary men. In 1594 no nobleman received so abundant a measure of adulation from the contemporary world of letters.[1] Thomas Nash justly described the Earl, when dedicating to him his 'Life of Jack Wilton' in 1594, as 'a dear lover and cherisher as well of the lovers of poets as of the poets themselves.' Nash addressed to him many affectionately phrased sonnets. The prolific sonnetteer Barnabe Barnes and the miscellaneous literary practitioner Gervase Markham confessed, respectively in 1593 and 1595, yearnings for Southampton's countenance in sonnets which glow hardly less ardently than Shakespeare's with admiration for his personal charm. Similarly John Florio, the Earl's Italian tutor, who is traditionally reckoned among Shakespeare's literary acquaintances,[2] wrote to Southampton in 1598, in his dedicatory epistle before his 'World of Words' (an Italian-English dictionary), 'as to me and many more, the glorious and gracious sunshine of your honour hath infused light and life.'

Shakespeare magnanimously and modestly described that *protégé* of Southampton, whom he deemed a specially dangerous rival, as an 'able' and a 'better' 'spirit,' 'a worthier pen,' a vessel 'of tall building and of goodly pride,' compared with whom he was himself 'a worthless boat.' He detected a touch of magic in the man's writing. His 'spirit,' Shakespeare hyperbolically declared, had been 'by spirits taught to write

---

[1] See Appendix IV. for a full account of Southampton's relations with Nash and other men of letters.

[2] See p. 85, note.

above a mortal pitch,' and 'an affable familiar ghost'
nightly gulled him with intelligence. Shake-

speare's dismay at the fascination exerted
on his patron by 'the proud full sail of his
[rival's] great verse' sealed for a time, he
declared, the springs of his own invention (lxxxvi.).

(margin) Shake-speare's fear of a rival poet.

There is no need to insist too curiously on the
justice of Shakespeare's laudation of 'the other
poet's' powers. He was presumably a new-comer in
the literary field who surprised older men of benevo-
lent tendency into admiration by his promise rather
than by his achievement. 'Eloquence and courtesy,'
wrote Gabriel Harvey at the time, 'are ever bountiful in
the amplifying vein;' and writers of amiability, Harvey
adds, habitually blazoned the perfections that they
hoped to see their young friends achieve, in language
implying that they had already achieved them. All
the conditions of the problem are satisfied by the
rival's identification with the young poet and scholar
Barnabe Barnes, a poetic panegyrist of Southampton
and a prolific sonnetteer, who was deemed by contemporary critics certain to prove a great poet. His
first collection of sonnets, 'Parthenophil and Parthenophe,' with many odes and madrigals interspersed,
was printed in 1593 ; and his second, 'A Centurie of
Spiritual Sonnets,' in 1595. Loud applause greeted
the first book, which included numerous adaptations
from the classical, Italian, and French poets, and disclosed, among many crudities, some fascinating lyrics
and at least one almost perfect sonnet (No. lxvi.,
'Ah, sweet content, where is thy sweet abode?')

Thomas Churchyard called Barnes 'Petrarch's scholar'; the learned Gabriel Harvey bade him 'go forward in maturity as he had begun in pregnancy,' and 'be the gallant poet, like Spenser;' Campion judged his verse to be 'heady and strong.' In a sonnet that Barnes addressed in this earliest volume to the 'virtuous' Earl of Southampton he declared that his patron's eyes were 'the heavenly lamps that give the Muses light,' and that his sole ambition was 'by flight to rise' to a height worthy of his patron's 'virtues.' Shakespeare sorrowfully pointed out in Sonnet lxxviii. that his lord's eyes

Barnabe Barnes probably the rival.

> Had taught the dumb on high to sing,
> And heavy ignorance aloft to fly,
> Had added feathers to the learned's wing,
> And given grace a double majesty ;

while in the following sonnet he asserted that the 'worthier pen' of his dreaded rival when lending his patron 'virtue' was guilty of plagiarism, for he 'stole that word' from his patron's 'behaviour.' The emphasis laid by Barnes on the inspiration that he sought from Southampton's 'gracious eyes' on the one hand, and his reiterated references to his patron's 'virtue' on the other, suggest that Shakespeare in these sonnets directly alluded to Barnes as his chief competitor in the hotly contested race for Southampton's favours. In Sonnet lxxxv. Shakespeare delares that 'he cries Amen to every hymn that able spirit [*i.e.* his rival] affords.' Very few poets of the day in England followed Ronsard's practice of bestowing the title of hymn on miscellaneous poems, but Barnes twice applies

the word to his poems of love.[1] When, too, Shakespeare in Sonnet lxxx. employs nautical metaphors to
indicate the relations of himself and his rival with
his patron —

> My saucy bark inferior far to his . . .
> Your shallowest help will hold me up afloat, —

he seems to write with an eye on Barnes's identical
choice of metaphor :

> My fancy's ship tossed here and there by these [sc. sorrow's floods]
> Still floats in danger ranging to and fro.
> How fears my thoughts' swift pinnace thine hard rock ![2]

Gervase Markham is equally emphatic in his
sonnet to Southampton on the potent influence of
his patron's 'eyes,' which, he says, crown
'the most victorious pen' — a possible reference to Shakespeare. Nash's poetic praises
of the Earl are no less enthusiastic, and are
of a finer literary temper than Markham's. But
Shakespeare's description of his rival's literary work
fits far less closely the verse of Markham and Nash
than the verse of their fellow-aspirant Barnes.

Other theories as to the rival's identity.

Many critics argue that the numbing fear of his
rival's genius and of its influence on his patron to
which Shakespeare confessed in the sonnets was
more likely to be evoked by the work of George
Chapman than by that of any other contemporary
poet. But Chapman had produced no conspicuously
'great verse' till he began his translation of Homer in
1598; and although he appended in 1610 to a complete

[1] Cf. *Parthenophil*, Madrigal i. line 12; Sonnet xvii. line 9.
[2] *Parthenophil*, Sonnet xci.

edition of his translation a sonnet to Southampton, it was couched in the coldest terms of formality, and it was one of a series of sixteen sonnets each addressed to a distinguished nobleman with whom the writer implies that he had no previous relations.[1] Drayton,

[1] Much irrelevance has been introduced into the discussion of Chapman's claim to be the rival poet. Professor Minto in his *Characteristics of English Poets*, p. 291, argued that Chapman was the man mainly because Shakespeare declared his competitor to be taught to write by 'spirits' — 'his compeers by night' — as well as by 'an affable familiar ghost' which gulled him with intelligence at night (lxxxvi. 5 seq.). Professor Minto saw in these phrases allusions to some remarks by Chapman in his *Shadows of Night* (1594), a poem on Night. There Chapman warned authors in one passage that the spirit of literature will often withhold itself from them unless it have 'drops of their blood like a heavenly familiar,' and in another place sportively invited 'nimble and aspiring wits' to join him in consecrating their endeavours to 'sacred night.' There is really no connection between Shakespeare's theory of the supernatural and nocturnal sources of his rival's influence with Chapman's trite allusion to the current faith in the power of 'nightly familiars' over men's minds and lives, or in Chapman's invitation to his literary comrades to honour Night with him. It is supererogatory to assume that Shakespeare had Chapman's phrases in his mind when alluding to superstitions which were universally acknowledged. It could be as easily argued on like grounds that Shakespeare was drawing on other authors. Nash in his prose tract called independently *The Terrors of the Night*, which was also printed in 1594, described the nocturnal habits of 'familiars' more explicitly than Chapman. The publisher Thomas Thorpe, in dedicating in 1600 Marlowe's translation of Lucan (bk. i.) to his friend Edward Blount, humorously referred to the same topic when he reminded Blount that 'this spirit [*i.e.* Marlowe], whose ghost or genius is to be seen walk the Churchyard [of St. Paul's] in at the least three or four sheets . . . was sometime a *familiar* of your own.' On the strength of these quotations, and accepting Professor Minto's line of argument, Nash, Thorpe, or Blount, whose 'familiar' is declared to have been no less a personage than Marlowe, has as good a claim as Chapman to be the rival poet of Shakespeare's sonnets. A second and equally impotent argument in Chapman's favour has been suggested. Chapman in his preface to his

Ben Jonson, and Marston have also been identified by various critics with 'the rival poet,' but none of these shared Southampton's bounty, nor are the terms which Shakespeare applies to his rival's verse specially applicable to the productions of any of them.

Many besides the 'dedicatory' sonnets are addressed to a handsome youth of wealth and rank, for whom the poet avows 'love,' in the Elizabethan sense of friendship.[1] Although no specific reference is made outside the twenty 'dedicatory' sonnets to the youth Sonnets of as a literary patron, and the clues to his friendship. identity are elsewhere vaguer, there is good ground for the conclusion that the sonnets of disinterested love or friendship also have Southampton for their subject. The sincerity of the poet's sentiment is often open to doubt in these poems, but they seem to illustrate a real intimacy subsisting between Shakespeare and a young Mæcenas.

translation of the *Iliads* (1611) denounces without mentioning any name 'a certain envious windsucker that hovers up and down, laboriously engrossing all the air with his luxurious ambition, and buzzing into every ear my detraction.' It is suggested that Chapman here retaliated on Shakespeare for his references to him as his rival in the sonnets; but it is out of the question that Chapman, were he the rival, should have termed those high compliments 'detraction.' There is no ground for identifying Chapman's 'windsucker' with Shakespeare (cf. Wyndham, p. 255). The strongest point in favour of the theory of Chapman's identity with the rival poet lies in the fact that each of the two sections of his poem *The Shadow of the Night* (1594) is styled a 'hymn,' and Shakespeare in Sonnet lxxxv. 6–7 credits his rival with writing 'hymns.' But Drayton, in his *Harmonie of the Church*, 1591, and Barnes, as we have just seen, both wrote 'hymns,' and the word was often loosely used in Elizabethan English, as in sixteenth-century French, in the general sense of 'poem.'

[1] See p. 127, note 1.

Extravagant compliment—'gross painting' Shakespeare calls it — was more conspicuous in the intercourse of patron and client during the last years of Elizabeth's reign than in any other epoch. For this result the sovereign herself was in part responsible. Contemporary schemes of literary compliment seemed infected by the feigned accents of amorous passion and false rhapsodies on her physical beauty with which men of letters servilely sought to satisfy the old Queen's incurable greed of flattery.[1] Sir

[1] Sir Walter Ralegh was wont to apostrophise his aged sovereign thus:

> Oh, hopeful love, my object and invention,
> Oh, true desire, the spur of my conceit,
> Oh, worthiest spirit, my mind's impulsion,
> Oh, eyes transparent, my affection's bait;
> Oh, princely form, my fancy's adamant,
> Divine conceit, my pain's acceptance,
> Oh, all in one! Oh, heaven on earth transparent!
> The seat of joy and love's abundance!

(Cf. *Cynthia*, a fragment in *Poems of Raleigh*, ed. Hannah, p. 33.) When Ralegh leaves Elizabeth's presence he tells us his 'forsaken heart' and his 'withered mind' were 'widowed of all the joys' they 'once possessed.' Only some 500 lines (the twenty-first book and a fragment of another book) survive of Ralegh's poem *Cynthia*, the whole of which was designed to prove his loyalty to the Queen, and all the extant lines are in the same vein as those I quote. The complete poem extended to twenty-two books, and the lines exceeded 10,000, or five times as many as in Shakespeare's sonnets. Richard Barnfield in his like-named poem of *Cynthia*, 1595, and Fulke Greville in sonnets addressed to Cynthia, also extravagantly described the Queen's beauty and graces. In 1599 Sir John Davies, poet and lawyer, apostrophised Elizabeth, who was then sixty-six years old, thus:

> Fair soul, since to the fairest body knit
> You give such lively life, such quickening power,
> Such sweet celestial influences to it
> As keeps it still in youth's immortal flower . . .
> O many, many years may you remain
> A happy angel to this happy land (*Nosce Teipsum*, dedication).

Davies published in the same year twenty-six 'Hymnes of Astrea' on

Philip Sidney described with admirable point the adulatory excesses to which less exalted patrons were habituated by literary dependents. He gave the warning that as soon as a man showed interest in poetry or its producers, poets straightway pronounced him 'to be most fair, most rich, most wise, most all.' 'You shall dwell upon superlatives . . . Your soule shall be placed with Dante's Beatrice.'[1] The warmth of colouring which distinguishes many of the sonnets

Extrava-
gances of
literary
compli-
ment.

that Shakespeare, under the guise of disinterested friendship, addressed to the youth can be matched at nearly all points in the adulation that patrons were in the habit of receiving from literary dependents in the style that Sidney described.[2]

Elizabeth's beauty and graces ; each poem forms an acrostic on the words ' Elizabetha Regina,' and the language of love is simulated on almost every page.

[1] *Apologie for Poetrie* (1595), ed. Shuckburgh, p. 62.

[2] Adulatory sonnets to patrons are met with in the preliminary or concluding pages of numerous sixteenth and seventeenth century books (*e.g.* the collection of sonnets addressed to James VI of Scotland in his *Essayes of a Prentise*, 1591, and the sonnets to noblemen before Spenser's *Faerie Queen*, at the end of Chapman's *Iliad*, and at the end of John Davies's *Microcosmos*, 1603). Other sonnets to patrons are scattered through collections of occasional poems such as Ben Jonson's *Forest* and *Underwoods* and Donne's *Poems*. Sonnets addressed to men are not only found in the preliminary pages but are occasionally interpolated in sonnet-sequences of fictitious love. Sonnet xi. in Drayton's sonnet-fiction called ' Idea ' (in 1599 edition) seems addressed to a man, in much the same manner as Shakespeare often addressed his hero ; and a few others of Drayton's sonnets are ambiguous as to the sex of their subject. John Soothern's eccentric collection of love-sonnets, *Pandora* (1584), has sonnets dedicatory to the Earl of Oxford ; and William Smith in his *Chloris* (1596) (a sonnet-fiction of the conventional kind) in two prefatory sonnets and in No. xlix. of the substantive collection invokes

Shakespeare assured his friend that he should never grow old (civ.), that the finest types of beauty and chivalry in mediæval romance lived again in him (cvi.), that absence from him was misery, and that his affection for him was unalterable. Hundreds of poets openly gave

Patrons habitually addressed in affectionate terms.

the affectionate notice of Edmund Spenser. Throughout Europe 'dedicatory' sonnets or poems to women betray identical characteristics to those that were addressed to men. The poetic addresses to the Countess of Bedford and other noble patronesses of Donne, Ben Jonson, and their colleagues are always affectionate, often amorous, in their phraseology, and akin in temper to Shakespeare's sonnets of friendship. Nicholas Breton, in his poem *The Pilgrimage to Paradise coyned with the Countess of Pembroke's Love*, 1592, and another work of his, *The Countess of Pembroke's Passion* (first printed from manuscript in 1867), pays the Countess, who was merely his literary patroness, an homage which is indistinguishable from the ecstatic utterances of a genuine and overmastering passion. The difference in the sex of the persons addressed by Breton and by Shakespeare seems to place their poems in different categories, but they both really belonged to the same class. They both merely display a *protégé's* loyalty to his patron, couched, according to current convention, in the strongest possible terms of personal affection. In Italy and France exactly the same vocabulary of adoration was applied by authors indifferently to patrons and patronesses. It is known that one series of Michael Angelo's impassioned sonnets was addressed to a young nobleman Tommaso dei Cavalieri, and another series to a noble patroness Vittoria Colonna, but the tone is the same in both, and internal evidence fails to enable the critic to distinguish between the two series. Only one English contemporary of Shakespeare published a long series of sonnets addressed to a man who does not prove on investigation to have been a professional patron. In 1595 Richard Barnfield appended to his poem *Cynthia* a set of twenty sonnets, in which he feignedly avowed affection for a youth called Ganymede. These poems do not belong to the same category as Shakespeare's, but to the category of sonnet-sequences of love in which it was customary to invoke a fictitious mistress. Barnfield explained that in his sonnets he attempted a variation on the conventional practice by fancifully adapting to the sonnet-form the second of Virgil's *Eclogues*, in which the shepherd Coridon apostrophises the shepherd-boy Alexis.

the like assurances to their patrons. Southampton was only one of a crowd of Mæcenases whose pane-gyrists, writing without concealment in their own names, credited them with every perfection of mind and body, and 'placed them,' in Sidney's apt phrase, 'with Dante's " Beatrice." '

Illustrations of the practice abound. Matthew Roydon wrote of his patron, Sir Philip Sidney:

> His personage seemed most divine,
> A thousand graces one might count
> Upon his lovely cheerful eyne.
> To heare him speak and sweetly smile
> You were in Paradise the while.

Edmund Spenser in a fine sonnet told his patron, Admiral Lord Charles Howard, that 'his good per-sonage and noble deeds' made him the pattern to the present age of the old heroes of whom 'the antique poets' were 'wont so much to sing.' This compli-ment, which Shakespeare turns to splendid account in Sonnet cvi., recurs constantly in contemporary sonnets of adulation.[1] Ben Jonson apostrophised the Earl of Desmond as 'my best-best lov'd.' Campion told Lord Walden, the Earl of Suffolk's undistinguished heir, that although his muse sought to express his love, 'the admired virtues' of the patron's youth

> Bred such despairing to his daunted Muse
> That it could scarcely utter naked truth.[2]

---

[1] Cf. Sonnet lix :

> Show me your image in some antique book . . .
> O sure I am the wits of former days
> To subjects worse have given admiring praise.

[2] Campion's *Poems*, ed. Bullen, pp. 148 seq. Cf. Shakespeare's sonnets :

> O how I faint when I of you do write. — (lxxx. 1.)
> Finding thy worth a limit past my praise. — (lxxxii 6.)

Dr. John Donne includes among his 'Verse Letters' to patrons and patronesses several sonnets of similar temper, one of which, acknowledging a letter of news from a patron abroad, concludes thus :

> And now thy alms is given, thy letter's read,
> The body risen again, the which was dead,
> And thy poor starveling bountifully fed.
> After this banquet my soul doth say grace,
> And praise thee for it and zealously embrace
> Thy love, though I think thy love in this case
> To be as gluttons', which say 'midst their meat
> They love that best of which they most do eat.[1]

The tone of yearning for a man's affection is sounded by Donne and Campion almost as plaintively in their sonnets to patrons as it was sounded by Shakespeare. There is nothing, therefore, in the vocabulary of affection which Shakespeare employed in his sonnets of friendship to conflict with the theory that they were inscribed to a literary patron with whom his intimacy was of the kind normally subsisting at the time between literary clients and their patrons.

We know Shakespeare had only one literary patron, the Earl of Southampton, and the view that that nobleman is the hero of the sonnets of 'friendship' is strongly corroborated by such definite details as can be deduced from the vague eulogies in those poems of the youth's gifts and graces. Every compliment, in fact, paid by Shakespeare to the youth, whether it be

---

[1] Donne's *Poems* (in Muses' Library), ii. 34. See also Donne's sonnets and verse-letters to Mr. Rowland Woodward and Mr. I. W.

vaguely or definitely phrased, applies to Southampton
without the least straining of the words.   In real life

Direct
references
to South-
ampton in
the sonnets
of friend-
ship.
beauty, birth, wealth, and wit sat 'crowned'
in the Earl, whom poets acclaimed the
handsomest of Elizabethan courtiers, as
plainly as in the hero of the poet's verse.
Southampton has left in his correspon-
dence ample proofs of his literary learning and taste,
and, like the hero of the sonnets, was 'as fair in
knowledge as in hue.' The opening sequence of
seventeen sonnets, in which a youth of rank and
wealth is admonished to marry and beget a son so
that 'his fair house' may not fall into decay, can only
have been addressed to a young peer like Southampton, who was as yet unmarried, had vast possessions,
and was the sole male representative of his family.
The sonnetteer's exclamation, 'You had a father, let
your son say so,' had pertinence to Southampton at
any period between his father's death in his boyhood
and the close of his bachelorhood in 1598.   To
no other peer of the day are the words exactly
applicable.   The 'lascivious comment' on his 'wanton
sport' which pursues the young friend through the
sonnets, and is so adroitly contrived as to add point
to the picture of his fascinating youth and beauty,
obviously associates itself with the reputation for sensual indulgence that Southampton acquired both at
Court, and, according to Nash, among men of letters.[1]

There is no force in the objection that the
young man of the sonnets of 'friendship' must have
been another than Southampton because the terms

[1] See p. 386, note.

in which he is often addressed imply extreme youth. In 1594, a date to which I refer most of the sonnets, Southampton was barely twenty-one, and the young man had obviously reached manhood. In Sonnet civ. Shakespeare notes that the first meeting between him and his friend took place three years before that poem was written, so that, if the words are to be taken literally, the poet may have at times embodied reminiscences of Southampton when he was only seventeen or eighteen.[1] But Shakespeare, already worn in worldly experience, passed his thirtieth birthday in 1594, and he proba- bly tended, when on the threshold of middle life, to exaggerate the youthfulness of the nobleman almost ten years his junior, who even later impressed his acquaintances by his boyish appearance and disposi- tion.[2] 'Young' was the epithet invariably applied to Southampton by all who knew anything of him even when he was twenty-eight. In 1601 Sir Robert Cecil referred to him as the 'poor young Earl.'

His youth- fulness.

But the most striking evidence of the identity of the

[1] Three years was the conventional period which sonnetteers allotted to the development of their passion. Cf. Ronsard, *Sonnets pour Hélène* (No. xiv.), beginning: 'Trois ans sont ja passez que ton œil me tient pris.'

[2] Octavius Cæsar at thirty-two is described by Mark Antony after the battle of Actium as the 'boy Cæsar' who 'wears the rose of youth' (*Antony and Cleopatra*, III. ii. 17 seq.). Spenser in his *Astrophel* apostrophises Sir Philip Sidney on his death near the close of his thirty-second year as 'oh wretched boy' (l. 133) and 'luckless boy' (l. 142). Conversely it was a recognised convention among son- netteers to exaggerate their own age. See p. 86, note.

youth of the sonnets of 'friendship' with Southampton is found in the likeness of feature and

The evi-
dence of
portraits.

complexion which characterises the poet's
description of the youth's outward appearance and the extant pictures of Southampton as a
young man. Shakespeare's many references to his
youth's 'painted counterfeit' (xvi., xxiv., xlvii.,
lxvii.) suggest that his hero often sat for his portrait.
Southampton's countenance survives in probably
more canvases than that of any of his contemporaries.
At least fourteen extant portraits have been identified
on good authority — nine paintings, three miniatures
(two by Peter Oliver and one by Isaac Oliver), and two
contemporary prints.[1]   Most of these, it is true,

---

[1] Two portraits, representing the Earl in early manhood, are at Welbeck Abbey, and are described above.   Of the remaining seven paintings, two are assigned to Van Somer, and represent the Earl in early
middle age; one, a half-length, a very charming picture, now belongs to
James Knowles, Esq., of Queen Anne's Lodge; the other, a full-
length in drab doublet and hose, is in the Shakespeare Memorial Gallery at Stratford-on-Avon.   Mireveldt twice painted the Earl at a later
period of his career; one of the pictures is now at Woburn Abbey, the
property of the Duke of Bedford, the other is at the National Portrait Gallery.   A fifth picture, assigned to Mytens, belongs to Viscount
Powerscourt; a sixth, by an unknown artist, belongs to Mr. Wingfield
Digby, and the seventh (in armour) is in the Master's Lodge at St. John's
College, Cambridge, where Southampton was educated.   The miniature
by Isaac Oliver, which also represents Southampton in late life, was
formerly in Dr. Lumsden Propert's collection.   It now belongs to a
collector at Hamburg.   The two miniatures assigned to Peter Oliver
belong respectively to Mr. Jeffery Whitehead and Sir Francis Cook,
Bart.   (Cf. Catalogue of Exhibition of Portrait Miniatures at the Burlington Fine Arts Club, London, 1889, pp. 32, 71, 100.)   In all the best
preserved of these portraits the eyes are blue and the hair a dark shade
of auburn.   Among the middle-life portraits Southampton appears to
best advantage in the one by Van Somer belonging to Mr. James Knowles.

Henry Wriothesley, third Earl of Southampton
as a young man, from the original picture at Welbeck Abbey.

portray their subject in middle age, when the roses of youth had faded, and they contribute nothing to the present argument. But the two portraits that are now at Welbeck, the property of the Duke of Portland, give all the information that can be desired of Southampton's aspect 'in his youthful morn.' [1] One of these pictures represents the Earl at twenty-one, and the other at twenty-five or twenty-six. The earlier portrait, which is reproduced on the opposite page, shows a young man resplendently attired. His doublet is of white satin; a broad collar, edged with lace, half covers a pointed gorget of red leather, embroidered with silver thread; the white trunks and knee-breeches are laced with gold; the sword-belt, embroidered in red and gold, is decorated at intervals with white silk bows; the hilt of the rapier is overlaid with gold; purple garters, embroidered in silver thread, fasten the white stockings below the knee. Light body armour, richly damascened, lies on the ground to the right of the figure; and a white-plumed helmet stands to the left on a table covered with a cloth of purple velvet embroidered in gold. Such gorgeous raiment suggests that its wearer bestowed much attention on his personal equipment. But the head is more interesting than the body. The eyes are blue, the cheeks pink, the complexion clear, and the expression sedate; rings are in the ears; beard and moustache are at an incipient stage, and are of the same bright auburn hue as the hair in a picture of Southampton's mother

---

[1] I describe these pictures from a personal inspection of them which the Duke kindly permitted me to make.

L

that is also at Welbeck.[1] But, however scanty is the down on the youth's cheek, the hair on his head is luxuriant. It is worn very long, and falls over and below the shoulder. The colour is now of walnut, but was originally of lighter tint.

The portrait depicting Southampton five or six years later shows him in prison, to which he was committed after his secret marriage in 1598. A cat and a book in a jewelled binding are on a desk at his right hand. Here the hair falls over both his shoulders in even greater profusion, and is distinctly blonde. The beard and thin upturned moustache are of brighter auburn and fuller than before, although still slight. The blue eyes and colouring of the cheeks show signs of ill-health, but differ little from those features in the earlier portrait.

From either of the two Welbeck portraits of Southampton might Shakespeare have drawn his picture of the youth in the Sonnets. Many times does he tell us that the youth is fair in complexion, and that his eyes are fair. In Sonnet lxviii., when he points to the youth's face as a map of what beauty was 'without all ornament, itself and true' — before fashion sanctioned the use of artificial 'golden tresses' — there can be little doubt that he had in mind the wealth of locks that fell about Southampton's neck.[2]

[1] Cf. Shakespeare's Sonnet iii. :

> Thou art thy mother's glass, and she in thee
> Calls back the lovely April of her prime.

[2] Southampton's singularly long hair procured him at times unwelcome attentions. When, in January 1598, he struck Ambrose Willoughby, an esquire of the body, for asking him to break off,

A few only of the sonnets that Shakespeare addressed to the youth can be allotted to a date subsequent to 1594; only two bear on the surface signs of a later composition.   In Sonnet lxx. the poet no longer credits his hero with juvenile wantonness, but with a ' pure, unstained prime,' which has ' passed by the ambush of young days.'   Sonnet cvii., apparently the last of the series, was penned almost a decade after the mass of its companions, for it makes references that cannot be mistaken to three events that took place in 1603 — to Queen Elizabeth's death, to the accession of James I, and to the release of the Earl of Southampton, who had been in prison since he was convicted in 1601 of complicity in the rebellion of the Earl of Essex. The first two events are thus described :

Sonnet cvii. the last of the series.

> The mortal moon hath her eclipse endured
> And the sad augurs mock their own presage;
> Incertainties now crown themselves assured
> And peace proclaims olives of endless age.

It is in almost identical phrase that every pen in the spring of 1603 was felicitating the nation on the unexpected turn of events, by which Elizabeth's crown had passed, without civil war, to the Scottish King, and thus the revolution that had been foretold as the inevitable

Allusion to Elizabeth's death.

owing to the lateness of the hour, a game of primero that he was playing in the royal chamber at Whitehall, the esquire Willoughby is stated to have retaliated by ' pulling off some of the Earl's locks.'   On the incident being reported to the Queen, she ' gave Willoughby, in the presence, thanks for what he did ' (*Sydney Papers,* ii. 83).

consequence of Elizabeth's demise was happily averted. Cynthia (*i.e.* the moon) was the Queen's recognised poetic appellation. It is thus that she figures in the verse of Barnfield, Spenser, Fulke Greville, and Ralegh, and her elegists involuntarily followed the same fashion. 'Fair Cynthia's dead' sang one.

> Luna's extinct ; and now beholde the sunne
> Whose beames soake up the moysture of all teares,

wrote Henry Petowe, in his 'A Fewe Aprill Drops Showered on the Hearse of Dead Eliza,' 1603. There was hardly a verse-writer who mourned her loss that did not typify it, moreover, as the eclipse of a heavenly body. One poet asserted that death 'veiled her glory in a cloud of night.' Another argued: 'Naught can eclipse her light, but that her star will shine in darkest night.' A third varied the formula thus :

> When winter had cast off her weed
> Our sun eclipsed did set. Oh ! light most fair.[1]

At the same time James was constantly said to have entered on his inheritance 'not with an olive branch in his hand, but with a whole forest of olives round about him, for he brought not peace to this kingdom alone' but to all Europe.[2]

'The drops of this most balmy time,' in this same sonnet, cvii., is an echo of another current strain of fancy. James came to England in a springtide of rarely rivalled clemency, which was reckoned of the

[1] These quotations are from *Sorrowes Joy*, a collection of elegies on Queen Elizabeth by Cambridge writers (Cambridge, 1603), and from Chettle's *England's Mourning Garment* (London, 1603).

[2] Gervase Markham's *Honour in her Perfection*, 1624.

happiest augury. 'All things look fresh,' one poet
sang, 'to greet his excellence.' 'The air, the seasons,

Allusions
to South-
ampton's
release
from
prison.
and the earth' were represented as in sympathy with the general joy in 'this sweetest
of all sweet springs.' One source of grief
alone was acknowledged : Southampton was
still a prisoner in the Tower, 'supposed as forfeit
to a confined doom.' All men, wrote Manningham,
the diarist, on the day following the Queen's death,
wished him at liberty.[1] The wish was fulfilled quickly.
On April 10, 1603, his prison gates were opened by
'a warrant from the king.' So bountiful a beginning
of the new era, wrote John Chamberlain to Dudley
Carleton two days later, 'raised all men's spirits,
. . . and the very poets with their idle pamphlets
promised themselves' great things.[2] Samuel Daniel
and John Davies celebrated Southampton's release
in buoyant verse.[3] It is improbable that Shakespeare remained silent. 'My love looks fresh,' he
wrote, in the concluding lines of Sonnet cvii., and
he repeated the conventional promise that he had
so often made before, that his friend should live in
his 'poor rhyme,' 'when tyrants' crests and tombs
of brass are spent.' It is impossible to resist the
inference that Shakespeare thus saluted his patron
on the close of his days of tribulation. Shakespeare's
genius had then won for him a public reputation that
rendered him independent of any private patron's

---

[1] Manningham's *Diary*, Camden Soc., p. 148.
[2] *Court and Times of James I*, I. i. 7.
[3] See Appendix IV.

favour, and he made no further reference in his writings to the patronage that Southampton had extended to him in earlier years. But the terms in which he greeted his former protector for the last time in verse, justify the belief that, during his remaining thirteen years of life, the poet cultivated friendly relations with the Earl of Southampton, and was mindful to the last of the encouragement that the young peer offered him while he was still on the threshold of the temple of fame.

X

THE SUPPOSED STORY OF INTRIGUE IN THE SONNETS

IT is hardly possible to doubt that had Shakespeare, who was more prolific in invention than any other poet, poured out in his sonnets his personal passions and emotions, he would have been carried by his imagination, at every stage, far beyond the beaten tracks of the conventional sonnetteers of his day. The imitative element in his sonnets is large enough to refute the assertion that in them as a whole he sought to 'unlock his heart.' It is likely enough that beneath all the conventional adulation bestowed by Shakespeare on Southampton there lay a genuine affection, but his sonnets to the Earl were no involuntary ebullitions of a devoted and disinterested friendship; they were celebrations of a patron's favour in the terminology — often raised by Shakespeare's genius to the loftiest heights of poetry — that was invariably consecrated to such a purpose by a current literary convention. Very few of Shakespeare's 'sugared sonnets' have a substantial right to be regarded as untutored cries of the soul. It is true that the sonnets in which the writer reproaches himself with sin, or gives expression to a sense of melancholy, offer at times a convincing illusion of autobiographic confessions; and it is just possible that they stand apart from the rest, and reveal the writer's inner consciousness, in which case they are not to be matched in any other of Shakespeare's literary compositions. But they may be, on the other hand, merely literary meditations, conceived by the greatest of dramatists, on infirmities incident to all human nature, and only attempted after the cue had been given by rival sonnetteers. At any rate, their energetic lines are often adapted from the less forcible and less coherent utterances of contemporary poets, and the themes are common to almost all Elizabethan collections of sonnets.[1] Shakespeare's noble sonnet on the ravages of lust (cxxix.), for example, treats with marvellous force and insight a stereotyped theme of sonnetteers,

---

[1] The fine exordium of Sonnet cxix.:

> What potions have I drunk of Siren tears,
> Distill'd from limbecks foul as hell within,

adopts expressions in Barnes's vituperative sonnet (No. xlix.), where, after denouncing his mistress as a 'siren,' the poet incoherently ejaculates:

> From my love's limbeck [sc. have I] still [di]stilled tears!

Almost every note in the scale of sadness or self-reproach is sounded from time to time in Petrarch's sonnets. Tasso in *Scelta delle Rime*, 1582, part ii. p. 26, has a sonnet (beginning 'Vinca fortuna homai, se sotto il peso') which adumbrates Shakespeare's Sonnets xxix. ('When in disgrace with fortune and men's eyes') and lxvi. ('Tired with all these, for restful death I cry'). Drummond of Hawthornden translated Tasso's sonnet in his sonnet (part i. No. xxxiii.); while Drummond's Sonnets xxv. ('What cruel star into this world was brought') and xxxii. ('If crost with all mishaps be my poor life') are pitched in the identical key.

and it may have owed its whole existence to Sir Philip Sidney's sonnet on ' Desire.' [1]

Only in one group, composed of six sonnets scattered through the collection, is there traceable a strand of wholly original sentiment, not to be readily defined, and boldly projecting from the web into which it is wrought. This series of six sonnets deals with a love adventure of no normal type. Sonnet cxliv. opens with the lines :

> Two loves I have of comfort and despair
> Which like two angels do suggest (*i.e.* tempt) me still :
> The better angel is a man right fair,
> The worser spirit a woman colour'd ill.[2]

The woman, the sonnetteer continues, has corrupted the man and has drawn him from his ' side.' Five

The youth's relations with the poet's mistress. other sonnets treat the same theme. In three addressed to the man (xl., xli., and xlii.) the poet mildly reproaches his youthful friend for having sought and won the favours of a woman whom he himself loved ' dearly,' but the trespass is forgiven on account of the friend's youth and

---

[1] Sidney's *Certain Sonnets* (No. xiii.) appended to *Astrophel and Stella* in the edition of 1598. In *Emaricdulfe : Sonnets written by E. C.*, 1595, Sonnet xxxvii. beginning 'O lust, of sacred love the foul corrupter,' even more closely resembles Shakespeare's sonnet in both phraseology and sentiment. E. C.'s rare volume is reprinted in the *Lamport Garland* (Roxburghe Club), 1881.

[2] Even this sonnet is adapted from Drayton. See Sonnet xxii. in 1599 edition :

> An evil spirit your beauty haunts me still . . .
> Thus am I still provoked to every evil
> By this good-wicked spirit, sweet Angel-Devil.

But Shakespeare entirely alters the point of the lines by contrasting the influence exerted on him by the woman with that exerted on him by a man.

beauty. In the two remaining sonnets Shakespeare addresses the woman (cxxxiii. and cxxxiv.), and he rebukes her for having enslaved not only himself but ' his next self ' — his friend. Shakespeare, in his denunciation elsewhere of a mistress's disdain of his advances, assigns her blindness, like all the professional sonnetteers, to no better defined cause than the perversity and depravity of womankind. In these six sonnets alone does he categorically assign his mistress's alienation to the fascinations of a dear friend or hint at such a cause for his mistress's infidelity. The definite element of intrigue that is developed here is not found anywhere else in the range of Elizabethan sonnet-literature. The character of the innovation and its treatment seem only capable of explanation by regarding it as a reflection of Shakespeare's personal experience. But how far he is sincere in his accounts of his sorrow in yielding his mistress to his friend in order to retain the friendship of the latter must be decided by each reader for himself. If all the words be taken literally, there is disclosed an act of self-sacrifice that it is difficult to parallel or explain. But it remains very doubtful if the affair does not rightly belong to the annals of gallantry. The sonnetteer's complacent condonation of the young man's offence chiefly suggests the deference that was essential to the maintenance by a dependent of peaceful relations with a self-willed and self-indulgent patron. Southampton's sportive and lascivious temperament might easily impel him to divert to himself the attention of an attractive woman by whom he saw that his poet was fascinated, and he was unlikely to tolerate any outspoken protest on the part of his *protégé*. There is no clue to the lady's identity, and speculation on the topic is useless. She may have given Shakespeare hints for his pictures of the 'dark lady,' but he treats that lady's obduracy conventionally, and his vituperation of her sheds no light on the personal history of the mistress who left him for his friend.

The emotions roused in Shakespeare by the episode, even if potent at the moment, were not likely to be deep-seated or enduring. And it is possible that a half-jesting reference, which would deprive Shakespeare's amorous adventure of serious import, was made to it by a literary comrade in a poem that was licensed for publication on September 3, 1594, and was published immediately under the title of 'Willobie his Avisa, or the True Picture of a Modest Maid and of a Chaste and Constant Wife.'[1] In this volume, which mainly consists of seventy-two cantos in varying numbers of six-line stanzas, the chaste heroine, Avisa, holds converse — in the opening section as a maid, and in the later section as a wife — with a series of passionate adorers. In every case she firmly repulses their advances. Midway through the book its alleged author — Henry Willobie — is introduced in his own person as an ardent admirer, and the last twenty-nine of the cantos rehearse his woes and Avisa's obduracy. To this section there is

(marginal note:) 'Willobie his Avisa.'

---

[1] The work was reprinted by Dr. Grosart in his *Occasional Issues*, 1880, and extracts from it appear in the New Shakspere Society's 'Allusion Books,' i. 169 seq.

prefixed an argument in prose (canto xliv.). It is there stated that Willobie, ' being suddenly affected with the contagion of a fantastical wit at the first sight of Avisa, pineth a while in secret grief. At length, not able any longer to endure the burning heat of so fervent a humour, [he] bewrayeth the secrecy of his disease unto his familiar friend *W. S.*, *who not long before had tried the courtesy of the like passion and was now newly recovered of the like infection.* Yet [W. S.], finding his friend let blood in the same vein, took pleasure for a time to see him bleed, and instead of stopping the issue, he enlargeth the wound with the sharp razor of willing conceit,' encouraging Willobie to believe that Avisa would ultimately yield 'with pains, diligence, and some cost in time.' ' The miserable comforter ' [W. S.], the passage continues, was moved to comfort his friend ' with an impossibility,' for one of two reasons. Either he 'now would secretly laugh at his friend's folly ' because he ' had given occasion not long before unto others to laugh at his own.' Or ' he would see whether another could play his part better than himself, and, in viewing after the course of this loving comedy,' would 'see whether it would sort to a happier end for this new actor than it did for *the old actor*. But at length this comedy was like to have grown to a tragedy by the weak and feeble estate that H. W. was brought unto,' owing to Avisa's unflinching rectitude. Happily, 'time and necessity ' effected a cure. In two succeeding cantos in verse W. S. is introduced in dialogue with Willobie, and he gives him, in *oratio recta*, light-hearted and mocking counsel which Willobie accepts with results disastrous to his mental health.

Identity of initials, on which the theory of Shakespeare's identity with H. W.'s unfeeling adviser mainly rests, is not a strong foundation,[1] and doubt is justifiable as to whether the story of 'Avisa' and her lovers is not fictitious. In a preface signed Hadrian Dorell, the writer, after mentioning that the alleged author (Willobie) was abroad, discusses somewhat enigmatically whether or no the work is 'a poetical fiction.' In a new edition of 1596 the same editor decides the question in the affirmative. But Dorell, while making this admission, leaves untouched the curious episode of 'W. S.' The mention of 'W. S.' as 'the old actor,' and the employment of theatrical imagery in discussing his relations with Willobie, must be coupled with the fact that Shakespeare, at a date when mentions of him in print were rare, was eulogised by name as the author of 'Lucrece' in some prefatory verses to the volume. From such considerations the theory of 'W. S.'s' identity with Willobie's acquaintance acquires substance. If we assume that it was Shakespeare who took a roguish delight in watching his friend Willobie suffer the disdain of 'chaste Avisa' because he had 'newly recovered' from the effects of

---

[1] W. S. are common initials, and at least two authors bearing them made some reputation in Shakespeare's day. There was a dramatist named Wentworth Smith (see p. 180, *infra*), and there was a William Smith who published a volume of love-lorn sonnets called *Chloris* in 1595. A specious argument might possibly be devised in favour of the latter's identity with Willobie's counsellor. But Shakespeare, of the two, has the better claim.

a like experience, it is clear that the theft of Shakespeare's mistress by another friend did not cause him deep or lasting distress. The allusions that were presumably made to the episode by the author of 'Avisa' bring it, in fact, nearer the confines of comedy than of tragedy.

The processes of construction which are discernible in Shakespeare's sonnets are thus seen to be identical with those that are discernible in the rest of his literary work. They present one more proof of his punctilious regard for the demands of public taste, and of his marvellous genius and skill in adapting and transmuting for his own purposes the labours of other workers in the field that for the moment engaged his attention. Most of Shakespeare's sonnets were produced in 1594 under the incitement of that freakish rage for sonnetteering which, taking its rise in Italy and sweeping over France on its way to England, absorbed for some half-dozen years in this country a greater volume of literary energy than has been applied to sonnetteering within the same space of time here or elsewhere before or since. The thousands of sonnets that were circulated in England between 1591 and 1597 were of every literary quality, from sublimity to inanity, and they illustrated in form and topic every known phase of sonnetteering activity. Shakespeare's collection, which was put together at haphazard and published surreptitiously many years after the poems were written, was a medley, at times reaching heights of literary excellence that none

Summary of conclusions respecting the sonnets.

other scaled, but as a whole reflecting the varied features of the sonnetteering vogue. Apostrophes to metaphysical abstractions, vivid picturings of the beauties of nature, adulation of a patron, idealisation of a *protégé's* regard for a nobleman in the figurative language of amorous passion, amiable compliments on a woman's hair or touch on the virginals, and vehement denunciation of the falseness and frailty of womankind — all appear as frequently in contemporary collections of sonnets as in Shakespeare's. He borrows very many of his competitors' words and thoughts, but he so fused them with his fancy as often to transfigure them. Genuine emotion or the writer's personal experience very rarely inspired the Elizabethan sonnet, and Shakespeare's sonnets proved no exception to the rule. A personal note may have escaped him involuntarily in the sonnets in which he gives voice to a sense of melancholy and self-remorse, but his dramatic instinct never slept, and there is no proof that he is doing more in those sonnets than produce dramatically the illusion of a personal confession. Only in one scattered series of six sonnets, where he introduced a topic, unknown to other sonnetteers, of a lover's supersession by his friend in a mistress's graces, does he seem to show independence of his comrades and draw directly on an incident in his own life, but even there the emotion is wanting in seriousness. The sole biographical inference deducible from the sonnets is that at one time in his career Shakespeare disdained no weapon of flattery in an endeavour to monopolise the bountiful patronage of a young man of rank. External evidence agrees with internal evidence in identifying the belauded patron with the Earl of Southampton, and the real value to a biographer of Shakespeare's sonnets is the corroboration they offer of the ancient tradition that the Earl of Southampton, to whom his two narrative poems were openly dedicated, gave Shakespeare at an early period of his literary career help and encouragement, which entitles the Earl to a place in the poet's biography resembling that filled by the Duke Alfonso D'Este in the biography of Ariosto, or like that filled by Margaret, duchess of Savoy, in the biography of Ronsard.

XI

THE DEVELOPMENT OF DRAMATIC POWER

But, all the while that Shakespeare was fancifully assuring his patron

> [How] to no other pass my verses tend
> Than of your graces and your gifts to tell,

his dramatic work was steadily advancing. To the winter season of 1595 probably belongs 'Midsummer Night's Dream.'[1] The comedy may well have been written to celebrate a marriage — perhaps the marriage of the universal patroness of poets, Lucy Harington, to Edward Russell, third Earl of Bedford, on December 12, 1594; or that of William Stanley, Earl of Derby, at Greenwich on January 24, 1594–5. The elaborate compliment to the Queen, 'a fair vestal throned by the west' (II. i. 157 seq.), was at once an acknowledgment of past marks of royal favour and an invitation for their extension to the future. Oberon's fanciful description (II. ii. 148–68) of the spot where he saw the little western flower called 'Love-in-idleness' that he bids Puck fetch for him, has been interpreted as a reminiscence of one of the scenic pageants with

'Mid-summer Night's Dream.'

[1] No edition appeared before 1600, and then two were published.

M

which the Earl of Leicester entertained Queen
Elizabeth on her visit to Kenilworth in 1575.[1] The
whole play is in the airiest and most graceful vein
of comedy.   Hints for the story can be traced to a
variety of sources — to Chaucer's 'Knight's Tale,' to
Plutarch's 'Life of Theseus,' to Ovid's 'Metamorphoses' (bk. iv.), and to the story of Oberon, the
fairy-king, in the French mediæval romance of 'Huon
of Bordeaux,' of which an English translation by
Lord Berners was first printed in 1534. The influence of John Lyly is perceptible in the raillery in
which both mortals and immortals indulge.   In the
humorous presentation of the play of 'Pyramus and
Thisbe' by the 'rude mechanicals' of Athens, Shakespeare improved upon a theme which he had already
employed in 'Love's Labour's Lost.'   But the final
scheme of the 'Midsummer Night's Dream' is of the
author's freshest invention, and by endowing — practically for the first time in literature — the phantoms
of the fairy world with a genuine and a sustained
dramatic interest, Shakespeare may be said to have
conquered a new realm for art.

More sombre topics engaged him in the comedy
of 'All's Well that Ends Well,' which may be ten-
'All's   tatively assigned to 1595. Meres, writing
Well.'   three years later, attributed to Shakespeare
a piece called 'Love's Labour's Won.' This title,
which is not otherwise known, may well be applied

---

[1] *Oberon's Vision*, by the Rev. W. J. Halpin (Shakespeare Society),
1843.   Two accounts of the Kenilworth *fêtes*, by George Gascoigne
and Robert Laneham respectively, were published in 1576.

to ' All's Well.' ' The Taming of The Shrew,' which
has also been identified with ' Love's Labour's Won,'
has far slighter claim to the designation. The plot
of ' All's Well,' like that of ' Romeo and Juliet,' was
drawn from Painter's ' Palace of Pleasure' (No.
xxxviii.). The original source is Boccaccio's ' Deca-
merone' (giorn. iii. nov. 9). Shakespeare, after his
wont, grafted on the touching story of Helena's love
for the unworthy Bertram the comic characters of the
braggart Parolles, the pompous Lafeu, and a clown
(Lavache) less witty than his compeers. Another
original creation, Bertram's mother, Countess of
Roussillon, is a charming portrait of old age. In
frequency of rhyme and other metrical characteristics
the piece closely resembles ' The Two Gentlemen,'
but the characterisation betrays far greater power,
and there are fewer conceits or crudities of style.
The pathetic element predominates. The heroine
Helena, whose ' pangs of despised love' are expressed
with touching tenderness, ranks with the greatest of
Shakespeare's female creations.

    ' The Taming of The Shrew ' — which, like ' All's
Well,' was first printed in the folio — was probably
composed soon after the completion of that solemn
comedy. It is a revision of an old play on lines
somewhat differing from those which Shakespeare

' Taming
of The
Shrew.'

had followed previously. From ' The
Taming of A Shrew,' a comedy first published in 1594,[1] Shakespeare drew the Induction and the scenes in which the hero Petruchio

[1] Reprinted by the Shakespeare Society in 1844.

conquers Catherine the Shrew. He first infused into them the genuine spirit of comedy. But while following the old play in its general outlines, Shakespeare's revised version added an entirely new underplot — the story of Bianca and her lovers, which owes something to the 'Supposes' of George Gascoigne, an adaptation of Ariosto's comedy called 'Gli Suppositi.' Evidence of style — the liberal introduction of tags of Latin and the exceptional beat of the doggerel — makes it difficult to allot the Bianca scenes to Shakespeare; those scenes were probably due to a coadjutor.

The Induction to 'The Taming of The Shrew' has a direct bearing on Shakespeare's biography, for the poet admits into it a number of literal references to Stratford and his native county. Such personalities are rare in Shakespeare's plays, and can only be paralleled in two of slightly later date — the 'Second Part of Henry IV' and the 'Merry Wives of Windsor.' All these local allusions may well be attributed to such a renewal of Shakespeare's personal relations

Stratford allusions in the Induction.

with the town as is indicated by external facts in his history of the same period. In the Induction the tinker, Christopher Sly, describes himself as 'Old Sly's son of Burton Heath.' Burton Heath is Barton-on-the-Heath, the home of Shakespeare's aunt, Edmund Lambert's wife, and of her sons. The tinker in like vein confesses that he has run up a score with Marian Hacket, the fat alewife of Wincot.[1] The references

[1] All these details are of Shakespeare's invention, and do not figure

to Wincot and the Hackets are singularly precise. The name of the maid of the inn is given as Cicely Hacket, and the alehouse is described in the stage direction as 'on a heath.'

Wincot was the familiar designation of three small Warwickshire villages, and a good claim has been set up on behalf of each to be the scene of Sly's drunken exploits. There is a very small hamlet named Wincot within four miles of Stratford, now consisting of a single farmhouse which was once an Elizabethan mansion; it is situated on what was doubtless in Shakespeare's day, before the land there was enclosed, an open heath. This Wincot forms part of the parish of Quinton, where, according to the parochial registers, a Hacket family resided in Shakespeare's day. On November 21, 1591, 'Sara Hacket, the daughter of Robert Hacket,' was baptised in Quinton church.[1] Yet by Warwickshire contemporaries the Wincot of 'The Taming of The Shrew' was unhesitatingly identified with Wilnecote, near Tamworth, on the Staffordshire border of Warwickshire, at some distance from Stratford. That

Wincot.

in the old play. But in the crude induction in the old play the non-descript drunkard is named without prefix 'Slie.' That surname, although it was very common at Stratford and in the neighbourhood, was borne by residents in many other parts of the country, and its appearance in the old play is not in itself, as has been suggested, sufficient to prove that the old play was written by a Warwickshire man. There are no other names or references in the old play that can be associated with Warwickshire.

[1] Mr. Richard Savage, the secretary and librarian of the Birthplace Trustees at Stratford, has generously placed at my disposal this interesting fact, which he lately discovered.

village, whose name was pronounced 'Wincot,' was celebrated for its ale in the seventeenth century, a distinction which is not shown by contemporary evidence to have belonged to any place of like name. The Warwickshire poet, Sir Aston Cokain, within half a century of the production of Shakespeare's 'Taming of The Shrew,' addressed to 'Mr. Clement Fisher of Wincott' (a well-known resident at Wilnecote) verses which begin

> *Shakspeare* your *Wincot* ale hath much renowned,
> That fox'd a Beggar so (by chance was found
> Sleeping) that there needed not many a word
> To make him to believe he was a Lord.

In the succeeding lines the writer promises to visit 'Wincot' (*i.e.* Wilnecote) to drink

> Such ale as *Shakspeare* fancies
> Did put Kit Sly into such lordly trances.

It is therefore probable that Shakespeare consciously invested the home of Kit Sly and of Kit's hostess with characteristics of Wilnecote as well as of the hamlet near Stratford.

Wilmcote, the native place of Shakespeare's mother, is also said to have been popularly pronounced 'Wincot.' A tradition which was first recorded by Capell as late as 1780 in his notes to 'The Taming of The Shrew' (p. 26) is to the effect that Shakespeare often visited an inn at 'Wincot' to enjoy the society of a 'fool who belonged to a neighbouring mill,' and the Wincot of this story is, we are told, locally associated with the village of Wilmcote. But the links that connect Shakespeare's tinker with Wilmcote are far slighter than those which connect him with Wincot and Wilnecote.

The mention of Kit Sly's tavern comrades —

> Stephen Sly and old John Naps of Greece,
> And Peter Turf and Henry Pimpernell —

was in all likelihood a reminiscence of contemporary Warwickshire life as literal as the name of the hamlet where the drunkard dwelt. There was a genuine Stephen Sly who was in the dramatist's day a self-assertive citizen of Stratford; and 'Greece,' whence 'old John Naps' derived his cognomen, is an obvious misreading of Greet, a hamlet by Winchmore in Gloucestershire, not far removed from Shakespeare's native town.

In 1597 Shakespeare turned once more to English history. From Holinshed's 'Chronicle,' and from a valueless but very popular piece, 'The Famous Victories of Henry V,' which was repeatedly acted between 1588 and 1595,[1] he worked up with splendid energy two plays on the reign of Henry IV. They form one continuous whole, but are known respectively as parts i. and ii. of 'Henry IV.' The 'Second Part of Henry IV' is almost as rich as the Induction to 'The Taming of The Shrew' in direct references to persons and districts familiar to Shakespeare. Two amusing scenes pass at the house of Justice Shallow in Gloucestershire, a county which touched the boundaries of Strat-

'Henry IV.'

---

[1] It was licensed for publication in 1594, and published in 1598.

ford (III. ii. and v. i.). When, in the second of these
scenes, the justice's factotum, Davy, asked his master
'to countenance William Visor of Woncot[1] against
Clement Perkes of the Hill,' the local references are
unmistakable. Woodmancote, where the family of
Visor or Vizard has flourished since the sixteenth
century, is still pronounced Woncot. The adjoining
Stinchcombe Hill (still familiarly known to natives as
'The Hill') was in the sixteenth century the home of
the family of Perkes. Very precise too are the allusions to the region of the Cotswold Hills, which were
easily accessible from Stratford. 'Will Squele, a
Cotswold man,' is noticed as one of Shallow's friends
in youth (III. ii. 23); and when Shallow's servant Davy
receives his master's instructions to sow 'the head-
land' 'with red wheat,' in the early autumn, there is
an obvious reference to the custom almost peculiar
to the Cotswolds of sowing 'red lammas' wheat at an
unusually early season of the agricultural year.[2]

The kingly hero of the two plays of 'Henry IV'
had figured as a spirited young man in 'Richard II';
he was now represented as weighed down by care
and age. With him are contrasted (in part i.) his
impetuous and ambitious subject Hotspur and (in

[1] The quarto of 1600 reads Woncote: all the folios read Woncot.
Yet Malone in the Variorum of 1803 introduced the new and unwarranted reading of Wincot, which has been unwisely adopted by
succeeding editors.

[2] These references are convincingly explained by Mr. Justice Mad-
den in his *Diary of Master Silence*, pp. 87 seq., 372–4. Cf. Blunt's
Dursley and its Neighbourhood; Huntley's *Glossary of the Cotswold
Dialect,* and Marshall's *Rural Economy of Cotswold* (1796).

both parts) his son and heir Prince Hal, whose boisterous disposition drives him from Court to seek adventures among the haunters of taverns. Hotspur is a vivid and fascinating portrait of a hot-headed soldier, courageous to the point of rashness, and sacrificing his life to his impetuous sense of honour. Prince Hal, despite his vagaries, is endowed by the dramatist with far more self-control and common sense.

On the first, as on every subsequent, production of 'Henry IV' the main public interest was concentrated neither on the King nor on his son, nor on Hotspur, but on the chief of Prince Hal's riotous companions. At the outset the propriety of that great creation was questioned on a political or historical ground of doubtful relevance. Shakespeare in both parts of 'Henry IV' originally named the chief of the prince's associates after Sir John Oldcastle, a character in the old play. But Henry Brooke, eighth Lord Cobham, who succeeded to the title early in 1597, and claimed descent from the historical Sir John Oldcastle, the Lollard leader, raised objection; and when the first part of the play was printed by the acting-company's authority in 1598 ('newly corrected' in 1599), Shake-

Falstaff. speare bestowed on Prince Hal's tun-bellied follower the new and deathless name of Falstaff. A trustworthy edition of the second part of 'Henry IV' also appeared with Falstaff's name substituted for that of Oldcastle in 1600. There the epilogue expressly denied that Falstaff had any characteristic in common with the martyr Oldcastle,

'Oldcastle died a martyr, and this is not the man.'
But the substitution of the name 'Falstaff' did not pass
without protest. It hazily recalled Sir John Fastolf,
an historical warrior who had already figured in
'Henry VI' and was owner at one time of the Boar's
Head Tavern in Southwark; according to traditional
stage directions,[1] the prince and his companions in
'Henry IV,' frequent the Boar's Head, Eastcheap.
Fuller in his 'Worthies,' first published in 1662, while
expressing satisfaction that Shakespeare had 'put
out' of the play Sir John Oldcastle, was eloquent
in his avowal of regret that 'Sir John Fastolf' was
'put in,' on the ground that it was making over
bold with a great warrior's memory to make him a
'Thrasonical puff and emblem of mock-valour.'

The offending introduction and withdrawal of
Oldcastle's name left a curious mark on literary
history. Humbler dramatists (Munday, Wilson,
Drayton, and Hathaway), seeking to profit by the
attention drawn by Shakespeare to the historical
Oldcastle, produced a poor dramatic version of Old-
castle's genuine history; and of two editions of 'Sir
John Oldcastle' published in 1600, one printed for
T[homas] P[avier] was impudently described on the
title-page as by Shakespeare.

But it is not the historical traditions which are
connected with Falstaff that give him his perennial
attraction. It is the personality that owes nothing
to history with which Shakespeare's imaginative

---

[1] First adopted by Theobald in 1733; cf. Halliwell-Phillipps,
ii. 257.

power clothed him. The knight's unfettered indulgence in sensual pleasures, his exuberant mendacity, and his love of his own ease are purged of offence by his colossal wit and jollity, while the contrast between his old age and his unreverend way of life supplies that tinge of melancholy which is inseparable from the highest manifestations of humour. The Elizabethan public recognised the triumphant success of the effort, and many of Falstaff's telling phrases, with the names of his foils, Justices Shallow and Silence, at once took root in popular speech. Shakespeare's purely comic power culminated in Falstaff; he may be claimed as the most humorous figure in literature.

In all probability 'The Merry Wives of Windsor,' a comedy inclining to farce, and unqualified by 'Merry any pathetic interest, followed close upon Wives of 'Henry IV.' In the epilogue to the 'Second Windsor.' Part of Henry IV' Shakespeare had written: 'If you be not too much cloyed with fat meat, our humble author will continue the story with Sir John in it . . . where for anything I know Falstaff shall die of a sweat, unless already a' be killed with your hard opinions.' Rowe asserts that 'Queen Elizabeth was so well pleased with that admirable character of Falstaff in the two parts of "Henry IV" that she commanded him to continue it for one play more, and to show him in love. Dennis, in the dedication of 'The Comical Gallant' (1702), noted that the 'Merry Wives' was written at the Queen's 'command and by her direction; and she was so eager to see it acted that she commanded it to be finished in fourteen days, and was afterwards, as tradition tells us, very well pleased with the representation.' In his 'Letters' (1721, p. 232) Dennis reduces the period of composition to ten days — 'a prodigious thing,' added Gildon,[1] 'where all is so well contrived and carried on without the least confusion.' The localisation of the scene at Windsor, and the complimentary references to Windsor Castle, corroborate the tradition that the comedy was prepared to meet a royal command. An imperfect draft of the play was printed by Thomas Creede in 1602;[2] the folio of 1623 first supplied a complete version. The plot was probably suggested by an Italian novel. A tale from Straparola's 'Notti' (ii. 2), of which an adaptation figured in the miscellany of novels called Tarleton's 'Newes out of Purgatorie' (1590), another Italian tale from the 'Pecorone' of Ser Giovanni Fiorentino (ii. 2), and a third romance, the Fishwife's tale of Brainford in the collection of stories called 'Westward for Smelts,'[3] supply incidents distantly resembling episodes in the play. Nowhere has Shakespeare so vividly reflected the bluff temper of contemporary middle-class society. The presentment of the buoyant domestic life of an Elizabethan country town bears distinct impress of Shakespeare's own experience. Again, there are literal references to the neigh-

[1] *Remarks*, p. 291.

[2] Cf. Shakespeare Society's reprint, 1842, ed. Halliwell.

[3] This collection of stories is said by both Malone and Steevens to have been published in 1603, although no edition earlier than 1620 is now known. The 1620 edition of *Westward for Smelts, written by Kinde Kit of Kingston*, was reprinted by the Percy Society in 1848. Cf. *Shakespeare's Library*, ed. Hazlitt, i. ii. 1–80.

bourhood of Stratford. Justice Shallow, whose coat-of-arms is described as consisting of 'luces,' is thereby openly identified with Shakespeare's early foe, Sir Thomas Lucy of Charlecote. When Shakespeare makes Master Slender repeat the report that Master Page's fallow greyhound was 'outrun on Cotsall' (I. i. 93), he testifies to his interest in the coursing matches for which the Cotswold district was famed.

The spirited character of Prince Hal was peculiarly congenial to its creator, and in 'Henry V' Shakespeare, during 1598, brought his 'Henry V.' career to its close. The play was performed early in 1599, probably in the newly built Globe Theatre. Again Thomas Creede printed, in 1600, an imperfect draft, which was thrice reissued before a complete version was supplied in the First Folio of 1623. The dramatic interest of 'Henry V' is slender. There is abundance of comic element, but death has removed Falstaff, whose last moments are described with the simple pathos that comes of a matchless art, and, though Falstaff's companions survive, they are thin shadows of his substantial figure. New comic characters are introduced in the person of three soldiers respectively of Welsh, Scottish, and Irish nationality, whose racial traits are contrasted with telling effect. The irascible Irishman, Captain Mac-Morris, is the only representative of his nation who figures in the long list of Shakespeare's *dramatis personæ*. The scene in which the pedantic but patriotic Welshman, Fluellen, avenges the sneers of the braggart Pistol at his nation's emblem, by forcing him to eat the leek, overflows in vivacious humour. The piece in its main current presents a series of loosely connected episodes in which the hero's manliness is displayed as soldier, ruler, and lover. The topic reached its climax in the victory of the English at Agincourt, which powerfully appealed to patriotic sentiment. Besides the 'Famous Victories,'[1] there was another lost piece on the subject, which Henslowe produced for the first time on November 28, 1595. 'Henry V' may be regarded as Shakespeare's final experiment in the dramatisation of English history, and it artistically rounds off the series of his 'histories' which form collectively a kind of national epic. For 'Henry VIII,' which was produced very late in his career, he was only in part responsible, and that 'history' consequently belongs to a different category.

A glimpse of autobiography may be discerned in the direct mention by Shakespeare in ' Henry V' of an exciting episode in current history. In the prologue to act v. Shakespeare foretold for Robert Devereux, second Earl of Essex, the close friend of his patron Southampton, an enthusiastic reception by the people of London when he should come home after 'broaching' rebellion in Ireland.

Essex and the rebellion of 1601.

> Were now the general of our gracious empress,
> As in good time he may, from Ireland coming,
> Bringing rebellion broached on his sword,
> How many would the peaceful city quit
> To welcome him! — (Act v. Chorus, ll. 30–4.)

Essex had set out on his disastrous mission as

[1] *Diary*, p. 61; see p. 167.

the would-be pacificator of Ireland on March 27, 1599. The fact that Southampton went with him probably accounts for Shakespeare's avowal of sympathy. But Essex's effort failed. He was charged, soon after 'Henry V' was produced, with treasonable neglect of duty, and he sought in 1601, again with the support of Southampton, to recover his position by stirring up rebellion in London. Then Shakespeare's reference to Essex's popularity with Londoners bore perilous fruit. The friends of the rebel leaders sought the dramatist's countenance. They paid 40s. to Augustine Phillips, a leading member of Shakespeare's company, to induce him to revive at the Globe Theatre 'Richard II' (beyond doubt Shakespeare's play), in the hope that its scene of the killing of a king might encourage a popular outbreak. Phillips subsequently deposed that he prudently told the conspirators who bespoke the piece that 'that play of Kyng Richard' was 'so old and so long out of use as that they should have small or no company at it.' None the less the performance took place on Saturday (February 7, 1601), the day preceding that fixed by Essex for the rising. The Queen, in a later conversation with William Lambarde (on August 4, 1601), complained that 'this tragedie' of 'Richard II,' which she had always viewed with suspicion, was played at the period with seditious intent 'forty times in open streets and houses.'[1] At the trial of Essex and his friends, Phillips gave evidence of the circumstances under which the tragedy was revived at the

---

[1] Nichols, *Progresses of Elizabeth*, iii. 552.

Globe Theatre. Essex was executed and South-ampton was imprisoned until the Queen's death. No proceedings were taken against the players,[1] but Shakespeare wisely abstained, for the time, from any public reference to the fate either of Essex or of his patron Southampton.

Such incidents served to accentuate Shakespeare's growing reputation. For several years his genius as dramatist and poet had been acknowledged by critics and playgoers alike, and his social and pro-fessional position had become considerable. Inside the theatre his influence was supreme. When, in 1598, the manager of the company rejected Ben Jonson's first comedy — his ' Every Man in his Humour ' — Shakespeare intervened, accord-ing to a credible tradition (reported by Rowe but denounced by Gifford), and procured a reversal of the decision in the interest of the unknown dramatist, who was his junior by nine years. He took a part when the piece was performed. Jonson was of a difficult and jealous temper, and subsequently he gave vent to an occasional expression of scorn at Shake-speare's expense; but, despite passing manifestations of his unconquerable surliness, there can be no doubt that Jonson cherished genuine esteem and affection for Shakespeare till death.[2] Within a very few years of Shakespeare's death Sir Nicholas L'Estrange, an

Marginal note: Shake-speare's popularity and influ-ence.

[1] Cf. Domestic MSS. (Elizabeth) in the Public Record Office, vol. cclxxviii. Nos. 78 and 85; and Calendar of Domestic State Papers, 1598-1601, pp. 575–8.

[2] Cf. Gilchrist, *Examination of the charges . . . of Jonson's Enmity towards Shakespeare*, 1808.

industrious collector of anecdotes, put into writing an anecdote for which he made Dr. Donne responsible, attesting the amicable relations that habitually subsisted between Shakespeare and Jonson. 'Shakespeare,' ran the story, 'was godfather to one of Ben Jonson's children, and after the christening, being in a deep study, Jonson came to cheer him up and asked him why he was so melancholy. "No, faith, Ben," says he, "not I, but I have been considering a great while what should be the fittest gift for me to bestow upon my godchild, and I have resolv'd at last." "I prythee, what?" says he. "I' faith, Ben, I'll e'en give him a dozen good Lattin spoons, and thou shalt translate them." ' [1]

The creator of Falstaff could have been no stranger to tavern life, and he doubtless took part with zest in the convivialities of men of letters.   Tradition
The Mer-   reports that Shakespeare joined, at the
maid meet-   Mermaid Tavern in Bread Street, those
ings.   meetings of Jonson and his associates which
Beaumont described in his poetical 'Letter' to Jonson:

> What things have we seen
> Done at the Mermaid? heard words that have been
> So nimble and so full of subtle flame,
> As if that every one from whence they came
> Had meant to put his whole wit in a jest,
> And had resolved to live a fool the rest
> Of his dull life.

---

[1] Latten is a mixed metal resembling brass. Pistol in *Merry Wives of Windsor* (act i. scene i. l. 165) likens Slender to a 'Latten Bilbo,' that is, a sword made of the mixed metal. Cf. *Anecdotes and Traditions*, edited from L'Estrange's MSS. by W. J. Thoms for the Camden Society, p. 2.

N

'Many were the wit-combats,' wrote Fuller of Shakespeare in his 'Worthies' (1662), 'betwixt him and Ben Jonson, which two I behold like a Spanish great galleon and an English man of war; Master Jonson (like the former) was built far higher in learning, solid but slow in his performances. Shakespear, with the Englishman of war, lesser in bulk, but lighter in sailing, could turn with all tides, tack about, and take advantage of all winds by the quickness of his wit and invention.'

Of the many testimonies paid to Shakespeare's literary reputation at this period of his career, the Meres's eu- most striking was that of Francis Meres. logy, 1598. Meres was a learned graduate of Cambridge University, a divine and schoolmaster, who brought out in 1598 a collection of apophthegms on morals, religion and literature which he entitled 'Palladis Tamia.' In the book he interpolated 'A comparative discourse of our English poets with the Greek, Latin, and Italian poets,' and there exhaustively surveyed contemporary literary effort in England. Shakespeare figured in Meres's pages as the greatest man of letters of the day. 'The Muses would speak Shakespeare's fine filed phrase,' Meres asserted, 'if they could speak English.' 'Among the English,' he declared, 'he was the most excellent in both kinds for the stage' (*i.e.* tragedy and comedy). The titles of six comedies ('Two Gentlemen of Verona,' 'Errors,' 'Love's Labour's Lost,' 'Love's Labour's Won,' 'Midsummer Night's Dream,' and 'Merchant of Venice') and of six tragedies ('Richard II,' 'Richard III,' 'Henry IV,' 'King

John,' 'Titus,' and 'Romeo and Juliet') were enumerated, and mention followed of his 'Venus and Adonis,' his 'Lucrece,' and his 'sugred[1] sonnets among his private friends.' These were cited as proof 'that the sweet witty soul of Ovid lives in mellifluous and honey-tongued Shakespeare.' In the same year a rival poet, Richard Barnfield, in 'Poems in Divers Humours,' predicted immortality for Shakespeare with no less confidence.

> And Shakespeare, thou whose honey-flowing vein
> (Pleasing the world) thy Praises doth obtain,
> Whose *Venus* and whose *Lucrece* (sweet and chaste)
> Thy name in Fame's immortal Book have placed.
> Live ever you, at least in fame live ever:
> Well may the Body die, but Fame dies never.

Shakespeare's name was thenceforth of value to unprincipled publishers, and they sought to palm off on their customers as his work the productions of inferior pens. Already, in 1595, Thomas Creede, the surreptitious printer of 'Henry V' and the 'Merry Wives,' had issued the crude 'Tragedie of Locrine,' as 'newly set foorth overseene and corrected by W. S.' It appropriated many passages from an older piece called 'Selimus,' which was possibly by Greene and certainly came

Value of his name to publishers.

---

[1] This, or some synonym, is the conventional epithet applied at the date to Shakespeare and his work. Weever credited such characters of Shakespeare as Tarquin, Romeo, and Richard III with 'sugred tongues' in his *Epigrams* of 1595. In the *Return from Parnassus* (1601?) Shakespeare is apostrophised as 'sweet Master Shakespeare.' Milton did homage to the tradition by writing of 'sweetest Shakespeare' in *L'Allegro*.

into being long before Shakespeare had written a line of blank verse. The same initials — 'W. S.'[1]— figured on the title-pages of 'The Puritaine, or the Widdow of Watling-streete' (printed by G. Eld in 1607), and of 'The True Chronicle Historie of Thomas, Lord Cromwell' (licensed August 11, 1602, and printed by Thomas Snodham in 1613). Shakespeare's full name appeared on the title-pages of 'The Life of Oldcastle' in 1600 (printed by T[homas] P[avier]), of 'The London Prodigall' in 1605 (printed by T. C. for Nathaniel Butter), and of 'The Yorkshire Tragedy' in 1608 (by R. B. for Thomas Pavier). None of these six plays have any internal claim to Shakespeare's authorship; nevertheless all were uncritically included in the third folio of his collected works (1664). Schlegel and a few other critics of repute have, on no grounds that merit acceptance, detected signs of Shakespeare's genuine work in one of the six, 'The Yorkshire Tragedy'; it is 'a coarse, crude, and vigorous impromptu,' which is clearly by a far less experienced hand.

[1] A hack-writer, Wentworth Smith, took a hand in producing thirteen plays, none of which are extant, for the theatrical manager, Philip Henslowe, between 1601 and 1603. *The Hector of Germanie*, an extant play 'made by W. Smith' and published 'with new additions' in 1615, was doubtless by Wentworth Smith, and is the only dramatic work by him that has survived. Neither internal nor external evidence confirms the theory that the six above-mentioned plays, which have been wrongly claimed for Shakespeare, were really by Wentworth Smith. The use of the initials 'W. S.' was not due to the publishers' belief that Wentworth Smith was the author, but to their endeavour to hoodwink their customers into a belief that the plays were by Shakespeare.

The fraudulent practice of crediting Shakespeare with valueless plays from the pens of comparatively dull-witted contemporaries was in vogue among enterprising traders in literature both early and late in the seventeenth century. The worthless old play on the subject of King John was attributed to Shakespeare in the reissues of 1611 and 1622. Humphrey Moseley, a reckless publisher of a later period, fraudulently entered on the 'Stationers' Register' on September 9, 1653, two pieces which he represented to be in whole or in part by Shakespeare, viz. 'The Merry Devill of Edmonton' and the 'History of Cardenio,' a share in which was assigned to Fletcher. 'The Merry Devill of Edmonton,' which was produced on the stage before the close of the sixteenth century, was entered on the 'Stationers' Register,' October 22, 1607, and was first published anonymously in 1608; it is a delightful comedy, abounding in both humour and romantic sentiment; at times it recalls scenes of the 'Merry Wives of Windsor,' but no sign of Shakespeare's workmanship is apparent. The 'History of Cardenio' is not extant.[1] Francis Kirkman, another active London publisher, who first printed William Rowley's 'Birth of Merlin' in 1662, described it on the title-page as 'written by William Shakespeare and William Rowley;' it was unwisely reprinted at Halle in a so-called 'Collection of pseudo-Shakespearean plays' in 1887.

But poems no less than plays, in which Shakespeare had no hand, were deceptively placed to his

[1] Cf. p. 258, *infra*.

credit as soon as his fame was established. In 1599 William Jaggard, a well-known pirate publisher, issued a poetic anthology which he entitled 'The

'The Passionate Pilgrim.' Passionate Pilgrim, by W. Shakespeare.' The volume opened with two sonnets by Shakespeare which were not previously in print, and there followed three poems drawn from the already published 'Love's Labour's Lost'; but the bulk of the volume was by Richard Barnfield and others.[1] A third edition of the 'Passionate Pilgrim' was printed in 1612 with unaltered title-page, although the incorrigible Jaggard had added two new poems which he silently filched from Thomas Heywood's 'Troia Britannica.' Heywood called attention to his own grievance in the dedicatory epistle before his 'Apology for Actors' (1612), and he added that Shakespeare resented the more substantial injury which the publisher had done him. 'I know,' wrote Heywood of Shakespeare, '[he was] much offended with M. Jaggard that (altogether unknown to him) presumed to make so bold with his name.' In the result

---

[1] There were twenty pieces in all. The five by Shakespeare are placed in the order i. ii. iii. v. xvi. Of the remainder, two — 'If music and sweet poetry agree' (No. viii.) and 'As it fell upon a day' (No. xx.) — were borrowed from Barnfield's *Poems in Divers Humours* (1598). 'Venus with Adonis sitting by her' (No. xi.) is from Bartholomew Griffin's *Fidessa* (1596); 'My flocks feed not' (No. xvii.) is adapted from Thomas Weelkes's *Madrigals* (1597); 'Live with me and be my love' is by Marlowe; and the appended stanza, entitled 'Love's Answer,' by Sir Walter Ralegh (No. xix.); 'Crabbed age and youth cannot live together' (No. xii.), is a popular song often quoted by the Elizabethan dramatists. Nothing has been ascertained of the origin and history of the remaining nine poems (iv. vi. vii. ix. x. xiii. xiv. xviii.).

the publisher seems to have removed Shakespeare's name from the title-page of a few copies. This is the only instance on record of a protest on Shakespeare's part against the many injuries which he suffered at the hands of contemporary publishers.

In 1601 Shakespeare's full name was appended to 'a poetical essaie on the Phœnix and the Turtle,' which was published by Edward Blount in an appendix to Robert Chester's 'Love's Martyr, or Rosalins complaint, allegorically shadowing the Truth of Love in the Constant Fate of the Phœnix and Turtle.' The drift of Chester's crabbed verse is not clear, nor can the praise of perspicuity be allowed to the appendix to which Shakespeare contributed, together with Marston, Chapman, Ben Jonson, and 'Ignoto.' The appendix is introduced by a new title-page running thus: 'Hereafter follow diverse poeticall Essaies on the former subject, viz: the Turtle and Phœnix. Done by the best and chiefest of our modern writers, with their names subscribed to their particular workes: never before extant.' Shakespeare's alleged contribution consists of thirteen four-lined stanzas in trochaics, each line being of seven syllables, with the rhymes disposed as in Tennyson's 'In Memoriam.' The concluding 'threnos' is in five three-lined stanzas, also in trochaics, each stanza having a single rhyme. The poet describes in enigmatic language the obsequies of the Phœnix and the Turtle-dove, who had been united in life by the ties of a purely spiritual love. The poem may be a mere play of fancy without recondite intention, or it

*The Phœnix and the Turtle.'

may be of allegorical import; but whether it bear
relation to pending ecclesiastical, political, or metaphysical controversy, or whether it interpret popular
grief for the death of some leaders of contemporary
society, is not easily determined.[1] Happily Shakespeare wrote nothing else of like character.

[1] A unique copy of Chester's *Love's Martyr* is in Mr. Christie-
Miller's library at Britwell. Of a reissue of the original edition in 1611
with a new title, *The Annals of Great Brittaine*, a copy (also unique) is
in the British Museum. A reprint of the original edition was prepared
for private circulation by Dr. Grosart in 1878, in his series of 'Occasional Issues.' It was also printed in the same year as one of the publications of the New Shakspere Society. Matthew Roydon in his elegy
on Sir Philip Sidney, appended to Spenser's *Colin Clouts Come Home
Again*, 1595, describes the part figuratively played in Sidney's obsequies
by the turtle-dove, swan, phœnix, and eagle, in verses that very closely
resemble Shakespeare's account of the funereal functions fulfilled by the
same four birds in his contribution to Chester's volume. This resemblance
suggests that Shakespeare's poem may be a fanciful adaptation of Roydon's elegiac conceits without ulterior significance. Shakespeare's concluding 'Threnos' is imitated in metre and phraseology by Fletcher in
his *Mad Lover* in the song 'The Lover's Legacy to his Cruel Mistress.'

XII

THE PRACTICAL AFFAIRS OF LIFE

SHAKESPEARE, in middle life, brought to practical affairs a singularly sane and sober temperament.

Shake-speare's practical tempera-ment. In 'Ratseis Ghost' (1605), an anecdotal biography of Gamaliel Ratsey, a notorious highwayman, who was hanged at Bedford on March 26, 1605, the highwayman is represented as compelling a troop of actors whom he met by chance on the road to perform in his presence. At the close of the performance Ratsey, according to the memoir, addressed himself to a leader of the company, and cynically urged him to practise the utmost frugality in London. 'When thou feelest thy purse well lined (the counsellor proceeded), buy thee some place or lordship in the country that, growing weary of playing, thy money may there bring thee to dignity and reputation.' Whether or no Ratsey's biographer consciously identified the highwayman's auditor with Shakespeare, it was the prosaic course of conduct marked out by Ratsey that Shakespeare literally followed. As soon as his position in his profession was assured, he devoted his energies to re-establishing the fallen fortunes of his family in his native place, and to acquiring for himself and his successors the status of gentlefolk.

His father's pecuniary embarrassments had steadily increased since his son's departure. Creditors harassed him unceasingly. In 1587 one Nicholas Lane pursued him for a debt for which he had become liable as surety for his brother Henry, who was still farming their father's lands at Snitterfield. Through 1588 and 1589 John Shakespeare retaliated with pertinacity on a debtor named John Tompson. But in 1591 a creditor, Adrian Quiney, obtained a writ of distraint against him, and although in 1592 he attested inventories taken on the death of two neighbours, Ralph Shaw and Henry Field, father of the London printer, he was on December 25 of the same year 'presented' as a recusant for absenting himself from Church. The commissioners reported that his absence was probably due to 'fear of process for debt.' He figures for the last time in the proceedings of the local court, in his customary *rôle* of defendant, on March 9, 1595. He was then joined with two fellow-traders — Philip Green, a chandler, and Henry Rogers, a butcher — as defendant in a suit brought by Adrian Quiney and Thomas Barker for the recovery of the sum of five pounds. Unlike his partners in the litigation, his name is not followed in the record by a mention of his calling, and when the suit reached a later stage his name was omitted altogether. These may be viewed as indications that in the course of the proceedings he finally retired from trade, which had been of late prolific in disasters for him. In January 1596–7 he conveyed a slip of land attached to his dwelling in Henley Street to one George Badger.

There is a likelihood that the poet's wife fared, in the poet's absence, no better than his father. The only contemporary mention made of her between her marriage in 1582 and her husband's death in 1616 is as the borrower at an unascertained date (evidently before 1595) of forty shillings from Thomas Whittington, who had formerly been her father's shepherd. The money was unpaid when Whittington died in 1601, and he directed his executor to recover the sum from the poet and distribute it among the poor of Stratford.[1]

His wife's debt.

It was probably in 1596 that Shakespeare returned, after nearly eleven years' absence, to his native town, and worked a revolution in the affairs of his family. The prosecutions of his father in the local court ceased. Thenceforth the poet's relations with Stratford were uninterrupted. He still resided in London for most of the year; but until the close of his professional career he paid the town at least one annual visit, and he was always formally described as 'of Stratford-on-Avon, gentleman.' He was no doubt there on August 11, 1596, when his only son, Hamnet, was buried in the parish church; the boy was eleven and a half years old.

At the same date the poet's father, despite his pecuniary embarrassments, took a step, by way of regaining his prestige, which must be assigned to the

---

[1] Halliwell-Phillipps, ii. 186.

poet's intervention.[1] He made application to the
College of Heralds for a coat-of-arms.[2] Then, as
now, the heralds when bestowing new coats-of-arms
commonly credited the applicant's family with an
imaginary antiquity, and little reliance need be placed
on the biographical or genealogical statements alleged
in grants of arms. The poet's father or the poet
himself when first applying to the College stated that
John Shakespeare, in 1568, while he was bailiff
of Stratford, and while he was by virtue of
that office a justice of the peace, had obtained from
Robert Cook, then Clarenceux herald, a 'pattern' or
sketch of an armorial coat. This allegation is not
noticed in the records of the College, and may be a
formal fiction designed by John Shakespeare and his
son to recommend their claim to the notice of the
heralds. The negotiations of 1568, if they were not
apocryphal, were certainly abortive; otherwise there
would have been no necessity for the further action
of 1596. In any case, on October 20, 1596, a draft,
which remains in the College of Arms, was pre-

The coat-of-arms.

---

[1] There is an admirable discussion of the question involved in the
poet's heraldry in *Herald and Genealogist*, i. 510. Facsimiles of all
the documents preserved in the College of Arms are given in *Miscellanea
Genealogica et Heraldica*, 2nd ser. 1886, i. 109. Halliwell-Phillipps
prints imperfectly one of the 1596 draft-grants, and that of 1599 (*Outlines*, ii. 56, 60), but does not distinguish between the character of the
negotiations of the two years.

[2] It is still customary at the College of Arms to inform an applicant
for a coat-of-arms who has a father alive that the application should be
made in the father's name, and the transaction conducted as if the
father were the principal. It was doubtless on advice of this kind that
Shakespeare was acting in the negotiations that are described below.

pared under the direction of William Dethick,
Garter King-of-Arms, granting John's request for
a coat-of-arms. Garter stated, with characteristic
vagueness, that he had been 'by credible report'
informed that the applicant's 'parentes and late antecessors were for theire valeant and faithfull service
advanced and rewarded by the most prudent prince
King Henry the Seventh of famous memorie, sythence
whiche tyme they have continewed at those partes [*i.e.*
Warwickshire] in good reputacion and credit;' and that
'the said John [had] maryed Mary, daughter and heiress
of Robert Arden, of Wilmcote, gent.' In consideration of these titles to honour, Garter declared that he
assigned to Shakespeare this shield, viz. : ' Gold, on a
bend sable, a spear of the first, and for his crest or cog-
nizance a falcon, his wings displayed argent, standing on
a wreath of his colours, supporting a spear gold steeled
as aforesaid.' In the margin of this draft-grant there
is a pen sketch of the arms and crest, and above them
is written the motto, ' Non Sans Droict.' [1] A second
copy of the draft, also dated in 1596, is extant at the
College. The only alterations are the substitution of
the word 'grandfather' for 'antecessors' in the account
of John Shakespeare's ancestry, and the substitution
of the word ' esquire ' for ' gent ' in the description of
his wife's father, Robert Arden. At the foot of this
draft, however, appeared some disconnected and
unverifiable memoranda which John Shakespeare or

[1] In a manuscript in the British Museum (*Harl. MS.* 6140, f. 45)
is a copy of the tricking of the arms of William ' Shakspere,' which is
described ' as a pattent per Will'm Dethike Garter, principale King of
Armes'; this is figured in French's *Shakespeareana Genealogica*, p. 524.

his son had supplied to the heralds, to the effect that
John had been bailiff of Stratford, had received a
'pattern' of a shield from Clarenceux Cook, was a
man of substance, and had married into a worshipful
family.[1]

Neither of these drafts was fully executed. It
may have been that the unduly favourable representations made to the College respecting John Shakespeare's social and pecuniary position excited suspicion even in the habitually credulous minds of the
heralds, or those officers may have deemed the
profession of the son, who was conducting the negotiation, a bar to completing the transaction. At any
rate, Shakespeare and his father allowed three years
to elapse before (as far as extant documents show)
they made a further endeavour to secure the coveted
distinction. In 1599 their efforts were crowned
with success. Changes in the interval among the
officials at the College may have facilitated the
proceedings. In 1597 the Earl of Essex had become
Earl Marshal and chief of the Heralds' College (the
office had been in commission in 1596); while the

---

[1] These memoranda, which were as follows, were first written without the words here enclosed in brackets; those words were afterwards
interlineated in the manuscript in a hand similar to that of the original
sentences:

'[This John shoeth] A patierne therof under Clarent Cookes hand
in paper. xx. years past. [The Q. officer and cheffe of the towne]

[A Justice of peace] And was a Baylife of Stratford uppo Avon
xv. or xvj. years past.

That he hathe lands and tenements of good wealth and substance
[500 li.]

That he mar[ried a daughter and heyre of Arden, a gent. of
worship.]'

great scholar and antiquary, William Camden, had joined the College, also in 1597, as Clarenceux King-of-Arms. The poet was favourably known to both Camden and the Earl of Essex, the close friend of the Earl of Southampton. His father's application now took a new form. No grant of arms was asked for. It was asserted without qualification that the coat, as set out in the draft-grants of 1596 had been *assigned* to John Shakespeare while he was bailiff, and the heralds were merely invited to give him a 'recognition' or 'exemplification' of it.[1] At the same time he asked permission for himself to impale, and his eldest son and other children to quarter, on ' his ancient coat-of-arms' that of the Ardens of Wilmcote, his wife's family. The College officers were characteristically complacent. A draft was prepared under the hands of Dethick, the Garter king, and of Camden, the Clarenceux King, granting the required 'exemplification' and authorising the required impalement and quartering. On one point only did Dethick and Camden betray conscientious scruples. Shakespeare and his father obviously desired the heralds to recognise the title of Mary Shakespeare (the poet's mother) to bear the arms of the great Warwickshire family of Arden, then seated at Park Hall. But the relationship, if it existed, was undetermined; the Warwickshire Ardens were gentry of influence in the county, and were certain to

[1] An 'exemplification' was invariably secured more easily than a new grant of arms. The heralds might, if they chose, tacitly accept, without examination, the applicant's statement that his family had borne arms long ago, and they thereby regarded themselves as relieved of the obligation of close inquiry into his present status.

protest against any hasty assumption of identity between their line and that of the humble farmer of Wilmcote.   After tricking the Warwickshire Arden coat in
the margin of the draft-grant for the purpose of indicating the manner of its impalement, the heralds on second
thoughts erased it.   They substituted in their sketch
the arms of an Arden family living at Alvanley in
the distant county of Cheshire.   With that stock there
was no pretence that Robert Arden of Wilmcote was
lineally connected; but the bearers of the Alvanley coat
were unlikely to learn of its suggested impalement
with the Shakespeare shield, and the heralds were less
liable to the risk of litigation.   But the Shakespeares
wisely relieved the College of all anxiety by omitting
to assume the Arden coat.   The Shakespeare arms
alone are displayed with full heraldic elaboration on the
monument above the poet's grave in Stratford Church;
they alone appear on the seal and on the tombstone of
his elder daughter, Mrs. Susanna Hall, impaled with the
arms of her husband;[1] and they alone were quartered
by Thomas Nash, the first husband of the poet's
granddaughter, Elizabeth Hall.[2]

Some objection was taken a few years later to the
grant even of the Shakespeare shield, but it was based
on vexatious grounds that could not be upheld.
Early in the seventeenth century Ralph Brooke, who
was York herald from 1593 till his death in 1625, and
was long engaged in a bitter quarrel with his fellow-

[1] On the gravestone of John Hall, Shakespeare's elder son-in-law,
the Shakespeare arms are similarly impaled with those of Hall.
[2] French *Shakespeareana Genealogica*, p. 413.

officers at the College, complained that the arms 'exemplified' to Shakespeare usurped the coat of Lord Mauley, on whose shield 'a bend sable' also figured. Dethick and Camden, who were responsible for any breach of heraldic etiquette in the matter, answered that the Shakespeare shield bore as much resemblance to the Mauley coat as to that of the Harley and the Ferrers families, which also bore 'a bend sable,' but that in point of fact it differed conspicuously from all three by the presence of a spear on the 'bend.' Dethick and Camden added, with customary want of precision, that the person to whom the grant was made had 'borne magistracy and was justice of peace at Strat-ford-on-Avon ; he maried the daughter and heire of Arderne, and was able to maintain that Estate.' [1]

Meanwhile, in 1597, the poet had taken openly in his own person a more effective step in the way of rehabilitating himself and his family in the eyes of Purchase of his fellow-townsmen. On May 4 he pur-New Place. chased the largest house in the town, known as New Place. It had been built by Sir Hugh Clopton more than a century before, and seems to have fallen into a ruinous condition. But Shakespeare paid for it, with two barns and two gardens, the then substantial sum of 60l. Owing to the sudden death of the vendor, William Under-

---

[1] The details of Brooke's accusation are not extant, and are only to be deduced from the answer of Garter and Clarenceux to Brooke's complaint, two copies of which are accessible : one is in the vol. W–Z at the Heralds' College, f. 276; and the other, slightly differing, is in Ashmole MS. 846, ix. f. 50. Both are printed in the *Herald and Genealogist*, i. 514.

o

hill, on July 7, 1597, the original transfer of the property was left at the time incomplete. Underhill's
son Fulk died a felon, and he was succeeded in the
family estates by his brother Hercules, who on
coming of age, May 1602, completed in a new deed
the transfer of New Place to Shakespeare.[1] On
February 4, 1597–8, Shakespeare was described as a
householder in Chapel Street ward, in which New
Place was situated, and as the owner of ten quarters
of corn. The inventory was made owing to the
presence of famine in the town, and only two inhabitants were credited with a larger holding. In the
same year (1598) he procured stone for the repair of
the house, and before 1602 had planted a fruit
orchard. He is traditionally said to have interested
himself in the garden, and to have planted with
his own hands a mulberry tree, which was long a
prominent feature of it. When this was cut down,
in 1758, numerous relics were made from it, and
were treated with an almost superstitious veneration.[2] Shakespeare does not appear to have permanently settled at New Place till 1611. In 1609

[1] *Notes and Queries*, 8th ser. v. 478.

[2] The tradition that Shakespeare planted the mulberry tree was not
put on record till it was cut down in 1758. In 1760 mention is made of
it in a letter of thanks in the corporation's archives from the Steward of
the Court of Record to the corporation of Stratford for presenting him
with a standish made from the wood. But, according to the testimony
of old inhabitants confided to Malone (cf. his *Life of Shakespeare*, 1790,
p. 118), the legend had been orally current in Stratford since Shakespeare's lifetime. The tree was perhaps planted in 1609, when a French-
man named Veron distributed a number of young mulberry trees through
the midland counties by order of James I, who desired to encourage
the culture of silk-worms (cf. Halliwell-Phillipps, i. 134, 411–16).

the house, or part of it, was occupied by the town clerk, Thomas Greene, 'alias Shakespeare,' who claimed to be the poet's cousin. His grandmother seems to have been a Shakespeare. He often acted as the poet's legal adviser.

It was doubtless under their son's guidance that Shakespeare's father and mother set on foot in November 1597 — six months after his acquisition of New Place — a lawsuit against John Lambert for the recovery of the mortgaged estate of Asbies in Wilmcote. The litigation dragged on for some years without result.

Three letters written during 1598 by leading men at Stratford are still extant among the Corporation's archives, and leave no doubt of the reputation for wealth and influence with which the purchase of New Place invested the poet in his fellow-townsmen's eyes. Abraham Sturley, who was once bailiff, writing early in 1598, apparently to a brother in London, says: 'This is one special remembrance from our father's motion. It seemeth by him that our countryman, Mr. Shakspere, is willing to disburse some money upon some odd yardland or other at Shottery, or near about us : he thinketh it a very fit pattern to move him to deal in the matter of our tithes. By the instructions you can give him thereof, and by the friends he can make therefor, we think it a fair mark for him to shoot at, and would do us much good.' Richard Quiney, another townsman, father of Thomas (afterwards one of Shakespeare's two sons-in-law),

Appeals for aid from his fellow-townsmen.

was, in the autumn of the same year, harassed by
debt, and on October 25 appealed to Shakespeare for
a loan of money. ' Loving countryman,' the application ran, ' I am bold of you as of a friend craving
your help with xxx*li.*' Quiney was staying at the
Bell Inn in Carter Lane, London, and his main business in the metropolis was to procure exemption for
the town of Stratford from the payment of a subsidy.
Abraham Sturley, writing to Quiney from Stratford
ten days later (on November 4, 1598), pointed out to
him that since the town was wholly unable, in consequence of the dearth of corn, to pay the tax, he hoped
' that our countryman, Mr. Wm. Shak., would procure
us money, which I will like of, as I shall hear when,
and where, and how.'

The financial prosperity to which this correspondence and the transactions immediately pre-
Financial ceding it point has been treated as one of
position the chief mysteries of Shakespeare's career,
before 1599. but the difficulties are gratuitous. There is
practically nothing in Shakespeare's financial position
that a study of the contemporary conditions of
theatrical life does not fully explain. It was not
until 1599, when the Globe Theatre was built, that
he acquired any share in the profits of a playhouse.
But his revenues as a successful dramatist and actor
were by no means contemptible at an earlier date.
His gains in the capacity of dramatist formed the
smaller source of income. The highest price known
to have been paid before 1599 to an author for a
play by the manager of an acting company was 11*l.*;

6*l.* was the lowest rate.[1]   A small additional gratuity —
rarely apparently exceeding ten shillings — was bestowed on a dramatist whose piece on its first production was especially well received ; and the author was
by custom allotted, by way of ' benefit,' a certain proportion of the receipts of the theatre on the production
of a play for the second time.[2]   Other sums, amounting at times to as much as 4*l.*, were bestowed on the
author for revising and altering an old play for a revival.
The nineteen plays which may be set to Shakespeare's
credit between 1591 and 1599, combined with such
revising work as fell to his lot during those eight
years, cannot consequently have brought him less
than 200*l.*, or some 20*l.* a year.   Eight or nine of
these plays were published during the period, but the

---

[1] I do not think we shall over-estimate the present value of Shakespeare's income if we multiply each of its items by eight, but it is difficult to state authoritatively the ratio between the value of money in
Shakespeare's time and in our own.   The money value of corn then
and now is nearly identical; but other necessaries of life — meat, milk,
eggs, wool, building materials, and the like — were by comparison ludi-
crously cheap in Shakespeare's day.   If we strike the average between
the low price of these commodities and the comparatively high price of
corn, the average price of necessaries will be found to be in Shakespeare's
day about an eighth of what it is now.   The cost of luxuries is also now
about eight times the price that it was in the sixteenth or seventeenth
century.   Sixpence was the usual price of a new quarto or octavo book
such as would now be sold at prices ranging between three shillings
and sixpence and six shillings.   Half a crown was charged for the best-
placed seats in the best theatres.   The purchasing power of one Elizabethan pound might be generally defined in regard to both necessaries and
luxuries as equivalent to that of eight pounds of the present currency.

[2] Cf. Henslowe's *Diary*, ed. Collier, pp. xxviii. seq.   After the
Restoration the receipts at the third performance were given for the
author's ' benefit.'

publishers operated independently of the author,
taking all the risks and, at the same time, all the receipts. The publication of Shakespeare's plays in
no way affected his monetary resources, although his
friendly relations with the printer Field doubtless
secured him, despite the absence of any copyright
law, some part of the profits in the large and continuous sale of his poems.

But it was as an actor that at an early date he
acquired a genuinely substantial and secure income.
There is abundance of contemporary evidence to show
that the stage was for an efficient actor an assured
avenue to comparative wealth. In 1590 Robert Greene
describes in his tract entitled 'Never too Late' a meeting with a player whom he took by his 'outward habit'
to be 'a gentleman of great living' and a 'substantial man.' The player informed Greene that he had
at the beginning of his career travelled on foot,
bearing his theatrical properties on his back, but he
prospered so rapidly that at the time of speaking 'his very share in playing apparel would not be
sold for 200*l.*' Among his neighbours 'where he
dwelt' he was reputed able 'at his proper cost to build
a windmill.' In the university play, 'The Return from
Parnassus' (1600?), a poor student enviously complains of the wealth and position which a successful
actor derived from his calling:

> England affords those glorious vagabonds,
> That carried erst their fardles on their backs,
> Coursers to ride on through the gazing streets,
> Sweeping it in their glaring satin suits,
> And pages to attend their masterships;

> With mouthing words that better wits had framed,
> They purchase lands and now esquires are made.[1]

The travelling actors, from whom the highwayman Gamaliel Ratsey extorted a free performance in
1604, were represented as men with the certainty
of a rich competency in prospect.[2]   An efficient
actor received in 1635 as large a regular salary
as 180*l*.   The lowest known valuation set an actor's
wages at 3*s*. a day, or about 45*l*. a year.   Shakespeare's emoluments as an actor before 1599 are
not likely to have fallen below 100*l*.; while the remuneration due to performances at Court or in noblemen's houses, if the accounts of 1594 be accepted
as the basis of reckoning, added some 15*l*.

Thus over 130*l*. (equal to 1,040*l*. of to-day) would
be Shakespeare's average annual revenue before 1599.
Such a sum would be regarded as a very large income
in a country town.   According to the author of
' Ratseis Ghost,' the actor, who may well have been
meant for Shakespeare, practised in London a strict
frugality, and there seems no reason why Shakespeare
should not have been able in 1597 to draw from his

---

[1] *Return from Parnassus*, act v. scene i. ll. 10–16.

[2] Cf. H[enry] P[arrot]'s *Laquei Ridiculosi or Springes for Wood-
cocks*, 1613.   Epigram No. 131, headed ' Theatrum Licencia ':

> Cotta's become a player most men know,
>   And will no long take such toyling paines
> For here's the spring (saith he) whence pleasures flow
>   And brings them damnable excessive gaines:
> That now are cedars growne from shrubs and sprigs,
>   Since Greene's *Tu Quoque* and those Garlicke Jigs.

Greene's *Tu Quoque* was a drolling piece very popular with the rougher
London playgoers, and ' Garlicke Jigs ' alluded derisively to step-dances
which won much esteem from patrons of the smaller playhouses.

savings 60*l.* wherewith to buy New Place. His
resources might well justify his fellow-townsmen's
opinion of his wealth in 1598, and suffice between 1597 and 1599 to meet his expenses, in re-
building the house, stocking the barns with grain, and
conducting various legal proceedings. But, according
to tradition, he had in the Earl of Southampton a
wealthy and generous friend who on one occasion
gave him a large gift of money to enable ' him to go
through with ' a purchase to which he had a mind.
A munificent gift, added to professional gains, leaves
nothing unaccounted for in Shakespeare's financial
position before 1599.

After 1599 his sources of income from the theatre
greatly increased. In 1635 the heirs of the actor
Richard Burbage were engaged in litigation
respecting their proprietary rights in the two
playhouses, the Globe and the Blackfriars
theatres. The documents relating to this litigation
supply authentic, although not very detailed, information of Shakespeare's interest in theatrical property.[1]
Richard Burbage, with his brother Cuthbert, erected
at their sole cost the Globe Theatre in the winter of
1598–9, and the Blackfriars Theatre, which their father
was building at the time of his death in 1597, was also
their property. After completing the Globe they
leased out, for twenty-one years, shares in the receipts
of the theatre to ' those deserving men Shakespeare,

Financial position after 1599.

---

[1] The documents which are now in the Public Record Office among
the papers relating to the Lord Chamberlain's Office, were printed in
full by Halliwell-Phillipps, i. 312–19.

Hemings, Condell, Philips, and others.' All the share-holders named were, like Burbage, active members of Shakespeare's company of players. The shares, which numbered sixteen in all, carried with them the obligation of providing for the expenses of the playhouse, and were doubtless in the first instance freely bestowed. Hamlet claims, in the play scene (III. ii. 293), that the success of his improvised tragedy deserved to 'get him a fellowship in a cry of players' — a proof that a successful dramatist might reasonably expect such a reward for a conspicuous effort. In 'Hamlet,' moreover, both a share and a half-share of 'a fellow-ship in a cry of players' are described as assets of enviable value (III. ii. 294–6). How many shares originally fell to Shakespeare there is no means of determining. Records of later subdivisions suggest that they did not exceed two. The Globe was an exceptionally large and popular playhouse. It would accommodate some two thousand spectators, whose places cost them sums varying between twopence and half a crown. The receipts were therefore considerable, hardly less than 25*l.* daily, or some 8,000*l.* a year. According to the documents of 1635, an actor-sharer at the Globe received above 200*l.* a year on each share, besides his actor's salary of 180*l.* Thus Shakespeare drew from the Globe Theatre, at the lowest estimate, more than 500*l.* a year in all.

His interest in the Blackfriars Theatre was comparatively unimportant, and is less easy to estimate. The often quoted documents on which Collier depended to prove him a substantial shareholder in that playhouse have long been proved to be forgeries. The pleas in the lawsuit of 1635 show that the Burbages, the owners, leased the Blackfriars Theatre after its establishment in 1597 for a long term of years to the master of the Children of the Chapel, but bought out the lessee at the end of 1609, and then 'placed' in it 'men-players which were Hemings, Condell, Shakespeare, &c.' To these and other actors they allotted shares in the receipts, the shares numbering eight in all. The profits were far smaller than at the Globe, and if Shakespeare held one share (certainty on the point is impossible), it added not more than 100*l.* a year to his income, and that not until 1610.

His remuneration as dramatist between 1599 and 1611 was also by no means contemptible. Prices paid to dramatists for plays rose rapidly in the early years of the seventeenth century,[1] while the value of the author's 'benefits' grew with the growing vogue of the theatre. The exceptional popularity of Shakespeare's plays after 1599 gave him the full advantage of higher rates of pecuniary reward in all directions, and the seventeen plays which were produced by him between that year and the close of his professional career in 1611 probably brought him an average return of 20*l.* each or 340*l.* in all — nearly 30*l.* a year. At the same time the increase in the number of Court performances under James I, and the additional favour bestowed on Shakespeare's

Later income.

---

[1] In 1613 Robert Daborne, a playwright of insignificant reputation, charged for a drama as much as 25*l. Alleyn Papers*, ed. Collier, p. 65.

company, may well have given that source of income the enhanced value of 20*l.* a year.[1]

Thus Shakespeare in the later period of his life was earning above 600*l.* a year in money of the period. With so large a professional income he could easily, with good management, have completed those purchases of houses and land at Stratford on which he laid out, between 1599 and 1613, a total sum of 970*l.*, or an annual average of 70*l.* These properties, it must be remembered, represented investments, and he drew rent from most of them. He traded, too, in agricultural produce. There is nothing inherently improbable in the statement of John Ward, the seventeenth-century vicar of Stratford, that in his last years ' he spent at the rate of a thousand a year, as I have heard,' although we may reasonably make allowance for exaggeration in the round figures.

Shakespeare realised his theatrical shares several years before his death in 1616, when he left, according to his will, 350*l.* in money in addition to an extensive real estate and numerous personal belong-

Incomes of fellow-actors.

ings. There was nothing exceptional in this comparative affluence. His friends and fellow-actors, Heming and Condell, amassed equally large, if not larger, fortunes. Burbage died in 1619 worth 300*l.* in land, besides personal property; while a contemporary actor and theatrical proprietor, Edward

[1] Ten pounds was the ordinary fee paid to actors for a performance at the Court of James I. Shakespeare's company appeared annually twenty times and more at Whitehall during the early years of James I's reign, and Shakespeare, as being both author and actor, doubtless received a larger share of the receipts than his colleagues.

Alleyn, purchased the manor of Dulwich for 10,000*l.* (in money of his own day), and devoted it, with much other property, to public uses, at the same time as he made ample provision for his family out of the residue of his estate. Gifts from patrons may have continued occasionally to augment Shakespeare's resources, but his wealth can be satisfactorily assigned to better attested agencies. There is no ground for treating it as of mysterious origin.[1]

Between 1599 and 1611, while London remained Shakespeare's chief home, he built up at Stratford a large landed estate which his purchase of New Place had inaugurated. In 1601 his father died, being buried on September 8. He apparently left no will, and the poet, as the eldest son, inherited the houses in Henley Street, the only portion of the property of the elder Shakespeare or of his wife which had not been alienated to creditors. Shakespeare permitted his mother to reside in one of the Henley Street houses till her death (she was buried September 9, 1608), and he

Formation of the estate at Stratford, 1601-10. derived a modest rent from the other. On May 1, 1602, he purchased for 320*l.* of the rich landowners William and John Combe of Stratford 107 acres of arable land near the town. The conveyance was delivered, in the poet's absence, to his brother Gilbert, 'to the use of the within named William Shakespere.'[2] A third purchase quickly followed. On September 28, 1602, at a Court Baron of the manor of Rowington, one

---

[1] Cf. Halliwell-Phillipps, i. 312-19; Fleay, *Stage*, pp. 324-8.

[2] Halliwell-Phillipps, ii. 17-19.

Walter Getley transferred to the poet a cottage and garden which were situated at Chapel Lane, opposite the lower grounds of New Place. They were held practically in fee-simple at the annual rental of 2s. 6d. It appears from the roll that Shakespeare did not attend the manorial court held on the day fixed for the transfer of the property at Rowington, and it was consequently stipulated then that the estate should remain in the hands of the lady of the manor until he completed the purchase in person. At a later period he was admitted to the copyhold, and he settled the remainder on his two daughters in fee. In April 1610 he purchased from the Combes 20 acres of pasture land, to add to the 107 of arable land that he had acquired of the same owners in 1602.

As early as 1598 Abraham Sturley had suggested that Shakespeare should purchase the tithes of Stratford. Seven years later, on July 24, 1605, he bought for 440l. of Ralph Huband an unexpired term of thirty-one years of a ninety-two years' lease of a moiety of the tithes of Stratford, Old Stratford, Bishopton, and Welcombe. The moiety was subject to a rent of 17l. to the Corporation, who were the reversionary owners on the lease's expiration, and of 5l. to John Barker, the heir of a former proprietor. The investment brought Shakespeare, under the most favourable circumstances, no more than an annuity of 38l.; and the refusal of persons who claimed an interest in the other moiety to acknowledge the full extent of their liability to the Corporation led that body to demand

The Stratford tithes.

from the poet payments justly due from others. After 1609 he joined with two interested persons, Richard Lane of Awston and Thomas Greene, the town clerk of Stratford, in a suit in Chancery to determine the exact responsibilities of all the tithe-owners, and in 1612 they presented a bill of complaint to Lord-chancellor Ellesmere, with what result is unknown. His acquisition of a part-ownership in the tithes was fruitful in legal embarrassments.

Shakespeare inherited his father's love of litigation, and stood rigorously by his rights in all his business relations. In March 1600 he recovered in London a debt of 7*l.* from one John Clayton. In July 1604, in the local court at Stratford, he sued one Philip Rogers, to whom he had supplied since the preceding March malt to the value of 1*l.* 19*s.* 10*d.*, and had on June 25 lent 2*s.* in cash. Rogers paid back 6*s.*, and Shakespeare sought the balance of the account, 1*l.* 15*s.* 10*d.* During 1608 and 1609 he was at law with another fellow-townsman, John Addenbroke. On February 15, 1609, Shakespeare, who was apparently represented by his solicitor and kinsman, Thomas Greene,[1] obtained judgment from a jury against Addenbroke for the payment of 6*l.*, and 1*l.* 5*s.* costs, but Addenbroke left the town, and the triumph proved barren. Shakespeare avenged himself by proceeding against one Thomas Horneby, who had acted as the absconding debtor's bail.[2]

Recovery of small debts.

---

[1] See p. 195.   [2] Halliwell-Phillipps, ii. 77–80.

XIII

MATURITY OF GENIUS

WITH an inconsistency that is more apparent than real, the astute business transactions of these years

Literary (1597–1611) synchronise with the produc-
work in tion of Shakespeare's noblest literary work
1599. — of his most sustained and serious efforts in comedy, tragedy, and romance. In 1599, after abandoning English history with 'Henry V,' he addressed himself to the composition of his three most perfect essays in comedy — 'Much Ado about Nothing,' 'As You Like It,' and 'Twelfth Night.' Their good-humoured tone seems to reveal their author in his happiest frame of mind; in each the gaiety and tenderness of youthful womanhood are exhibited in fascinating union; while Shakespeare's lyric gift bred no sweeter melodies than the songs with which the three plays are interspersed. At the same time each comedy enshrines such penetrating reflections on mysterious problems of life as mark the stage of maturity in the growth of the author's intellect. The first two of the three plays were entered on the 'Stationers' Registers' before August 4, 1600, on which day a prohibition was set on their publication, as well as on the publication of 'Henry V' and of Ben

Jonson's ' Every Man in his Humour.'   This was one
of the many efforts of the acting company to stop the
publication of plays in the belief that the practice was
injurious to their rights.   The effort was only partially
successful.   ' Much Ado,' like ' Henry V,' was published before the close of the year.   Neither 'As You
Like It' nor 'Twelfth Night,' however, was printed
till it appeared in the folio.

In 'Much Ado,' which appears to have been
written in 1599, the brilliant and spirited comedy of
Benedick and Beatrice, and of the blundering watchmen Dogberry and Verges, is wholly original; but the
' Much   sombre story of Hero and Claudio, about which
Ado.'   the comic incident revolves, is drawn from
an Italian source, either from Bandello (novel. xxii.)
through Belleforest's 'Histoires Tragiques,' or from
Ariosto's 'Orlando Furioso' through Sir John Harington's translation (canto v.).   Ariosto's version, in which
the injured heroine is called Ginevra, and her lover
Ariodante, had been dramatised before.   According
to the accounts of the Court revels, ' A Historie of
Ariodante and Ginevra was showed before her
Majestie on Shrovetuesdaie at night' in 1583.[1]
Throughout Shakespeare's play the ludicrous and
serious aspects of humanity are blended with a con-
vincing naturalness.   The popular comic actor
William Kemp filled the *rôle* of Dogberry, and
Cowley appeared as Verges.   In both the Quarto of
1600 and the Folio of 1623 these actors' names are

---

[1] *Accounts of the Revels*, ed. Peter Cunningham (Shakespeare
Society), p. 177; *Variorum Shakespeare*, 1821, iii. 406.

prefixed by a copyist's error to some of the speeches
allotted to the two characters (act iv. scene ii.).

'As You Like It,' which quickly followed, is a
dramatic adaptation of Lodge's romance, 'Rosa-
'As You   lynde, Euphues Golden Legacie' (1590), but
Like It.'   Shakespeare added three new characters
of first-rate interest — Jaques, the meditative cynic;
Touchstone, the most carefully elaborated of all
Shakespeare's fools; and the hoyden Audrey. Hints
for the scene of Orlando's encounter with Charles the
Wrestler, and for Touchstone's description of the
diverse shapes of a lie, were clearly drawn from a
book called 'Saviolo's Practise,' a manual of the art
of self-defence, which appeared in 1595 from the pen
of Vincentio Saviolo, an Italian fencing-master in
the service of the Earl of Essex. None of Shakespeare's comedies breathes a more placid temper or
approaches more nearly to a pastoral drama. Yet
there is no lack of intellectual or poetic energy in the
enunciation of the contemplative philosophy which is
cultivated in the Forest of Arden. In Rosalind, Celia,
Phœbe, and Audrey four types of youthful womanhood are contrasted with the liveliest humour.

The date of 'Twelfth Night' is probably 1600,
'Twelfth   and its name, which has no reference to the
Night.'   story, doubtless commemorates the fact that
it was designed for a Twelfth Night celebration.
'The new map with the augmentation of the Indies,'
spoken of by Maria (act iii. sc. ii. 86), was a respect-
ful reference to the great map of the world or 'hydro-
graphical description' which was first issued with

P

Hakluyt's 'Voyages' in 1599 or 1600, and first disclosed the full extent of recent explorations of the
'Indies' in the New World and the Old.[1]　Like
the 'Comedy of Errors,' 'Twelfth Night' achieved
the distinction early in its career of a presentation at
an Inn of Court.　It was produced at Middle Temple
Hall on February 2, 1601–2, and Manningham, a barrister who was present, described the performance.[2]
Manningham wrote that the piece was 'much like the
"Comedy of Errors" or "Menechmi" in Plautus, but
most like and neere to that in Italian called "Inganni."'
Two sixteenth-century Italian plays entitled 'Gl' Inganni' ('The Cheats'), and a third called 'Gl' Ingan-
nati,' bear resemblance to 'Twelfth Night.'　It is
just possible that Shakespeare had recourse to the
last, which was based on Bandello's novel of Nicuola,[3]
and was first published at Siena in 1538.　But in all
probability he drew the story solely from the 'Historie of Apolonius and Silla,' which was related in
'Riche his Farewell to Militarie Profession' (1581).
The author of that volume, Barnabe Riche, translated
the tale either direct from Bandello's Italian novel
or from the French rendering of Bandello's work in
Belleforest's 'Histoires Tragiques.'　Romantic pathos,

---

[1] It was reproduced by the Hakluyt Society to accompany *The
Voyages and Workes of John Davis the Navigator*, ed. Captain A. H.
Markham, 1880.　Cf. Mr. Coote's note on the *New Map*, lxxxv.–
xcv.　A paper on the subject by Mr. Coote also appears in *New Shakspere Society's Tansactions*, 1877–9, pt. i. pp. 88–100.

[2] *Diary*, Camden Soc. p. 18; the Elizabethan Stage Society
repeated the play on the same stage on February 10, 11, and 12,
1897.　　　　　　　　　[3] Bandello's *Novelle*, ii. 36.

as in 'Much Ado,' is the dominant note of the main plot of 'Twelfth Night,' but Shakespeare neutralises the tone of sadness by his mirthful portrayal of Malvolio, Sir Toby Belch, Sir Andrew Aguecheek, Fabian, the clown Feste, and Maria, all of whom are his own creations. The ludicrous gravity of Malvolio proved exceptionally popular on the stage.

In 1601 Shakespeare made a new departure by drawing a plot from North's noble translation of 'Plutarch's Lives.'[1] Plutarch is the king of biographers, and the deference which Shakespeare paid his work by adhering to the phraseology wherever it was practicable illustrates his literary discrimination. On Plutarch's lives of Julius Cæsar, Brutus, and Antony, Shakespeare based his historical tragedy of 'Julius Cæsar.' Weever, in 1601, in his 'Mirror of Martyrs,' plainly refers to the masterly speech in the Forum at Cæsar's funeral which Shakespeare put into Antony's mouth. There is no suggestion of the speech in Plutarch; hence the composition of 'Julius Cæsar' may be held to have preceded the issue of Weever's book in 1601. The general topic was already familiar on the stage. Polonius told Hamlet how, when he was at the university, he 'did enact Julius Cæsar; he was kill'd in the Capitol: Brutus kill'd him.'[2] A play of the same title was known as early as 1589, and was acted in 1594 by Shakespeare's company. Shakespeare's piece is a penetrating study of political life, and, although the

'Julius Cæsar,' 1601.

---

[1] First published in 1579; 2nd edit. 1595.
[2] *Hamlet*, act iii. sc. ii. ll. 109–10.

murder and funeral of Cæsar form the central episode and not the climax, the tragedy is thoroughly well planned and balanced. Cæsar is ironically depicted in his dotage. The characters of Brutus, Antony, and Cassius, the real heroes of the action, are exhibited with faultless art. The fifth act, which presents the battle of Philippi in progress, proves ineffective on the stage, but the reader never relaxes his interest in the fortunes of the vanquished Brutus, whose death is the catastrophe.

While ' Julius Cæsar ' was winning its first laurels on the stage, the fortunes of the London theatres were menaced by two manifestations of unreasoning prejudice on the part of the public. The earlier manifestation, although speciously the more serious, was in effect innocuous. The puritans of the city of London had long agitated for the suppression of all theatrical performances, and it seemed as if the agitators triumphed when they induced the Privy Council on June 22, 1600, to issue to the officers of the Corporation of London and to the justices of the peace of Middlesex and Surrey an order forbidding the maintenance of more than two playhouses — one in Middlesex (Alleyn's newly erected playhouse, the 'Fortune' in Cripplegate), and the other in Surrey (the 'Globe' on the Bankside). The contemplated restriction would have deprived very many actors of employment, and driven others to seek a precarious livelihood in the provinces. Happily, disaster was averted by the failure of the municipal authorities and the magistrates of Surrey and Middlesex to make the order operative. All the London theatres that were already in existence went on their way unchecked.[1]

More calamitous was a temporary reverse of fortune which Shakespeare's company, in common with the other companies of adult actors, suffered soon afterwards at the hands, not of fanatical enemies of the drama, but of playgoers who were its avowed supporters. The company of boy-actors, chiefly recruited from the choristers of the Chapel Royal, and known as 'the Children of the Chapel,' had since 1597 been installed at the new theatre in Blackfriars, and after 1600 the fortunes of the veterans, who occupied rival stages, were put in jeopardy by the extravagant outburst of public favour that the boys' performances evoked. In 'Hamlet,' the play which followed 'Julius Cæsar,' Shakespeare pointed out the perils of the situation.[2] The adult

The strife between adult and boy actors.

[1] On December 31, 1601, the Lords of the Council sent letters to the Lord Mayor of London and to the Magistrates of Surrey and Middlesex expressing their surprise that no steps had yet been taken to limit the number of playhouses in accordance with 'our order set down and prescribed about a year and a half since.' But nothing followed, and no more was heard officially of the Council's order until 1619, when the Corporation of London remarked on its practical abrogation at the same time as they directed the suppression (which was not carried out) of the Blackfriars Theatre. All the documents on this subject are printed from the Privy Council Register by Halliwell-Phillipps, i. 307–9.

[2] The passage, act ii. sc. ii. 348–94, which deals in ample detail with the subject, only appears in the folio version of 1623. In the first quarto a very curt reference is made to the misfortunes of the 'tragedians of the city':

> Y' faith, my lord, noveltie carries it away,
> For the principal publike audience that
> Came to them are turned to private playes
> And to the humours of children.

'Private playes' were plays acted by amateurs, with whom the 'Children' might well be classed.

actors, Shakespeare asserted, were prevented from
performing in London through no falling off in their
efficiency, but by the 'late innovation' of the children's
vogue.[1]   They were compelled to go on tour in the
provinces, at the expense of their revenues and reputation, because 'an aery [*i.e.* nest] of children, little
eyases [*i.e.* young hawks]' dominated the theatrical
world, and monopolised public applause.   'These
are now the fashion,' the dramatist lamented,[2] and he
made the topic the text of a reflection on the fickle-
ness of public taste :

> HAMLET.   Do the boys carry it away ?
> ROSENCRANTZ.   Ay that they do, my lord, Hercules and his load too.
> HAMLET.   It is not very strange; for my uncle is King of Denmark,
> and those that would make mows at him while my father lived, give
> twenty, forty, fifty, a hundred ducats apiece for his picture in little.

Jealousies in the ranks of the dramatists accent-
uated the actors' difficulties.   Ben Jonson was, at the
end of the sixteenth century, engaged in a fierce
personal quarrel with two of his fellow-dramatists,
Marston and Dekker.   The adult actors generally
avowed sympathy with Jonson's foes.   Jonson, by
way of revenge, sought an offensive alliance with 'the
Children of the Chapel.'   Under careful tuition the
boys proved capable of performing much the same
pieces as the men.   To 'the children' Jonson offered

[1] All recent commentators follow Steevens in interpreting the 'late
innovation' as the Order of the Privy Council of June 1600, restricting
the number of the London playhouses to two; but that order, which
was never put in force, in no way affected the actors' fortunes.   The
First Quarto's reference to the perils attaching to the 'noveltie' of the
boys' performances indicates the true meaning.

[2] *Hamlet*, act ii. sc. ii. 349–64.

in 1600 his comical satire of 'Cynthia's Revels,' in which he held up to ridicule Dekker, Marston, and their actor-friends. The play, when acted by 'the children' at the Blackfriars Theatre, was warmly welcomed by the audience. Next year Jonson repeated his manœuvre with greater effect. He learnt that Marston and Dekker were conspiring with the actors of Shakespeare's company to attack him in a piece called 'Satiro-Mastix, or the Untrussing of the Humorous Poet.' He anticipated their design by producing, again with 'the Children of the Chapel,' his 'Poetaster,' which was throughout a venomous invective against his enemies — dramatists and actors alike. Shakespeare's company retorted by producing Dekker and Marston's 'Satiro-Mastix' at the Globe Theatre next year. But Jonson's action had given new life to the vogue of the children. Playgoers took sides in the struggle, and their attention was for a season riveted, to the exclusion of topics more germane to their province, on the actors' and dramatists' boisterous war of personalities.[1]

---

[1] At the moment offensive personalities seemed to have infected all the London theatres. On May 10, 1601, the Privy Council called the attention of the Middlesex magistrates to the abuse covertly levelled by the actors of the 'Curtain' at gentlemen 'of good desert and quality,' and directed the magistrates to examine all plays before they were produced (*Privy Council Register*). Jonson subsequently issued an 'apologetical dialogue' (appended to printed copies of the *Poetaster*), in which he somewhat truculently qualified his hostility to the players:

> Now for the players 'tis true I tax'd them
> And yet but some, and those so sparingly
> As all the rest might have sat still unquestioned,
> Had they but had the wit or conscience

In his detailed references to the conflict in
'Hamlet' Shakespeare protested against the
abusive comments on the men-actors of 'the
common stages' or public theatres which
were put into the children's mouths. Rosen-
crantz declared that the children 'so berattle [*i.e.* assail]
the common stages — so they call them — that many
wearing rapiers are afraid of goose-quills, and dare
scarce come thither [*i.e.* to the public theatres].'
Hamlet in pursuit of the theme pointed out that the
writers who encouraged the vogue of the 'child-
actors' did them a poor service, because when the
boys should reach men's estate they would run the
risk, if they continued on the stage, of the same insults
and neglect which now threatened their seniors.

Shake-
speare's
references
to the
struggle.

HAMLET. What are they children? Who maintains 'em? how are
they escoted [*i.e.* paid]? Will they pursue the quality [*i.e.* the actor's
profession] no longer than they can sing? Will they not say afterwards,
if they should grow themselves to common players — as it is most like,
if their means are no better — their writers do them wrong to make
them exclaim against their own succession?

ROSENCRANTZ. Faith, there has been much to do on both sides,
and the nation holds it no sin to tarre [*i.e.* incite] them to controversy;
there was for a while no money bid for argument, unless the poet and
the player went to cuffs in the question.

HAMLET. Is it possible?

GUILDENSTERN. O, there has been much throwing about of brains!

To think well of themselves. But impotent they
Thought each man's vice belonged to their whole tribe;
And much good do it them. What they have done against me
I am not moved with, if it gave them meat
Or got them clothes, 'tis well; that was their end,
Only amongst them I am sorry for
Some better natures by the rest so drawn
To run in that vile line.

Shakespeare clearly favoured the adult actors in their rivalry with the boys, but he wrote more like a disinterested spectator than an active partisan when he made specific reference to the strife between the poet Ben Jonson and the players. In the prologue to 'Troilus and Cressida' which he penned in 1603, he warned his hearers with obvious allusion to Ben Jonson's battles that he hesitated to identify himself with either actor or poet.[1] Passages in Ben Jonson's 'Poetaster,' moreover, pointedly suggest that Shakespeare cultivated so assiduously an attitude of neutrality that Jonson acknowledged him to be qualified for the *rôle* of peacemaker. The gentleness of disposition with which Shakespeare was invariably credited by his friends would have well fitted him for such an office.

Jonson figures personally in the 'Poetaster' under the name of Horace. Episodically Horace and his friends, Tibullus and Gallus, eulogise the work and genius of another character, Virgil, in terms so closely resembling those which Jonson is known to have applied to Shakespeare that they may be regarded as intended to apply to him (act v. sc. i.). Jonson points out that Virgil, by his penetrating intuition, achieved the great effects which others laboriously sought to reach through rules of art.

Jonson's 'Poetaster.'

His learning labours not the school-like gloss
That most consists of echoing words and terms . . .
Nor any long or far-fetched circumstance —
Wrapt in the curious generalities of arts —

---

[1] See p. 229, note 1, *ad. fin.*

> But a direct and analytic sum
> Of all the worth and first effects of arts.
> And for his poesy, 'tis so rammed with life
> That it shall gather strength of life with being,
> And live hereafter, more admired than now.

Tibullus gives Virgil equal credit for having in his writings touched with telling truth upon every vicissitude of human existence.

> That which he hath writ
> Is with such judgment laboured and distilled
> Through all the needful uses of our lives
> That, could a man remember but his lines,
> He should not touch at any serious point
> But he might breathe his spirit out of him.

Finally, Virgil in the play is nominated by Cæsar to act as judge between Horace and his libellers, and he advises the administration of purging pills to the offenders. That course of treatment is adopted with satisfactory results.[1]

As against this interpretation, one contemporary witness has been held to testify that Shakespeare stemmed the tide of Jonson's embittered activity by no peace-making interposition, but by joining his foes, and by administering, with their aid, the identical course of medicine which in the 'Poetaster' is meted out to his enemies. In the same year (1601) as the 'Poetaster' was produced, 'The Return from Parnassus' —a third piece in a trilogy of plays — was 'acted by

---

[1] The proposed identification of Virgil in the 'Poetaster' with Chapman has little to recommend it. Chapman's literary work did not justify the commendations which were bestowed on Virgil in the play.

the students in St. John's College, Cambridge.' In
this piece, as in its two predecessors, Shakespeare
received, both as a playwright and a poet, high commendation, although his poems were judged to reflect
somewhat too largely 'love's lazy foolish languish-
ment.' The actor Burbage was introduced in his
own name instructing an aspirant to the actor's
profession in the part of Richard the Third, and the
familiar lines from Shakespeare's play —

> Now is the winter of our discontent
> Made glorious summer by this sun of York —

are recited by the pupil as part of his lesson. Subsequently in a prose dialogue between Shakespeare's
fellow-actors Burbage and Kempe, Kempe remarks
of University dramatists, 'Why, here's our fellow
Shakespeare puts them all down; aye, and Ben Jonson, too. O! that Ben Jonson is a pestilent fellow.
He brought up Horace, giving the poets a pill; but
our fellow Shakespeare hath given him a purge that
made him bewray his credit.' Burbage adds: 'He is
a shrewd fellow, indeed.' This perplexing passage
has been held to mean that Shakespeare took a
decisive part against Jonson in the controversy with
Dekker and Dekker's actor-friends. But such a conclusion is nowhere corroborated, and seems
to be confuted by the eulogies of Virgil
in the 'Poetaster' and by the general handling of the theme in 'Hamlet.' The words
quoted from 'The Return from Parnassus' hardly
admit of a literal interpretation. Probably the
'purge' that Shakespeare was alleged by the author

Shake-
speare's
alleged
partisan-
ship.

of 'The Return from Parnassus' to have given Jonson meant no more than that Shakespeare had signally outstripped Jonson in popular esteem. As the author of 'Julius Cæsar,' he had just proved his command of topics that were peculiarly suited to Jonson's vein,[1] and had in fact outrun his churlish comrade on his own ground.

[1] The most scornful criticism that Jonson is known to have passed on any composition by Shakespeare was aimed at a passage in *Julius Cæsar*, and as Jonson's attack is barely justifiable on literary grounds, it is fair to assume that the play was distasteful to him from other considerations. 'Many times,' Jonson wrote of Shakespeare in his *Timber*, 'hee fell into those things [which] could not escape laughter: As when hee said in the person of *Cæsar*, one speaking to him [*i.e.* Cæsar]; *Cæsar, thou dost me wrong.* Hee [*i.e.* Cæsar] replyed: *Cæsar did never wrong, butt with just cause:* and such like, which were ridiculous.' Jonson derisively quoted the same passage in the induction to *The Staple of News* (1625): 'Cry you mercy, you did not wrong but with just cause.' Possibly the words that were ascribed by Jonson to Shakespeare's character of *Cæsar* appeared in the original version of the play, but owing perhaps to Jonson's captious criticism they do not figure in the Folio version, the sole version that has reached us. The only words there that correspond with Jonson's quotation are Cæsar's remark:

> Know, Cæsar doth not wrong, nor without cause
> Will he be satisfied

(act iii. sc. i. ll. 47-8). The rhythm and sense seem to require the re-insertion after the word 'wrong' of the phrase 'but with just cause,' which Jonson needlessly reprobated. Leonard Digges (1588-1635), one of Shakespeare's admiring critics, emphasises the superior popularity of Shakespeare's *Julius Cæsar* in the theatre to Ben Jonson's Roman play of *Catiline*, in his eulogistic lines on Shakespeare (published after Digges's death in the 1640 edition of Shakespeare's *Poems*):

> So have I seen when Cæsar would appear,
> And on the stage at half-sword parley were
> Brutus and Cassius — oh, how the audience
> Were ravish'd, with what wonder they went thence;
> When some new day they would not brook a line
> Of tedious, though well-laboured, Catiline.

At any rate, in the tragedy that Shakespeare brought out in the year following the production of 'Julius Cæsar,' he finally left Jonson and all friends and foes lagging far behind both in achievement and reputation. This new exhibition of the force of his genius re-established, too, the ascendency of the adult actors who interpreted his work, and the boys' supremacy was quickly brought to an end. In 1602 Shakespeare produced 'Hamlet,' 'that piece of his which most kindled English hearts.' The story of the 'Hamlet,' Prince of Denmark had been popular on the 1602. stage as early as 1589 in a lost dramatic version by another writer—doubtless Thomas Kyd, whose tragedies of blood, 'The Spanish Tragedy' and 'Jeronimo,' long held the Elizabethan stage. To that lost version of 'Hamlet' Shakespeare's tragedy certainly owed much.[1] The story was also accessible in the

---

[1] I wrote on this point in the article on Thomas Kyd in the *Dictionary of National Biography* (vol. xxxi.) : 'The argument in favour of Kyd's authorship of a pre-Shakespearean play (now lost) on the subject of Hamlet deserves attention. Nash in 1589, when describing [in his preface to *Menaphon*] the typical literary hack, who at almost every point suggests Kyd, notices that in addition to his other accomplishments "he will afford you whole Hamlets, I should say handfuls of tragical speeches." Other references in popular tracts and plays of like date prove that in an early tragedy concerning Hamlet there was a ghost who cried repeatedly, "Hamlet, revenge!" and that this expression took rank in Elizabethan slang beside the vernacular quotations from [Kyd's sanguinary tragedy of] *Jeronimo*, such as "What outcry calls me from my naked bed," and "Beware, Hieronimo, go by, go by." The resemblance between the stories of *Hamlet* and *Jeronimo* suggests that the former would have supplied Kyd with a congenial plot. In *Jeronimo* a father seeks to avenge his son's murder; in *Hamlet* the theme is the same with the

'Histoires Tragiques,' of Belleforest, who adapted it from the 'Historia Danica' of Saxo Grammaticus.[1] No English translation of Belleforest's 'Hystorie of Hamblet' appeared before 1608; Shakespeare doubtless read it in the French. But his authorities give little hint of what was to emerge from his study of them.

Burbage created the title-part in Shakespeare's tragedy, and its success on the stage led to the play's publication immediately afterwards. The bibliography of 'Hamlet' offers a puzzling problem. On July 26, 1602, 'A Book called the Revenge of Hamlet, Prince

The prob-
lem of its
publica-
tion.

of Denmark, as it was lately acted by the Lord Chamberlain his Servants,' was entered on the Stationers' Company's Registers, and it was published in quarto next year by N[icholas]

position of father and son reversed. In *Jeronimo* the avenging father resolves to reach his end by arranging for the performance of a play in the presence of those whom he suspects of the murder of his son, and there is good ground for crediting the lost tragedy of *Hamlet* with a similar play-scene. Shakespeare's debt to the lost tragedy is a matter of conjecture, but the stilted speeches of the play-scene in his *Hamlet* read like intentional parodies of Kyd's bombastic efforts in *The Spanish Tragedy*, and it is quite possible that they were directly suggested by an almost identical episode in a lost *Hamlet* by the same author.' Shakespeare elsewhere shows acquaintance with Kyd's work. He places in the mouth of Kit Sly in *The Taming of The Shrew* the current phrase 'Go by, Jeronimy,' from *The Spanish Tragedy*. Shakespeare quotes verbatim a line from the same piece in *Much Ado About Nothing* (I. i. 271): 'In time the savage bull doth bear the yoke;' but Kyd practically borrowed that line from Watson's *Passionate Centurie* (No. xlvii.), where Shakespeare may have met it.

[1] Cf. Gericke und Max Moltke, *Hamlet-Quellen*, Leipzig, 1881. The story was absorbed into Scandinavian mythology: cf. *Ambales-Saga*, edited by Mr. Israel Gollancz, 1898.

L[ing] and John Trundell. The title-page stated that the piece had been 'acted divers times in the city of

The First Quarto, 1603.

London, as also in the two Universities of Cambridge and Oxford and elsewhere.' The text here appeared in a rough and imperfect state. In all probability it was a piratical and carelessly transcribed copy of Shakespeare's first draft of the play, in which he drew largely on the older piece.

A revised version, printed from a more complete and accurate manuscript, was published in 1604 as 'The Tragical History of Hamlet Prince of Denmark, by William Shakespeare, newly imprinted and en-

The Second Quarto, 1604.

larged to almost as much again as it was, according to the true and perfect copy.' This was printed by I[ames] R[oberts] for ●the publisher N[icholas] L[ing]. The concluding words — 'according to the true and perfect copy' — of the title-page of the second quarto were intended to stamp its predecessor as surreptitious and unauthentic. But it is clear that the second quarto was not a perfect version of the play. It was itself printed from a copy which had been curtailed for acting purposes.

A third version (long the *textus receptus*) figured in the folio of 1623. Here many passages, not to be found in the quartos, appear for the first time, but a

The Folio Version.

few others that appear in the quartos are omitted. The folio text probably came nearest to the original manuscript; but it, too, followed an acting copy which had been abbreviated somewhat less drastically than the second quarto and in a

different fashion.[1]　Theobald in his 'Shakespeare
Restored' (1726) made the first scholarly attempt to
form a text from a collation of the First Folio with
the second quarto, and Theobald's text with further
embellishments by Sir Thomas Hanmer, Edward
Capell, and the Cambridge editors of 1866, is now
generally adopted.

'Hamlet' was the only drama by Shakespeare
that was acted in his lifetime at the two Universities.
It has since attracted more attention from actors,
playgoers, and readers of all capacities than any other
of Shakespeare's plays.　Its world-wide popularity

Popularity
of 'Ham-
let.'

from its author's day to our own, when it is
as warmly welcomed in the theatres of France
and Germany as in those of England and
America, is the most striking of the many testimonies
to the eminence of Shakespeare's dramatic instinct.
At a first glance there seems little in the play to
attract the uneducated or the unreflecting.　'Hamlet'
is mainly a psychological effort, a study of the reflec-
tive temperament in excess.　The action develops
slowly; at times there is no movement at all.　Except
'Antony and Cleopatra,' which exceeds it by sixty
lines, the piece is the longest of Shakespeare's plays,
while the total length of Hamlet's speeches far exceeds
that of those allotted by Shakespeare to any other
of his characters.　Humorous relief is, it is true,

---

[1] Cf. *Hamlet* — parallel texts of the first and second quarto, and
first folio — ed. Wilhelm Vietor, Marburg, 1891; *The Devonshire
Hamlets*, 1860, parallel texts of the two quartos edited by Mr. Sam
Timmins; *Hamlet*, ed. George Macdonald, 1885, a study with the text
of the folio.

effectively supplied to the tragic theme by Polonius and the grave-diggers, and if the topical references to contemporary theatrical history (ii. ii. 350–89) could only count on an appreciative reception from an Elizabethan audience, the pungent censure of actors' perennial defects is calculated to catch the ear of the average playgoer of all ages. But it is not to these subsidiary features that the universality of the play's vogue can be attributed. It is the intensity of interest which Shakespeare contrives to excite in the character of the hero that explains the position of the play in popular esteem. The play's un-rivalled power of attraction lies in the pathetic fascination exerted on minds of almost every calibre by the central figure — a high-born youth of chivalric instincts and finely developed intellect, who, when stirred to avenge in action a desperate private wrong, is foiled by introspective workings of the brain that paralyse the will.

Although the difficulties of determining the date of 'Troilus and Cressida' are very great, there are many grounds for assigning its composition to the early days of 1603. In 1599 Dekker and Chettle were engaged by Henslowe to prepare for the Earl of Nottingham's company — a rival of Shakespeare's company — a play of 'Troilus and Cressida,' of which no trace survives. It doubtless suggested the topic to Shakespeare. On February 7, 1602–3, James Roberts obtained a license for 'the booke of Troilus and Cresseda as yt is acted by my

'Troilus and Cressida.'

Q

Lord Chamberlens men,' *i.e.* Shakespeare's company.[1]
Roberts printed the second quarto of ' Hamlet' and
others of Shakespeare's plays ; but his effort to publish 'Troilus' proved abortive, owing to the interposition of the players.   Roberts's ' book' was probably
Shakespeare's play.   The metrical characteristics
of Shakespeare's 'Troilus and Cressida' — the regularity of the blank verse — powerfully confirm the
date of composition which Roberts's license suggests.
Six years later, however, on January 28, 1608–9, a
new license for the issue of 'a booke called the history of Troylus and Cressida' was granted to other
publishers, Richard Bonian and Henry Walley,[2] and
these publishers, more fortunate than Roberts, soon
printed a quarto with Shakespeare's full name as
author.   The text seems fairly authentic, but exceptional obscurity attaches to the circumstances of
the publication.   Some copies of the book bear an
ordinary type of title-page stating that the piece was
printed ' as it was acted by the King's majesties
servants at the Globe.'   But in other copies, which
differ in no way in regard to the text of the play,
there was substituted for this title-page a more pretentious announcement running : 'The famous Historie of Troylus and Cresseid, excellently expressing
the beginning of their loues with the conceited wooing
of Pandarus, prince of Lacia.'   After this pompous
title-page there was inserted, for the first and only
time in the case of a play by Shakespeare that was

[1] Arber's *Transcript of the Stationers' Registers*, iii. 226.
[2] *Ib.* iii. 400.

published in his lifetime, an advertisement or preface. In this interpolated page an anonymous scribe, writing in the name of the publishers, paid bombastic and high-flown compliments to Shakespeare as a writer of 'comedies,' and defiantly boasted that the 'grand possessers' — *i.e.* the owners — of the manuscript deprecated its publication. By way of enhancing the value of what were obviously stolen wares, it was falsely added that the piece was new and unacted. This address was possibly the brazen reply of the publishers to a more than usually emphatic protest on the part of players or dramatist against the printing of the piece. The editors of the Folio evinced distrust of the quarto edition by printing their text from a different copy showing many deviations, which were not always for the better.

The work, which in point of construction shows signs of haste, and in style is exceptionally unequal, is the least attractive of the efforts of Shakespeare's middle life. The story is based on a romantic legend of the Trojan war, which is of mediæval

Treatment of the theme.

origin. Shakespeare had possibly read Chapman's translation of Homer's 'Iliad,' but he owed his plot to Chaucer's 'Troilus and Cresseid' and Lydgate's 'Troy Book.' In defiance of his authorities he presented Cressida as a heartless coquette; the poets who had previously treated her story — Boccaccio, Chaucer, Lydgate, and Robert Henryson — had imagined her as a tender-hearted, if frail, beauty, with claims on their pity rather than on their scorn. But Shakespeare's innovation is dramatically effective, and accords with strictly moral canons. The charge frequently brought against the dramatist that in 'Troilus and Cressida' he cynically invested the Greek heroes of classical antiquity with contemptible characteristics is ill supported by the text of the play. Ulysses, Nestor, and Agamemnon figure in Shakespeare's play as brave generals and sagacious statesmen, and in their speeches Shakespeare concentrated a marvellous wealth of pithily expressed philosophy, much of which has fortunately obtained proverbial currency. Shakespeare's conception of the Greeks followed traditional lines except in the case of Achilles, whom he transforms into a brutal coward. And that portrait quite legitimately interpreted the selfish, unreasoning, and exorbitant pride with which the warrior was credited by Homer and his imitators.

Shakespeare's treatment of his theme cannot therefore be fairly construed, as some critics construe it, into a petty-minded protest against the honour paid to the ancient Greeks and to the form and sentiment of their literature by more learned dramatists of the day, like Ben Jonson and Chapman. Although Shakespeare knew the Homeric version of the Trojan war, he worked in 'Troilus and Cressida' upon a mediæval romance, which was practically uninfluenced either for good or evil by the classical spirit.[1]

[1] Less satisfactory is the endeavour that has been made by Mr. F. G. Fleay and Mr. George Wyndham to treat *Troilus and Cressida* as Shakespeare's contribution to the embittered controversy of 1601–2, between

Despite the association of Shakespeare's company with the rebellion of 1601, and its difficulties with the children of the Chapel Royal, he and his fellow-actors

Jonson and Marston and Dekker and their actor-friends, and to represent it as a pronouncement against Jonson. According to this fanciful view, Shakespeare held up Jonson to savage ridicule in Ajax, while in Thersites he denounced Marston, despite Marston's intermittent antagonism to Jonson, which entitled him to freedom from attack by Jonson's foes. The appearance of the word 'mastic' in the line (I. iii. 73) 'When rank Thersites opes his mastic jaws' is treated as proof of Shakespeare's identification of Thersites with Marston, who used the pseudonym 'Therio-mastix' in his *Scourge of Villainy*. It would be as reasonable to identify him with Dekker, who wrote the greater part of *Satiro-mastix*. 'Mastic' is doubtless an adjective formed without recondite significance from the substantive 'mastic,' *i.e.* the gum commonly used at the time for stopping decayed teeth. No hypothesis of a polemical intention is needed to account for Shakespeare's conception of Ajax or Thersites. There is no trait in either character as depicted by Shakespeare which a reading of Chapman's *Homer* would fail to suggest. The controversial interpretation of the play is in conflict with chronology (for *Troilus* cannot, on any showing, be assigned to the period of the war between Jonson and Dekker, in 1601–2), and it seems confuted by the facts and arguments already adduced in the discussion of the theatrical conflict (see pp. 213–19). If more direct disproof be needed, it may be found in Shakespeare's prologue to *Troilus*, where there is a good-humoured and expressly pacific allusion to the polemical aims of Jonson's *Poetaster*. Jonson had introduced into his play 'an *armed* prologue' on account, he asserted, of his enemies' menaces. Shakespeare, after describing in his prologue to *Troilus* the progress of the Trojan war before his story opened, added that his 'prologue' presented itself '*arm'd*,' not to champion 'author's pen or actor's voice,' but simply to announce in a guise befitting the warlike subject-matter that the play began in the middle of the conflict between Greek and Trojan, and not at the beginning. These words of Shakespeare put out of court any interpretation of Shakespeare's play that would represent it as a contribution to the theatrical controversy.

retained its hold on Court favour till the close of Eliza-

Queen
Elizabeth's
death,
March 26,
1603.
beth's reign.   As late as February 2, 1603, the company entertained the dying Queen at Richmond.   Her death on March 26, 1603, drew from Shakespeare's early eulo-
gist, Chettle, a vain appeal to him under the fanciful name of Melicert, to

> Drop from his honied muse one sable teare,
> To mourne her death that gracèd his desert,
> And to his laies opened her royal eare.[1]

But except on sentimental grounds, the Queen's death justified no lamentation on the part of Shakespeare. On the withdrawal of one royal patron he and his friends at once found another, who proved far more liberal and appreciative.

On May 19, 1603, James I, very soon after his accession, extended to Shakespeare and other mem-
bers of the Lord Chamberlain's company a very marked and valuable recognition.   To them he granted under royal letters patent a license 'freely to use and exercise the arte and facultie of playing comedies, tragedies, histories, enterludes, moralls, pastoralles, stage-plaies, and such other like as they have already studied, or hereafter shall use or studie as well for the recreation of our loving subjectes as for our solace and pleasure, when we shall thinke good to see them during our pleasure.'   The Globe Theatre was noted as the customary scene of their labours, but permission was granted to them to per-

---

[1] *England's Mourning Garment*, 1603, sign. D. 3.

form in the town-hall or moot-hall of any country
James I's
patronage. town. Nine actors are named. Lawrence
Fletcher stands first on the list; he had
already performed before James in Scotland in 1599
and 1601. Shakespeare comes second and Burbage
third. The company to which they belonged was
thenceforth styled the King's company; its members
became 'the King's Servants,' and they took rank with
the Grooms of the Chamber.[1] Shakespeare's plays
were thenceforth repeatedly performed in James's
presence, and Oldys related that James wrote Shakespeare a letter in his own hand, which was at one
time in the possession of Sir William D'Avenant,
and afterwards, according to Lintot, in that of John
Sheffield, first duke of Buckingham.

In the autumn and winter of 1603 the prevalence
of the plague led to the closing of the theatres in
London. The King's players were compelled to
make a prolonged tour in the provinces, which
entailed some loss of income. For two months from
the third week in October, the Court was temporarily installed at Wilton, the residence of William
Herbert, third earl of Pembroke, and late in November the company was summoned by the royal officers

[1] At the same time the earl of Worcester's company was taken
into the Queen's patronage, and its members were known as 'the
Queen's servants,' while the earl of Nottingham's company was taken
into the patronage of the Prince of Wales, and its members were
known as the Prince's servants. This extended patronage of actors by
the royal family was noticed as especially honourable to the King by one
of his contemporary panegyrists, Gilbert Dugdale, in his *Time Triumphant*, 1604, sig. B.

to perform in the royal presence. The actors travelled from Mortlake to Salisbury 'unto the Courte aforesaide,' and their performance took place at Wilton House on December 2. They received next day 'upon the Councells warrant' the large sum of 30*l.* 'by way of his majesties reward.'[1] Many other gracious marks of royal favour followed. On March 15, 1604, Shakespeare and eight other actors of the company walked from the Tower of London to Westminster in the procession which accompanied the King on his formal entry into London. Each actor received four-and-a-half yards of scarlet cloth to wear as a cloak on the occasion, and in the document authorising the grant Shakespeare's name stands first on the list.[2] The dramatist Dekker was author of a somewhat bombastic account of the elaborate ceremonial, which rapidly ran through three editions. On

---

[1] The entry, which appears in the accounts of the Treasurer of the Chamber, was first printed in 1842 in Cunningham's *Extracts from the Accounts of the Revels at Court*, p. xxxiv. A comparison of Cunningham's transcript with the original in the Public Record Office (*Audit Office-Declared Accounts*, Treasurer of the Chamber, bundle 388, roll 41) shows that it is accurate. The earl of Pembroke was in no way responsible for the performance at Wilton House. At the time, the Court was formally installed in his house (cf. *Cal. State Papers*, Dom. 1603–10, pp. 47–59), and the Court officers commissioned the players to perform there, and paid all their expenses. The alleged tradition, recently promulgated for the first time by the owners of Wilton, that *As You Like It* was performed on the occasion, is unsupported by contemporary evidence.

[2] The grant is transcribed in the New Shakspere Society's *Transactions*, 1877–9, Appendix II., from the Lord Chamberlain's papers in the Public Record Office, where it is now numbered 660. The number allotted it in the *Transactions* is obsolete.

April 9, 1604, the King gave further proof of his
friendly interest in the fortunes of his actors by
causing an official letter to be sent to the Lord
Mayor of London and the Justices of the Peace for
Middlesex and Surrey, bidding them 'permit and
suffer' the King's players to 'exercise their playes'
at their 'usual house,' the Globe.[1]   Four months
later — in August — every member of the company
was summoned by the King's order to attend at
Somerset House during the fortnight's sojourn
there of the Spanish ambassador extraordinary,
Juan Fernandez de Velasco, duke de Frias, and
Constable of Castile, who came to London to ratify
the treaty of peace between England and Spain,
and was magnificently entertained by the English
Court.[2]   Between All Saints' Day [November 1]

[1] A contemporary copy of this letter, which declared the Queen's
players acting at the Fortune and the Prince's players at the Curtain
to be entitled to the same privileges as the King's players, is at Dulwich
College (cf. G. F. Warner's *Catalogue of the Dulwich Manuscripts*,
pp. 26-7).   Collier printed it in his *New Facts* with fraudulent additions, in which the names of Shakespeare and other actors figured.

[2] Mr. Halliwell-Phillipps, in his *Outlines*, i. 213, cites a royal order
to this effect, but gives no authority, and I have sought in vain for the
document at the Public Record Office, at the British Museum, and
elsewhere.   But there is no reason to doubt the fact that Shakespeare
and his fellow-actors took part, as Grooms of the Chamber, in the
ceremonies attending the Constable's visit to London.   In the unprinted accounts of Edmund Tilney, master of the revels, for the
year October 1603 to October 1604, charge is made for his three
days' attendance with four men to direct the entertainments 'at the
receaving of the Constable of Spayne' (Public Record Office, *Declared
Accounts*, Pipe Office Roll 2805).   The magnificent festivities culminated in a splendid banquet given in the Constable's honour by James I
at Whitehall on Sunday, August $\frac{19}{29}$ — the day on which the treaty

and the ensuing Shrove Tuesday, which fell early
in February 1605, Shakespeare's company gave no
fewer than eleven performances at Whitehall in the
royal presence.[1]

was signed.   In the morning all the members of the royal household
accompanied the Constable in formal procession from Somerset House.
After the banquet, at which the earls of Pembroke and Southampton
acted as stewards, there was a ball, and the King's guests subsequently
witnessed exhibitions of bear baiting, bull baiting, rope dancing, and
feats of horsemanship.   (Cf. Stow's *Chronicle*, 1631, pp. 845-6, and
a Spanish pamphlet, *Relacion de la jornada del exc^mo Condestabile
di Castilla*, etc., Antwerp, 1604, 4to, which was summarised in
Ellis's *Original Letters*, 2nd series, vol. iii. pp. 207-15, and was partly
translated in Mr. W. B. Rye's *England as seen by Foreigners*, pp. 117-
24).

[1] At the Bodleian Library (MS. Rawlinson, A 204) are the original
accounts of Lord Stanhope of Harrington, Treasurer of the Chamber
for various (detached) years in the early part of James I's reign.   These
documents show that Shakespeare's company acted at Court on
November 1 and 4, December 26 and 28, 1604, and on January 7
and 8, February 2 and 3, and the evenings of the following Shrove
Sunday, Shrove Monday, and Shrove Tuesday, 1605.

XIV

THE HIGHEST THEMES OF TRAGEDY

UNDER the incentive of such exalted patronage, Shakespeare's activity redoubled, but his work shows 'Othello' none of the conventional marks of literature and 'Measure for Measure.' that is produced in the blaze of Court favour. The first six years of the new reign saw him absorbed in the highest themes of tragedy, and an unparalleled intensity and energy, which bore few traces of the trammels of a Court, thenceforth illumined every scene that he contrived.   To 1604 the composition of two plays can be confidently assigned, one of which — 'Othello' — ranks with Shakespeare's greatest achievements ; while the other — 'Measure for Measure'— although as a whole far inferior to 'Othello,' contains one of the finest scenes (between Angelo and Isabella, II. ii. 43 seq.) and one of the greatest speeches (Claudio on the fear of death, III. i. 116–30) in the range of Shakespearean drama.   'Othello' was doubtless the first new piece by Shakespeare that was acted before James.   It was produced at Whitehall on November 1.   'Measure for Measure' followed on December 26.[1]   Neither was printed in Shakespeare's

---

[1] These dates are drawn from a memorandum of plays performed at Court in 1604 and 1605 which is among Malone's manuscripts in the

lifetime.   The plots of both ultimately come from the
same Italian collection of novels — Giraldi Cinthio's
'Hecatommithi,' which was first published in 1565.

Cinthio's painful story of 'Othello' (decad. iii.
nov. 3) is not known to have been translated into
English before Shakespeare dramatised it.   He followed its main drift with fidelity, but he introduced
the new characters of Roderigo and Emilia, and he
invested the catastrophe with new and fearful intensity
by making Iago's cruel treachery known to Othello at
the last, after Iago's perfidy has impelled the noblehearted Moor in his groundless jealousy to murder
his gentle and innocent wife Desdemona.   Iago became in Shakespeare's hands the subtlest of all studies
of intellectual villainy and hypocrisy.   The whole
tragedy displays to magnificent advantage the dramatist's fully matured powers.   An unfaltering equi-

Bodleian Library, and was obviously derived by Malone from authentic
documents that were in his day preserved at the Audit Office in Somerset
House.   The document cannot now be traced at the Public Record
Office, whither the Audit Office papers have been removed since
Malone's death.   Peter Cunningham professed to print the original
document in his accounts of the revels at Court (Shakespeare Society,
1842, pp. 203 seq.), but there is no doubt that he forged his so-called
transcript, and that the additions which he made to Malone's memorandum were the outcome of his fancy.   Collier's assertion in his *New
Particulars*, p. 57, that Othello was first acted at Sir Thomas Egerton's
residence at Harefield on August 6, 1602, was based solely on a document among the Earl of Ellesmere's MSS. at Bridgwater House, which
purported to be a contemporary account by the clerk, Sir Arthur Mayn-
waring, of Sir Thomas Egerton's household expenses.   This document,
which Collier reprinted in his *Egerton Papers* (Camden Soc.), p. 343,
was authoritatively pronounced by experts in 1860 to be 'a shameful
forgery' (cf. Ingleby's *Complete View of the Shakspere Controversy*,
1861, pp. 261-5).

librium is maintained in the treatment of plot and characters alike.

Cinthio made the perilous story of 'Measure for Measure' the subject not only of a romance, but of a tragedy called 'Epitia.' Before Shakespeare wrote his play, Cinthio's romance had been twice rendered into English by George Whetstone. Whetstone had not only given a somewhat altered version of the Italian romance in his unwieldy play of 'Promos and Cassandra' (in two parts of five acts each, 1578), but he had also freely translated it in his collection of prose tales, 'Heptameron of Civil Discources' (1582). Yet there is every likelihood that Shakespeare also knew Cinthio's play, which, unlike his romance, was untranslated; the leading character, who is by Shakespeare christened Angelo, was known by another name to Cinthio in his story, but Cinthio in his play (and not in his novel) gives the character a sister named Angela, which doubtless suggested Shakespeare's designation.[1] In the hands of Shakespeare's predecessors the tale is a sordid record of lust and cruelty. But Shakespeare prudently showed scant respect for their handling of the narrative. By diverting the course of the plot at a critical point he not merely proved his artistic ingenuity, but gave dramatic dignity and moral elevation to a degraded and repellent theme. In the old versions Isabella yields her virtue as the price of her brother's life. The central fact of Shakespeare's play is Isabella's inflexible and unconditional chastity. Other of Shakespeare's altera-

[1] Dr. Garnett's *Italian Literature*, 1898, p. 227.

tions, like the Duke's abrupt proposal to marry Isabella, seem hastily conceived. But his creation of the pathetic character of Mariana 'of the moated grange' — the legally affianced bride of Angelo, Isabella's would-be seducer — skilfully excludes the possibility of a settlement (as in the old stories) between Isabella and Angelo on terms of marriage. Shakespeare's argument is throughout philosophically subtle. The poetic eloquence in which Isabella and the Duke pay homage to the virtue of chastity, and the many expositions of the corruption with which unchecked sexual passion threatens society, alternate with coarsely comic interludes which suggest the vanity of seeking to efface natural instincts by the coercion of law. There is little in the play that seems designed to recommend it to the Court before which it was first performed. But the two emphatic references to a ruler's dislike of mobs, despite his love of his people, were perhaps penned in deferential allusion to James I, whose horror of crowds was notorious. In act I. sc. i. 67–72 the Duke remarks:

> I love the people
> But do not like to stage me to their eyes.
> Though it do well, I do not relish well
> Their loud applause and aves vehement.
> Nor do I think the man of safe discretion
> That does affect it.

Of like tenor is the succeeding speech of Angelo (act II. sc. iv. 27–30):

> The general [*i.e.* the public], subject to a well-wish'd King, . . .
> Crowd to his presence, where their untaught love
> Must needs appear offence.

In 'Macbeth,' his 'great epic drama,' which he began in 1605 and completed next year, Shakespeare employed a setting wholly in harmony with the accession of a Scottish king. The story was drawn from Holinshed's 'Chronicle of Scottish History,' with occasional reference, perhaps, to earlier Scottish sources.[1] The supernatural machinery of the three witches accorded with the King's super-stitious faith in demonology; the dramatist lavished his sympathy on Banquo, James's ancestor; while Macbeth's vision of kings who carry 'twofold balls and treble sceptres' (IV. i. 20) plainly adverted to the union of Scotland with England and Ireland under James's sway. The allusion by the porter (act II. iii. 9) to the 'equivocator . . . who committed treason' was perhaps suggested by the notorious defence of the doctrine of equivocation made by the Jesuit Henry Garnett, who was executed early in 1606 for his share in the 'Gunpowder Plot.' The piece was not printed until 1623. It is in its existing shape the shortest of all Shakespeare's plays, and it is possible that it survives only in an abbreviated acting version. Much scenic elaboration characterised the production. Dr. Simon Forman witnessed a performance of the tragedy at the Globe in April 1611 and noted that Macbeth and Banquo entered the stage on horseback, and that Banquo's ghost was materially represented (III. iv. 40 seq.). Like 'Othello,' the play ranks with the noblest tragedies either of the modern or the ancient world. The characters of hero and heroine

'Macbeth.'

---

[1] Letter by Mrs. Stopes in *Athenæum*, July 25, 1896.

— Macbeth and his wife — are depicted with the utmost subtlety and insight. In three points 'Macbeth' differs somewhat from other of Shakespeare's productions in the great class of literature to which it belongs. The interweaving with the tragic story of supernatural interludes in which Fate is weirdly personified is not exactly matched in any other of Shakespeare's tragedies. In the second place, the action proceeds with a rapidity that is wholly without parallel in the rest of Shakespeare's plays. Nowhere, moreover, has Shakespeare introduced comic relief into a tragedy with bolder effect than in the porter's speech after the murder of Duncan (II. iii. 1 seq.). The theory that this passage was from another hand does not merit acceptance.[1] It cannot, however, be overlooked that the second scene of the first act — Duncan's interview with the 'bleeding sergeant' — falls so far below the style of the rest of the play as to suggest that it was an interpolation by a hack of the theatre. The resemblances between Thomas Middleton's later play of 'The Witch' (1610) and portions of 'Macbeth' may safely be ascribed to plagiarism on Middleton's part. Of two songs which according to the stage directions were to be sung during the representation of 'Macbeth' (III. v. and IV. i.), only the first line of each is noted there, but songs beginning with the same lines are set out in full in Middleton's play; they were probably by Middleton, and were interpolated by actors in a stage version of 'Macbeth' after its original production.

[1] Cf. *Macbeth*, ed. Clark and Wright, Clarendon Press Series.

'King Lear,' in which Shakespeare's tragic genius moved without any faltering on Titanic

'King Lear.' heights, was written during 1606, and was produced before the Court at Whitehall on the night of December 26 of that year.[1] It was entered on the 'Stationers' Registers' on November 26, 1607, and two imperfect editions, published by Nathaniel Butter, appeared in the following year; neither exactly corresponds with the other or with the improved and fairly satisfactory text of the Folio. The three versions present three different playhouse transcripts. Like its immediate predecessor, 'Macbeth,' the tragedy was mainly founded on Holinshed's 'Chronicle.' The leading theme had been dramatised as early as 1593, but Shakespeare's attention was no doubt directed to it by the publication of a crude dramatic adaptation of Holinshed's version in 1605 under the title of 'The True Chronicle History of King Leir and his three Daughters — Gonorill, Ragan, and Cordella.' Shakespeare did not adhere closely to his original. He invested the tale of Lear with a hopelessly tragic conclusion, and on it he grafted the equally distressing tale of Gloucester and his two sons, which he drew from Sidney's 'Arcadia.'[2] Hints for the speeches of Edgar when feigning madness were drawn from Harsnet's 'Declaration of Popish

[1] This fact is stated on the title-page of the Quartos.

[2] Sidney tells the story in a chapter entitled 'The pitiful state and story of the Paphlagonian unkind King and his blind son; first related by the son, then by his blind father' (bk. ii. chap. 10, ed. 1590, 4to; pp. 132–3, ed. 1674, fol.).

R

Impostures,' 1603.   In every act of 'Lear' the pity and
terror of which tragedy is capable reach their climax.
Only one who has something of the Shakespearean
gift of language could adequately characterise the
scenes of agony — 'the living martyrdom' — to which
the fiendish ingratitude of his daughters condemns
the abdicated king — 'a very foolish, fond old man,
fourscore and upward.'   The elemental passions burst
forth in his utterances with all the vehemence of the
volcanic tempest which beats about his defence-
less head in the scene on the heath.   The brutal
blinding of Gloucester by Cornwall exceeds in horror
any other situation that Shakespeare created, if we
assume that he was not responsible for the like scenes
of mutilation in 'Titus Andronicus.'   'At no point in
'Lear' is there any loosening of the tragic tension.
The faithful half-witted lad who serves the king as
his fool plays the jesting chorus on his master's
fortune in penetrating earnest and deepens the deso-
lating pathos.

Although Shakespeare's powers showed no sign
of exhaustion, he reverted in the year following the
colossal effort of 'Lear' (1607) to his earlier habit
'Timon of of collaboration, and with another's aid com-
Athens.'   posed two dramas — 'Timon of Athens' and
'Pericles.'   An extant play on the subject of 'Timon
of Athens' was composed in 1600[1] but there is nothing to show that Shakespeare and his coadjutor were
acquainted with it.   They doubtless derived a part

---

[1] It was edited for the Shakespeare Society in 1842 by Dyce, who
owned the manuscript.

of their story from Painter's 'Palace of Pleasure,'
and from a short digression in Plutarch's 'Life of
Marc Antony,' where Antony is described as emulating the life and example of 'Timon Misanthropos
the Athenian.'   The dramatists may, too, have
known a dialogue of Lucian entitled 'Timon,' which
Boiardo had previously converted into a comedy
under the name of 'Il Timone.'   Internal evidence
makes it clear that Shakespeare's colleague was
responsible for nearly the whole of acts iii. and v.
But the character of Timon himself and all the scenes
which he dominates are from Shakespeare's pen.
Timon is cast in the mould of Lear.

There seems some ground for the belief that
Shakespeare's coadjutor in 'Timon' was George
Wilkins, a writer of ill-developed dramatic power,
who, in 'The Miseries of Enforced Marriage' (1607),
first treated the story that afterwards served for the
plot of 'The Yorkshire Tragedy.'   At any rate,
'Pericles.' Wilkins may safely be credited with portions of 'Pericles,' a romantic play which
can be referred to the same year as 'Timon.'   Shakespeare contributed only acts iii. and v. and parts of
iv., which together form a self-contained whole, and
do not combine satisfactorily with the remaining
scenes.   The presence of a third hand, of inferior
merit to Wilkins, has been suspected, and to this col-
laborator (perhaps William Rowley, a professional re-
viser of plays who could show capacity on occasion)
are best assigned the three scenes of purposeless coarse-
ness which take place in or before a brothel (iv. ii., v.,

and vi.). From so distributed a responsibility the piece naturally suffers. It lacks homogeneity and the story is helped out by dumb shows and prologues. But a matured felicity of expression characterises Shakespeare's own contributions, narrating the romantic quest of Pericles for his daughter Marina, who was born and abandoned in a shipwreck. At many points he here anticipated his latest dramatic effects. The shipwreck is depicted (act IV. i.) as impressively as in the 'Tempest,' and Marina and her mother Thaisa enjoy many experiences in common with Perdita and Hermione in the 'Winter's Tale.' The prologues, which were not by Shakespeare, were spoken by an actor representing the mediæval poet John Gower, who in the fourteenth century had versified Pericles's story in his 'Confessio Amantis' under the title of 'Apollonius of Tyre.' It is also found in a prose translation (from the French), which was printed in Lawrence Twyne's 'Patterne of Painfull Adventures' in 1576, and again in 1607. After the play was produced George Wilkins, one of the alleged coadjutors, based on it a novel called 'The Painful Adventures of Pericles, Prynce of Tyre, being the True history of the Play of Pericles as it was lately presented by the worthy and ancient Poet, John Gower' (1608). The play was issued as by William Shakespeare in a mangled form in 1608, and again in 1611, 1619, 1630, and 1635. It was not included in Shakespeare's collected works till 1664.

In May 1608 Edward Blount entered in the

'Stationers' Registers,' by the authority of Sir George Buc, the licenser of plays, a 'booke called "Anthony and Cleopatra."' No copy of this date is known, and once again the company probably hindered the publication. The play was first printed in the folio of 1623. The source of the tragedy is the life of Antonius in North's 'Plutarch.' Shakespeare closely followed the historical narrative, and assimilated not merely its temper, but, in the first three acts, much of its phraseology. A few short scenes are original, but there is no detail in such a passage, for example, as Enobarbus's gorgeous description of the pageant of Cleopatra's voyage up the Cydnus to meet Antony (II. ii. 194 seq.), which is not to be matched in Plutarch. In the fourth and fifth acts Shakespeare's method changes and he expands his material with magnificent freedom.[1] The whole theme is in his hands instinct with a dramatic grandeur which lifts into sublimity even Cleopatra's moral worthlessness and Antony's criminal infatuation. The terse and caustic comments which Antony's level-headed friend Enobarbus, in the *rôle* of chorus, passes on the action accentuates its significance. Into the smallest as into the greatest personages Shakespeare breathed all his vitalising fire. The 'happy valiancy' of the style, too, — to use Coleridge's admirable phrase, — sets the tragedy very near the zenith of Shakespeare's achievement, and while differentiating it

---

[1] Mr. George Wyndham, in his introduction to his edition of North's *Plutarch*, i. pp. xciii.–c., gives an excellent criticism of the relations of Shakespeare's play to Plutarch's life of Antonius.

from ' Macbeth,' ' Othello,' and ' Lear ' renders it a
very formidable rival.

'Coriolanus' (first printed from a singularly bad
text in 1623) similarly owes its origin to the biography

'Corio-   of the hero in North's 'Plutarch,' although
lanus.'   Shakespeare may have first met the story in
Painter's ' Palace of Pleasure ' (No. iv.). He again
adhered to the text of Plutarch with the utmost
literalness, and at times — even in the great crises of the
action — repeated North's translation word for word.[1]
But the humorous scenes are wholly of Shakespeare's
invention, and the course of the narrative was at times
slightly changed for purposes of dramatic effect. The
metrical characteristics prove the play to have been
written about the same period, as ' Antony and Cleo-

---

[1] See the whole of Coriolanus's great speech on offering his services
to Aufidius, the Volscian general, IV. v. 71–107 :

> My name is Caius Marcius, who hath done
> To thee particularly and to all the Volsces,
> Great hurt and mischief; thereto witness may
> My surname, Coriolanus . . . to do thee service.

North's translation of *Plutarch* gives in almost the same terms Coriolanus's speech on the occasion. It opens: ' I am Caius Martius, who
hath done to thyself particularly, and to all the Volsces generally,
great hurt and mischief, which I cannot deny for my surname of
Coriolanus that I bear.' Similarly Volumnia's stirring appeal to her son
and her son's proffer of submission, in act v. sc. iii. 94–193, reproduce
with equal literalness North's rendering of *Plutarch*. ' If we held our
peace, my son,' Volumnia begins in North, ' the state of our raiment
would easily betray to thee what life we have led at home since thy
exile and abode abroad; but think now with thyself,' and so on. The
first sentence of Shakespeare's speech runs:

> Should we be silent and not speak, our raiment
> And state of bodies would bewray what life
> We have led since thy exile. Think with thyself . . .

patra,' probably in 1609. In its austere temper it contrasts at all points with its predecessor. The courageous self-reliance of Coriolanus's mother, Volumnia, is severely contrasted with the submissive gentleness of Virgilia, Coriolanus's wife. The hero falls a victim to no sensual flaw, but to unchecked pride of caste, and there is a searching irony in the emphasis laid on the ignoble temper of the rabble, who procure his overthrow. By way of foil, the speeches of Menenius give dignified expression to the maturest political wisdom. The dramatic interest throughout is as single and as unflaggingly sustained as in 'Othello.'

XV

THE LATEST PLAYS

In 'Cymbeline,' 'The Winter's Tale,' and 'The Tempest,' the three latest plays that came from his unaided pen, Shakespeare dealt with roman-

The latest plays.

tic themes which all end happily, but he instilled into them a pathos which sets them in a category of their own apart alike from comedy and tragedy. The placidity of tone conspicuous in these three plays (none of which was published in his life-time) has been often contrasted with the storm and stress of the great tragedies that preceded them. But the commonly accepted theory that traces in this change of tone a corresponding development in the author's own emotions ignores the objectivity of Shake-speare's dramatic work. All phases of feeling lay within the scope of his intuition, and the successive order in which he approached them bore no expli-cable relation to substantive incident in his private life or experience. In middle life, his temperament, like that of other men, acquired a larger measure of gravity and his thought took a profounder cast than characterised it in youth. The highest topics of tragedy were naturally more congenial to him, and

were certain of a surer handling when he was nearing his fortieth birthday than at an earlier age. The
serenity of meditative romance was more in harmony
with the fifth decade of his years than with the
second or third. But no more direct or definite
connection can be discerned between the progressive stages of his work and the progressive stages
of his life. To seek in his biography for a chain of
events which should be calculated to stir in his own
soul all or any of the tempestuous passions that ani-
mate his greatest plays is to under-estimate and to
misapprehend the resistless might of his creative
genius.

In 'Cymbeline' Shakespeare freely adapted a fragment of British history taken from Holinshed, inter-
'Cymbe-   weaving with it a story from Boccaccio's
line.'   'Decameron' (day 2, novel ix.). Ginevra,
whose falsely suspected chastity is the theme of the
Italian novel, corresponds to Shakespeare's Imogen.
Her story is also told in the tract called 'Westward
for Smelts,' which had already been laid under contribution by Shakespeare in the 'Merry Wives.'[1] The
by-plot of the banishment of the lord, Belarius,
who in revenge for his expatriation kidnapped the
king's young sons and brought them up with him
in the recesses of the mountains, is Shakespeare's
invention. Although most of the scenes are laid
in Britain in the first century before the Christian era, there is no pretence of historical vraisem-
blance. With an almost ludicrous inappropriateness

[1] See p. 172 and note 2.

the British king's courtiers make merry with technical terms peculiar to Calvinistic theology, like ' grace ' and 'election.'[1] The action, which, owing to the combination of three threads of narrative, is exceptionally varied and intricate, wholly belongs to the region of romance. On Imogen, who is the central figure of the play, Shakespeare lavished all the fascination of his genius. She is the crown and flower of his conception of tender and artless womanhood. Her husband Posthumus, her rejected lover Cloten, her would-be seducer Iachimo, are contrasted with her and with each other with consummate ingenuity. The mountainous retreat in which Belarius and his fascinating boy-companions play their part has points of resemblance to the Forest of Arden in ' As You Like It ' ; but life throughout ' Cymbeline ' is grimly earnest, and the mountains nurture little of the contemplative quiet which characterises existence in the Forest of Arden. The play contains the splendid lyric ' Fear no more the heat of the sun ' (IV. ii. 258 seq.). The 'pitiful mummery' of the vision of Posthumus (v. iv. lines 30 seq.) must have been supplied by another hand. Dr. Forman, the astrologer who kept notes of some of his experiences as a playgoer, saw ' Cymbeline ' acted either in 1610 or 1611.

' A Winter's Tale ' was seen by Dr. Forman at the Globe on May 15, 1611, and it seems to have been

---

[1] In I. i. 136–7 Imogen is described as ' past grace ' in the theological sense. In I. ii. 30–1 the Second Lord remarks : 'If it be a sin to make a true election, she is damned.'

acted at Court on November 5 following.[1] It is based
'A Win-   upon Greene's popular romance which was
ter's Tale.' called ' Pandosto ' in the first edition of 1588,
and in numerous later editions, but was ultimately in
1648 re-christened ' Dorastus and Fawnia.'   Shakespeare followed Greene, his early foe, in allotting a
seashore to Bohemia — an error over which Ben Jonson
and many later critics have made merry.[2] A few lines
were obviously drawn from that story of Boccaccio
with which Shakespeare had dealt just before in
' Cymbeline.'[3] But Shakespeare created the high-
spirited Paulina and the thievish pedlar Autolycus,
whose seductive roguery has become proverbial, and
he invented the reconciliation of Leontes, the irration-
ally jealous husband, with Hermione, his wife, whose
dignified resignation and forbearance lend the story
its intense pathos. In the boy Mamilius, the poet
depicted childhood in its most attractive guise, while
the courtship of Florizel and Perdita is the perfection
of gentle romance. The freshness of the pastoral

---

[1] See p. 255 note 1.   Camillo's reflections on the ruin that attends
those who ' struck anointed kings ' have been regarded, not quite conclusively, as specially designed to gratify James I (i. ii. 358 seq.).

[2] Conversations with Drummond, p. 16.

[3] In Winter's Tale (iv. iv. 760 seq.) Autolycus threatens that
the clown's son ' shall be flayed alive; then 'nointed over with honey,
set on the head of a wasp's nest,' etc.   In Boccaccio's story the villain
Ambrogiuolo (Shakespeare's Iachimo), after ' being bounden to the
stake and anointed with honey,' was ' to his exceeding torment not
only slain but devoured of the flies and wasps and gadflies wherewith
that country abounded ' (cf: Decameron, translated by John Payne,
1893, i. 164).

incident surpasses that of all Shakespeare's presentations of country life.

✓ 'The Tempest' was probably the latest drama that Shakespeare completed. In the summer of 1609 a fleet bound for Virginia, under the command of Sir George Somers, was overtaken by a storm off the West Indies, and the admiral's ship, the 'Sea-Venture,' was driven on the coast of the hitherto unknown Bermuda Isles. There they remained ten months, pleasurably impressed by the mild beauty of the climate, but sorely tried by the hogs which overran the island and by mysterious noises which led them to imagine that spirits and devils had made the island their home. Somers and his men were given up for lost, but they escaped from Bermuda in two boats of cedar to Virginia in May 1610, and the news of their adventures and of their safety was carried to England by some of the seamen in September 1610. The sailors' arrival created vast public excitement in London. At least five accounts were soon published of the shipwreck and of the mysterious island, previously uninhabited by man, which had proved the salvation of the expedition. 'A Discovery of the Bermudas, otherwise called the Ile of Divels,' written by Sylvester Jourdain or Jourdan, one of the survivors, appeared as early as October. A second pamphlet describing the disaster was issued by the Council of the Virginia Company in December, and a third by one of the leaders of the expedition, Sir Thomas Gates. Shakespeare, who mentions the 'still vexed Bermoothes' (i. i. 229), incorporated

'Tempest.'

in 'The Tempest' many hints from Jourdain, Gates, and the other pamphleteers. The references to the gentle climate of the island on which Prospero is cast away, and to the spirits and devils that infested it, seem to render its identification with the newly discovered Bermudas unquestionable. But Shakespeare incorporated the result of study of other books of travel. The name of the god Setebos whom Caliban worships is drawn from Eden's translation of Magellan's 'Voyage to the South Pole' (in the 'Historie of Travell,' 1577), where the giants of Patagonia are described as worshipping a 'great devil they call Setebos.' No source for the complete plot has been discovered, but the German writer, Jacob Ayrer, who died in 1605, dramatised a somewhat similar story in 'Die schöne Sidea,' where the adventures of Prospero, Ferdinand, Ariel, and Miranda are roughly anticipated.[1] English actors were performing at Nuremberg, where Ayrer lived, in 1604 and 1606, and may have brought reports of the piece to Shakespeare. Or perhaps both English and German plays had a common origin in some novel that has not yet been traced. Gonzalo's description of an ideal commonwealth (II. i. 147 seq.) is derived from Florio's translation of Montaigne's essays (1603), while into Prospero's great speech renouncing his practice of magical art (v. i. 33–57) Shakespeare wrought reminiscences of Golding's translation of Medea's invocation in Ovid's 'Metamorphoses'

---

[1] Printed in Cohn's *Shakespeare in Germany.*

(vii. 197–206).[1]   Golding's rendering of Ovid had been one of Shakespeare's best-loved books in youth.

A highly ingenious theory, first suggested by Tieck, represents 'The Tempest' (which, excepting 'Macbeth' and the 'Two Gentlemen,' is the shortest of Shakespeare's plays) as a masque written to celebrate the marriage of Princess Elizabeth (like Miranda, an island-princess) with the Elector Frederick.   This marriage took place on February 14, 1612–13, and 'The Tempest' formed one of a series of nineteen plays which were performed at the nuptial festivities in May 1613.   But none of the other plays produced seem to have been new; they were all apparently chosen because they were established favourites at Court and on the public stage, and neither in subject-matter or language bore obviously specific relation to the joyous occasion.   But 1613 is, in fact, on more substantial ground far too late a date to which to assign the composition of 'The Tempest.'   According to information which was accessible to Malone, the play had 'a being and a name' in the autumn of 1611, and was no doubt written some months before.[2]

---

[1] Golding's translation of Ovid's *Metamorphoses*, edit. 1612, p. 82b. The passage begins :

> Ye ayres and windes, ye elves of hills, ye brookes and woods alone.

[2] *Variorum Shakespeare*, 1821, XV. 423.   In the early weeks of 1611 Shakespeare's company presented no less than fifteen plays at Court. Payment of 150l. was made to the actors for their services on February 12, 1610–11.   The council's warrant is extant in the *Bodleian Library* MS. Rawl. A 204 (f. 305).   The plays performed were not specified by name, but some by Shakespeare were beyond doubt amongst them, and possibly 'The Tempest.'   A forged page which was inserted in a detached

The plot, which revolves about the forcible expulsion
of a ruler from his dominions, and his daughter's
wooing by the son of the usurper's chief ally, is,
moreover, hardly one that a shrewd playwright would
deliberately choose as the setting of an official epitha-
lamium in honour of the daughter of a monarch so
sensitive about his title to the crown as James I.[1]

In the theatre and at court the early representations of 'The Tempest' evoked unmeasured applause.
The success owed something to the beautiful lyrics
which were dispersed through the play and had been
set to music by Robert Johnson, a lutenist in high
repute.[2]

Like its predecessor, 'A Winter's Tale,' 'The
Tempest' long maintained its first popularity in the

account-book of the Master of the Court-Revels for the years 1611
and 1612 at the Public Record Office, and was printed as genuine
in Peter Cunningham's *Extracts from the Revels' Accounts*, p. 210,
supplies among other entries two to the effect that 'The Tempest' was
performed at Whitehall at Hallowmas (*i.e.* November 1) 1611,
and that 'A Winter's Tale' followed four days later, on November 5.
Though these entries are fictitious, the information they offer may be
true. Malone doubtless based his positive statement respecting the
date of the composition of 'The Tempest' in 1611 on memoranda made
from papers then accessible at the Audit Office, but now, since the
removal of those archives to the Public Record Office, mislaid. All
the forgeries introduced into the Revels' accounts are well considered
and show expert knowledge (see p. 235, note 1). The forger of the
1612 entries probably worked either on the published statement of
Malone, or on fuller memoranda left by him among his voluminous
manuscripts.

[1] Cf. *Universal Review*, April 1889, article by Dr. Richard Garnett.

[2] Harmonised scores of Johnson's airs for the songs 'Full Fathom
Five' and 'Where the Bee Sucks' are preserved in Wilson's 'Cheerful
Ayres and Ballads set for Three Voices,' 1660.

theatre, and the vogue of the two pieces drew a passing sneer from Ben Jonson. In the Induction to his
'Bartholomew Fair,' first acted in 1614, he wrote:
'If there be never a servant-monster in the Fair, who
can help it he [*i.e.* the author] says? nor a nest of
Antics. He is loth to make nature afraid in his
plays like those that beget Tales, Tempests, and such
like Drolleries.' The 'servant-monster' was an obvious allusion to Caliban, and 'the nest of Antics'
was a glance at the satyrs who figure in the sheep-
shearing feast in 'A Winter's Tale.'

Nowhere did Shakespeare give rein to his
imagination with more imposing effect than in 'The
Tempest.' As in 'Midsummer Night's
Dream,' magical or supernatural agencies
are the mainsprings of the plot. But the
tone is marked at all points by a solemnity and pro-
fundity of thought and sentiment which are lacking
in the early comedy. The serious atmosphere has
led critics, without much reason, to detect in the
scheme of 'The Tempest' something more than
the irresponsible play of poetic fancy. Many of the
characters have been represented as the outcome of
speculation respecting the least soluble problems of
human existence. Little reliance should be placed
on such interpretations. The creation of Miranda
is the apotheosis in literature of tender, ingenuous
girlhood unsophisticated by social intercourse, but
Shakespeare had already sketched the outlines of
the portrait in 'Marina' and 'Perdita,' the youthful
heroines respectively of 'Pericles' and 'A Winter's

*Fanciful interpreta-
tions of
'The Tem-
pest.'*

Tale,' and these two characters were directly developed from romantic stories of girl-princesses, cast by misfortune on the mercies of nature, to which Shakespeare had recourse for the plots of the two plays. It is by accident, and not by design, that in Ariel appear to be discernible the capabilities of human intellect when detached from physical attributes. Ariel belongs to the same world as Puck, although he is delineated in the severer colours that were habitual to Shakespeare's fully developed art. Caliban — Ariel's antithesis — did not owe his existence to any conscious endeavour on Shakespeare's part to typify human nature before the evolution of moral sentiment.[1] Caliban is an imaginary portrait, conceived with matchless vigour and vividness of the aboriginal savage of the New World, descriptions of whom abounded in contemporary travellers' speech and writings, and universally excited the liveliest curiosity.[2] In Prospero, the guiding providence of the romance, who resigns his magic power in the closing scene, traces have been sought of the lineaments of the dramatist himself, who in this play probably bade farewell to the enchanted work of his life. Prospero is in the story a scholar-prince of rare intellectual attainments, whose engrossing study of the mysteries

[1] Cf. Browning, *Caliban upon Setebos;* Daniel Wilson, *Caliban, or the Missing Link* (1873); and Renan, *Caliban* (1878), a drama continuing Shakespeare's play.

[2] When Shakespeare wrote *Troilus and Cressida* he had formed some conception of a character of the Caliban type. Thersites says of Ajax (III. iii. 264), ' He's grown a very land-fish, languageless, a monster.'

s

of science has given him command of the forces of nature. His magnanimous renunciation of his magical faculty as soon as by its exercise he has restored his shattered fortunes is in perfect accord with the general conception of his just and philosophical temper. Any other justification of his final act is superfluous.

While there is every indication that in 1611 Shakespeare abandoned dramatic composition, there seems Unfinished little doubt that he left with the manager of plays. his company unfinished drafts of more than one play which others were summoned at a later date to complete. His place at the head of the active dramatists was at once filled by John Fletcher, and Fletcher, with some aid possibly from his friend Philip Massinger, undertook the working up of Shakespeare's unfinished sketches. On September 9, 1653, the publisher Humphrey Moseley obtained a license for the publication of a play which he described as 'History of Cardenio, by Fletcher and Shakespeare.' This was probably identical with The lost the lost play, 'Cardenno,' or 'Cardenna,' play of which was twice acted at Court by Shake- 'Cardenio.' speare's company in 1613 — in May during the Princess Elizabeth's marriage festivities, and on June 8 before the duke of Savoy's ambassador.[1] Moseley, whose description may have been fraudulent,[2]

---

[1] Treasurer's accounts in Rawl. MS., A 239, leaf 47 (in the Bodleian), printed in New Shakspere Society's *Transactions*, 1895–6, part ii. p. 419.

[2] *The Merry Devill of Edmonton*, a comedy which was first published in 1608, was also re-entered by Moseley for publication on September 9, 1653, as the work of Shakespeare (see p. 181, *supra*).

failed to publish the piece, and nothing is otherwise
known of it with certainty; but it was no doubt a
dramatic version of the adventures of the lovelorn
Cardenio which are related in the first part of 'Don
Quixote' (ch. xxiii.–xxxvii.). Cervantes's amorous
story, which first appeared in English in Thomas
Shelton's translation in 1612, offers much incident in
Fletcher's vein. When Lewis Theobald, the Shakespearean critic, brought out his 'Double Falshood,
or the Distrest Lovers,' in 1727, he mysteriously
represented that the play was based on an unfinished
and unpublished draft of a play by Shakespeare.
The story of Theobald's piece is the story of Cardenio, although the characters are renamed. There
is nothing in the play as published by Theobald
to suggest Shakespeare's hand,[1] but Theobald doubtless took advantage of a tradition that Shakespeare
and Fletcher had combined to dramatise the Cer-
vantic theme.

Two other pieces, 'The Two Noble Kinsmen' and
'Henry VIII,' which are attributed to a similar partner-
ship, survive.[2] 'The Two Noble Kinsmen' was first
'Two printed in 1634, and was written, accord-
Noble ing to the title-page, 'by the memorable
Kinsmen.' worthies of their time, Mr. John Fletcher

---

[1] Dyce thought he detected traces of Shirley's workmanship, but it
was possibly Theobald's unaided invention.

[2] The 1634 quarto of the play was carefully edited for the New
Shakspere Society by Mr. Harold Littledale in 1876. See also
Spalding, *Shakespeare's Authorship of 'Two Noble Kinsmen,'* 1833,
reprinted by New Shakspere Society, 1876; Spalding in *Edinburgh
Review*, 1847; *Transactions*, New Shakspere Society, 1874.

and Mr William Shakespeare, gentlemen.' It was included in the folio of Beaumont and Fletcher of 1679. On grounds alike of æsthetic criticism and metrical tests, a substantial portion of the play was assigned to Shakespeare by Charles Lamb, Coleridge, and Dyce. The last included it in his edition of Shakespeare. Coleridge detected Shakespeare's hand in act I., act II. sc. i., and act III. sc. i. and ii. In addition to those scenes, act IV. sc. iii. and act V. (except sc. ii.) were subsequently placed to his credit. Some recent critics assign much of the alleged Shakespearean work to Massinger, and they narrow Shakespeare's contribution to the first scene (with the opening song, 'Roses their sharp spines being gone') and act V. sc. i. and iv.[1] An exact partition is impossible, but frequent signs of Shakespeare's workmanship are unmistakable. All the passages for which Shakespeare can on any showing be held responsible develop the main plot, which is drawn from Chaucer's 'Knight's Tale' of Palamon and Arcite, and seems to have been twice dramatised previously. A lost play, 'Palæmon and Arcyte,' by Richard Edwardes, was acted at Court in 1566, and a second piece, called 'Palamon and Arsett' (also lost), was purchased by Henslowe in 1594. The non-Shakespearean residue of 'The Two Noble Kinsmen' is disfigured by indecency and triviality, and is of no literary value.

A like problem is presented by 'Henry VIII.'

[1] Cf. Mr. Robert Boyle in *Transactions* of the New Shakspere Society, 1882.

The play was nearly associated with the final scene in the history of that theatre which was identified with the triumphs of Shakespeare's career. 'Henry VIII' was in course of performance at the Globe Theatre on June 29, 1613, when the firing of some cannon incidental to the performance set fire to the playhouse, which was burned down. The theatre 'Henry VIII.' was rebuilt next year, but the new fabric never acquired the fame of the old. Sir Henry Wotton, describing the disaster on July 2, entitled the piece that was in process of representation at the time as 'All is True representing some principal pieces in the Reign of Henry VIII.'[1] The

---

[1] *Reliquiæ Wottonianæ*, 1675, pp. 425-6. Wotton adds 'that the piece was set forth with many extraordinary circumstances of Pomp and Majesty, even to the matting of the Stage; the Knights of the Order, with their Georges and Garters, the Guards with their embroidered Coats, and the like: sufficient in truth within a while to make greatness very familiar, if not ridiculous. Now King *Henry* making a Masque at the Cardinal *Wolsey's* House, and certain Canons being shot off at his entry, some of the paper or other stuff wherewith one of them was stopped, did light on the Thatch, where being thought at first but an idle smoak, and their eyes more attentive to the show, it kindled inwardly, and ran round like a train, consuming within less than an hour the whole House to the very grounds. This was the fatal period of that vertuous fabrique; wherein yet nothing did perish, but wood and straw and a few forsaken cloaks; only one man had his breeches set on fire, that would perhaps have broyled him, if he had not by the benefit of a provident wit put it out with bottle[d] ale.' John Chamberlain writing to Sir Ralph Winwood on July 8, 1613, briefly mentions that the theatre was burnt to the ground in less than two hours, owing to the accidental ignition of the thatch roof through the firing of cannon 'to be used in the play.' The audience escaped unhurt though they had 'but two narrow doors to get out' (Winwood's *Memorials*, iii. p. 469). A similar account was sent by the Rev. Thomas Lorkin to Sir Thomas Puckering, Bart., from London, June 30, 1613. 'The fire broke out,' Lorkin writes, 'no longer

play of 'Henry VIII' that is commonly allotted to
Shakespeare is loosely constructed, and the last act ill
coheres with its predecessors. The whole resembles an
'historical masque.' It was first printed in the folio of
Shakespeare's works in 1623, but shows traces of more
hands than one. The three chief characters — the king,
Queen Katharine of Arragon, and Cardinal Wolsey
— bear clear marks of Shakespeare's best workmanship; but only act I. sc. i., act II. sc. iii. and iv.
(Katharine's trial), act III. sc. ii. (except ll. 204–460),
act V. sc. i., can on either æsthetic or metrical grounds
be confidently assigned to him. These portions may,
according to their metrical characteristics, be dated,
like the 'Winter's Tale,' about 1611. There are good
grounds for assigning nearly all the remaining thirteen
scenes to the pen of Fletcher, with occasional aid from
Massinger. Wolsey's familiar farewell to Cromwell
(act III. sc. ii. ll. 204–460) is the only passage the
authorship of which excites really grave embarrass-
ment. It recalls at every point the style of Fletcher,
and nowhere that of Shakespeare. But the Fletcherian
style, as it is here displayed, is invested with a greatness that is not matched elsewhere in Fletcher's work.
That Fletcher should have exhibited such faculty once

since than yesterday, while Burbage's company were acting at the Globe
the play of *Henry VIII'* (*Court and Times of James I*, 1848, vol. i.
p. 253). A contemporary sonnet on 'the pittifull burning of the Globe
playhouse in London,' first printed by Haslewood ' from an old manuscript volume of poems' in the *Gentleman's Magazine* for 1816, was
again printed by Halliwell-Phillipps (i. pp. 310–11) from an authentic
manuscript in the library of Sir Matthew Wilson, Bart., of Eshton Hall,
Yorkshire.

and once only is barely credible, and we are driven to the alternative conclusion that the noble valediction was by Shakespeare, who in it gave proof of his versatility by echoing in a glorified key the habitual strain of Fletcher, his colleague and virtual successor. James Spedding's theory that Fletcher hastily completed Shakespeare's unfinished draft for the special purpose of enabling the company to celebrate the marriage of Princess Elizabeth and the Elector Palatine, which took place on February 14, 1612–13, seems fanciful. During May 1613, according to an extant list, nineteen plays were produced at Court in honour of the event, but 'Henry VIII' is not among them.[1] The conjecture that Massinger and Fletcher alone collaborated in 'Henry VIII' (to the exclusion of Shakespeare altogether) does not deserve serious consideration.[2]

[1] *Bodl. MS.* Rawl. A 239; cf. Spedding in *Gentleman's Magazine*, 1850, reprinted in New Shakspere Society's *Transactions*, 1874.
[2] Cf. Mr. Robert Boyle in New Shakspere Society's *Transactions*, 1884.

XVI

THE CLOSE OF LIFE

THE concluding years of Shakespeare's life (1611–16) were mainly passed at Stratford. It is probable that in 1611 he disposed of his shares in the Globe and Blackfriars theatres. He owned none at the date of his death. But until 1614 he paid frequent visits to London, where friends in sympathy with his work were alone to be found. His plays continued to form the staple of Court performances. In May 1613, during the Princess Elizabeth's marriage festivities, Heming, Shakespeare's former colleague, produced at Whitehall no less than seven of his plays, viz. 'Much Ado,' 'Tempest,' 'Winter's Tale,' 'Sir John Falstaff' (*i.e.* 'Merry Wives'), 'Othello,' 'Julius Cæsar,' and 'Hotspur' (doubtless '1 Henry IV ').[1] Of his actor-friends, one of the chief, Augustine Phillips, had died in 1605, leaving by will ' to my fellowe, William Shakespeare, a thirty-shillings piece of gold.' With Burbage, Heming, and Condell his relations remained close to the end. Burbage, according to a poetic elegy, made his reputation by creating the leading parts in Shakespeare's greatest tragedies. Hamlet,

Plays at Court in 1613.

Actor-friends.

1 Halliwell-Phillipps, ii. 87.

Othello, and Lear were *rôles* in which he gained especial renown. But Burbage and Shakespeare were popularly credited with co-operation in less solemn enterprises. They were reputed to be companions in many sportive adventures. The sole anecdote of Shakespeare that is positively known to have been recorded in his lifetime relates that Burbage, when playing Richard III, agreed with a lady in the audience to visit her after the perform-ance; Shakespeare, overhearing the conversation, anticipated the actor's visit, and met Burbage on his arrival with the quip that 'William the Conqueror was before Richard the Third.'[1]

Such gossip possibly deserves little more accept-ance than the later story, in the same key, which credits Shakespeare with the paternity of Sir William D'Avenant. The latter was baptised at Oxford on March 3, 1605, as the son of John D'Avenant, the landlord of the Crown Inn, where Shakespeare lodged in his journeys to and from Stratford. The story of Shakespeare's parental relation to D'Avenant was long current in Oxford, and was at times com-placently accepted by the reputed son. Shakespeare is known to have been a welcome guest at John D'Avenant's house, and another son, Robert, boasted of the kindly notice which the poet took of him as a child.[2] It is safer to adopt the less compro-mising version which makes Shakespeare the god-

[1] Manningham, *Diary*, March 13, 1601, Camd. Soc. p. 39.
[2] Cf. Aubrey, *Lives;* Halliwell-Phillipps, ii. 43; and art. Sir William D'Avenant, in the *Dictionary of National Biography*.

father of the boy William instead of his father. But the antiquity and persistence of the scandal belie the assumption that Shakespeare was known to his contemporaries as a man of scrupulous virtue. Ben Jonson and Drayton — the latter a Warwickshire man — seem to have been Shakespeare's closest literary friends in his latest years.

At Stratford, in the words of Nicholas Rowe, 'the latter part of Shakespeare's life was spent, as all men of good sense will wish theirs may be, in ease, retirement, and the conversation of his friends.' As a resident in the town, he took a full share of social and civic responsibilities. On October 16, 1608, he stood chief godfather to William, son of Henry Walker, a mercer and alderman. On September 11, 1611, when he had finally settled in New Place, his name appeared in the margin of a folio page of donors (including all the principal inhabitants of Stratford) to a fund that was raised 'towards the charge of prosecuting the bill in Parliament for the better repair of the highways.'

Final settlement at Stratford.

Meanwhile his own domestic affairs engaged some of his attention. Of his two surviving children — both daughters — the eldest, Susannah, had married, on June 5, 1607, John Hall (1575–1635), a rising physician of puritan leanings, and in the following February there was born the poet's only granddaughter, Elizabeth Hall. On September 9, 1608, the poet's mother was buried in the parish church, and on February 4, 1613, his third brother Richard. On July 15, 1613, Mrs. Hall preferred,

Domestic affairs.

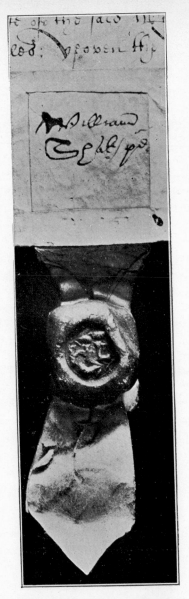

SHAKESPEARE'S AUTOGRAPH SIGNATURE APPENDED TO
THE PURCHASE-DEED OF A HOUSE IN BLACKFRIARS
ON MARCH 10, 1612-13.

Reproduced from the original document now preserved in the Guildhall
Library, London.

with her father's assistance, a charge of slander against one Lane in the ecclesiasical court at Worcester; the defendant, who had apparently charged the lady with illicit relations with one Ralph Smith, did not appear, and was excommunicated.

In the same year (1613), when on a short visit to London, he invested a small sum of money in a new
Purchase of a house in Black-friars. property. This was his last investment in real estate. He then purchased a house, the ground-floor of which was a haberdasher's shop, with a yard attached. It was situated within six hundred feet of the Blackfriars Theatre — on the west side of St. Andrew's Hill, formerly termed Puddle Hill or Puddle Dock Hill, in the near neighbourhood of what is now known as Ireland Yard. The former owner, Henry Walker, a musician, had bought the property for 100*l.* in 1604. Shakespeare in 1613 agreed to pay him 140*l.* The deeds of conveyance bear the date of March 10 in that year.[1] Next day, on March 11, Shakespeare executed another deed (now in the British Museum) which stipulated that 60*l.* of the purchase-money was to remain on mortgage until the following Michaelmas. The money was unpaid at Shakespeare's death. In both purchase-deed and mortgage-deed Shakespeare's signature was witnessed by, among others, Henry Lawrence, 'servant' or clerk to Robert Andrewes, the

[1] The indenture prepared for the purchaser is in the Halliwell-Phillipps collection, which was sold to Mr. Marsden J. Perry of Providence, Rhode Island, U. S. A., in January 1897. That held by the vendor is in the Guildhall Library.

scrivener who drew the deeds, and Lawrence's seal, bearing his initials ' H. L.,' was stamped in each case on the parchment tag across the head of which Shakespeare wrote his name. In all three documents — the two indentures and the mortgage-deed — Shakespeare is described as ' of Stratford-on-Avon, in the Countie of Warwick, Gentleman.' There is no reason to suppose that he acquired the house for his own residence. He at once leased the property to John Robinson, already a resident in the neighbourhood.

With puritans and puritanism Shakespeare was not in sympathy,[1] and he could hardly have viewed with unvarying composure the steady progress that puritanism was making among his fellow-townsmen. Nevertheless a preacher, doubtless of puritan proclivities, was entertained at Shakespeare's residence, New Place, after delivering a sermon in the spring of 1614. The incident might serve to illustrate Shakespeare's characteristic placability, but his son-in-law

---

[1] Shakespeare's references to puritans in the plays of his middle and late life are so uniformly discourteous that they must be judged to reflect his personal feeling. The discussion between Maria and Sir Andrew Aguecheek regarding Malvolio's character in *Twelfth Night* (II. iii. 153 seq.) runs :

> MARIA. Marry, sir, sometimes he is a kind of puritan.
> SIR ANDREW. O! if I thought that, I'd beat him like a dog.
> SIR TOBY. What, for being a puritan ? thy exquisite reason, dear knight.
> SIR ANDREW. I have no exquisite reason for 't, but I have reason good enough.

In *Winter's Tale* (IV. iii. 46) the Clown, after making contemptuous references to the character of the shearers, remarks that there is ' but one puritan amongst them, and he sings psalms to hornpipes.' Cf. the allusions to ' grace ' and ' election ' in *Cymbeline*, p. 250, note 1.

SHAKESPEARE'S AUTOGRAPH SIGNATURE APPENDED TO
A DEED MORTGAGING HIS HOUSE IN BLACKFRIARS
ON MARCH 11, 1612–13.

Reproduced from the original document now preserved in the British
Museum.

Hall, who avowed sympathy with puritanism, was probably in the main responsible for the civility.[1]   In July John Combe, a rich inhabitant of Stratford, died and left 5*l*. to Shakespeare.   The legend that Shakespeare alienated him by composing some doggerel on his practice of lending money at ten or twelve per cent. seems apocryphal, although it is quoted by Aubrey and accepted by Rowe.[2]   Combe's death involved Shakespeare more conspicuously than before in civic affairs. Combe's heir William no sooner succeeded to his father's lands than he, with a neighbouring owner,

[1] The town council of Stratford-on-Avon, whose meeting-chamber almost overlooked Shakespeare's residence of New Place, gave curious proof of their puritanic suspicion of the drama on February 7, 1612, when they passed a resolution that plays were unlawful and 'the sufferance of them against the orders heretofore made and against the example of other well-governed cities and boroughs,' and the council was therefore 'content,' the resolution ran, that 'the penalty of x*s*. imposed [on players heretofore] be x*li*. henceforward.' Ten years later the King's players were bribed by the council to leave the city without playing (see the present writer's *Stratford-on-Avon*, p. 270).

[2] The lines as quoted by Aubrey (*Lives*, ed. Clark, ii. 226) run:

> Ten-in-the-hundred the Devil allows,
> But Combe will have twelve he sweares and he vowes;
> If any man ask, who lies in this tomb?
> Oh! ho! quoth the Devil, 'tis my John-a-Combe.

Rowe's version opens somewhat differently:

> Ten-in-the-hundred lies here ingrav'd.
> 'Tis a hundred to ten, his soul is not sav'd.

The lines, in one form or another, seem to have been widely familiar in Shakespeare's lifetime, but were not ascribed to him.   The first two in Rowe's version were printed in the epigrams by H[enry] P[arrot], 1608, and again in Camden's *Remains*, 1614.   The whole first appeared in Richard Brathwaite's *Remains* in 1618 under the heading: 'Upon one John Combe of Stratford upon Aven, a notable Usurer, fastened upon a Tombe that he had Caused to be built in his Life Time.

Arthur Mannering, steward of Lord-Chancellor Ellesmere (who was ex-officio lord of the manor), attempted

to enclose the common fields, which belonged
to the Corporation of Stratford, about his
estate at Welcombe. The Corporation re-
solved to offer the scheme a stout resistance.
Shakespeare had a twofold interest in the matter by
virtue of his owning the freehold of 106 acres at Welcombe and Old Stratford, and as joint owner — now
with Thomas Greene, the town clerk — of the tithes of
Old Stratford, Welcombe, and Bishopton. His interest in his freeholds could not have been prejudicially
affected, but his interest in the tithes might be depreci-
ated by the proposed enclosure. Shakespeare consequently joined with his fellow-owner Greene in obtaining from Combe's agent Replingham in October 1614
a deed indemnifying both against any injury they
might suffer from the enclosure. But having thus
secured himself against all possible loss, Shakespeare
threw his influence into Combe's scale. In November
1614 he was on a last visit to London, and Greene,
whose official position as town clerk compelled him
to support the Corporation in defiance of his private
interests, visited him there to discuss the position of
affairs. On December 23, 1614, the Corporation in
formal meeting drew up a letter to Shakespeare im-
ploring him to aid them. Greene himself sent to the
dramatist 'a note of inconveniences [to the Corporation that] would happen by the enclosure.' But
although an ambiguous entry of a later date (September 1615) in the few extant pages of Greene's

ungrammatical diary has been unjustifiably tortured
into an expression of disgust on Shakespeare's part
at Combe's conduct,[1] it is plain that, in the spirit of
his agreement with Combe's agent, he continued to
lend Combe his countenance.   Happily Combe's
efforts failed, and the common lands remain un-
enclosed.

At the beginning of 1616 Shakespeare's health
was failing.   He directed Francis Collins, a solicitor of
Warwick, to draft his will, but, though it was prepared
for signature on January 25, it was for the time laid
aside.   On February 10, 1616, Shakespeare's younger
daughter, Judith, married, at Stratford parish church,
Thomas Quiney, four years her junior, a son of an old
friend of the poet.   The ceremony took place apparently without public asking of the banns and before
a license was procured.   The irregularity led to
the summons of the bride and bridegroom to the
ecclesiastical court at Worcester and the imposition
of a fine.   According to the testimony of John Ward,

---

[1] The clumsy entry runs: 'Sept. Mr. Shakespeare tellyng J.
Greene that I was not able to beare the encloseing of Welcombe.'
J. Greene is to be distinguished from Thomas Greene, the writer of the
diary.   The entry therefore implies that Shakespeare told J. Greene
that the writer of the diary, Thomas Greene, was not able to bear the
enclosure.   Those who represent Shakespeare as a champion of popular
rights have to read the 'I' in 'I was not able' as 'he.'   Were that
the correct reading, Shakespeare would be rightly credited with telling
J. Greene that he disliked the enclosure;   but palæographers only
recognise the reading 'I.'   Cf. *Shakespeare and the Enclosure of
Common Fields at Welcombe*, a facsimile of Greene's diary, now at
the Birthplace, Stratford, with a transcript by Mr. E. J. L. Scott, edited
by Dr. C. M. Ingleby, 1885.

the vicar, Shakespeare entertained at New Place his two friends, Michael Drayton and Ben Jonson, in this same spring of 1616, and ' had a merry meeting,' but 'itt seems drank too hard, for Shakespeare died of a feavour there contracted.' A popular local legend, which was not recorded till 1762,[1] credited Shakespeare with engaging at an earlier date in a prolonged and violent drinking bout at Bidford, a neighbouring village,[2] but his achievements as a hard drinker may be dismissed as unproven. The cause of his death is undetermined, but probably his illness seemed likely to take a fatal turn in March, when he revised and signed the will that had been drafted in the previous January. On Tuesday, April 23, he died at the age of fifty-two.[3]

Death.

On Thursday, April 25 (O.S.) the poet was buried inside Stratford Church, near the northern wall of the chancel, in which, as part-owner of the tithes, and consequently one of the lay-rectors, he had a right of interment. Hard by was the charnel-house, where bones dug up from the churchyard were deposited. Over the poet's grave were inscribed the lines :

Burial.

> Good friend, for Jesus' sake forbeare
> To dig the dust enclosed heare;
> Bleste be the man that spares these stones,
> And curst be he that moves my bones.

---

[1] *British Magazine*, June 1762.

[2] Cf. Malone, *Shakespeare*, 1821, ii. 500–2; Ireland, *Confessions*, 1805, p. 34; Green, *Legend of the Crab Tree*, 1857.

[3] The date is in the old style, and is equivalent to May 3 in the new; Cervantes, whose death is often described as simultaneous, died at Madrid ten days earlier — on April 13, in the old style, or April 23, 1616, in the new.

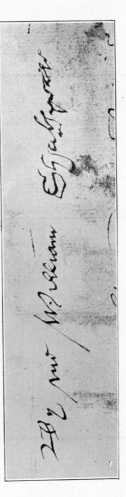

THREE AUTOGRAPH SIGNATURES SEVERALLY WRITTEN BY SHAKESPEARE ON
THE THREE SHEETS OF HIS WILL, ON MARCH 25, 1616.

Reproduced from the original document now at Somerset House, London.

According to one William Hall, who described a visit to Stratford in 1694,[1] these verses were penned by Shakespeare to suit 'the capacity of clerks and sextons, for the most part a very ignorant set of people.' Had this curse not threatened them, Hall proceeds, the sexton would not have hesitated in course of time to remove Shakespeare's dust to 'the bone-house.' As it was, the grave was made seventeen feet deep, and was never opened, even to receive his wife, although she expressed a desire to be buried with her husband.

Shakespeare's will, the first draft of which was drawn up before January 25, 1616, received many interlineations and erasures before it was signed in the ensuing March. Francis Collins, the solicitor of Warwick, and Thomas Russell, 'esquier,' of Stratford, were the overseers; it was proved by John Hall, the poet's son-in-law and joint-executor with Mrs. Hall, in London on June 22 following. The religious exordium is in conventional phraseology, and gives no clue to Shakespeare's personal religious opinions. What those opinions were, we have neither the means nor the warrant for discussing. But while it is possible to quote from the plays many contemptuous references to the puritans and their doctrines, we may dismiss as idle gossip Davies's irresponsible report that 'he dyed a papist.' The name of Shakespeare's wife was omitted from the original draft of the will, but by an interlineation

The will.

---

[1] Hall's letter was published as a quarto pamphlet at London in 1884, from the original, now in the Bodleian Library, Oxford.

T

in the final draft she received his second best bed with its furniture. No other bequest was made her.

Bequest to his wife. Several wills of the period have been discovered in which a bedstead or other article of household furniture formed part of a wife's inheritance, but none except Shakespeare's is forthcoming in which a bed forms the sole bequest. At the same time the precision with which Shakespeare's will accounts for and assigns to other legatees every known item of his property refutes the conjecture that he had set aside any portion of it under a previous settlement or jointure with a view to making independent provision for his wife. Her right to a widow's dower — i.e. to a third share for life in freehold estate — was not subject to testamentary disposition, but Shakespeare had taken steps to prevent her from benefiting — at any rate to the full extent — by that legal arrangement. He had barred her dower in the case of his latest purchase of freehold estate, viz., the house at Blackfriars.[1] Such pro-

---

[1] Mr. Charles Elton, Q.C., has been kind enough to give me a legal opinion on this point. He wrote to me on December 9, 1897: 'I have looked to the authorities with my friend Mr. Herbert Mackay, and there is no doubt that Shakespeare barred the dower.' Mr. Mackay's opinion is couched in the following terms: 'The conveyance of the Blackfriars estate to William Shakespeare in 1613 shows that the estate was conveyed to Shakespeare, Johnson, Jackson, and Hemming as joint tenants, and therefore the dower of Shakespeare's wife would be barred unless he were the survivor of the four bargainees.' That was a remote contingency, which did not arise, and Shakespeare always retained the power of making 'another settlement when the trustees were shrinking.' Thus the bar was for practical purposes perpetual, and disposes of Mr. Halliwell-Phillipps's assertion that

cedure is pretty conclusive proof that he had the intention of excluding her from the enjoyment of his possessions after his death. But, however plausible the theory that his relations with her were from first to last wanting in sympathy, it is improbable that either the slender mention of her in the will or the barring of her dower was designed by Shakespeare to make public his indifference or dislike. Local tradition subsequently credited her with a wish to be buried in his grave; and her epitaph proves that she inspired her daughters with genuine affection. Probably her ignorance of affairs and the infirmities of age (she was past sixty) combined to unfit her in the poet's eyes for the control of property, and, as an act of ordinary prudence, he committed her to the care of his elder daughter, who inherited, according to such information as is accessible, some of his own shrewdness, and had a capable adviser in her husband.

This elder daughter, Susannah Hall, was, according to the will, to become the mistress of New Place, and practically of all the poet's estate. She received (with remainder to her issue in strict entail) New Place, all the land, barns, and gardens at and near Stratford (except the tenement in Chapel Lane), and the house in Blackfriars, London, while she and her husband were appointed executors and residuary legatees, with full rights over nearly all the poet's household furniture and personal belong-

His heiress.

Shakespeare's wife was entitled to dower in one form or another from all his real estate. Cf. *Davidson on Conveyancing;* Littleton, sect. 45; *Coke upon Litt'eton,* ed. Hargrave, p. 379*b*, note 1.

ings.   To their only child and the testator's granddaughter, or 'niece,' Elizabeth Hall, was bequeathed
the poet's plate, with the exception of his broad silver
and gilt bowl, which was reserved for his younger
daughter, Judith. To his younger daughter he also left,
with the tenement in Chapel Lane (in remainder to the
elder daughter), 150*l.* in money, of which 100*l.*, her
marriage portion, was to be paid within a year, and
another 150*l.* to be paid to her if alive three years
after the date of the will.[1]   To the poet's sister, Joan
Hart, whose husband, William Hart, predeceased the
testator by only six days, he left, besides a contingent reversionary interest in Judith's pecuniary legacy, his wearing apparel, 20*l.* in money, a life interest
in the Henley Street property, with 5*l.* for each of
her three sons, William, Thomas, and Michael.   To
the poor of Stratford he gave 10*l.*, and to Mr. Thomas

Legacies   Combe (apparently a brother of William,
to friends.   of the enclosure controversy) his sword.
To each of his Stratford friends, Hamlett Sadler,
William Reynoldes, Anthony Nash, and John
Nash, and to each of his 'fellows' (*i.e.* theatrical
colleagues in London), John Heming, Richard Burbage, and Henry Condell, he left xxvj*s.* viij*d.*, with
which to buy memorial rings.   His godson, William
Walker, received ' xx ' shillings in gold.

Before 1623[2] an elaborate monument, by a London

---

[1] A hundred and fifty pounds is described as a substantial jointure
in *Merry Wives*, III. iii. 1. 49.

[2] Leonard Digges, in commendatory verses before the First Folio of
1623, wrote that Shakespeare's works would be alive

[When] Time dissolves thy Stratford monument.

sculptor of Dutch birth, Gerard Johnson, was erected
The tomb. to Shakespeare's memory in the chancel of
the parish church.[1] It includes a half-length
bust, depicting the dramatist on the point of writing.
The fingers of the right hand are disposed as if
holding a pen, and under the left hand lies a quarto
sheet of paper. The inscription, which was apparently by a London friend, runs :

> Judicio Pylium, genio Socratem, arte Maronem,
>   Terra tegit, populus mæret, Olympus habet.

> Stay passenger, why goest thou by so fast?
> Read, if thou canst, whom envious death hath plast
> Within this monument; Shakespeare with whome
> Quick nature dide; whose name doth deck ys tombe
> Far more than cost; sith all yt he hath writt
> Leaves living art but page to serve his witt.

> Obiit ano. doi 1616   Ætatis 53   Die 23 Ap.

At the opening of Shakespeare's career Chettle
wrote of his ' civil demeanour ' and of the reports of
Personal   ' his uprightness of dealing which argues his
character. honesty.' In 1601 — when near the zenith of
his fame — he was apostrophised as 'sweet Master
Shakespeare ' in the play of ' The Return from
Parnassus,' and that adjective was long after associated with his name. In 1604 one Anthony Scoloker
in a poem called ' Daiphantus ' bestowed on him the
epithet 'friendly.' After the close of his career
Jonson wrote of him: ' I loved the man and do

---

[1] Cf. Dugdale, *Diary*, 1827, p. 99 ; see under article on Bernard
Janssen in the *Dictionary of National Biography*.

honour his memory, on this side idolatry as much as any. He was, indeed, honest and of an open and free nature.' [1] No other contemporary left on record any definite impression of Shakespeare's personal character, and the 'Sonnets,' which alone of his literary work can be held to throw any illumination on a personal trait, mainly reveal him in the light of one who was willing to conform to all the conventional methods in vogue for strengthening the bonds between a poet and a great patron. His literary practices and aims were those of contemporary men of letters, and the difference in the quality of his work and theirs was due not to conscious endeavour on his part to act otherwise than they, but to the magic and involuntary working of his genius. He seemed unconscious of his marvellous superiority to his professional comrades. The references in his will to his fellow-actors, and the spirit in which (as they announce in the First Folio) they approached the task of collecting his works after his death, corroborate the description of him as a sympathetic friend of gentle, unassuming mien. The later traditions brought together by Aubrey depict him as 'very good company, and of a very ready and pleasant smooth wit,' and there is much in other early posthumous references to suggest a genial, if not a convivial, temperament, linked to a quiet turn for good-humoured satire. But Bohemian ideals and modes of life had no genuine attraction for Shakespeare. His extant work attests his 'copious' and

---

[1] 'Timber,' in *Works*, 1641.

continuous industry,[1] and with his literary power and sociability there clearly went the shrewd capacity of a man of business. Pope had just warrant for the surmise that he

> For gain not glory winged his roving flight,
> And grew immortal in his own despite.

His literary attainments and successes were chiefly valued as serving the prosaic end of providing permanently for himself and his daughters. His highest ambition was to restore among his fellow-townsmen the family repute which his father's misfortunes had imperilled. Ideals so homely are reckoned rare among poets, but Chaucer and Sir Walter Scott, among writers of exalted genius, vie with Shakespeare in the sobriety of their personal aims and in the sanity of their mental attitude towards life's ordinary incidents.

[1] John Webster, the dramatist, made vague reference in the address before his 'White Divel' in 1612 to 'the right happy and copious industry of M. Shakespeare, M. Decker, and M. Heywood.'

XVII

SURVIVORS AND DESCENDANTS

SHAKESPEARE'S widow died on August 6, 1623, at the age of sixty-seven, and was buried near her husband inside the chancel two days later. Some affectionately phrased Latin elegiacs — doubtless from Dr. Hall's pen — were inscribed on a brass plate fastened to the stone above her grave.[1] The younger daughter, Judith, resided with her husband, Thomas Quiney, at The Cage, a house which he leased in Bridge Street from 1616 till 1652. There he carried on the trade of a vintner, and took part in municipal affairs, acting as a councillor from 1617 and as chamberlain in 1621–2 and 1622–3; but after 1630 his affairs grew embarrassed, and he left Stratford late in 1652 for London, where he seems to have died a few months later. Of his three sons by Judith, the eldest, Shakespeare (baptised on November 23, 1616), was buried in Stratford Churchyard on May 8, 1617; the second son,

The survivors.

Mistress Judith Quiney.

---

[1] The words run: 'Heere lyeth interred the bodye of Anne, wife of Mr. William Shakespeare, who depted. this life the 6th day of August, 1623, being of the age of 67 yeares.

'Vbera, tu, mater, tu lac vitamq. dedisti,
   Vae mihi; pro tanto munere saxa dabo!
Quam mallem, amoueat lapidem bonus Angel[us] ore,
   Exeat ut Christi Corpus, imago tua.
Sed nil vota valent; venias cito, Christe; resurget,
   Clausa licet tumulo, mater, et astra petet.'

Richard (baptised on February 9, 1617–18), was buried on January 28, 1638–9; and the third son, Thomas (baptised on January 23, 1619–20), was buried on February 26, 1638–9. Judith survived her husband, sons, and sister, dying at Stratford on February 9, 1661–2, in her seventy-seventh year.

The poet's elder daughter, Mrs. Susannah Hall, re-sided at New Place till her death. Her sister Judith alienated to her the Chapel Place tenement before

Mistress Susannah Hall. 1633, but that, with the interest in the Stratford tithes, she soon disposed of. Her husband, Dr. John Hall, died on November 25, 1635. In 1642, James Cooke, a surgeon in attendance on some Royalist troops stationed at Stratford, visited Mrs. Hall and examined manu-scripts in her possession, but they were apparently of her husband's, not of her father's, composition.[1] From July 11 to 13, 1643, Queen Henrietta Maria, while jour-neying from Newark to Oxford, was billeted on Mrs. Hall at New Place for three days, and was visited there by Prince Rupert. Mrs. Hall was buried beside her husband in Stratford Churchyard on July 11, 1649, and a rhyming inscription, describing her as 'witty above her sex,' was engraved on her tomb-stone. The whole inscription ran: 'Heere lyeth ye. body of Svsanna, wife to John Hall, Gent. ye. davghter of William Shakespeare, Gent. She deceased ye. 11th of Jvly, A.D. 1649, aged 66.

> 'Witty above her sexe, but that's not all,
> Wise to Salvation was good Mistress Hall,

---

[1] Cf. Hall, *Select Observations*, ed. Cooke, 1657.

Something of Shakespere was in that, but this
Wholy of him with whom she's now in blisse.
Then, passenger, ha'st ne're a teare,
    To weepe with her that wept with all?
That wept, yet set herselfe to chere
    Them up with comforts cordiall.
Her Love shall live, her mercy spread,
When thou hast ne're a teare to shed.'

Mrs. Hall's only child, Elizabeth, was the last
surviving descendant of the poet.   In April 1626 she
married her first husband, Thomas Nash of
Stratford (*b.* 1593), who studied at Lincoln's
Inn, was a man of property, and, dying
childless at New Place on April 4, 1647, was buried
in Stratford Church next day.   At Billesley, a village
four miles from Stratford, on June 5, 1649, Mrs. Nash
married, as a second husband, a widower, John Bernard
or Barnard of Abington, Northamptonshire, who was
knighted by Charles II in 1661.   About the same
date she seems to have abandoned New Place for her
husband's residence at Abington.   Dying without
issue, she was buried there on February 17, 1669-70.
Her husband survived her four years, and was buried
beside her.[1]   On her mother's death in 1649 Lady
Barnard inherited under the poet's will the land near
Stratford, New Place, the house at Blackfriars, and (on
the death of the poet's sister, Joan Hart, in 1646) the
houses in Henley Street, while her father, Dr. Hall, left
her in 1635 a house at Acton with a meadow.   She
sold the Blackfriars house, and apparently the Stratford land, before 1667.   By her will, dated January

The last
descen-
dant.

---

[1] Baker, *Northamptonshire*, i. 10; *New Shaksp. Soc. Trans.*
1880-5, pt. ii. pp. 13†-15†.

1669–70, and proved in the following March, she left small bequests to the daughters of Thomas Hathaway, of the family of her grandmother, the poet's wife. The houses in Henley Street passed to her cousin, Thomas Hart, the grandson of the poet's sister Joan, and they remained in the possession of Thomas's direct descendants till 1806 (the male line expired on the death of John Hart in 1800). By her will Lady Barnard also ordered New Place to be sold, and it was purchased on May 18, 1675, by Sir Edward Walker, through whose daughter Barbara, wife of Sir John Clopton, it reverted to the Clopton family. Sir John rebuilt it in 1702. On the death of his son Hugh in 1752, it was bought by the Rev. Francis Gastrell (*d.*1768), who demolished the new building in 1759.[1]

Of Shakespeare's three brothers, only one, Gilbert, seems to have survived him. Edmund, the youngest brother, 'a player,' was buried at St. Saviour's Church, Southwark, 'with a forenoone knell of the great bell,' on December 31, 1607 ; he was in his twenty-eighth year. Richard, John Shakespeare's third son, died at Stratford in February 1613, aged 29. 'Gilbert Shakespeare adolescens,' who was buried at Stratford on February 3, 1611–12, was doubtless son of the poet's next brother Gilbert; the latter, having nearly completed his forty-sixth year, could scarcely be described as 'adolescens'; his death is not recorded, but according to Oldys he survived to a patriarchal age.

Shakespeare's brothers.

[1] Halliwell-Phillipps, *Hist. of New Place*, 1864, fol.

XVIII

AUTOGRAPHS, PORTRAITS, AND MEMORIALS

MUCH controversy has arisen over the spelling of
the poet's surname.   It has been proved capable of
four thousand variations.[1]   The name of the
Spelling of
the poet's   poet's father is entered sixty-six times in
surname.   the council books of Stratford, and is spelt
in sixteen ways.   The commonest form is 'Shax-
peare.'   Five autographs of the poet of undisputed
authenticity are extant; his signature to the indenture
Autograph   relating to the purchase of the property in
signatures. Blackfriars, dated March 10, 1612–13 (since
1841 in the Guildhall Library); his signature to the
mortgage-deed relating to the same purchase, dated
March 11, 1612–13 (since 1858 in the British Museum),
and the three signatures on the three sheets of his
will, dated March 25, 1615–16 (now at Somerset
House).   In all the signatures some of the letters are
represented by recognised signs of abbreviation.   The
signature to the first document is 'William Shakspere,'
though in all other portions of the deeds the name is

[1] Wise, *Autograph of William Shakespeare . . . together with* 4,000
ways of spelling the name, Philadelphia, 1869.

spelt 'Shakespeare.' The signature to the second
document has been interpreted both as Shakspere and
Shakspeare. The ink of the first signature in the
will has now faded almost beyond decipherment, but
that it was 'Shakspere' may be inferred from the
facsimile made by Steevens in 1776. The second and
third signatures to the will, which are also somewhat
difficult to decipher, have been read both as Shakspere
and Shakspeare; but a close examination suggests
that whatever the second signature may be, the third
is 'Shakespeare.' Shakspere is the spelling of the
alleged autograph in the British Museum copy of
Florio's 'Montaigne,' but the genuineness of that
signature is disputable.[1] Shakespeare was the form
adopted in the full signature appended to the dedicatory epistles of the 'Venus and Adonis' of 1593 and
the 'Lucrece' of 1594, volumes which were produced
under the poet's supervision. It is the spelling
adopted on the title-pages of the majority of contemporary editions of his works, whether or not produced
under his supervision. It is adopted in almost all
the published references to the poet during the seventeenth century. It appears in the grant of arms in
1596, in the license to the players of 1603, and in the
text of all the legal documents relating to the poet's
property. The poet, like most of his contemporaries,
acknowledged no finality on the subject. According
to the best authority, he spelt his surname in two
ways when signing his will. There is consequently

[1] See the article on Florio, John, in the *Dictionary of National
Biography*, and Sir Frederick Madden's *Observations on an Autograph
of Shakspere*, 1838.

no good ground for abandoning the form Shakespeare which is sanctioned by legal and literary custom.[1]

Aubrey reported that Shakespeare was 'a handsome well-shap't man,' but no portrait exists which can be said with absolute certainty to have been executed during his lifetime, although one has recently been discovered with a good claim to that distinction. Only two of the extant portraits are positively known to have been produced within a short period after his death. These are the bust in Stratford Church and the frontispiece to the folio of 1623. Each is an inartistic attempt at a posthumous likeness. There is considerable discrepancy between the two; their main points of resemblance are the baldness on the top of the head and the fulness of the hair about the ears. The bust was by Gerard Johnson or Janssen, who was a Dutch stonemason or tombmaker settled in Southwark. It was set up in the church before 1623, and is a rudely carved specimen of mortuary sculpture. There are marks about the forehead and ears which suggest that the face was fashioned from a death mask, but the workmanship is at all points clumsy. The round face and eyes present a heavy, unintellectual expression. The bust was originally coloured, but in 1793 Malone caused it to be whitewashed. In 1861 the whitewash was removed, and the colours, as far as traceable, restored. The eyes are light hazel, the hair and beard auburn. There

Shake-speare's portraits.

The Stratford bust.

---

[1] Cf. Halliwell-Phillipps *New Lamps or Old*, 1880; Malone, *Inquiry*, 1796.

have been numberless reproductions, both engraved and photographic. It was first engraved — very imperfectly — for Rowe's edition in 1709; then by Vertue for Pope's edition of 1725; and by Gravelot for Hanmer's edition in 1744. A good engraving by William Ward appeared in 1816. A phototype and a chromo-phototype, issued by the New Shakspere Society, are the best reproductions for the purposes of study. The pretentious painting known as the 'Stratford' portrait, and presented in 1867 by W. O. Hunt, town clerk of Stratford, to the Birthplace Museum, where it is very prominently displayed, was probably painted from the bust late in the eighteenth century; it lacks either historic or artistic interest.

The 'Stratford' portrait.

The engraved portrait — nearly a half-length — which was printed on the title-page of the folio of 1623, was by Martin Droeshout. On the opposite page lines by Ben Jonson congratulate 'the graver' on having satisfactorily 'hit' the poet's 'face.' Jonson's testimony does no credit to his artistic discernment; the expression of countenance, which is very crudely rendered, is neither distinctive nor lifelike. The face is long and the forehead high; the top of the head is bald, but the hair falls in abundance over the ears. There is a scanty moustache and a thin tuft under the lower lip. A stiff and wide collar, projecting horizontally, conceals the neck. The coat is closely buttoned and elaborately bordered, especially at the shoulders. The dimensions of the head and face are disproportionately large as

Droeshout's engraving.

compared with those of the body. In the unique proof
copy which belonged to Halliwell-Phillipps (now with
his collection in America) the tone is clearer than in
the ordinary copies, and the shadows are less darkened
by cross-hatching and coarse dotting. The engraver,
Martin Droeshout, belonged to a Flemish family of
painters and engravers long settled in London, where
he was born in 1601. He was thus fifteen years old
at the time of Shakespeare's death in 1616, and it is
consequently improbable that he had any personal
knowledge of the dramatist. The engraving was
doubtless produced by Droeshout very shortly before
the publication of the First Folio in 1623, when he
had completed his twenty-second year. It thus
belongs to the outset of the engraver's professional
career, in which he never achieved extended practice
or reputation. A copy of the Droeshout engraving,
by William Marshall, was prefixed to Shakespeare's
'Poems' in 1640, and William Faithorne made
another copy for the frontispiece of the edition of
'The Rape of Lucrece' published in 1655.

There is little doubt that young Droeshout in
fashioning his engraving worked from a painting, and
The 'Droe- there is a likelihood that the original picture
shout'   from which the youthful engraver worked has
painting. lately come to light. As recently as 1892
Mr. Edgar Flower, of Stratford-on-Avon, discovered
in the possession of Mr. H. C. Clements, a private
gentleman with artistic tastes residing at Peckham
Rye, a portrait alleged to represent Shakespeare.
The picture, which was faded and somewhat worm-

eaten, dated beyond all doubt from the early years of
the seventeenth century. It was painted on a panel
formed of two planks of old elm, and in the upper
left-hand corner was the inscription 'Willm Shakespeare, 1609.' Mr. Clements purchased the portrait
of an obscure dealer about 1840, and knew nothing
of its history, beyond what he set down on a slip of
paper when he acquired it. The note that he then
wrote and pasted on the box in which he preserved
the picture ran as follows : 'The original portrait of
Shakespeare, from which the now famous Droeshout
engraving was taken and inserted in the first collected
edition of his works, published in 1623, being seven
years after his death. The picture was painted nine
[veré seven] years before his death, and consequently
sixteen [veré fourteen] years before it was published.
. . . The picture was publicly exhibited in London
seventy years ago, and many thousands went to see it.'
In all its details and in its comparative dimensions,
especially in the disproportion between the size of
the head and that of the body, this picture is
identical with the Droeshout engraving. Though
coarsely and stiffly drawn, the face is far more
skilfully presented than in the engraving, and the
expression of countenance betrays some artistic
sentiment which is absent from the print. Connois-
seurs, including Sir Edward Poynter, Mr. Sidney
Colvin, and Mr. Lionel Cust, have almost unreservedly pronounced the picture to be anterior in
date to the engraving, and they have reached the
conclusion that in all probability Martin Droeshout

U

directly based his work upon the painting. Influences
of an early seventeenth-century Flemish school are
plainly discernible in the picture, and it is just possible
that it is the production of an uncle of the young engraver Martin Droeshout, who bore the same name
as his nephew, and was naturalised in this country on
January 25, 1608, when he was described as a 'painter
of Brabant.' Although the history of the portrait
rests on critical conjecture and on no external contemporary evidence, there seems good ground for regarding it as a portrait of Shakespeare painted in his
lifetime — in the forty-fifth year of his age. No other
pictorial representation of the poet has equally serious
claims to be treated as contemporary with himself, and
it therefore presents features of unique interest. On
the death of its owner, Mr. Clements, in 1895, the
painting was purchased by Mrs. Charles Flower, and
was presented to the Memorial Picture Gallery at
Stratford, where it now hangs. No attempt at restoration has been made. A photogravure forms the
frontispiece to the present volume.[1]

Of the same type as the Droeshout engraving,
although less closely resembling it than the picture
just described, is the ' Ely House ' portrait, (now the
property of the Birthplace Trustees at Stratford),

---

[1] Mr. Lionel Cust, director of the National Portrait Gallery, who has
little doubt of the genuineness of the picture, gave an interesting account
of it at a meeting of the Society of Antiquaries on December 12, 1895.
Mr. Cust's paper is printed in the Society's *Proceedings*, second series,
vol. xvi. p. 42. Mr. Salt Brassington, the librarian of the Shakespeare
Memorial Library, has given a careful description of it in the *Illustrated
Catalogue of the Pictures in the Memorial Gallery*, 1896, pp. 78–83.

which formerly belonged to Thomas Turton, Bishop of Ely, and it is inscribed ' Æ. 39 x. 1603.'[1] This painting is of high artistic value. The features are of a far more attractive and intellectual cast than in either the Droeshout painting or engraving, and the many differences in detail raise doubts as to whether the person represented can have been intended for Shakespeare. Experts are of opinion that the picture was painted early in the seventeenth century.

Early in Charles II's reign Lord Chancellor Clarendon added a portrait of Shakespeare to his great gallery in his house in St. James's. Mention is made of it in a letter from the diarist John Evelyn to his friend Samuel Pepys in 1689, but Clarendon's collection was dispersed at the end of the seventeenth century and the picture has not been traced.[2]

Of the numerous extant paintings which have been described as portraits of Shakespeare, only the Later 'Droeshout' portrait and the 'Ely House' portraits. portrait, both of which are at Stratford, bear any definable resemblance to the folio engraving or the bust in the church.[3] In spite of their admitted

---

[1] *Harper's Magazine*, May 1897.

[2] Cf. *Evelyn's Diary and Correspondence*, iii. 444.

[3] Numberless portraits have been falsely identified with Shakespeare, and it would be futile to attempt to make the record of the pretended portraits complete. Upwards of sixty have been offered for sale to the National Portrait Gallery since its foundation in 1856, and not one of these has proved to possess the remotest claim to authenticity. The following are some of the wholly unauthentic portraits that have attracted public attention: Three portraits assigned to Zucchero, who left England in 1580, and cannot have had any relations with Shakespeare — one in the Art Museum, Boston, U.S.A.; another, formerly

imperfections, those presentments can alone be held indisputably to have been honestly designed to depict the poet's features. They must be treated as the standards of authenticity in judging of the genuineness of other portraits claiming to be of an early date.

Of other alleged portraits which are extant, the most famous and interesting is the ' Chandos ' portrait, now in the National Portrait Gallery. Its pedigree suggests that it was intended to represent the poet, but numerous and conspicuous divergences from the authenticated likenesses show that it was painted from fanciful descriptions of him some years after his death. The face is bearded, and rings adorn the ears. Oldys reported that it was from the brush of Burbage, Shakespeare's fellow-actor, who had some reputation as a limner,[1] and that it had belonged to Joseph Taylor, an actor contemporary with Shakespeare. These rumours are not corroborated; but there is no doubt that it was at one time the property of D'Avenant, and that it subsequently belonged successively to the actor Betterton and to Mrs. Barry the actress. In 1693 Sir Godfrey Kneller made a copy

The 'Chandos' portrait.

the property of Richard Cosway, R.A., and afterwards of Mr. J. A. Langford of Birmingham (engraved in mezzotint by H. Green); and a third belonging to the Baroness Burdett-Coutts, who purchased it in 1862. At Hampton Court is a wholly unauthentic portrait of the Chandos type, which was at one time at Penshurst; it bears the legend ' Ætatis suæ 34 ' (cf. Law's *Cat. of Hampton Court*, p. 234). A portrait inscribed ' ætatis suæ 47, 1611,' belonging to Clement Kingston of Ashbourne, Derbyshire, was engraved in mezzotint by G. F. Storm in 1846.

[1] In the picture-gallery at Dulwich is ' a woman's head on a boord done by Mr. Burbidge, ye actor ' — a well-authenticated example of the actor's art.

as a gift for Dryden. After Mrs. Barry's death in 1713 it was purchased for forty guineas by Robert Keck, a barrister of the Inner Temple. At length it reached the hands of one John Nichols, whose daughter married James Brydges, third duke of Chandos. In due time the Duke became the owner of the picture, and it subsequently passed, through Chandos's daughter, to her husband, the first Duke of Buckingham, whose son, the second Duke of Buckingham, sold it with the rest of his effects at Stowe in 1848, when it was purchased by the Earl of Ellesmere. The latter presented it to the nation. Edward Capell many years before presented a copy by Ranelagh Barret to Trinity College, Cambridge, and other copies are attributed to Sir Joshua Reynolds and Ozias Humphrey (1783). It was engraved by George Vertue in 1719 for Pope's edition (1725), and often later, one of the best engravings being by Vandergucht. A good lithograph from a tracing by Sir George Scharf was published by the trustees of the National Portrait Gallery in 1864. The Baroness Burdett-Coutts purchased in 1875 a portrait of similar type, which is said, somewhat doubtfully, to have belonged to John lord Lumley, who died in 1609, and to have formed part of a collection of portraits of the great men of his day at his house, Lumley Castle, Durham. Its early history is not positively authenticated, and it may well be an early copy of the 'Chandos' portrait. The 'Lumley' painting was finely chromo-lithographed in 1863 by Vincent Brooks.

The so-called 'Jansen' or 'Janssens' portrait, which

belongs to Lady Guendolen Ramsden, daughter of the
Duke of Somerset, and is now at her residence at Bulstrode, was first doubtfully identified about 1770, when in the possession of Charles
Jennens. Janssens did not come to England before
Shakespeare's death. It is a fine portrait, but is
unlike any other that has been associated with the
dramatist. An admirable mezzotint by Richard
Earlom was issued in 1811.

The 'Felton' portrait, a small head on a panel, with
a high and very bald forehead (belonging
since 1873 to the Baroness Burdett-Coutts),
was purchased by S. Felton of Drayton, Shropshire,
in 1792, of J. Wilson, the owner of the Shakespeare
Museum in Pall Mall; it bears a late inscription, 'Gul.
Shakespear 1597, R. B.' [i.e. Richard Burbage]. It
was engraved by Josiah Boydell for George Steevens
in 1797, and by James Neagle for Isaac Reed's edition
in 1803. Fuseli declared it to be the work of a Dutch
artist, but the painters Romney and Lawrence regarded it as of English workmanship of the sixteenth
century. Steevens held that it was the original picture whence both Droeshout and Marshall made their
engravings, but there are practically no points of resemblance between it and the prints.

The 'Soest' or 'Zoust' portrait—in the possession
of Sir John Lister-Kaye of the Grange,
Wakefield—was in the collection of Thomas
Wright, painter, of Covent Garden in 1725, when
John Simon engraved it. Soest was born twenty-one
years after Shakespeare's death, and the portrait is

WILLIAM SHAKESPEARE.

From a plaster-cast of the terra-cotta bust now in the possession of the Garrick Club.

only on fanciful grounds identified with the poet.   A chalk drawing by Joseph Michael Wright, obviously inspired by the Soest portrait, is the property of Sir Arthur Hodgson of Clopton House, and is on loan at the Memorial Gallery, Stratford.

Miniatures.   A well-executed miniature by Hilliard, at one time in the possession of William Somerville the poet, and now the property of Sir Stafford North-cote, bart., was engraved by Agar for vol. ii. of the 'Variorum Shakespeare' of 1821, and in Wivell's 'Inquiry,' 1827.   It has little claim to attention as a portrait of the dramatist.   Another miniature (called the 'Auriol' portrait), of doubtful authenticity, for-merly belonged to Mr. Lumsden Propert, and a third is at Warwick Castle.

The Garrick Club bust.   A bust, said to be of Shakespeare, was discovered in 1845 bricked up in a wall in Spode & Copeland's china warehouse in Lincoln's Inn Fields. The warehouse had been erected on the site of the Duke's Theatre, which was built by D'Avenant in 1660.   The bust, which is of black terra-cotta, and bears traces of Italian workmanship, is believed to have adorned the proscenium of the Duke's Theatre.   It was acquired by the surgeon William Clift, from whom it passed to Clift's son-in-law, Richard (afterwards Sir Richard) Owen the natural-ist.   The latter sold it to the Duke of Devonshire, who presented it in 1851 to the Garrick Club, after having two copies made in plaster.   One of these copies is now in the Shakespeare Memorial Gallery at Stratford, and from it an engraving has been made for reproduction in this volume.

The Kesselstadt death-mask was discovered by Dr. Ludwig Becker, librarian at the ducal palace at Darmstadt, in a rag-shop at Mayence in 1849. The features resemble those of an alleged portrait of Shakespeare (dated 1637) which Dr. Becker purchased in 1847. This picture had long been in the possession of the family of Count Francis von Kesselstadt of Mayence, who died in 1843. Dr. Becker brought the mask and the picture to England in 1849, and Richard Owen supported the theory that the mask was taken from Shakespeare's face after death, and was the foundation of the bust in Stratford Church. The mask was for a long time in Dr. Becker's private apartments at the ducal palace, Darmstadt.[1] The features are singularly attractive; but the chain of evidence which would identify them with Shakespeare is incomplete.[2]

Alleged death-mask.

A monument, the expenses of which were defrayed

[1] It is now the property of Frau Oberst Becker, the discoverer's daughter-in-law. Darmstadt, Heidelbergerstrasse 111.

[2] Some account of Shakespeare's portraits will be found in the following works: James Boaden, *Inquiry into various Pictures and Prints of Shakespeare*, 1824; Abraham Wivell, *Inquiry into Shakespeare's Portraits*, 1827, with engravings by B. and W. Holl; George Scharf, *Principal Portraits of Shakespeare*, 1864; J. Hain Friswell, *Life-Portraits of Shakespeare*, 1864; William Page, *Study of Shakespeare's Portraits*, 1876; Ingleby, *Man and Book*, 1877, pp. 84 seq.; J. Parker Norris, *Portraits of Shakespeare*, Philadelphia, 1885, with numerous plates; *Illustrated Cat. of Portraits in Shakespeare's Memorial at Stratford*, 1896. In 1885 Mr. Walter Rogers Furness issued, at Philadelphia, a volume of composite portraits, combining the Droeshout engraving and the Stratford bust with the Chandos, Jansen, Felton, and Stratford portraits.

by public subscription, was set up in the Poets'
Corner in Westminster Abbey in 1741. Pope
and the Earl of Burlington were among
the promoters. The design was by William
Kent, and the statue of Shakespeare was executed
by Peter Scheemakers.[1] Another statue was executed
by Roubiliac for Garrick, who bequeathed it to the
British Museum in 1779. A third statue, freely
adapted from the works of Scheemakers and Roubiliac, was executed for Baron Albert Grant and was
set up by him as a gift to the metropolis in Leicester
Square, London, in 1879. A fourth statue (by Mr.
J. Q. A. Ward) was placed in 1882 in the Central
Park, New York. A fifth in bronze, by M. Paul Four-
nier, which was erected in Paris in 1888 at the expense
of an English resident, Mr. W. Knighton, stands at the
point where the Avenue de Messine meets the Boule-
vard Haussmann. A sixth memorial in sculpture, by
Lord Ronald Gower, the most elaborate and ambitious
of all, stands in the garden of the Shakespeare Memorial buildings, and was unveiled in 1888; Shakespeare
is seated on a high pedestal; below, at each side of
the pedestal, stand figures of four of Shakespeare's
principal characters: Lady Macbeth, Hamlet, Prince
Hal, and Sir John Falstaff.

At Stratford, the Birthplace, which was acquired
by the public in 1846 and converted into a museum, is,
with Anne Hathaway's cottage (which was acquired
by the Birthplace Trustees in 1892), a place of pilgrimage for visitors from all parts of the globe. The

(marginal note:) Memorials in sculpture.

---

[1] Cf. *Gentleman's Magazine*, 1741, p. 105.

27,038 persons who visited it in 1896 and the 26,510 persons who visited it in 1897 represented over forty nationalities. The site of the demolished New Place, with the gardens, was also purchased by public subscription in 1861, and now forms a public garden. Of a new memorial building on the river-bank at Stratford, consisting of a theatre, picture-gallery, and library, the foundation-stone was laid on April 23, 1877. The theatre was opened exactly two years later, when 'Much Ado about Nothing' was performed, with Helen Faucit (Lady Martin) as Beatrice and Barry Sullivan as Benedick. Performances of Shakespeare's plays have since been given annually during April. The library and picture-gallery were opened in 1881.[1] A memorial Shakespeare library was opened at Birmingham on April 23, 1868, to commemorate the tercentenary of 1864, and, although destroyed by fire in 1879, was restored in 1882; it now possesses nearly ten thousand volumes relating to Shakespeare.

[1] *A History of the Shakespeare Memorial, Stratford-on-Avon*, 1882; *Illustrated Catalogue of Pictures in the Shakespeare Memorial*, 1896.

XIX

BIBLIOGRAPHY

ONLY two of Shakespeare's works — his narrative poems 'Venus and Adonis' and 'Lucrece'— were published with his sanction and co-operation. These poems were the first specimens of his work to appear in print, and they passed in his lifetime through a greater number of editions than any of his plays. At the time of his death in 1616 there had been printed in quarto seven editions of his 'Venus and Adonis' (1593, 1594, 1596, 1599, 1600, and two in 1602), and five editions of his 'Lucrece' (1594, 1598, 1600, 1607, 1616). There was only one lifetime edition of the 'Sonnets,' Thorpe's surreptitious venture of 1609;[1] but three editions were issued of the piratical 'Passionate Pilgrim,' which was fraudulently assigned to Shakespeare by the publisher William Jaggard, although it only contained a few occasional poems by him (1599, 1600 no copy known, and 1612).

Quartos of the poems in the poet's lifetime.

Of posthumous editions in quarto of the two

---

[1] This was facsimiled in 1862, and again by Mr. Griggs in 1880.

narrative poems in the seventeenth century, there
were two of 'Lucrece' — viz. in 1624 ('the
sixth edition') and in 1655 (with John
Quarles's 'Banishment of Tarquin')— and
there were as many as six editions of 'Venus' (1617,
1620, 1627, two in 1630 and 1636), making thirteen
editions in all in forty-three years.   No later editions
of these two poems were issued in the seventeenth
century.   They were next reprinted together with
'The Passionate Pilgrim' in 1707, and thenceforth
they usually figured, with the addition of the 'Sonnets,'
in collected editions of Shakespeare's works.

A so-called first collected edition of Shakespeare's
'Poems' in 1640 (London, by T. Cotes for I. Benson)
was mainly a reissue of the 'Sonnets,'
but it omitted six (Nos. xviii., xix., xliii.,
lvi., lxxv., and lxxvi.) and it included the
twenty poems of 'The Passionate Pilgrim, with
some other pieces by other authors.   Marshall's copy
of the Droeshout engraving of 1623 formed the
frontispiece. There were prefatory poems by Leonard
Digges and John Warren, as well as an address 'to the
reader' signed with the initials of the publisher. There
Shakespeare's 'Sonnets' were described as 'serene,
clear, and elegantly plain ; such gentle strains as shall
re-create and not perplex your brain. No intricate
or cloudy stuff to puzzle intellect. Such as will raise
your admiration to his praise.'   A chief point of interest in the volume of 'Poems' of 1640 is the fact
that the 'Sonnets' were printed then in a different
order to that which was followed in the volume of

1609. Thus the poem numbered lxvii. in the original edition opens the reissue, and what has been regarded as the crucial poem beginning

Two loves I have of comfort and despair,

which was in 1609 numbered cxliv., takes the thirty-second place in 1640. In most cases a more or less fanciful general title was placed in the second edition at the head of each sonnet, but in a few instances a single title serves for short sequences of two or three sonnets which are printed as independent poems continuously without spacing. The poems drawn from 'The Passionate Pilgrim' are intermingled with the 'Sonnets,' together with extracts from Thomas Heywood's 'General History of Women,' although no hint is given that they are not Shakespeare's work. The edition concludes with three epitaphs on Shakespeare and a short section entitled 'An addition of some excellent poems to those precedent by other Gentlemen.' The volume is of great rarity. An exact reprint was published in 1885.

Of Shakespeare's plays there were in print in 1616 only sixteen (all in quarto), or eighteen if we Quartos of include the 'Contention,' the first draft of the plays '2 Henry VI' (1594 and 1600), and 'The in the poet's life- True Tragedy,' the first draft of '3 Henry time.   VI' (1595 and 1600). These sixteen quartos were publishers' ventures, and were undertaken without the co-operation of the author.

Two of the plays, published thus, reached five editions before 1616, viz. 'Richard III' (1597, 1598,

1602, 1605, 1612) and '1 Henry IV' (1598, 1599, 1604, 1608, 1615).

Three reached four editions, viz. 'Richard II' (1597, 1598, 1608 supplying the deposition scene for the first time, 1615), 'Hamlet' (1603 imperfect, 1604, 1605, 1611), and 'Romeo and Juliet' (1597 imperfect, 1599, two in 1609).

Two reached three editions, viz. 'Henry V' (1600 imperfect, 1602, and 1608) and 'Pericles' (two in 1609, 1611).

Four reached two editions, viz. 'Midsummer Night's Dream' (both in 1600), 'Merchant of Venice,' (both in 1600), 'Lear' (both in 1608), and 'Troilus and Cressida' (both in 1609).

Five achieved only one edition, viz. 'Love's Labour's Lost' (1598), '2 Henry IV' (1600), 'Much Ado' (1600), 'Titus' (1600), 'Merry Wives' (1602 imperfect).

Three years after Shakespeare's death — in 1619 — there appeared a second edition of 'Merry Wives' Posthu- (again imperfect) and a fourth of 'Pericles.' mous 'Othello' was first printed posthumously in quartos of the plays. 1622 (4to), and in the same year sixth editions of 'Richard III' and '1 Henry IV' appeared.[1] The largest collections of the original quartos —

[1] Lithographed facsimiles of most of these volumes, with some of the quarto editions of the poems (forty-eight volumes in all), were prepared by Mr. E. W. Ashbee, and issued to subscribers by Halliwell-Phillipps between 1862 and 1871. A cheaper set of quarto facsimiles, undertaken by Mr. W. Griggs, and issued under the supervision of Dr. F. J. Furnivall, appeared in forty-three volumes between 1880 and 1889.

each of which only survives in four, five, or six copies — are in the libraries of the Duke of Devonshire, the British Museum, and Trinity College, Cambridge, and in the Bodleian Library.[1] All the quartos were issued in Shakespeare's day at sixpence each.

In 1623 the first attempt was made to give the world a complete edition of Shakespeare's plays. The First Folio. Two of the dramatist's intimate friends and fellow-actors, John Heming and Henry Condell, were nominally responsible for the venture, but it seems to have been suggested by a small syndicate of printers and publishers, who undertook all pecuniary responsibility. Chief of the syndicate was William Jaggard, printer since 1617 to the City of London, who was established in business in Fleet Street at the east end of St. Dunstan's Church. As the piratical publisher of 'The Passionate Pilgrim' he had long known the commercial value of Shakespeare's work. In 1613 he had extended his business by purchasing the stock and rights of a rival pirate, The publishing syndicate. James Roberts, who had printed the quarto editions of the 'Merchant of Venice' and 'Midsummer Night's Dream' in 1600 and the complete quarto of 'Hamlet' in 1604. Roberts had enjoyed for nearly twenty years the right to print 'the players' bills,' or programmes, and he made over

---

[1] Perfect copies range in price, according to their rarity, from 200*l.* to 300*l.* In 1864, at the sale of George Daniel's library, quarto copies of 'Love's Labour's Lost' and of 'Merry Wives' (first edition) each fetched 346*l.* 10*s.* On May 14, 1897, a copy of the quarto of 'The Merchant of Venice' (printed by James Roberts in 1600) was sold at Sotheby's for 315*l.*

that privilege to Jaggard with his other literary property.   It was to the close personal relations with the
playhouse managers into which the acquisition of the
right of printing 'the players' bills' brought Jaggard
after 1613 that the inception of the scheme of the
'First Folio' may safely be attributed.   Jaggard associated his son Isaac with the enterprise.   They alone
of the members of the syndicate were printers.   Their
three partners were publishers or booksellers only.
Two of these, William Aspley and John Smethwick,
had already speculated in plays of Shakespeare.   Aspley had published with another in 1600 the 'Second
Part of Henry IV' and 'Much Ado about Nothing,'
and in 1609 half of Thorpe's impression of Shakespeare's 'Sonnets.'   Smethwick, whose shop was in
St. Dunstan's Churchyard, Fleet Street, near Jaggard's, had published in 1611 two late editions of
'Romeo and Juliet' and one of 'Hamlet.'   Edward
Blount, the fifth partner, was an interesting figure in
the trade, and, unlike his companions, had a true
taste in literature.   He had been a friend and admirer of Christopher Marlowe, and had actively engaged in the posthumous publication of two of
Marlowe's poems.   He had published that curious
collection of mystical verse entitled 'Love's Martyr,'
one poem in which, 'a poetical essay of the Phœnix
and the Turtle,' was signed 'William Shakespeare.'[1]

The First Folio was doubtless printed in Jaggard's
printing office near St. Dunstan's Church.   Upon
Blount probably fell the chief labour of seeing the

[1] See p. 183.

work through the press. It was in progress throughout 1623, and had so far advanced by November 8,
1623, that on that day Edward Blount and Isaac
(son of William) Jaggard obtained formal license
from the Stationers' Company to publish sixteen
of the twenty hitherto unprinted plays that it was
intended to include. The pieces, whose approaching
publication for the first time was thus announced,
were of supreme literary interest. The titles ran:
'The Tempest,' 'The Two Gentlemen,' 'Measure
for Measure,' 'Comedy of Errors,' 'As You Like It,'
'All's Well,' 'Twelfth Night,' 'Winter's Tale,' '3
Henry VI,' 'Henry VIII,' 'Coriolanus,' 'Timon,' 'Julius
Cæsar,' 'Macbeth,' 'Antony and Cleopatra,' and 'Cymbeline.' Four other hitherto unprinted dramas for
which no license was sought figured in the volume,
viz. 'King John,' '1 and 2 Henry VI,' and 'The Taming of The Shrew'; but each of these plays was based
by Shakespeare on a play of like title which had been
published at an earlier date, and the absence of a license
was doubtless due to an ignorant misconception on the
part either of the Stationers' Company's officers or of
the editors of the volume as to the true relations subsisting between the old pieces and the new. The only play
by Shakespeare that had been previously published
and was not included in the First Folio was 'Pericles.'

Thirty-six pieces in all were thus brought together.
The volume consisted of nearly one thousand double-
column pages and was sold at a pound a copy. Steevens
estimated that the edition numbered 250 copies. The
book was described on the title-page as published by

x

Edward Blount and Isaac Jaggard, and in the colophon as printed at the charges of 'W. Jaggard, I. Smithweeke, and W. Aspley,' as well as of Blount.[1] On the title-page was engraved the Droeshout portrait. Commendatory verses were supplied by Ben Jonson, Hugh Holland, Leonard Digges, and I. M., perhaps Jasper Maine. The dedication was addressed to the brothers William Herbert, earl of Pembroke, the lord chamberlain, and Philip Herbert, earl of Montgomery, and was signed by Shakespeare's friends and fellow-actors, Heming and Condell. The same signatures were appended to a succeeding address 'to the great variety of readers.' In both addresses the two actors made pretension to a larger responsibility for the enterprise than they really incurred, but their motives in identifying themselves with the venture were doubtless irreproachable. They disclaimed (they wrote) 'ambition either of selfe-profit or fame in undertaking the design,' being solely moved by anxiety to 'keepe the memory of so worthy a friend and fellow alive as was our Shakespeare.' 'It had bene a thing we confesse worthie to haue bene wished,' they inform the reader, 'that the author himselfe had liued to haue set forth and ouerseen his owne writings. . . .' A list of contents follows the address to the readers.

The title-page states that all the plays were printed 'according to the true originall copies.' The dedicators wrote to the same effect. 'As where (before) we were abus'd with diuerse stolne and surreptitious

The prefatory matter.

---

[1] Cf. *Bibliographica*, i. 489 seq.

copies, maimed and deformed by the frauds and
stealthes of incurious impostors that expos'd them;
even those are now offer'd to your view cur'd and
perfect in their limbes, and all the rest absolute in
their numbers as he conceived them.'   There is no
doubt that the whole volume was printed from the
acting versions in the possession of the manager of
the company with which Shakespeare had been associated.   But it is doubtful if any play were printed
exactly as it came from his pen.   The First Folio
text is often markedly inferior to that of the six-
The value   teen pre-existent quartos, which, although
of the text.   surreptitiously and imperfectly printed, followed playhouse copies of far earlier date.   From
the text of the quartos the text of the First Folio differs
invariably, although in varying degrees.   The quarto
texts of ' Love's Labour's Lost,' ' Midsummer Night's
Dream,' and ' Richard II,' for example, differ very
largely and always for the better from the folio texts.
On the other hand, the folio repairs the glaring defects of the quarto versions of 'The Merry Wives of
Windsor' and of ' Henry V.'   In the case of twenty
of the plays in the First Folio no quartos exist for
comparison, and of these twenty plays, ' Coriolanus,'
' All's Well,' and ' Macbeth ' present a text abounding
in corrupt passages.

The plays are arranged under three headings —
' Comedies,' ' Histories,' and ' Tragedies ' —
The order   and each division is separately paged.   The
of the   arrangement of the plays in each division
plays.   follows no principle.   The comedy section begins

with the 'Tempest' and ends with the 'Winter's Tale.' The histories more justifiably begin with 'King John' and end with 'Henry VIII.' The tragedies begin with 'Troilus and Cressida' and end with 'Cymbeline.' This order has been usually followed in subsequent collected editions.

As a specimen of typography the First Folio is not to be commended. There are a great many con-
The typog- temporary folios of larger bulk far more
raphy.   neatly and correctly printed. It looks as though Jaggard's printing office were undermanned. The misprints are numerous and are especially conspicuous in the pagination. The sheets seem to have been worked off very slowly, and corrections were made while the press was working, so that the copies struck off later differ occasionally from the earlier copies. One mark of carelessness on the part of the compositor or corrector of the press, which is common to all copies, is that 'Troilus and Cressida,' though in the body of the book it opens the section of tragedies, is not mentioned at all in the list of contents, and the play is unpaged except on its second and third pages, which bear the numbers 79 and 80.

Three copies are known which are distinguished by more interesting irregularities, in each case unique.
Unique   The copy in the Lenox Library in New York
copies.   includes a cancel duplicate of a leaf of 'As You Like It' (sheet R of the comedies), and the title-page bears the date 1622 instead of 1623; but it is suspected that the figures were tampered with outside the printing office.[1] Samuel Butler, successively head

[1] This copy was described in the *Variorum Shakespeare* of 1821

master of Shrewsbury and Bishop of Lichfield and
Coventry, possessed a copy of the First Folio in which
a proof leaf of 'Hamlet' was bound up with the
corrected leaf.[1]

The most interesting irregularity yet noticed appears in one of the two copies of the book belonging
to the Baroness Burdett-Coutts. This copy is known
as the Sheldon Folio, having formed in the seventeenth century part of the library of Ralph Sheldon
of Weston Manor in the parish of Long Compton,
Warwickshire.[2] In the Sheldon Folio the opening
page of 'Troilus and Cressida,' of which the
recto or front is occupied by the prologue
and the verso or back by the opening lines
of the text of the play, is followed by a superfluous
leaf. On the recto or front of the unnecessary leaf[3]
are printed the concluding lines of 'Romeo and Juliet'
in place of the prologue to 'Troilus and Cressida.'
At the back or verso are the opening lines of 'Troilus and Cressida' repeated from the preceding page.

The Sheldon copy.

(xxi. 449) as in the possession of Messrs. J. and A. Arch, booksellers, of
Cornhill. It was subsequently sold at Sotheby's in 1855 for 163*l*. 16*s*.

[1] I cannot trace the present whereabouts of this copy, but it is
described in the *Variorum Shakespeare* of 1821, xxi. 449–50.

[2] The copy seems to have been purchased by a member of the
Sheldon family in 1628, five years after publication. There is a note
in a contemporary hand which says it was bought for 3*l*. 15*s*., a
somewhat extravagant price. The entry further says that it cost three
score pounds of silver, words that I cannot explain. The Sheldon
family arms are on the sides of the volume, and there are many
manuscript notes in the margin, interpreting difficult words, correcting
misprints, or suggesting new readings.

[3] It has been mutilated by a former owner, and the signature of the
leaf is missing, but it was presumably G G 3.

The presence of a different ornamental headpiece on each page proves that the two are not taken from the same setting of the type.   At a later page in the Sheldon copy the concluding lines of 'Romeo and Juliet' are duly reprinted at the close of the play, and on the verso or back of the leaf, which supplies them in their right place, is the opening passage, as in other copies, of 'Timon of Athens.'   These curious confusions attest that while the work was in course of composition the printers or editors of the volume at one time intended to place 'Troilus and Cressida,' with the prologue omitted, after 'Romeo and Juliet.'   The last page of 'Romeo and Juliet' is in all copies numbered 79, an obvious misprint for 77; the first leaf of 'Troilus' is paged 78; the second and third pages of 'Troilus' are numbered 79 and 80.   It was doubtless suddenly determined while the volume was in the press to transfer 'Troilus and Cressida' to the head of the tragedies from a place near the end, but the numbers on the opening pages which indicated its first position were clumsily retained, and to avoid the extensive typographical corrections that were required by the play's change of position, its remaining pages were allowed to go forth unnumbered.[1]

It is difficult to estimate how many copies survive of the First Folio, which is intrinsically and extrinsically the most valuable volume in the whole range

[1] Correspondents inform me that two copies of the First Folio, one formerly belonging to Leonard Hartley and the other to Bishop Virtue of Portsmouth, showed a somewhat similar irregularity. Both copies were bought by American booksellers, and I have not been able to trace them.

of English literature. It seems that about 140 copies
Estimated
number of
extant
copies.
have been traced within the past century.
Of these fewer than twenty are in a perfect state, that is, with the portrait *printed*
(*not inlaid*) *on* the title-page, and the flyleaf facing
it, with all the pages succeeding it, intact and
uninjured. (The flyleaf contains Ben Jonson's
verses, attesting the truthfulness of the portrait.)
Excellent copies in this enviable state are in the
Grenville Library at the British Museum, and in
the libraries of the Duke of Devonshire, the Earl of
Crawford, the Baroness Burdett-Coutts, and Mr. A. H.
Huth. Of these probably the finest and cleanest is
the 'Daniel' copy belonging to the Baroness Burdett-
Coutts. It measures 13 inches by 8¼, and was purchased by its present owner for 716*l*. 2*s*. at the sale
of George Daniel's library in 1864. Some twenty
more copies are defective in the preliminary pages,
but are unimpaired in other respects. There remain
about a hundred copies which have sustained serious
damage at various points.

A reprint of the First Folio unwarrantably purporting to be exact was published in 1807–8.[1] The
Reprints of
the First
Folio.
best reprint was issued in three parts by
Lionel Booth in 1861, 1863, and 1864. The
valuable photo-zincographic reproduction
undertaken by Sir Henry James, under the direction
of Howard Staunton, was issued in sixteen folio parts
between February 1864 and October 1865. A reduced

---

[1] Cf. *Notes and Queries*, 1st ser., vii. 47.

photographic facsimile, too small to be legible, appeared
in 1876, with a preface by Halliwell-Phillipps.

The Second Folio edition was printed in 1632 by
Thomas Cotes for Robert Allot and William Aspley,
each of whose names figures as publisher on different
copies. To Allot Blount had transferred, on
November 16, 1630, his rights in the sixteen
plays which were first licensed for publication in 1623.[1] The Second Folio was reprinted from
the First; a few corrections were made in the
text, but most of the changes were arbitrary and
needless. Charles I's copy is at Windsor, and
Charles II's at the British Museum. The 'Perkins
Folio,' now in the Duke of Devonshire's possession,
in which John Payne Collier introduced forged emendations, was a copy of that of 1632.[2] The Third
Folio — for the most part a faithful reprint of the
Second — was first published in 1663 by Peter
Chetwynde, who reissued it next year with
the addition of seven plays, six of which have no

The Second Folio.

The Third Folio

---

[1] Arber, *Stationers' Registers*, iii. 242–3.

[2] On January 31, 1852, Collier announced in the *Athenæum*, that
this copy, which had been purchased by him for thirty shillings, and
bore on the outer cover the words ' *Tho. Perkins his Booke*,' was annotated throughout by a former owner in the middle of the seventeenth
century. Shortly afterwards Collier published all the ' essential ' manuscript readings in a volume entitled *Notes and Emendations to the Plays
of Shakespeare.* Next year he presented the folio to the Duke of
Devonshire. A warm controversy as to the date and genuineness of
the corrections followed, but in 1859 all doubt as to their origin was set
at rest by Mr. N. E. S. A. Hamilton of the manuscript department of
the British Museum, who in letters to the *Times* of July 2 and 16 pronounced all the manuscript notes to be recent fabrications in a simulated seventeenth-century hand.

claim to admission among Shakespeare's works.
'Unto this impression,' runs the title-page of 1664,
'is added seven Playes never before printed in folio,
viz. : Pericles, Prince of Tyre. The London Prodigall. The History of Thomas Ld. Cromwell. Sir
John Oldcastle, Lord Cobham. The Puritan Widow.
A Yorkshire Tragedy. The Tragedy of Locrine.'
The six spurious pieces which open the volume were
attributed by unprincipled publishers to Shakespeare
in his lifetime. Fewer copies of the Third Folio are
reputed to be extant than of the Second or Fourth
owing to the destruction of many unsold impressions
The Fourth in the Fire of London in 1666. The Fourth
Folio. Folio, printed in 1685 'for H. Herringman,
E. Brewster, R. Chiswell, and R. Bentley,' reprints the
folio of 1664 without change except in the way of
modernising the spelling; it repeats the spurious
pieces.

Since 1685 some two hundred independent
editions of the collected works have been published
Eigh- in Great Britain and Ireland, and many
teenth-
century thousand editions of separate plays. The
editors. eighteenth-century editors of the collected
works endeavoured with varying degrees of success
to purge the text of the numerous incoherences
of the folios, and to restore, where good taste or
good sense required it, the lost text of the contemporary quartos. It is largely owing to a due co-ordi-
nation of the results of the efforts of the eighteenth-
century editors by their successors in the present
century that Shakespeare's work has become intelli-

gible to general readers unversed in textual criticism, and has won from them the veneration that it merits.[1]

√ Nicholas Rowe, a popular dramatist of Queen Anne's reign, and poet laureate to George I, was the first critical editor of Shakespeare. He produced an edition of his plays in six octavo volumes in 1709.

Nicholas Rowe, 1674–1718. A new edition in eight volumes followed in 1714, and another hand added a ninth volume which included the poems. Rowe prefixed a valuable life of the poet embodying traditions which were in danger of perishing without a record. His text followed that of the Fourth Folio. The plays were printed in the same order except that he transferred the spurious pieces from the beginning to the end. Rowe did not compare his text with that of the First Folio or of the quartos, but in the case of 'Romeo and Juliet' he met with an early quarto while his edition was passing through the press, and inserted at the end of the play the prologue which is only met with in the quartos. He made a few happy emendations, some of which coincide accidentally with the readings of the First Folio; but his text is deformed by many palpable errors. His practical experience as a playwright induced him, however, to prefix for the first time a list of *dramatis personæ* to each play, to divide and number acts and scenes on rational principles, and to mark the

[1] The best account of eighteenth-century criticism of Shakespeare is to be found in the preface to the Cambridge edition by Mr. Aldis Wright. The memoirs of the various editors in the *Dictionary of National Biography* supply useful information. I have made liberal use of these sources in the sketch given in the following pages.

entrances and exits of the characters. Spelling, punctuation, and grammar he corrected and modernised.

The poet Pope was Shakespeare's second editor. His edition in six quarto volumes was completed in

Alexander Pope, 1688–1744.

1725. The poems, edited by Dr. George Sewell, with an essay on the rise and progress of the stage, and a glossary, appeared in a seventh volume. Pope had few qualifications for the task, and the venture was a commercial failure. In his preface Pope, while he fully recognised Shakespeare's native genius, deemed his achievement deficient in artistic quality. Pope claimed to have collated the text of the Fourth Folio with that of all preceding editions, and although his work indicates that he had access to the First Folio and some of the quartos, it is clear that his text was based on that of Rowe. His innovations are numerous, and are derived from 'his private sense and conjecture,' but they are often plausible and ingenious. He was the first to indicate the place of each new scene, and he improved on Rowe's subdivision of the scenes. A second edition of Pope's version in ten duodecimo volumes appeared in 1728 with Sewell's name on the title-page as well as Pope's. There were few alterations in the text, though a preliminary table supplied a list of twenty-eight quartos. Other editions followed in 1735 and 1768. The last was printed at Garrick's suggestion at Birmingham from Baskerville's types.

Pope found a rigorous critic in Lewis Theobald, who although contemptible as a writer of original verse and

prose proved himself the most inspired of all the textual critics of Shakespeare. Pope savagely
avenged himself on his censor by holding him
up to ridicule as the hero of the 'Dunciad.'
Theobald first displayed his critical skill in 1726 in a
volume which deserves to rank as a classic in English
literature.   The title runs 'Shakespeare Restored, or
a specimen of the many errors as well committed as
unamended by Mr. Pope in his late edition of this
poet, designed not only to correct the said edition but
to restore the true reading of Shakespeare in all the
editions ever yet publish'd.'   There at page 137 appears Theobald's great emendation in Shakespeare's
account of Falstaff's death (Henry V, ii. iii. 17):
'His nose was as sharp as a pen and a' babbled of
green fields,' in place of the reading in the old copies,
'His nose was as sharp as a pen and a table of
green fields.' In 1733 Theobald brought out his
edition of Shakespeare in seven volumes.   In 1740 it
reached a second issue.   A third edition was published
in 1752.   Others are dated 1772 and 1773.   It is
stated that 12,860 copies in all were sold.   Theobald
made the First Folio the basis of his text, although he
failed to adopt all the correct readings of that version,
but over 300 corrections or emendations which he
made in his edition have become part and parcel of
the authorised canon.   Theobald's principles of textual criticism were as enlightened as his practice was
triumphant.   'I ever labour,' he wrote to Warburton,
'to make the smallest deviation that I possibly can
from the text; never to alter at all where I can by

Lewis
Theobald,
1688–1744.

any means explain a passage with sense; nor ever
by any emendation to make the author better when it
is probable the text came from his own hands.'
Theobald has every right to the title of the Porson of
Shakespearean criticism.[1] The following are favourable specimens of his insight. In ' Macbeth ' (I. vii. 6)
for ' this bank and school of time,' he substituted
the familiar ' bank and shoal of time.' In ' Antony
and Cleopatra ' the old copies (v. ii. 87) made
Cleopatra say of Antony :

> For his bounty,
> There was no winter in 't; an Anthony it was
> That grew the more by reaping.

For the gibberish ' an Anthony it was,' Theobald read
' an autumn 'twas,' and thus gave the lines true point
and poetry. A third notable instance, somewhat
more recondite, is found in ' Coriolanus ' (II. i. 59–60)
where Menenius asks the tribunes in the First Folio
version ' What harm can your besom conspectuities
[*i.e.* vision or eyes] glean out of this character ? '
Theobald replaced the meaningless epithet ' besom '
by ' bisson ' (*i.e.* purblind), a recognised Elizabethan
word which Shakespeare had already employed in
' Hamlet ' (II. ii. 529).[2]

---

[1] Mr. Churton Collins's admirable essay on Theobald's textual
criticism of Shakespeare entitled ' The Porson of Shakespearean Critics,'
is reprinted from the *Quarterly Review* in his *Essays and Studies*,
1895, pp. 263 seq.

[2] Collier doubtless followed Theobald's hint when he pretended to
have found in his ' Perkins Folio ' the extremely happy emendation (now
generally adopted) of ' bisson multitude ' for ' bosom multiplied ' in
Coriolanus's speech :

> How shall this bisson multitude digest
> The senate's courtesy? — (*Coriolanus*, III. i. 131-2.)

The fourth editor was Sir Thomas Hanmer, a country gentleman without much literary culture, but possessing a large measure of mother wit. He was speaker in the House of Commons for a few months in 1714, and retiring soon afterwards from public life devoted his leisure to a thoroughgoing scrutiny of Shakespeare's plays. His edition, which was the earliest to pretend to typographical beauty, was printed at the Oxford University Press in 1744 in six quarto volumes. It contained a number of good engravings by Gravelot after designs by Francis Hayman, and was long highly valued by book collectors. No editor's name was given. In forming his text, Hanmer depended exclusively on his own ingenuity. He made no recourse to the old copies. The result was a mass of common sense emendations, some of which have been permanently accepted.[1] Hanmer's edition was reprinted in 1770–1.

Sir Thomas Hanmer, 1677–1746.

In 1747 Bishop Warburton produced a revised version of Pope's edition in eight volumes. Warburton was hardly better qualified for the task than Pope, and such improvements as he introduced are mainly borrowed from Theobald and Hanmer. On both these critics he arrogantly and unjustly heaped abuse in his preface. The Bishop was consequently criticised with appro-

Bishop Warburton, 1698–1779.

---

[1] A happy example of his shrewdness may be quoted from *King Lear*, III. vi. 72, where in all previous editions Edgar's enumeration of various kinds of dogs included the line 'Hound or spaniel brach or hym [or him].' For the last word Hanmer substituted 'lym,' which was the Elizabethan synonym for bloodhound.

priate severity for his pretentious incompetence by many writers; among them, by Thomas Edwards, whose 'Supplement to Warburton's Edition of Shakespeare' first appeared in 1747, and, having been renamed 'The Canons of Criticism' next year in the third edition, passed through as many as seven editions by 1765.

Dr. Johnson, the sixth editor, completed his edition in eight volumes in 1765, and a second issue followed three years later. Although he made some independent collation of the quartos, his textual labours were slight, and his verbal notes show little close knowledge of sixteenth and seventeenth century literature. But in his preface and elsewhere he displays a genuine, if occasionally sluggish, sense of Shakespeare's greatness, and his massive sagacity enabled him to indicate convincingly Shakespeare's triumphs of characterisation.

Dr. Johnson, 1709–83.

The seventh editor, Edward Capell, advanced on his predecessors in many respects. He was a clumsy writer, and Johnson declared, with some justice, that he 'gabbled monstrously,' but his collation of the quartos and the First and Second Folios was conducted on more thorough and scholarly methods than any of his predecessors, not excepting Theobald. His industry was untiring, and he is said to have transcribed the whole of Shakespeare ten times. Capell's edition appeared in ten small octavo volumes in 1768. He showed himself well versed in Elizabethan literature in a volume of notes which appeared in 1774, and in three further

Edward Capell, 1713–81.

volumes, entitled ' Notes, Various Readings, and the School of Shakespeare,' which were not published till 1783, two years after his death. The last volume, 'The School of Shakespeare,' consisted of 'authentic extracts from divers English books that were in print in that author's time,' to which was appended 'Notitia Dramatica; or, Tables of Ancient Plays (from their beginning to the Restoration of Charles II).'

George Steevens, whose saturnine humour involved him in a lifelong series of literary quarrels with rival students of Shakespeare, made invaluable contributions to Shakespearean study. In 1766 he reprinted twenty of the plays from the quartos. Soon afterwards he revised Johnson's edition without much assistance from the Doctor, and his revision, which embodied numerous improvements, appeared in ten volumes in 1773. It was long regarded as the standard version. Steevens's antiquarian knowledge alike of Elizabethan history and literature was greater than that of any previous editor; his citations of parallel passages from the writings of Shakespeare's contemporaries, in elucidation of obscure words and phrases, have not been exceeded in number or excelled in aptness by any of his successors. All commentators of recent times are more deeply indebted in this department of their labours to Steevens than to any other critic. But he lacked taste as well as temper, and excluded from his edition Shakespeare's sonnets and poems, because, he wrote, 'the strongest Act of Parliament that could be framed would fail to compel readers into their service.' [1]

George Steevens, 1736–1800.

1 Edition of 1793, vol. i. p. 7.

The second edition of Johnson and Steevens's version appeared in ten volumes in 1778. The third
edition, published in ten volumes in 1785, was revised by Steevens's friend, Isaac Reed (1742–1807), a
scholar of his own type. The fourth and last edition
published in Steevens's lifetime was prepared by
himself in fifteen volumes in 1793. As he grew
older, he made some reckless changes in the text,
chiefly with the unhallowed object of mystifying
those engaged in the same field. With a malignity
that was not without humour, he supplied, too, many
obscene notes to coarse expressions, and he pretended
that he owed his indecencies to one or other of two
highly respectable clergymen, Richard Amner and
John Collins, whose surnames were in each instance
appended. He had known and quarrelled with both.
Such proofs of his perversity justified the title which
Gifford applied to him of 'the Puck of Commentators.'

Edmund Malone, who lacked Steevens's quick wit
and incisive style, was a laborious and amiable archæ-
ologist, without much ear for poetry or delicate literary taste. He threw abundance of
new light on Shakespeare's biography, and
on the chronology and sources of his works, while
his researches into the beginnings of the English
stage added a new chapter of first-rate importance to
English literary history. To Malone is due the first
rational 'attempt to ascertain the order in which the
plays attributed to Shakespeare were written.' His
earliest results on the topic were contributed to

Edmund
Malone,
1741–1812.

Y

Steevens's edition of 1778. Two years later he published, as a supplement to Steevens's work, two volumes containing a history of the Elizabethan stage, with reprints of Arthur Brooke's 'Romeus and Juliet,' Shakespeare's Poems, and the plays falsely ascribed to him in the Third and Fourth Folios. A quarrel with Steevens followed, and was never closed. In 1787 Malone issued 'A Dissertation on the Three Parts of King Henry VI,' tending to show that those plays were not originally written by Shakespeare. In 1790 appeared his edition of Shakespeare in ten volumes, the first in two parts.

What is known among booksellers as the 'First Variorum' edition of Shakespeare was prepared by Steevens's friend, Isaac Reed, after Steevens's death. It was based on a copy of Steevens's work of 1793, which had been enriched with numerous manuscript additions, and it embodied the published notes and prefaces of preceding editors. It was published in twenty-one volumes in 1803. The 'Second Variorum' edition, which was mainly a reprint of the first, was published in twenty-one volumes in 1813. The 'Third Variorum' was prepared for the press by James Boswell the younger, the son of Dr. Johnson's biographer. It was based on Malone's edition of 1790, but included massive accumulations of notes left in manuscript by Malone at his death. Malone had been long engaged on a revision of his edition, but died in 1812, before it was completed. Boswell's 'Malone,' as the new work is often called, appeared in twenty-one volumes in 1821. It is the most valu-

Variorum editions.

able of all collected editions of Shakespeare's works, but the three volumes of preliminary essays on Shakespeare's biography and writings, and the illustrative notes brought together in the final volume, are confusedly arranged and are unindexed; many of the essays and notes break off abruptly at the point at which they were left at Malone's death. A new 'Variorum' edition, on an exhaustive scale, was undertaken by Mr. H. Howard Furness of Philadelphia, and eleven volumes have appeared since 1871 ('Romeo and Juliet,' 'Macbeth,' 'Hamlet,' 2 vols., 'King Lear,' 'Othello,' 'Merchant of Venice,' 'As You Like It,' 'Tempest,' 'Midsummer Night's Dream,' and 'Winter's Tale').

Of nineteenth-century editors who have prepared collective editions of Shakespeare's work with original annotations those who have most successfully pursued the great traditions of the eighteenth century are Alexander Dyce, Howard Staunton, Nikolaus Delius, and the Cambridge editors William George Clark (1821–78) and Dr. Aldis Wright.

Nineteenth-century editors.

Alexander Dyce was almost as well read as Steevens in Elizabethan literature, and especially in the drama of the period, and his edition of Shakespeare in nine volumes, which was first published in 1857, has many new and valuable illustrative notes and a few good textual emendations, as well as a useful glossary; but Dyce's annotations are not always adequate, and often tantalise the reader by their brevity. Howard Staunton's

Alexander Dyce, 1798–1869.

edition first appeared in three volumes between 1868
and 1870. He also was well read in contemporary literature and was an acute textual critic. His introductions bring together
much interesting stage history. Nikolaus Delius's
edition was issued at Elberfeld in seven volumes between 1854 and 1861. Delius's text
is formed on sound critical principles and is to
be trusted thoroughly. A fifth edition in two volumes
appeared in 1882. The Cambridge edition, which
first appeared in nine volumes between 1863
and 1866, exhaustively notes the textual
variations of all preceding editions, and
supplies the best and fullest *apparatus criticus*. (Of
new editions, one dated 1887 is also in nine volumes,
and another, dated 1893, in forty volumes.)

Howard
Staunton,
1810–74.

Nikolaus
Delius,
1813–88.

The Cam-
bridge
edition,
1863–6.

Other editors of the complete works of Shakespeare of the nineteenth century, whose labours,
although of some value, present fewer distinctive characteristics are: William Harness (1825, 8 vols.);
Samuel Weller Singer (1826, 10 vols., printed at the
Chiswick Press for William Pickering, illustrated by Stothard and others; reissued in
1856 with essays by William Watkiss
Lloyd); Charles Knight, with discursive notes and
pictorial illustrations by F. W. Fairholt and others
('Pictorial edition,' 8 vols., including biography
and the doubtful plays, 1838–43, often reissued
under different designations); Bryan Waller Procter,
i.e. Barry Cornwall (1839–43, 3 vols.); John
Payne Collier (1841–4, 8 vols.; another edition,

Other
nineteenth-
century
editions.

8 vols., privately printed, 1878, 4to); Samuel
Phelps, the actor (1852-4, 2 vols.; another edition,
1882-4); J. O. Halliwell (1853-61, 15 vols. folio, with
an encyclopædic collection of annotations of earlier
editors and pictorial illustrations); Richard Grant
White (Boston, U.S.A., 1857-65, 12 vols.); W. J.
Rolfe (New York, 1871-96, 40 vols.); the Rev.
H. N. Hudson (the Harvard edition, Boston, 1881,
20 vols.). The latest complete annotated editions
published in this country are, 'The Henry Irving
Shakespeare,' edited by F. A. Marshall and others —
especially useful for notes on stage history (8 vols.
1888-90) — and 'The Temple Shakespeare,' concisely
edited by Mr. Israel Gollancz (38 vols. 12mo, 1894-6).

Of one-volume editions of the unannotated text,
the best are the Globe, edited by W. G. Clark and
Dr. Aldis Wright (1864, and constantly reprinted —
since 1891 with a new and useful glossary); the
Leopold (1876, from the text of Delius, with preface
by Dr. Furnivall); and the Oxford, edited by Mr.
W. J. Craig (1894).

XX

POSTHUMOUS REPUTATION

SHAKESPEARE defied at every stage in his career the laws of the classical drama. He rode roughshod over the unities of time, place, and action. There were critics in his day who zealously championed the ancient rules, and viewed with distrust any infringement of them. But the force of Shakespeare's genius — its revelation of new methods of dramatic art — was not lost on the lovers of the ancient ways; and even those who, to assuage their consciences, entered a formal protest against his innovations, soon swelled the chorus of praise with which his work was welcomed by contemporary playgoers, cultured and uncultured alike. The unauthorised publishers of 'Troilus and Cressida' in 1608 faithfully echoed public opinion when they prefaced to the work the note : 'This author's comedies are so framed to the life that they serve for the most common commentaries of all actions of our lives, showing such a dexterity and power of wit that the most displeased with plays are pleased with his comedies. . . . So much and such savoured salt of wit is in his comedies that they seem for their height of pleasure to be born in the sea that brought forth Venus.'

Anticipating the final verdict, the editors of the
first Folio wrote, seven years after Shakespeare's
death: 'These plays have had their trial already and
stood out all appeals.'[1] Ben Jonson, the staunch-
est champion of classical canons, noted that Shakespeare 'wanted art,' but he allowed him,
in verses prefixed to the First Folio, the
first place among all dramatists, including those of Greece and Rome, and claimed that all
Europe owed him homage:

Ben Jon-
son's tri-
ute.

> Triumph, my Briton, thou hast one to show,
> To whom all scenes of Europe homage owe.
> He was not of an age, but for all time.

n 1630 Milton penned in like strains an epitaph on
the great heir of fame ' :

> What needs my Shakespeare for his honoured bones
> The labour of an age in pilèd stones?
> Or that his hollowed reliques should be hid
> Under a star-y-pointing pyramid?
> Dear son of memory, great heir of fame,
> What need'st thou such weak witness of thy name?
> Thou in our wonder and astonishment
> Hast built thyself a lifelong monument.

A writer of fine insight who veiled himself under the initials I. M. S.[2] contributed to the Second

---

[1] Cf. the opening line of Matthew Arnold's Sonnet on Shakespeare :

Others abide our question. Thou art free.

[2] These letters have been interpreted as standing for the inscription
In Memoriam Scriptoris ' as well as for the name of the writer. In the
atter connection, they have been variously and inconclusively read as
asper Mayne (Student), a young Oxford writer; as John Marston
Student or Satirist); and as John Milton (Senior or Student).

Folio of 1632 a splendid eulogy.   The opening lines
declare ' Shakespeare's freehold' to have been :

> A mind reflecting ages past, whose clear
> And equal surface can make things appear
> Distant a thousand years, and represent
> Them in their lively colours' just extent.

It was his faculty

> To outrun hasty time, retrieve the fates,
> Roll back the heavens, blow ope the iron gates
> Of death and Lethe, where (confused) lie
> Great heaps of ruinous mortality.

Milton and I. M. S. were followed within ten years
by critics of tastes so varied as the dramatist of do-
mesticity Thomas Heywood, the gallant lyrist Sir
John Suckling, the philosophic and 'ever-memorable'
John Hales of Eton, and the untiring versifier of the
stage and court, Sir William D'Avenant.   Before 1640
Hales is said to have triumphantly established, in a
public dispute held with men of learning in his rooms
at Eton, the proposition that 'there was no subject
of which any poet ever writ but he could produce it
much better done in Shakespeare.'[1]   Leonard Digges

---

[1] Charles Gildon, in 1694, in 'Some Reflections on Mr. Rymer's
Short View of Tragedy,' which he addressed to Dryden, gives the
classical version of this incident.   'To give the world,' Gildon informs
Dryden, 'some satisfaction that Shakespear has had as great a Venera-
tion paid his Excellence by men of unquestion'd parts as this I now
express of him, I shall give some account of what I have heard from
your Mouth, Sir, about the noble Triumph he gain'd over all the
Ancients by the Judgment of the ablest Critics of that time.   The
Matter of Fact (if my Memory fail me not) was this.   Mr. *Hales* of Eaton
affirm'd that he wou'd shew all the Poets of Antiquity outdone by
Shakespear, in all the Topics, and common places made use of in Poetry.
The Enemies of Shakespear wou'd by no means yield him so much
Excellence : so that it came to a Resolution of a trial of skill upon that

(in the 1640 edition of the 'Poems') asserted that every revival of Shakespeare's plays drew crowds to pit, boxes, and galleries alike.   At a little later date, Shakespeare's plays were the 'closet companions' of Charles I's 'solitudes.'[1]

After the Restoration public taste in England veered towards the French and classical dramatic models.[2]   Shakespeare's work was subjected to some unfavourable criticism as the product of nature to the exclusion of art, but the eclipse proved more partial and temporary than is commonly admitted.   The pedantic censure of Thomas Rymer on the score of Shakespeare's indifference to the classical canons attracted attention, but awoke in England no substantial echo.   In his 'Short View of Tragedy' (1692) Rymer mainly concentrated his attention on 'Othello,' and reached the eccentric conclusion that it was 'a bloody farce without salt or savour.'   In Pepys's eyes 'The Tempest' had 'no great wit,' and 'Midsummer Night's Dream' was the most insipid and ridiculous play; yet this

1660-1702.

Subject; the place agreed on for the Dispute was Mr. Hales's Chamber at Eaton; a great many Books were sent down by the Enemies of this Poet, and on the appointed day my Lord Falkland, Sir John Suckling, and all the Persons of Quality that had Wit and Learning, and interested themselves in the Quarrel, met there, and upon a thorough Disquisition of the point, the Judges chose by agreement out of this Learned and Ingenious Assembly unanimously gave the Preference to Shakespear.   And the Greek and Roman Poets were adjudg'd to Vail at least their Glory in that of the English Hero.'

[1] Milton, *Iconoclastes*, 1690, pp. 9-10.

[2] Cf. *Evelyn's Diary*, November 26, 1661 : 'I saw Hamlet, Prince of Denmark, played, but now the old plays began to disgust the refined age, since His Majesty's being so long abroad.'

exacting critic witnessed thirty-six performances of
twelve of Shakespeare's plays between October 11,
1660, and February 6, 1668–9, seeing ' Hamlet '
four times, and ' Macbeth,' which he admitted to be
' a most excellent play for variety,' nine times.
Dryden's   Dryden, the literary dictator of the day,
view.   repeatedly complained of Shakespeare's in-
equalities— 'he is the very Janus of poets.'[1]   But in
almost the same breath Dryden declared that Shakespeare was held in as much veneration among Englishmen as Æschylus among the Athenians, and that ' he
was the man who of all modern and perhaps ancient
poets had the largest and most comprehensive soul. . . .
When he describes anything, you more than see it—
you feel it too.'[2]   In 1693, when Sir Godfrey Kneller
presented Dryden with a copy of the Chandos portrait
of Shakespeare, the poet acknowledged the gift thus

TO SIR GODFREY KNELLER

Shakespear, thy Gift, I place before my sight;
With awe, I ask his Blessing 'ere I write;
With Reverence look on his Majestick Face;
Proud to be less, but of his Godlike Race.
His Soul Inspires me, while thy Praise I write,
And I, like *Teucer*, under *Ajax* fight.

Writers of Charles II's reign of such opposite
temperaments as Margaret Cavendish, duchess of

[1] *Conquest of Granada*, 1672.
[2] *Essay on Dramatic Poesie*, 1668.   Some interesting, if more
qualified, criticism by Dryden also appears in his preface to an adaptation of 'Troilus and Cressida' in 1679.   In the prologue to his and
D'Avenant's adaptation of 'The Tempest' in 1676, he wrote:

But Shakespeare's magic could not copied be;
Within that circle none durst walk but he.

Newcastle, and Sir Charles Sedley vigorously argued for Shakespeare's supremacy. As a girl the sober duchess declares she fell in love with Shakespeare. In her 'Sociable Letters,' which were published in 1664, she enthusiastically, if diffusely, described how Shakespeare creates the illusion that he had been 'transformed into every one of those persons he hath described,' and suffered all their emotions. When she witnessed one of his tragedies she felt persuaded that she was witnessing an episode in real life. 'Indeed,' she concludes, 'Shakespeare had a clear judgment, a quick wit, a subtle observation, a deep apprehension, and a most eloquent elocution.' The profligate Sedley, in a prologue to the 'Wary Widdow,' a comedy by one Higden, produced in 1693, apostrophised Shakespeare thus:

> Shackspear whose fruitfull Genius, happy wit
> Was fram'd and finisht at a lucky hit
> The pride of Nature, and the shame of Schools,
> Born to Create, and not to Learn from Rules.

Many adaptations of Shakespeare's plays were contrived to meet current sentiment of a less admirable type. But they failed efficiently to supersede the originals. Dryden and D'Avenant converted 'The Tempest' into an opera (1670). D'Avenant single-handed adapted 'The Two Noble Kinsmen' (1668) and 'Macbeth' (1674). Dryden dealt similarly with 'Troilus' (1679); Thomas Duffett with 'The Tempest' (1675); Shadwell with 'Timon' (1678); Nahum Tate with 'Richard II' (1681), 'Lear' (1681), and 'Coriolanus' (1682); John

Restoration adaptations.

Crowne with 'Henry VI' (1681); D'Urfey with 'Cym
beline' (1682); Ravenscoft with 'Titus Andronicus'
(1687); Otway with 'Romeo and Juliet' (1692), and
John Sheffield, duke of Buckingham, with 'Julius
Cæsar' (1692). But during the same period the chief
actor of the day, Thomas Betterton, won his spurs as
the interpreter of Shakespeare's leading parts, often
in unrevised versions. Hamlet was accounted that
actor's masterpiece.[1] 'No succeeding tragedy for
several years,' wrote Downes, the prompter at Betterton's theatre, 'got more reputation or money to the
company than this.'

From the accession of Queen Anne to the present
day the tide of Shakespeare's reputation, both on the
From 1702 stage and among critics, has flowed onward
onwards. almost uninterruptedly. The censorious
critic, John Dennis, in his 'Letters' on Shakespeare's
'genius,' gave his work in 1711 whole-hearted commendation; and two of the greatest men of letters of
the eighteenth century, Pope and Johnson, although
they did not withhold all censure, paid him, as we have
seen, the homage of becoming his editor. The school
of textual criticism which Theobald and Capell founded
in the middle years of the century has never ceased
its activity since their day.[2] Edmund Malone's devotion at the end of the eighteenth century to the biog-

---

[1] Cf. *Shakspere's Century of Praise*, 1591–1693, New Shakspere
Society, ed. Ingleby and Toulmin Smith, 1879; and *Fresh Allusions*,
ed. Furnivall, 1886.

[2] Cf. W. Sidney Walker, *Critical Examination of the Text of
Shakespeare*, 1859.

raphy of the poet and the contemporary history of the stage secured for him a vast band of disciples, of whom Joseph Hunter and John Payne Collier well deserve mention. But of all Malone's successors, James Orchard Halliwell, afterwards Halliwell-Phillipps (1820–89), has made the most important additions to our knowledge of Shakespeare's biography.

Meanwhile, at the beginning of the nineteenth century, there arose a third school to expound exclusively the æsthetic excellence of the plays. In its inception the æsthetic school owed much to the methods of Schlegel and other admiring critics of Shakespeare in Germany. But Coleridge in his 'Notes and Lectures'[1] and Hazlitt in his 'Characters of Shakespeare's Plays' (1817) are the best representatives of the æsthetic school in this or any other country. Although Professor Dowden, in his 'Shakespeare, his Mind and Art' (1874), and Mr. Swinburne in his 'Study of Shakespeare' (1880), are worthy followers, Coleridge and Hazlitt remain as æsthetic critics unsurpassed. In the effort to supply a fuller interpretation of Shakespeare's works—textual, historical, and æsthetic—two publishing societies have done much valuable work. 'The Shakespeare Society' was founded in 1841 by Collier, Halliwell, and their friends, and published some forty-eight volumes before its dissolution in 1853.

[1] See *Notes and Lectures on Shakespeare and other Poets by S. T. Coleridge, now first collected by T. Ashe*, 1883. Coleridge hotly resented the remark, which he attributed to Wordsworth, that a German critic first taught us to think correctly concerning Shakespeare. (Coleridge to Mudford, 1818; cf. Dyke Campbell's memoir of Coleridge, p. cv.). But there is much to be said for Wordsworth's general view (see p. 344, note 1).

The New Shakspere Society, which was founded by Dr. Furnivall in 1874, issued during the ensuing twenty years twenty-seven publications, illustrative mainly of the text and of contemporary life and literature.

√In 1769 Shakespeare's 'jubilee' was celebrated for three days (September 6–8) at Stratford, under the direction of Garrick, Dr. Arne, and Boswell. The festivities were repeated on a small scale in April 1827 and April 1830. 'The Shakespeare tercentenary festival,' which was held at Stratford from April 23 to May 4, 1864, claimed to be a national celebration.[1]

Stratford festivals.

On the English stage the name of every eminent actor since Betterton, the great actor of the period of the Restoration, has been identified with Shakespearean parts. Steele, writing in the 'Tatler' (No. 167) in reference to Betterton's funeral in the cloisters of Westminster Abbey on May 2, 1710, instanced his rendering of Othello as proof of an unsurpassable talent in realising Shakespeare's subtlest conceptions on the stage. One great and welcome innovation in Shakespearean acting is closely associated with Betterton's name. He encouraged the substitution, that was inaugurated by Killigrew, of women for boys in female parts. The first *rôle* that was professionally rendered by a woman in a public theatre was that of Desdemona in 'Othello,'

On the English stage.

The first appearance of actresses in Shakespearean parts.

---

[1] R. E. Hunter, *Shakespeare and the Tercentenary Celebration,* 1864.

apparently on December 8, 1660.[1] The actress on this occasion is said to have been Mrs. Margaret Hughes, Prince Rupert's mistress; but Betterton's wife, who was at first known on the stage as Mrs. Saunderson, was the first actress to present a series of Shakespeare's great female characters. Mrs. Betterton gave her husband powerful support, from 1663 onwards, in such *rôles* as Ophelia, Juliet, Queen Catherine, and Lady Macbeth.   Betterton formed a school of actors who carried on his traditions for many years after his death. Robert Wilks (1670–1732) as Hamlet, and Barton Booth (1681–1733) as Henry VIII and Hotspur, were popularly accounted no unworthy successors.   Colley Cibber (1671–1757) as actor, theatrical manager, and dramatic critic was both a loyal disciple of Betterton and a lover of Shakespeare, though his vanity and his faith in the ideals of the Restoration incited him to perpetrate many outrages on Shakespeare's text when preparing it for theatrical representation. His notorious adaptation of 'Richard III,' which was first produced in 1700, long held the stage to the exclusion of the original version.   But towards the middle of the eighteenth century all earlier efforts to interpret Shakespeare in the playhouse were eclipsed in public esteem by the concentrated energy and intelligence of David Garrick.   Garrick's enthusiasm for the poet

---

[1] Thomas Jordan, a very humble poet, wrote a prologue to notify the new procedure, and referred to the absurdity of the old custom:

> For to speak truth, men act, that are between
> Forty and fifty, wenches of fifteen,
> With bone so large and nerve so uncompliant,
> When you call DESDEMONA, enter GIANT.

and his histrionic genius riveted Shakespeare's hold on public taste. His claim to have restored to the stage the text of Shakespeare — purified of Restoration defilements — cannot be allowed without serious qualifications. Garrick had no scruple in presenting plays of Shakespeare in versions that he or his friends had recklessly garbled. He supplied 'Romeo and Juliet' with a happy ending; he converted 'The Taming of The Shrew' into the farce of 'Katherine and Petruchio,' 1754; he introduced radical changes in 'Antony and Cleopatra,' 'Two Gentlemen of Verona,' 'Cymbeline,' and 'Midsummer Night's Dream.' Nevertheless, no actor has won an equally exalted reputation in so vast and varied a repertory of Shakespearean *rôles*. His triumphant début as Richard III in 1741 was followed by equally successful performances of Hamlet, Lear, Macbeth, King John, Romeo, Falconbridge, Othello, Leontes, Benedick, and Antony in 'Antony and Cleopatra.' Garrick was not quite undeservedly buried in Westminster Abbey on February 1, 1779, at the foot of Shakespeare's statue.

David Garrick, 1717–79.

Garrick was ably seconded by Mrs. Clive (1711–85), Mrs. Cibber (1714–66), and Mrs. Pritchard (1711–68). Mrs. Cibber as Constance in 'King John,' and Mrs. Pritchard in Lady Macbeth, excited something of the same enthusiasm as Garrick in Richard III and Lear. There were, too, contemporary critics who judged rival actors to show in certain parts powers equal, if not superior, to those of Garrick. Charles Macklin (1697?–1797) for nearly half a century, from

1735 to 1785, gave many hundred performances of a
masterly rendering of Shylock. The character had,
for many years previous to Macklin's assumption of it,
been allotted to comic actors, but Macklin effectively
concentrated his energy on the tragic significance of
the part with an effect that Garrick could not surpass.
Macklin was also reckoned successful in Polonius and
Iago. John Henderson, the Bath Roscius (1747–85),
who, like Garrick, was buried in Westminster Abbey,
derived immense popularity from his representation
of Falstaff; while in subordinate characters like
Mercutio, Slender, Jaques, Touchstone, and Sir Toby
Belch, John Palmer (1742?–1798) was held to approach perfection. But Garrick was the accredited
chief of the theatrical profession until his death. He
was then succeeded in his place of predominance by
John Philip Kemble, who derived invaluable support
from his association with one abler than himself,
his sister, Mrs. Siddons.

Somewhat stilted and declamatory in speech,
Kemble enacted a wide range of characters of
John Philip Kemble, 1757–1823. Shakespearean tragedy with a dignity that
won the admiration of Pitt, Sir Walter
Scott, Charles Lamb, and Leigh Hunt.
Coriolanus was regarded as his masterpiece, but his
renderings of Hamlet, King John, Wolsey, the Duke in
' Measure for Measure,' Leontes, and Brutus satisfied
Mrs. Sarah Siddons, 1755–1831. the most exacting canons of contemporary
theatrical criticism. Kemble's sister, Mrs.
Siddons, was the greatest actress that Shake-
speare's countrymen have known. Her noble and

z

awe-inspiring presentation of Lady Macbeth, her Constance, her Queen Katherine, have, according to the best testimony, not been equalled even by the achievements of the eminent actresses of France.

During the present century the most conspicuous histrionic successes in Shakespearean drama have been won by Edmund Kean, whose triumphant rendering of Shylock on his first appearance at Drury Lane Theatre on January 26, 1814, is one of the most stirring incidents in the history of the English stage. Kean defied the rigid convention of the 'Kemble School,' and gave free rein to his impetuous passions. Besides Shylock, he excelled in Richard III, Othello, Hamlet, and Lear. No less a critic than Coleridge declared that to see him act was like 'reading Shakespeare by flashes of lightning.'. Among other Shakespearean actors of Kean's period a high place was allotted by public esteem to George Frederick Cooke (1756–1811), whose Richard III, first given in London at Covent Garden Theatre, October 31, 1801, was accounted his masterpiece. Charles Lamb, writing in 1822, declared that of all the actors who flourished in his time, Robert Bensley 'had most of the swell of soul,' and Lamb gave with a fine enthusiasm in his 'Essays of Elia' an analysis (which has become classical) of Bensley's performance of Malvolio. But Bensley's powers were rated more moderately by more experienced playgoers.[1] Lamb's praises of Mrs. Jordan (1762–1816) in Ophelia, Helena, and Viola in 'Twelfth Night,' are

Edmund Kean, 1787–1833.

---

[1] *Essays of Elia*, ed. Canon Ainger, pp. 180 seq.

corroborated by the eulogies of Hazlitt and Leigh Hunt. In the part of Rosalind Mrs. Jordan is reported on all sides to have beaten Mrs. Siddons out of the field.

The torch thus lit by Garrick, by the Kembles, and by Kean and his contemporaries was worthily kept alive by William Charles Macready, a cultivated and conscientious actor, who, during a professional career

William Charles Macready, 1793–1873. of more than forty years (1810–51), assumed every great part in Shakespearean tragedy. Although Macready lacked the classical bearing of Kemble or the intense passion of Kean, he won as the interpreter of Shakespeare the whole-hearted suffrages of the educated public. Macready's chief associate in women characters was Helen Faucit (afterward Lady Martin), whose refined impersonations of Imogen, Beatrice, Juliet, and Rosalind form an attractive chapter in the history of the stage.

The most notable tribute paid to Shakespeare by any actor-manager of recent times was paid by Samuel Phelps (1804–78), who gave during his

Recent revivals. tenure of Sadler's Wells Theatre between 1844 and 1862 competent representations of all the plays save 'Troilus and Cressida,' and 'Titus Andronicus.' Sir Henry Irving, who since 1878 has been ably seconded by Miss Ellen Terry, has revived at the Lyceum Theatre between 1874 and the present time eleven plays ('Hamlet,' 'Macbeth,' 'Othello,' 'Richard III,' 'The Merchant of Venice,' 'Much Ado about Nothing,' 'Twelfth Night,' 'Romeo and Juliet,' 'King Lear,' 'Henry VIII,' and 'Cymbeline'), and has given each of them all the advantage they can derive from thoughtful acting as well as from lavish scenic elaboration.[1] But theatrical revivals of plays of Shakespeare are in England intermittent, and no theatrical manager since Phelps's retirement has sought systematically to illustrate on the stage the full range of Shakespearean drama. Far more in this direction has been attempted in Germany.[2] In one respect the history of recent Shakespearean representations can be viewed by the literary student with unqualified satisfaction. Although some changes of text or some rearrangement of the scenes are found imperative in all theatrical representations of Shakespeare, a growing public sentiment in England and elsewhere has for many years favoured as loyal an adherence to the authorised version of the plays as is practicable on the part of theatrical managers; and the evil traditions of the stage which sanctioned the perversions of the eighteenth century are happily well-nigh extinct.

Music and art in England owe much to Shakespeare's influence. From Thomas Morley, Purcell, Matthew Locke, and Arne to William Linley, Sir Henry Bishop, and Sir Arthur Sullivan, every distinguished musician has sought to improve on his predecessor's setting of one or more of Shakespeare's songs, or has composed concerted

In music and art.

---

[1] *Hamlet* in 1874-5 and *Macbeth* in 1888-9 were each performed by Sir Henry Irving for 200 nights in uninterrupted succession; these are the longest continuous runs that any of Shakespeare's plays are known to have enjoyed. [2] See p. 346.

music in illustration of some of his dramatic themes.[1]
In art, the publisher John Boydell organised in 1787
a scheme for illustrating scenes in Shakespeare's
work by the greatest living English artists. Some
fine pictures were the result. A hundred and sixty-
eight were painted in all, and the artists whom
Boydell employed included Sir Joseph Reynolds,
George Romney, Thomas Stothard, John Opie,
Benjamin West, James Barry, and Henry Fuseli.
All the pictures were exhibited from time to time,
between 1789 and 1804, at a gallery specially built
for the purpose in Pall Mall, and in 1802 Boydell
published a collection of engravings of the chief
pictures. The great series of paintings was dispersed
by auction in 1805. Few eminent artists of later
date, from Daniel Maclise to Sir John Millais, have
lacked the ambition to interpret some scene or character of Shakespearean drama.

In America no less enthusiasm for Shakespeare
has been manifested than in England. Editors and
In Amer- critics are hardly less numerous there, and
ica.   some criticism from American pens, like that
of James Russell Lowell, has reached the highest
literary level. Nowhere, perhaps, has more labour
been devoted to the study of his works than that
given by Mr. H. H. Furness of Philadelphia to the
preparation of his 'New Variorum' edition. The
Barton collection of Shakespeareana in the Boston
Public Library is one of the most valuable extant,
and the elaborate catalogue (1878-80) contains some

---

[1] Cf. Alfred Roffe, *Shakspere Music*, 1878; *Songs in Shakspere
. . . set to Music*, 1884, New Shakspere Society.

2,500 entries. First of Shakespeare's plays to be represented in America, 'Richard III' was performed in New York in March 1750. More recently Edwin Forrest, Junius Brutus Booth, Edwin Booth, Charlotte Cushman, and Miss Ada Rehan have maintained on the American stage the great traditions of Shakespearean acting ; while Mr. E. A. Abbey has devoted high artistic gifts to pictorial representation of scenes from the plays.

The Bible, alone of literary compositions, has been translated more frequently or into a greater number Transla- of languages than the works of Shakespeare. tions. The progress of his reputation in Germany, France, Italy, and Russia was somewhat slow at the outset. But in Germany the poet has received for nearly a century and a half a recognition scarcely less pronounced than that accorded him in America and in his own country. Three of Shakespeare's plays, now In Ger- in the Zurich Library, were brought thither many. by J. R. Hess from England in 1614. As early as 1626 'Hamlet,' 'King Lear,' and 'Romeo and Juliet' were acted at Dresden, and a version of 'The Taming of The Shrew' was played there and elsewhere at the end of the seventeenth century. But such mention of Shakespeare as is found in German literature between 1640 and 1740 only indicates a knowledge on the part of German readers either of Dryden's criticisms or of the accounts of him printed in English encyclopædias.[1] The earliest sign of a direct acquaint-

[1] Cf. D. G. Morhoff, *Unterricht von der teutschen Sprache und Poesie*, Kiel, 1682, p. 250.

ance with the plays is a poor translation of 'Julius
Cæsar' into German by Baron C. W. von Borck,
formerly Prussian minister in London, which was published at Berlin in 1741. A worse rendering of 'Romeo
and Juliet' followed in 1758. Meanwhile J. C. Gott-
sched (1700–66), an influential man of letters, warmly
denounced Shakespeare in a review of Von Borck's
effort in 'Beiträge zur deutschen Sprache' and elsewhere. Lessing came without delay to Shakespeare's
rescue, and set his reputation, in the estimation of the
German public, on that exalted pedestal which it has
not ceased to occupy. It was in 1759, in a journal
entitled 'Litteraturbriefe,' that Lessing first claimed
for Shakespeare superiority, not only to the French
dramatists Racine and Corneille, who hitherto had
dominated European taste, but to all ancient or
modern poets. Lessing's doctrine, which he developed in his 'Hamburgische Dramaturgie' (Hamburg,
1767, 2 vols. 8vo), was at once accepted by the poet
Johann Gottfried Herder in the 'Blätter von deutschen
Art und Kunst,' 1771. Christopher Martin Wieland
(1733–1813) in 1762 began a prose translation which
Johann Joachim Eschenburg (1743–1820) completed
Zurich, 13 vols., 1775–84). Between 1797 and 1833
there appeared at intervals the classical German rendering by August Wilhelm von Schlegel and Ludwig Tieck, leaders of the romantic school of
German literature, whose creed embodied, as
one of its first articles, an unwavering veneration for Shakespeare. Schlegel translated only seventeen plays, and his workmanship excels that of the

German transla- tions.

rest of the translation. Tieck's part in the undertaking was mainly confined to editing translations by
various hands. Many other German translations in
verse were undertaken during the same period, — by
J. H. Voss and his sons (Leipzig, 1818-29), by J. W
O. Benda (Leipzig, 1825-6), by J. Körner (Vienna,
1836), by A. Böttger (Leipzig, 1836-7), by E. Ortlepp
(Stuttgart, 1838-9), and by A. Keller and M. Rapp
(Stuttgart, 1843-6). The best of more recent German
translations is that by a band of poets and eminent men
of letters, including Friedrich von Bodenstedt, Ferdi
nand Freiligrath, and Paul Heyse (Leipzig, 1867-71, 38
vols.). Most of these versions have been many times
reissued, but, despite the high merits of Von Bodenstedt
and his companions' performance, Schlegel and Tieck's
achievement still holds the field. Schlegel's lectures on
'Shakespeare and the Drama,' which were delivered
at Vienna in 1808, and were translated into English
in 1815, are worthy of comparison with those of Cole
ridge, who owed much to their influence. Wordsworth
in 1815 declared that Schlegel and his disciples first
marked out the right road in æsthetic criticism, and
enjoyed at the moment superiority over all English
æsthetic critics of Shakespeare.[1] Subsequently Goethe

[1] In his ' Essay Supplementary to the Preface ' in the edition of his
Poems of 1815, Wordsworth wrote: 'The Germans only, of foreign
nations, are approaching towards a knowledge of what he [*i.e.* Shake
speare] is. In some respects they have acquired a superiority over the
fellow-countrymen of the poet; for among us, it is a common — I might
say an established — opinion that Shakespeare is justly praised when he is
pronounced to be " a wild irregular genius in whom great faults are com
pensated by great beauties." How long may it be before this misconcep
tion passes away and it becomes universally acknowledged that the judg
ment of Shakespeare . . . is not less admirable than his imagination? . .

poured forth, in his voluminous writings, a mass of criticism even more illuminating and appreciative than Schlegel's.[1] Although Goethe deemed Shakespeare's works unsuited to the stage, he adapted ' Romeo and Juliet ' for the Weimar Theatre, while Schiller prepared ' Macbeth ' (Stuttgart, 1801). Heine published in 1838 charming studies of Shakespeare's heroines(English translation 1895), and acknowledged only one defect in Shakespeare — that he was an Englishman.

During the last half-century textual, æsthetic, and biographical criticism has been pursued in Germany with unflagging industry and energy; and although laboured and supersubtle theorising characterises much German æsthetic criticism, its mass and variety testify to the impressiveness of the appeal that Shakespeare's work has made to the German intellect. The vain effort to stem the current of Shakespearean worship made by the dramatist, J. R. Benedix, in ' Die Shakespearomanie ' (Stuttgart, 1873, 8vo), stands practically alone. In studies of the text and metre Nikolaus Delius (1813–88) should, among recent German writers, be accorded the first place; in studies of the biography and stage history Friedrich Karl Elze (1821–89); in æsthetic studies Friedrich Alexander Theodor Kreyssig (1818–79), author of ' Vorlesungen über Shakespeare ' (Berlin, 1858 and 1874), and ' Shakespeare-Fragen ' (Leipzig, 1871). Ulrici's ' Shakespeare's Dramatic Art ' (first published at Halle in

Modern German writers on Shakespeare.

[1] Cf. *Wilhelm Meister*

1839) and Gervinus's Commentaries (first published at Leipzig in 1848–9), both of which are familiar in English translations, are suggestive but unconvincing æsthetic interpretations. The German Shakespeare Society, which was founded at Weimar in 1865, has published thirty-four year-books (edited successively by Von Bodenstedt, Delius, Elze, and F. A. Leo); each contains useful contributions to Shakespearean study.

Shakespeare has been no less effectually nation-alised on the German stage. The three great actors —

On the Ger-man stage. Frederick Ulrich Ludwig Schroeder (1744–1816) of Hamburg, Ludwig Devrient (1784–1832), and his nephew Gustav Emil Devrient (1803–72) — largely derived their fame from their successful assumptions of Shakespearean characters. Another of Ludwig Devrient's nephews, Eduard (1801–77), also an actor, prepared, with his son Otto, an acting German edition (Leipzig, 1873 and following years). An acting edition by Wilhelm Oechelhaeuser appeared previously at Berlin in 1871. Twenty-eight of the thirty-seven plays assigned to Shakespeare are now on recognised lists of German acting plays, including all the histories.[1] In 1895 as many as 706 performances of twenty-five of Shakespeare's plays were given in German theatres.[2] In 1896 no fewer than 910 performances were given of twenty-three plays. In 1897 performances of twenty-four plays reached a total of 930 — an average of

---

[1] Cf. *Jahrbuch der Deutsche Shakespeare-Gesellschaft* for 1894.
[2] *Ib.* for 1896, p. 438.

nearly three Shakespearean representations a day in
the German-speaking districts of Europe.[1] It is
not only in capitals like Berlin and Vienna that the
representations are frequent and popular. In towns
like Altona, Breslau, Frankfort-on-the-Maine, Hamburg, Magdeburg, and Rostock, Shakespeare is acted
constantly and the greater number of his dramas is
regularly kept in rehearsal. 'Othello,' 'Hamlet,'
'Romeo and Juliet,' and 'The Taming of The Shrew'
usually prove most attractive. Of the many German
musical composers who have worked on Shakespearean themes, Mendelssohn (in 'Midsummer Night's
Dream'), Schumann, and Franz Schubert (in setting
separate songs) have achieved the greatest success.

In France Shakespeare won recognition after a
longer struggle than in Germany. Cyrano de Ber-

In France. gerac (1619–55) plagiarised 'Cymbeline,'
'Hamlet,' and 'The Merchant of Venice'
in his 'Agrippina.' About 1680 Nicolas Clement,
Louis XIV's librarian, allowed Shakespeare imagina-

---

[1] The exact statistics for 1896 and 1897 were: 'Othello,' acted
135 and 121 times for the respective years; 'Hamlet,' 102 and 91;
'Romeo and Juliet,' 95 and 118; 'Taming of The Shrew,' 91 and 92;
'The Merchant of Venice,' 84 and 62; 'A Midsummer Night's Dream,'
68 and 92; 'A Winter's Tale,' 49 and 65; 'Much Ado about Nothing,'
47 and 32; 'Lear,' 41 and 34; 'As You Like It,' 37 and 29;
'Comedy of Errors,' 29 and 43; 'Julius Cæsar,' 27 and 29; 'Macbeth,' 10 and 12; 'Timon of Athens,' 7 and 0; 'The Tempest,' 5
and 1; 'Antony and Cleopatra,' 2 and 4; 'Coriolanus,' 0 and 20;
'Cymbeline,' 0 and 4; 'Richard II,' 15 and 5; 'Henry IV,' Part I,
26 and 23, Part II, 6 and 13; 'Henry V,' 4 and 7; 'Henry VI,' Part
I, 3 and 5, Part II, 2 and 2; 'Richard III,' 25 and 26 (*Jahrbuch der
Deutsche Shakespeare-Gesellschaft* for 1897, pp. 306 seq., and for 1898,
pp. 440 seq.).

tion, natural thoughts, and ingenious expression, but
deplored his obscenity.[1] Half a century elapsed before
public attention in France was again directed to Shakespeare.[2] The Abbé Prévost, in his periodical 'Le
Pour et Contre' (1733 seq.), acknowledged his power.
But it is to Voltaire that his countrymen owe, as he himself boasted, their first effective introduction to Shakespeare. Voltaire studied Shakespeare thoroughly on
his visit to England between 1726 and 1729, and his
influence is visible in his own dramas. In his 'Lettres
Philosophiques' (1731), afterwards reissued as 'Lettres
sur les Anglais,' 1734 (Nos. xviii. and xix.), and in
his 'Lettre sur la Tragédie' (1731), he expressed
admiration for Shakespeare's genius, but attacked his
Voltaire's   want of taste and art. He described him as
strictures.   'le Corneille de Londres, grand fou d'ailleurs,
mais il a des morceaux admirables.' Writing to the
Abbé des Fontaines in November 1735, Voltaire admitted many merits in 'Julius Cæsar,' on which he
published 'Observations' in 1764. Johnson replied to
Voltaire's general criticism in the preface to his edition
(1765), and Mrs. Elizabeth Montagu in 1769 in a separate volume, which was translated into French in
1777. Diderot made, in his 'Encyclopédie,' the first
stand in France against the Voltairean position, and
increased opportunities of studying Shakespeare's
works increased the poet's vogue. Twelve plays
were translated in De La Place's 'Théâtre Anglais'

---

[1] Jusserand, *A French Ambassador*, p. 56.
[2] Cf. Al. Schmidt, *Voltaire's Verdienst von der Einführung
Shakespeares in Frankreich*, Königsberg, 1864.

(1745–8). Jean-François Ducis (1733–1816) adapted without much insight six plays for the French stage, beginning in 1769 with 'Hamlet,' his version of which was acted with applause. In 1776 Pierre Le Tourneur began a bad prose translation (completed in 1782) of all Shakespeare's plays, and declared him to be 'the god of the theatre.' Voltaire protested against this estimate in a new remonstrance consisting of two letters, of which the first was read before the French Academy on August 25, 1776. Here Shakespeare was described as a barbarian, whose works — 'a huge dunghill' — concealed some pearls.

Although Voltaire's censure was rejected by the majority of later French critics, it expressed a sentiment born of the genius of the nation, and made an impression that was only gradually effaced. Marmontel, La Harpe, Marie Joseph Chénier, and Châteaubriand, in his 'Essai sur Shakespeare,' 1801, inclined to Voltaire's view; but Madame de Staël wrote effectively on the other side in her 'De la Littérature,' 1804 (i. caps. 13, 14, ii. 5). 'At this day,' wrote Wordsworth in 1815, 'the French critics have abated nothing of their aversion to "this darling of our nation." "The English with their bouffon de Shakespeare" is as familiar an expression among them as in the time of Voltaire. Baron Grimm is the only French writer who seems to have perceived his infinite superiority to the first names of the French theatre, — an advantage which the Parisian critic owed to his German

French critics' gradual emancipation from Voltairean influence.

blood and German education.'[1] The revision of Le Tourneur's translation by François Guizot and A. Pichot in 1821 gave Shakespeare a fresh advantage. Paul Duport, in 'Essais Littéraires sur Shakespeare' (Paris, 1828, 2 vols.), was the last French critic of repute to repeat Voltaire's censure unreservedly. Guizot, in his 'Sur la Vie et les Œuvres de Shakespeare' (reprinted separately from the translation of 1821), as well as in his 'Shakespeare et son Temps' (1852); Villemain in a general essay,[2] and Barante in a study of 'Hamlet,'[3] acknowledged the mightiness of Shakespeare's genius with comparatively few qualifications. Other complete translations followed — by Francisque Michel (1839), by Benjamin Laroche (1851), and by Emil Montégut (1867); but the best is that in prose by François Victor Hugo (1859–66), whose father, Victor Hugo the poet, published a rhapsodical eulogy in 1864. Alfred Mézières's 'Shakespeare, ses Œuvres et ses Critiques' (Paris, 1860), is a saner appreciation.

Meanwhile 'Hamlet' and 'Macbeth,' 'Othello' and a few other Shakespearean plays, became stock pieces on the French stage. A powerful impetus to theatrical representation of Shakespeare in France was given by the perform-

On the French stage.

---

[1] Frederic Melchior, Baron Grimm (1723–1807), for some years a friend of Rousseau and the correspondent of Diderot and the *encyclopédistes*, scattered many appreciative references to Shakespeare in his voluminous *Correspondance Littéraire Philosophique et Critique*, extending over the period 1753-70, the greater part of which was published in 16 vols. 1812-13.

[2] *Mélanges Historiques*, 1827, iii. 141-87.

[3] *Ibid.* 1824, iii. 217-34.

ance in Paris of the chief plays by a strong company of English actors in the autumn of 1827. 'Hamlet' and 'Othello' were acted successively by Charles Kemble and Macready; Edmund Kean appeared as Richard III, Othello, and Shylock; Miss Smithson, who became the wife of Hector Berlioz the musician, filled the *rôles* of Ophelia, Juliet, Desdemona, Cordelia, and Portia. French critics were divided as to the merits of the performers, but most of them were enthusiastic in their commendations of the plays.[1] Alfred de Vigny prepared a version of 'Othello' for the Théâtre-Français in 1829 with eminent success. An adaptation of 'Hamlet' by Alexandre Dumas was first performed in 1847, and a rendering by the Chevalier de Châtelain (1864) was often repeated. George Sand translated 'As You Like It' (Paris, 1856) for representation by the Comédie Française on April 12, 1856. 'Lady Macbeth' has been represented in recent years by Madame Sarah Bernhardt, and 'Hamlet' by M. Mounet-Sully of the Théâtre-Français.[2] Four French musicians — Berlioz in his symphony of 'Romeo and Juliet,' Gounod in his opera of 'Romeo and Juliet,' Ambroise Thomas in his opera of 'Hamlet,' and Saint-Saëns in his opera of 'Henry VIII' — have sought with public

[1] Very interesting comments on these performances appeared day by day in the Paris newspaper *La Globe.* They were by Charles Magnin, who reprinted them in his *Causeries et Méditations Historiques et Littéraires* (Paris, 1843, ii. 62 seq.).

[2] Cf. Lacroix, *Histoire de l'Influence de Shakespeare sur le Théâtre Français,* 1867; *Edinburgh Review,* 1849, pp. 39–77; Elze, *Essays,* pp. 193 seq.; M. Jusserand, *Shakespeare en France sous l'Ancien Régime,* Paris, 1898.

approval to interpret musically portions of Shakespeare's work.

In Italy Shakespeare was little known before the
present century.   Such references as eighteenth-century Italian writers made to him were based

In Italy.   on remarks by Voltaire.[1]   The French adaptation of 'Hamlet' by Ducis was issued in Italian
blank verse (Venice, 1774, 8vo).   Complete translations of all the plays made direct from the English
were issued by Michele Leoni in verse at Verona,
1819–22, and by Carlo Rusconi in prose at Padua
in 1831 (new edit. Turin, 1858–9).   'Othello' and
'Romeo and Juliet' have been very often translated
into Italian separately.   The Italian actors, Madame
Ristori (as Lady Macbeth), Salvini (as Othello), and
Rossi rank among Shakespeare's most effective inter-
preters.   Verdi's operas on Macbeth, Othello, and
Falstaff (the last two with libretti by Boito) betray
a close and appreciative study of Shakespeare.

Two complete translations have been published in
Dutch : one in prose by A. S. Kok (Amsterdam, 1873–
80), the other in verse by Dr. L. A. J. Bur-
In Holland.   gersdijk (Leyden, 1884–8, 12 vols.)

In Eastern Europe, Shakespeare first became
known through French and German translations.
Into Russian 'Romeo and Juliet' was translated in
1772, 'Richard III' in 1783, and 'Julius Cæsar' in
1786.   Sumarakow translated Ducis's version
In Russia.   of 'Hamlet' in 1784 for stage purposes,

---

[1] Cf. Giovanni Andres, *Dell' Origine Progressi e Stato attuale
'd ogni Letteratura*, 1782.

while the Empress Catherine II adapted the 'Merry Wives' and 'King John.' Numerous versions of all the chief plays followed ; and in 1865 there appeared at St. Petersburg the best translation in verse (direct from the English), by Nekrasow and Gerbel. A prose translation, by N. Ketzcher, begun in 1862, was completed in 1879. Gerbel issued a Russian translation of the 'Sonnets' in 1880, and many critical essays in the language, original or translated, have been published. Almost every play has been represented in Russian on the Russian stage.[1]

A Polish version of 'Hamlet' was acted at Lemberg in 1797; and as many as sixteen plays now
In Poland. hold a recognised place among Polish acting plays. The standard Polish translation of Shakespeare's collected works appeared at Warsaw in 1875 (edited by the Polish poet Kraszewski), and is reckoned among the most successful renderings in a foreign tongue.

In Hungary, Shakespeare's greatest works have since the beginning of the century been highly
In Hungary. appreciated by students and by playgoers. A complete translation into Hungarian appeared at Kaschau in 1824. At the National Theatre at Budapest no less than twenty-two plays have been of late years included in the actors' repertory.[2]

---

[1] Cf. *New Shaksp. Soc. Trans.* 1880–5, pt. ii. 431 seq.

[2] Cf. *Ungarische Revue* (Budapest) January 1881, pp. 81–2; and August Greguss's *Shakspere . . . elsö kötet : Shakspere pálydja*, Budapest, 1880 (an account in Hungarian of Shakespeare's Life and Works).

2 A

Other complete translations have been published in Bohemian (Prague, 1874), in Swedish (Lund, 1847– 51), in Danish (1845–50), and Finnish (Helsing'fors, 1892–5). In Spanish a complete translation is in course of publication (Madrid, 1885 seq.), and the eminent Spanish critic Menéndez y Pelayo has set Shakespeare above Calderon. In Armenian, although only three plays ('Hamlet,' 'Romeo and Juliet,' and 'As You Like It') have been issued, the translation of the whole is ready for the press. Separate plays have appeared in Welsh, Portuguese, Friesic, Flemish, Servian Roumanian, Maltese, Ukrainian, Wallachian, Croatian, modern Greek, Latin, Hebrew, and Japanese; while a few have been rendered into Bengali, Hindustani, Marathi,[1] Gujarati, Urdu, Kanarese, and other languages of India, and have been acted in native theatres.

In other countries.

[1] Cf. *Macmillan's Magazine*, May 1880.

XXI

GENERAL ESTIMATE

No estimate of Shakespeare's genius can be adequate. In knowledge of human character, in General estimate. wealth of humour, in depth of passion, in fertility of fancy, and in soundness of judgment he has no rival. It is true of him, as of no other writer, that his language and versification adapt themselves to every phase of sentiment, and sound every note in the scale of felicity. Some defects are to be acknowledged, but they sink into insignificance when measured by the magnitude of his achievement. Sudden transitions, elliptical expressions, mixed metaphors, indefensible verbal quibbles, and fantastic conceits at times create an atmosphere of obscurity. The student is perplexed, too, by obsolete words and by some hopelessly corrupt readings. But when the whole of Shakespeare's vast work is scrutinised with due attention, the glow of his imagination is seen to leave few passages wholly unillumined. Some of his plots are hastily constructed and inconsistently developed, but the intensity of the interest with which he contrives to invest the personality of his heroes and heroines triumphs over halting or

digressive treatment of the story in which they have
their being. Although he was versed in the technicalities of stagecraft, he occasionally disregarded its
elementary conditions. But the success of his presentments of human life and character depended
little on his manipulation of theatrical machinery.
His unassailable supremacy springs from the versatile
working of his insight and intellect, by virtue of
which his pen limned with unerring precision almost
every gradation of thought and emotion that animates
the living stage of the world.

Shakespeare's mind, as Hazlitt suggested, contained within itself the germs of all faculty and feeling.
He knew intuitively how every faculty and feeling
would develop in any conceivable change of fortune.
Men and women — good or bad, old or young, wise
or foolish, merry or sad, rich or poor — yielded their
secrets to him, and his genius enabled him to give
being in his pages to all the shapes of humanity that
present themselves on the highway of life. Each
of his characters gives voice to thought or passion
with an individuality and a naturalness that rouse
in the intelligent playgoer and reader the
illusion that they are overhearing men and
women speak unpremeditatingly among
themselves, rather than that they are reading written speeches or hearing written speeches
recited. The more closely the words are studied,
the completer the illusion grows. Creatures of the
imagination — fairies, ghosts, witches — are delineated
with a like potency, and the reader or spectator

Character of Shake-speare's achieve-ment.

feels instinctively that these supernatural entities could not speak, feel, or act otherwise than Shakespeare represents them. The creative power of poetry was never manifested to such effect as in the corporeal semblances in which Shakespeare clad the spirits of the air.

So mighty a faculty sets at naught the common limitations of nationality, and in every quarter of the globe to which civilised life has penetrated Shakespeare's power is recognised. All the world over, language is applied to his creations that ordinarily applies to beings of flesh and blood. Hamlet and Othello, Lear and Macbeth, Falstaff and Shylock, Brutus and Romeo, Ariel and Caliban, are studied in almost every civilised tongue as if they were historic personalities, and the chief of the impressive phrases that fall from their lips are rooted in the speech of civilised humanity. To Shakespeare the intellect of the world, speaking in divers accents, applies with one accord his own words: 'How noble in reason! how infinite in faculty! in apprehension how like a god!'

Its universal recognition.

APPENDIX

APPENDIX

———◆◇◆———

I

THE SOURCES OF BIOGRAPHICAL KNOWLEDGE

THE scantiness of contemporary records of Shakespeare's career
has been much exaggerated. An investigation extending over

Contempo- two centuries has brought together a mass of detail
rary records which far exceeds that accessible in the case of any
abundant. other contemporary professional writer. Nevertheless,
some important links are missing, and at some critical points
appeal to conjecture is inevitable. But the fully ascertained
facts are numerous enough to define sharply the general direction that Shakespeare's career followed. Although the clues
are in some places faint, the trail never altogether eludes the
patient investigator.

Fuller, in his 'Worthies' (1662), attempted the first
biographical notice of Shakespeare, with poor results. Aubrey,
First in his gossiping 'Lives of Eminent Men,'[1] based his
efforts in ampler information on reports communicated to him
biography. by William Beeston (*d.* 1682), an aged actor, whom
Dryden called 'the chronicle of the stage,' and who was doubtless in the main a trustworthy witness. A few additional details
were recorded in the seventeenth century by the Rev. John
Ward (1629–1681), vicar of Stratford-on-Avon from 1662 to
1668, in a diary and memorandum-book written between 1661

---

[1] Compiled between 1669 and 1696; first printed in *Letters from the Bodleian,*
1813, and admirably re-edited for the Clarendon Press during the present year by
the Rev. Andrew Clark (2 vols.).

and 1663 (ed. C. A. Severn, 1839) ; by the Rev. William Fulman, whose manuscripts are at Corpus Christi College, Oxford (with valuable interpolations made before 1708 by the Rev. Richard Davies, vicar of Saperton, Gloucestershire) ; by John Dowdall, who recorded his experiences of travel through Warwickshire in 1693 (London, 1838) ; and by William Hall, who described a visit to Stratford in 1694 (London, 1884, from Hall's letter among the Bodleian MSS.). Phillips in his 'Theatrum Poetarum' (1675), and Langbaine in his 'English Dramatick Poets' (1691), confined themselves to elementary criticism. In 1709 Nicholas Rowe prefixed a more ambitious memoir than had yet been attempted to his edition of the plays and embodied some hitherto unrecorded Stratford and London traditions with which the actor Thomas Betterton supplied him. A little fresh gossip was collected by William Oldys and was printed from his manuscript 'Adversaria' (now in the British Museum) as an appendix to Yeowell's 'Memoir of Oldys,' 1862. Pope, Johnson, and Steevens, in the biographical prefaces to their editions, mainly repeated the narratives of their predecessor, Rowe.

In the Prolegomena to the Variorum editions of 1803, 1813 and especially in that of 1821 there was embodied a mass of Biograph- fresh information derived by Edmund Malone from ers of the systematic researches among the parochial records nineteenth of Stratford, the manuscripts accumulated by the century. actor Alleyn at Dulwich, and official papers of state preserved in the public offices in London (now collected in the Public Record Office). The available knowledge of Elizabethan stage history as well as of Shakespeare's biography, was thus greatly extended. John Payne Collier, in his 'History of English Dramatic Poetry' (1831), in his 'New Facts' about Shakespeare (1835), his 'New Particulars' (1836), and his 'Further Particulars' (1839), and in his editions of Henslowe's 'Diary' and the 'Alleyn Papers' for the Shakespeare Society, while occasionally throwing some further light on obscure places, foisted on Shakespeare's biography a series of ingeniously forged documents which have greatly perplexed succeeding biographers.[1] Joseph Hunter in 'New Illustrations of Shake-

[1] See p. 367-3.

peare' (1845) and George Russell French's 'Shakespeareana
Genealogica' (1869) occasionally supplemented Malone's researches.   James Orchard Halliwell (afterwards Halliwell-
Phillipps) printed separately, between 1850 and 1884, in various
privately issued publications, all the Stratford archives and
extant legal documents bearing on Shakespeare's career, many
of them for the first time.   In 1881 Halliwell-Phillipps began the
collective publication of materials for a full biography in his
'Outlines of the Life of Shakespeare'; this work was generously
enlarged in successive editions until it acquired massive proportions; in the fourth and last edition of 1887 it numbered near
1,000 pages.   Mr. Frederick Gard Fleay, in his 'Shakespeare
Manual' (1876), in his 'Life of Shakespeare' (1886), in his
History of the Stage' (1890), and his 'Biographical Chronicle
of the English Drama' (1891), adds much useful information
respecting stage history and Shakespeare's relations with his
fellow-dramatists, mainly derived from a study of the original
editions of the plays of Shakespeare and of his contemporaries;
but unfortunately many of Mr. Fleay's statements and conjectures are unauthenticated.   For notices of Stratford, R. B.
Wheler's 'History and Antiquities' (1806), John R. Wise's

Stratford   'Shakespere, his Birthplace and its Neighbourhood'
topo-   (1861), the present writer's 'Stratford-on-Avon to
graphy.   the Death of Shakespeare' (1890), and Mrs. C. C.
Stopes's 'Shakespeare's Warwickshire Contemporaries' (1897)
may be consulted.   Wise appends to his volume a tentative
glossary of words still used in Warwickshire to be found in
Shakspere.'   The parish registers of Stratford have been edited
by Mr. Richard Savage for the Parish Registers Society, 1898-9.
Nathan Drake's 'Shakespeare and his Times' (1817) and G. W.
Thornbury's 'Shakespeare's England' (1856) collect much
material respecting Shakespeare's social environment.

The chief monographs on special points in Shakespeare's
biography are Dr. Richard Farmer's 'Essay on the Learning of

Specialised   Shakespeare' (1767), reprinted in the Variorum
studies in   editions; Octavius Gilchrist's 'Examination of the
biography.   Charges . . . of Ben Jonson's Enmity towards
Shakespeare' (1808); W. J. Thoms's 'Was Shakespeare ever
a Soldier?' (1849), a study based on an erroneous identification

of the poet with another William Shakespeare ; Lord Campbell's 'Shakespeare's Legal Acquirements Considered' (1859); John Charles Bucknill's 'Medical Knowledge of Shakespeare' (1860); C. F. Green's 'Shakespeare's Crab-Tree, with its Legend' (1862); C. H. Bracebridge's 'Shakespeare no Deer-stealer' (1862); William Blades's 'Shakspere and Typography' (1872); and D. H. Madden's 'Diary of Master William Silence (Shakespeare and Sport),' 1897. A full epitome of the biographical information accessible at the date of publication is supplied in Karl Elze's 'Life of Shakespeare' (Halle, 1876; English translation, 1888), with which Elze's 'Essays' from the publications of the German Shakespeare Society (English translation, 1874) are worth studying. A less ambitious effort of the same kind by Samuel Neil (1861) is seriously injured by the writer's acceptance of Collier's forgeries. Professor Dowden's 'Shakespeare Primer' (1877) and his 'Introduction to Shakespeare' (1893), and Dr. Furnivall's 'Introduction to the Leopold Shakespeare,' are all useful summaries of leading facts.

Useful epitomes.

Francis Douce's 'Illustrations of Shakespeare' (1807, new edit. 1839), 'Shakespeare's Library' (ed. J. P. Collier and W. C. Hazlitt, 1875), 'Shakespeare's Plutarch' (ed. Skeat, 1875), and 'Shakespeare's Holinshed' (ed. W. G. Boswell-Stone, 1896) are of service in tracing the sources of Shakespeare's plots. Alexander Schmidt's 'Shakespeare Lexicon' (1874) and Dr. E. A. Abbott's 'Shakespearean Grammar' (1869, new edit. 1893) are valuable aids to a study of the text. Useful concordances to the Plays have been prepared by Mrs. Cowden-Clarke (1845), to the Poems by Mrs. H. H. Furness (Philadelphia, 1875), and to Plays and Poems, in one volume, with references to numbered lines, by John Bartlett (London and New York, 1895).[1] A 'Handbook Index' by J. O. Halliwell (privately printed 1866) gives lists of obsolete words and phrases, songs, proverbs, and plants mentioned in the works of Shakespeare. An unprinted glossary prepared by Richard Warner

Aids to study of plots and text.

Concordances.

---

[1] The earliest attempts at a concordance were *A Complete Verbal Index to the Plays*, by F. Twiss (1805), and *An Index to the Remarkable Passages and Words*, by Samuel Ayscough (1827), but these are now superseded.

between 1750 and 1770 is at the British Museum (Addit. MSS. 10472–542). Extensive bibliographies are given in Lowndes's 'Library Manual' (ed. Bohn); in Franz Thimm's 'Shakespeariana' (1864 and 1871); in the 'Encyclopædia Britannica,' 9th edit. (skilfully classified by Mr. H. R. Tedder); and in the 'British Museum Catalogue' (the Shakespearean entries in which, comprising 3,680 titles, were separately published in 1897).

Bibliographies.

The valuable publications of the Shakespeare Society, the New Shakspere Society, and of the Deutsche Shakespeare-Gesellschaft, comprising contributions alike to the æsthetic, textual, historical, and biographical study of Shakespeare, are noticed above (see pp. 333–4, 346). To the critical studies, on which comment has already been made (see p. 333), — viz. Coleridge's 'Notes and Lectures,' 1883, Hazlitt's 'Characters of Shakespeare's Plays,' 1817, Professor Dowden's 'Shakespeare: his Mind and Art,' 1875, and Mr. A. C. Swinburne, 'A Study of Shakespeare,' 1879, — there may be added the essays on Shakespeare's heroines respectively by Mrs. Jameson in 1833 and Lady Martin in 1885; Dr. Ward's 'English Dramatic Literature' (1875, new edit. 1898); Richard G. Moulton's 'Shakespeare as a Dramatic Artist' (1885); 'Shakespeare Studies' by Thomas Spencer Baynes (1893); F. S. Boas's 'Shakspere and his Predecessors' (1895), and Georg Brandes's 'William Shakespeare' — an elaborately critical but somewhat fanciful study — in Danish (Copenhagen, 1895, 8vo), in German (Leipzig, 1895), and in English (London, 1898, 2 vols. 8vo).

Critical studies.

The intense interest which Shakespeare's life and work have long universally excited has tempted unprincipled or sportively mischievous writers from time to time to deceive the public by the forgery of documents purporting to supply new information. The forgers were especially active at the end of the last century and during the middle years of the present century, and their frauds have caused students so much perplexity that it may be useful to warn them against those Shakespearean forgeries which have obtained the widest currency.

Shakespearean forgeries.

The earliest forger to obtain notoriety was John Jordan

(1746–1809), a resident at Stratford-on-Avon, whose most important achievement was the forgery of the will of
Shakespeare's father; but many other papers in
Jordan's 'Original Collections on Shakespeare and
Stratford-on-Avon' (1780), and 'Original Memoirs and Historical Accounts of the Families of Shakespeare and Hart,' are open
to the gravest suspicion.[1]

John Jordan, 1746–1809.

The best-known Shakespearean forger of the eighteenth
century was William Henry Ireland (1777–1835), a barrister's
clerk, who, with the aid of his father, Samuel Ireland
(1740?–1800), an author and engraver of some repute,
produced in 1796 a volume of forged papers claiming
to relate to Shakespeare's career. The title ran : ' Miscellaneous
Papers and Legal Instruments under the Hand and Seal of
William Shakespeare, including the tragedy of " King Lear " and
a small fragment of " Hamlet " from the original MSS. in the
possession of Samuel Ireland.' On April 2, 1796, Sheridan and
Kemble produced at Drury Lane Theatre a bombastic tragedy
in blank verse entitled ' Vortigern ' under the pretence that it
was by Shakespeare, and had been recently found among the
manuscripts of the dramatist that had fallen into the hands of the
Irelands.   The piece, which was published, was the invention of
young Ireland.   The fraud of the Irelands, which for some time
deceived a section of the literary public, was finally exposed by
Malone in his valuable 'Inquiry into the Authenticity of the
Ireland MSS.' (1796).   Young Ireland afterwards published his
'Confessions' (1805).   He had acquired much skill in copying
Shakespeare's genuine signature from the facsimile in Steevens's
edition of Shakespeare's works of the mortgage-deed of the
Blackfriars house of 1612–13,[2] and, besides conforming to that
style of handwriting in his forged deeds and literary compositions, he inserted copies of the signature on the title-pages
of many sixteenth-century books, and often added notes in
the same feigned hand on their margins.   Numerous sixteenth-
century volumes embellished by Ireland in this manner are
extant, and his forged signatures and marginalia have been
frequently mistaken for genuine autographs of Shakespeare.

The Ireland forgeries, 1796.

---

[1] Jordan's *Collections*, including this fraudulent will of Shakespeare's father,
were printed privately by J. O. Halliwell-Phillipps in 1864.   [2] See p. 267.

But Ireland's and Jordan's frauds are clumsy compared with those that belong to the present century. Most of the works Forgeries relating to the biography of Shakespeare or the promulga- history of the Elizabethan stage produced by John ted by Col- Payne Collier, or under his supervision, between 1835 lier and others, and 1849 are honeycombed with forged references 1835–1849. to Shakespeare, and many of the forgeries have been admitted unsuspectingly into literary history. The chief of these forged papers I arrange below in the order of dates that have been allotted to them by their manufacturers.[1]

1589 (November). Appeal from the Blackfriars players (16 in number) to the Privy Council for favour. Shakespeare's name stands twelfth. From the manuscripts at Bridgewater House, belonging to the Earl of Ellesmere. First printed in Collier's 'New Facts regarding the Life of Shakespeare,' 1835.

1596 (July). List of inhabitants of the Liberty of Southwark, Shakespeare's name appearing in the sixth place. First printed in Collier's 'Life of Shakespeare,' 1858, p. 126.

1596. Petition of the owners and players of the Blackfriars Theatre to the Privy Council in reply to an alleged petition of the inhabitants requesting the closing of the playhouse. Shakespeare's name is fifth on the list of petitioners. This forged paper is in the Public Record Office, and was first printed in Collier's 'History of English Dramatic Poetry' (1831), vol. i. p. 297, and has been constantly reprinted as if it were genuine.[2]

---

[1] Reference has already been made to the character of the manuscript corrections made by Collier in a copy of the Second Folio of 1632, known as the Perkins folio. See p. 312, n. 2, *supra*. The chief authorities on the subject of the Collier forgeries are: *An Inquiry into the Genuineness of the Manuscript Corrections in Mr. J. Payne Collier's Annotated Shakspere Folio, 1632, and of certain Shaksperian Documents likewise published by Mr. Collier*, by N. E. S. A. Hamilton, London, 1860; *A Complete View of the Shakespeare Controversy concerning the Authenticity and Genuineness of Manuscript Matter affecting the Works and Biography of Shakspere, published by J. Payne Collier as the Fruits of his Researches*, by C. M. Ingleby, LL.D. of Trinity College, Cambridge, London, 1861; *Catalogue of the Manuscripts and Muniments of Alleyn's College of God's Gift at Dulwich*, by George F. Warner, M.A., 1881; *Notes on the Life of James Payne Collier, with a Complete List of his Works and an Account of such Shakespeare Documents as are believed to be spurious*, by Henry B. Wheatley, London, 1884.

[2] See *Calendar of State Papers*, Domestic, 1595-7, p. 310.

1596 (*circa*). A letter signed H. S. (*i.e.* Henry, Earl of Southampton), addressed to Sir Thomas Egerton, praying
   protection for the players of the Blackfriars Theatre,
   and mentioning Burbage and Shakespeare by name.
   First printed in Collier's 'New Facts.'

1596 (*circa*). A list of sharers in the Blackfriars Theatre,
   with the valuation of their property, in which Shakespeare is credited with four shares, worth 933*l*. 6*s*. 8*d*.
   This was first printed in Collier's 'New Facts,' 1835,
   p. 6, from the Egerton MSS. at Bridgewater House.

1602 (August 6). Notice of the performance of ' Othello ' by
   Burbage's 'players' before Queen Elizabeth when on
   a visit to Sir Thomas Egerton, the lord-keeper, at
   Harefield, in a forged account of disbursements by
   Egerton's steward, Arthur Mainwaringe, from the
   manuscripts at Bridgewater House, belonging to the
   Earl of Ellesmere.   Printed in Collier's 'New Particulars regarding the Works of Shakespeare,' 1836,
   and again in Collier's edition of the 'Egerton Papers,'
   1840 (Camden Society), pp. 342–3.

1603 (October 3).   Mention of 'Mr. Shakespeare of the
   Globe' in a letter at Dulwich from Mrs. Alleyn to her
   husband; part of the letter is genuine.   First published
   in Collier's ' Memoirs of Edward Alleyn,' 1841, p. 63.[1]

1604 (April 9).   List of the names of eleven players of the
   King's Company fraudulently appended to a genuine
   letter at Dulwich College from the Privy Council
   bidding the Lord Mayor permit performances by the
   King's players.   Printed in Collier's 'Memoirs of
   Edward Alleyn,' 1841, p. 68.[2]

1605 (November–December).   Forged entries in Master of
   the Revels' account-books (now at the Public Record
   Office) of performances at Whitehall by the King's players of the ' Moor of Venice ' — *i.e.* 'Othello ' — on November 1, and of ' Measure for Measure ' on December
   26.   Printed in Peter Cunningham's 'Extracts from
   the Accounts of the Revels at Court' (pp. 203–4), pub-

[1] See Warner's *Catalogue of Dulwich MSS*. pp. 24–6.
[2] Cf. *ibid*. pp 26–7.

lished by the Shakespeare Society in 1842. Doubtless based on Malone's trustworthy memoranda (now
in Bodleian Library) of researches among genuine
papers formerly at the Audit Office at Somerset
House.[1]

1607. Notes of performances of 'Hamlet' and 'Richard II'
by the crews of the vessels of the East India Company's fleet off Sierra Leone. First printed in 'Narratives of Voyages towards the North-West, 1496–1631,'
edited by Thomas Rundall for the Hakluyt Society,
1849, p. 231, from what purported to be an exact
transcript 'in the India Office' of the 'Journal of
William Keeling,' captain of one of the vessels in
the expedition. Keeling's manuscript journal is still
at the India Office, but the leaves that should contain
these entries are now, and have long been, missing
from it.

1609 (January 4). A warrant appointing Robert Daborne,
William Shakespeare, and others instructors of the
Children of the Revels. From the Bridgewater
House MSS. first printed in Collier's 'New Facts,'
1835.

1609 (April 6). List of persons assessed for poor rate in
Southwark, April 6, 1609, in which Shakespeare's
name appears. First printed in Collier's 'Memoirs of
Edward Alleyn,' 1841, p. 91. The forged paper is at
Dulwich.[2]

1611 (November). Forged entries in Master of the Revels'
account-books (now at the Public Record Office) of
performances at Whitehall by the King's Players of
the 'Tempest' on November 1, and of the 'Winter's
Tale' on November 5. Printed in Peter Cunningham's
'Extracts from the Revels Accounts,' p. 210. Doubtless based on Malone's trustworthy memoranda of
researches among genuine papers formerly at the
Audit Office at Somerset House.[3]

[1] See p. 235, n. 1, *supra.*
[2] Cf Warner's *Dulwich MSS.* pp. 30–1.
[3] See p. 255, n. 1, *supra.*

2 B

II

THE BACON–SHAKESPEARE CONTROVERSY

THE apparent contrast between the homeliness of Shakespeare's Stratford career and the breadth of observation and knowledge displayed in his literary work has evoked the fantastic theory that Shakespeare was not the author of the literature that passes under his name, and perverse attempts have been made to assign his works to his great contemporary, Francis Bacon (1561–1626), the great contemporary prose-writer, philosopher, and lawyer. It is argued that Shakespeare's plays embody a general omniscience (especially a knowledge of law) which was possessed by no contemporary except Bacon; that there are many close parallelisms between passages in Shakespeare's and passages in Bacon's works,[1] and that Bacon makes

Its source.

---

[1] Most of those that are commonly quoted are phrases in ordinary use by all writers of the day. The only point of any interest raised in the argument from parallelisms of expression centres about a quotation from Aristotle which Bacon and Shakespeare not merely both make, but make in what looks at a first glance to be the same erroneous form. Aristotle wrote in his *Nicomachean Ethics*, i. 8, that young men were unfitted for the study of *political* philosophy. Bacon, in the *Advancement of Learning* (1605), wrote: ' Is not the opinion of Aristotle worthy to be regarded wherein he saith that young men are not fit auditors of *moral* philosophy?' (bk. ii. p. 255, ed. Kitchin). Shakespeare, about 1603, in *Troilus and Cressida*, II. ii. 166, wrote of ' young men whom Aristotle thought unfit to hear *moral* philosophy. But the alleged error of substituting *moral* for *political* philosophy in Aristotle's text is more apparent than real. By ' political ' philosophy Aristotle, as his context amply shows, meant the ethics of civil society, which are hardly distinguishable from what is commonly called ' morals.' In the summary paraphrase of Aristotle's *Ethics* which was translated into English from the Italian, and published in 1547, the passage to which both Shakespeare and Bacon refer is not rendered literally, but its general drift is given as a warning that moral philosophy is not a fit subject for study by youths who are naturally passionate and headstrong. Such an interpretation of Aristotle's language is common among sixteenth and seventeenth century writers. In a French translation of the *Ethics* by the Comte de Plessis, pub-

enigmatic references in his correspondence to secret 'recrea-
tions' and 'alphabets' and concealed poems for which his
alleged employment as a concealed dramatist can alone account.

Toby
Matthew's
letter.
Toby Matthew wrote to Bacon (as Viscount St.
Albans) at an uncertain date after January 1621 :
'The most prodigious wit that ever I knew of my
nation and of this side of the sea is of your Lordship's name,
though he be known by another.'[1]   This unpretending sentence
is distorted into conclusive evidence that Bacon wrote works
of commanding excellence under another's name, and among
them probably Shakespeare's plays.   According to the only
sane interpretation of Matthew's words, his 'most prodigious
wit' was some Englishman named Bacon whom he met abroad
— probably a pseudonymous Jesuit like most of Matthew's
friends.   (The real surname of Father Thomas Southwell, who
was a learned Jesuit domiciled chiefly in the Low Countries,
was Bacon.   He was born in 1592 at Sculthorpe, near Walsingham, Norfolk, being son of Thomas Bacon of that place, and
he died at Watten in 1637.)

Joseph C. Hart (U. S. Consul at Santa Cruz, d. 1855), in his
'Romance of Yachting' (1848), first raised doubts of Shake-
speare's authorship.   There followed in a like temper
Chief ex-
ponents.
'Who wrote Shakespeare?' in 'Chambers's Journal,'
August 7, 1852, and an article by Miss Delia Bacon
in 'Putnams' Monthly,' January 1856.   On the latter was based
'The Philosophy of the Plays of Shakespeare unfolded by
Delia Bacon,' with a neutral preface by Nathaniel Hawthorne,
London and Boston, 1857.   Miss Delia Bacon, who was the first
to spread abroad a spirit of scepticism respecting the established
facts of Shakespeare's career, died insane on September 2,

---

lished at Paris in 1553, the passage is rendered ' parquoy le ieune enfant n'est suffisant
auditeur de la science civile;' and an English commentator (in a manuscript note
written about 1605 in a copy of the book in the British Museum) turned the sentence
into English thus: 'Whether a young man may be a fitte scholler of *morall* philo-
sophie.'   In 1622 an Italian essayist, Virgilio Malvezzi, in his preface to his *Discorsi
sopra Cornelio Tacito*, has the remark, ' E non è discordante da questa mia
opinione Aristotele, il qual dice, che i giovani non sono buoni ascultatori delle
morali' (cf. Spedding, *Works of Bacon*, i. 739, iii. 440).

[1] Cf. Birch, *Letters of Bacon*, 1763, p. 392.   A foolish suggestion has been made
that Matthew was referring to Francis Bacon's brother Anthony, who died in 1601;
Matthew was writing of a man who was alive more than twenty years later.

1859.[1] Mr. William Henry Smith, a resident in London, seems first to have suggested the Baconian hypothesis in 'Was Lord Bacon the author of Shakespeare's plays ?— a letter to Lord Ellesmere' (1856), which was republished as 'Bacon and Shakespeare' (1857). The most learned exponent of this strange theory was Nathaniel Holmes, an American lawyer, who published at New York in 1866 'The Authorship of the Plays attributed to Shakespeare,' a monument of misapplied ingenuity (4th ed. 1886, 2 vols.). Bacon's 'Promus of Formularies and Elegancies,' a commonplace book in Bacon's handwriting in the British Museum (London, 1883), was first edited by Mrs. Henry Pott, a voluminous advocate of the Baconian theory; it contained many words and phrases common to the works of Bacon and Shakespeare, and Mrs. Pott pressed the argument from parallelisms of expression to its extremest limits. The Baconian theory has found its widest acceptance in America. There it achieved its wildest manifestation in the book called 'The Great Cryptogram : Francis Bacon's Cypher in the so-called Shakespeare Plays ' (Chicago and London, 1887, 2 vols.), which was the work of Mr. Ignatius Donnelly of Hastings, Minnesota. The author pretended to have discovered among Bacon's papers a numerical cypher which enabled him to pick out letters appearing at certain intervals in the pages of Shakespeare's First Folio, and the selected letters formed words and sentences categorically stating that Bacon was author of the plays. Many refutations have been published of Mr. Donnelly's arbitrary and baseless contention.

Its vogue in America.

A Bacon Society was founded in London in 1885 to develop and promulgate the unintelligible theory, and it inaugurated a magazine (named since May 1893 'Baconiana'). A quarterly periodical also called 'Baconiana,' and issued in the same interest, was established at Chicago in 1892. 'The Bibliography of the Shakespeare-Bacon Controversy' by W. H. Wyman, Cincinnati, 1884, gives the titles of two hundred and fifty-five books or pamphlets on both sides of the subject, published since 1848 ; the list was continued during 1886 in 'Shakespeariana,' a monthly journal published

Extent of the literature.

---

[1] Cf. *Life* by Theodore Bacon, London, 1888.

at Philadelphia, and might now be extended to fully twice its original number.

The abundance of the contemporary evidence attesting Shakespeare's responsibility for the works published under his name gives the Baconian theory no rational right to a hearing; while such authentic examples of Bacon's effort to write verse as survive prove beyond all possibility of contradiction that, great as he was as a prose-writer and a philosopher, he was incapable of penning any of the poetry assigned to Shakespeare. Defective knowledge and illogical or casuistical argument alone render any other conclusion possible.

III

THE YOUTHFUL CAREER OF THE EARL OF SOUTHAMPTON

FROM the dedicatory epistles addressed by Shakespeare to the Earl of Southampton in the opening pages of his two narrative poems, 'Venus and Adonis' (1593) and 'Lucrece' (1594),[1] from the account given by Sir William D'Avenant, and recorded by Nicholas Rowe, of the earl's liberal bounty to the poet,[2] and, from the language of the sonnets, it is abundantly clear that Shakespeare enjoyed very friendly relations with Southampton from the time when his genius was nearing its maturity. No contemporary document or tradition gives the faintest suggestion that Shakespeare was the friend or *protégé* of any man of rank other than Southampton ; and the student of Shakespeare's biography has reason to ask for some information respecting him who enjoyed the exclusive distinction of serving Shakespeare as his patron.

Southampton and Shakespeare.

Southampton was a patron worth cultivating. Both his parents came of the New Nobility, and enjoyed vast wealth. His father's father was Lord Chancellor under Henry VIII, and when the monasteries were dissolved, although he was faithful to the old religion, he was granted rich estates in Hampshire, including the Abbeys of Titchfield and Beaulieu in the New Forest. He was created Earl of Southampton early in Edward VI's reign, and, dying shortly afterwards, was succeeded by his only son, the father of Shakespeare's friend. The second Earl loved magnificence in his household. ' He was highly reverenced and favoured of all that were of his own rank, and bravely attended and served by the

Parentage.

---

[1] See pp. 4, 77, 127.   [2] See p. 126.

best gentlemen of those countries wherein he lived. His muster-roll never consisted of four lacqueys and a coachman, but of a whole troop of at least a hundred well-mounted gentlemen and yeomen.'[1] The second Earl remained a Catholic, like his father, and a chivalrous avowal of sympathy with Mary Queen of Scots procured him a term of imprisonment in the year preceding his distinguished son's birth. At a youthful age he married a lady of fortune, Mary Browne, daughter of the first Viscount Montague, also a Catholic. Her portrait, now at Welbeck, was painted in her early married days, and shows regularly formed features beneath bright auburn hair. Two sons and a daughter were the issue of the union. Shakespeare's friend, the second son, was borne at her father's residence, Cowdray House, near Midhurst, on October 6, 1573. He was thus Shakespeare's junior by nine years and a half. 'A goodly boy, God bless him!' exclaimed the gratified father, writing of his birth to a friend.[2] But the father barely survived the boy's infancy. He died at the early age of thirty-five — two days before the child's eighth birthday. The elder son was already dead. Thus, on October 4, 1581, the second and only surviving son became third Earl of Southampton, and entered on his great inheritance.[3]

Birth on Oct. 6, 1573.

As was customary in the case of an infant peer, the little Earl became a royal ward — 'a child of state'— and Lord Burghley, the Prime Minister, acted as the boy's guardian in the Queen's behalf. Burghley had good reason to be satisfied with his ward's intellectual promise. 'He spent,' wrote a contemporary, 'his childhood and other younger terms in the study of good letters.' At the age of twelve, in the autumn of 1585, he was admitted to St. John's College, Cambridge, 'the sweetest nurse of knowledge in all the University.' Southampton breathed easily the cultured

Education.

[1] Gervase Markham, *Honour in his Perfection*, 1624.

[2] *Loseley MSS.* ed. A. J. Kempe, p. 240.

[3] His mother, after thirteen years of widowhood, married in 1594 Sir Thomas Heneage, Vice-Chamberlain of Queen Elizabeth's household; but he died within a year, and in 1596 she took a third husband, Sir William Hervey, who distinguished himself in military service in Ireland and was created a peer as Lord Hervey by James I.

atmosphere. Next summer he sent his guardian, Burghley, an essay in Ciceronian Latin on the somewhat cynical text that 'All men are moved to the pursuit of virtue by the hope of reward.' The argument, if unconvincing, is precocious. 'Every man,' the boy tells us, 'no matter how well or how ill endowed with the graces of humanity, whether in the enjoyment of great honour or condemned to obscurity, experiences that yearning for glory which alone begets virtuous endeavour.' The paper, still preserved at Hatfield, is a model of caligraphy; every letter is shaped with delicate regularity, and betrays a refinement most uncommon in boys of thirteen.[1] Southampton remained at the University for some two years, graduating M.A. at sixteen, in 1589. Throughout his after life he cherished for his college 'great love and affection.'

Before leaving Cambridge, Southampton entered his name at Gray's Inn. Some knowledge of law was deemed needful in one who was to control a landed property that was not only large already but likely to grow.[2] Meanwhile he was sedulously cultivating his literary tastes. He took into his 'pay and patronage' John Florio, the well-known author and Italian tutor, and was soon, according to Florio's testimony, as thoroughly versed in Italian as 'teaching or learning' could make him.

'When he was young,' wrote a later admirer, 'no ornament of youth was wanting in him;' and it was naturally to the Court that his friends sent him at an early age to display his varied graces. He can hardly have been more than seventeen when he was presented to his Sovereign. She showed him kindly notice, and the Earl of Essex, her brilliant favourite, acknowledged his fascination. Thenceforth Essex displayed in

---

[1] By kind permission of the Marquis of Salisbury I lately copied out this essay at Hatfield.

[2] In 1588 his brother-in-law, Thomas Arundel, afterwards first Lord Arundel or Wardour (husband of his only sister, Mary), petitioned Lord Burghley to grant him an additional tract of the New Forest about his house at Beaulieu. Although in his 'nonage,' Arundel wrote, the Earl was by no means 'of the smallest hope.' Arundel, with almost prophetic insight, added that the Earl of Pembroke was Southampton's 'most feared rival' in the competition for the land in question. Arundel was referring to the father of that third Earl of Pembroke who, despite the absence of evidence, has been described as Shakespeare's friend of the sonnets (cf. *Calendar of Hatfield MSS.* iii. 365).

is welfare a brotherly interest which proved in course of time a very doubtful blessing.

While still a boy, Southampton entered with as much est into the sports and dissipations of his fellow-courtiers as into their literary and artistic pursuits. At tennis, in jousts and tournaments, he achieved distinction; nor was he a stranger to the delights of gambling at primero. In 1592, when he was in his eighteenth year, he was recognised as the most handsome and accomplished of all the young lords who frequented the royal presence. In the autumn of that year Elizabeth paid Oxford a visit in state. Southampton was in the throng of noblemen who bore her company. In a Latin poem describing the brilliant ceremonial, which was published at the time at the University Press, eulogy was lavished without stint on all the Queen's attendants; but the academic poet declared that Southampton's personal attractions exceeded those of any other in the royal train. 'No other youth who was present,' he wrote, 'was more beautiful than this prince of Hampshire (*quo non formosior alter affuit*), nor more distinguished in the arts of learning, although as yet tender down scarce bloomed on his cheek.' The last words testify to Southampton's boyish appearance.[1] Next year it was rumoured that his 'external grace' was to receive signal recognition by his admission, despite his juvenility, to the Order of the Garter. 'There be no Knights of the Garter new chosen as yet,' wrote a well-informed courtier on May 3, 1593, 'but there were four nominated.'[2] Three were eminent public servants, but first on the list stood the name of young Southampton. The purpose did not take effect, but the compliment of nomination was, at his age, without precedent outside the circle of the Sovereign's kinsmen. On November 17, 1595, he appeared in the lists set up in the Queen's presence in honour of the

Marginal notes: Recognition of Southampton's youthful beauty.

---

[1] Cf. *Apollinis et Musarum* Εὐκτικὰ Εἰδύλλια, Oxford, 1592, reprinted in *Elizabethan Oxford* (Oxford Historical Society), edited by Charles Plummer, xxix. 94:

> Post hunc (*i.e.* Earl of Essex) insequitur clarâ de stirpe Dynasta,
> Iure suo diues quem South-Hamptonia magnum
> Vendicat heroem; quo non formosior alter
> Affuit, aut doctâ iuuenis præstantior arte;
> Ora licet tenerâ vix dum lanugine vernent.

Marginal note: Comes South-Hamptoniæ.

[2] Historical MSS Commission, 7th Report (Appendix), p 521*b*.

thirty-seventh anniversary of her accession. The poet George Peele pictured in blank verse the gorgeous scene, and likened the Earl of Southampton to that ancient type of chivalry, Bevis of Southampton, so 'valiant in arms,' so 'gentle and debonair,' did he appear to all beholders.[1]

But clouds were rising on this sunlit horizon. Southampton, a wealthy peer without brothers or uncles, was the only male representative of his house. A lawful heir was essential to the entail of his great possessions. Early marriages — child-marriages — were in vogue in all ranks of society, and Southampton's mother and guardian regarded matrimony at a tender age as especially incumbent on him in view of his rich heritage. When he was seventeen Burghley accordingly offered him a wife in the person of his granddaughter, Lady Elizabeth Vere, eldest daughter of his daughter Anne and of the Earl of Oxford. The Countess of Southampton approved the match, and told Burghley that her son was not averse from it. Her wish was father to the thought. Southampton declined to marry to order, and, to the confusion of his friends, was still a bachelor when he came of age in 1594. Nor even then did there seem much prospect of his changing his condition. He was in some ways as young for his years in inward disposition as in outward appearance. Although gentle and amiable in most relations of life, he could be childishly self-willed and impulsive, and outbursts of anger involved him, at Court and elsewhere, in many petty quarrels which were with difficulty settled without bloodshed. Despite his rank and wealth, he was consequently accounted by many ladies of far too uncertain a temper to sustain marital responsibilities with credit. Lady Bridget Manners, sister of his friend the Earl of Rutland, was in 1594 looking to matrimony for means of release from the servitude of a lady-in-waiting to the Queen. Her guardian suggested that Southampton or the Earl of Bedford, who was intimate with Southampton and exactly of his age, would be an eligible suitor. Lady Bridget dissented. Southampton and his friend were, she objected, 'so young,' 'fantastical,' and volatile ('so easily carried away') that should ill fortune

Reluctance to marry.

[1] Peele's *Anglorum Feriæ*.

efall her mother, who was 'her only stay,' she 'doubted
their carriage of themselves.' She spoke, she said, from
observation.[1]

In 1595, at two-and-twenty, Southampton justified Lady

Intrigue Bridget's censure by a public proof of his fallibility. The
with Eliza- fair mistress Vernon (first cousin of the Earl of
beth Ver- Essex), a passionate beauty of the Court, cast her
non. spell on him. Her virtue was none too stable, and
in September the scandal spread that Southampton was courting her 'with too much familiarity.'

The entanglement with 'his fair mistress' opened a new
chapter in Southampton's career, and life's tempests began in
earnest. Either to free himself from his mistress's toils, or to
divert attention from his intrigue, he in 1596 withdrew from
Court and sought sterner occupation. Despite his mistress's
lamentations, which the Court gossips duly chronicled, he played
part with his friend Essex, in the military and naval expedition
to Cadiz in 1596, and in that to the Azores in 1597. He developed a martial ardour which brought him renown, and Mars
(his admirers said) vied with Mercury for his allegiance. He
travelled on the Continent, and finally, in 1598, he accepted a
subordinate place in the suite of the Queen's Secretary, Sir

Marriage Robert Cecil, who was going on an embassy to
in 1598. Paris. But Mistress Vernon was still fated to be his
evil genius, and Southampton learnt while in Paris
that her condition rendered marriage essential to her decaying
reputation. He hurried to London and, yielding his own
scruples to her entreaties, secretly made her his wife during the
few days he stayed in this country. The step was full of peril.
To marry a lady of the Court without the Queen's consent
infringed a prerogative of the Crown by which Elizabeth set
exaggerated store.

---

[1] *Cal. of the Duke of Rutland's MSS.* i. 321. Barnabe Barnes, who was one of
Southampton's poetic admirers, addressed a crude sonnet to 'the Beautiful Lady, The
Lady Bridget Manners,' in 1593, at the same time as he addressed one to Southampton. Both are appended to Barnes's collection of sonnets and other poems
entitled *Parthenophe and Parthenophil* (cf. Arber's *Garner,* v. 486). Barnes
apostrophises Lady Bridget as 'fairest and sweetest'

> Of all those sweet and fair flowers,
> The pride of chaste Cynthia's [*i e.* Queen Elizabeth's] rich crown.

The story of Southampton's marriage was soon public property. His wife quickly became a mother, and when he crossed
the Channel a few weeks later to revisit her he was received by
pursuivants, who had the Queen's orders to carry him to the Fleet
prison. For the time his career was ruined. Although he was
soon released from gaol, all avenues to the Queen's favour were
closed to him. He sought employment in the wars in Ireland,
but high command was denied him. Helpless and hopeless, he
late in 1600 joined Essex, another fallen favourite, in fomenting
a rebellion in London, in order to regain by force the positions
each had forfeited. The attempt at insurrection failed, and
the conspirators stood their trial on a capital charge of treason

Imprison-   on February 19, 1600–1. Southampton was con-
ment,   demned to die, but the Queen's Secretary pleaded
1601–3.   with her that 'the poor young Earl, merely for the
love of Essex, had been drawn into this action,' and his punish-
ment was commuted to imprisonment for life. Further mitiga-
tion was not to be looked for while the Queen lived. But Essex,
Southampton's friend, had been James's sworn ally. The first
act of James I as monarch of England was to set Southampton
free (April 10, 1603). After a confinement of more than two
years, Southampton resumed, under happier auspices, his place
at Court.

Southampton's later career does not directly concern the
student of Shakespeare's biography. After Shakespeare had

Later   congratulated Southampton on his liberty in his
career.   Sonnet cvii., there is no trace of further relations
between them, although there is no reason to doubt that they
remained friends to the end. Southampton on his release from
prison was immediately installed a Knight of the Garter, and
was appointed Governor of the Isle of Wight, while an Act of
Parliament relieved him of all the disabilities incident to his
conviction of treason. He was thenceforth a prominent figure
in Court festivities. He twice danced a correnta with the
Queen at the magnificent entertainment given at Whitehall on
August 19, 1604, in honour of the Constable of Castile, the
special ambassador of Spain, who had come to sign a treaty of
peace between his Sovereign and James I.[1] But home politics

[1] See p. 233, n. 2.

proved no congenial field for the exercise of Southampton's energies. Quarrels with fellow-courtiers continued to jeopardise his fortunes. With Sir Robert Cecil, with Philip Herbert, Earl of Montgomery, and with the Duke of Buckingham he had violent disputes. It was in the schemes for colonising the New World that Southampton found an outlet for his impulsive activity. He helped to equip expeditions to Virginia, and acted as treasurer of the Virginia Company. The map of the country commemorates his labours as a colonial pioneer. In his honour were named Southampton Hundred, Hampton River, and Hampton Roads in Virginia. Finally, in the summer of 1624, at the age of fifty-one, Southampton, with characteristic spirit, took command of a troop of English volunteers which was raised to aid the Elector Palatine, husband of James I's daughter Elizabeth, in his struggle with the Emperor and the Catholics of Central Europe. With him went his eldest son, Lord Wriothesley. Both on landing in the Low Countries were attacked by fever. The younger man succumbed at once. The Earl regained sufficient strength to accompany his son's body

Death on Nov. 10, 1624.

to Bergen-op-Zoom, but there, on November 10, he himself died of a lethargy. Father and son were both buried in the chancel of the church of Titch-field, Hampshire, on December 28. Southampton thus outlived Shakespeare by more than eight years.

IV

THE EARL OF SOUTHAMPTON AS A LITERARY PATRON

SOUTHAMPTON'S close relations with men of letters of his time give powerful corroboration of the theory that he was the patron whom Shakespeare commemorated in the sonnets. From earliest to latest manhood — throughout the dissipations of Court life, amid the torments that his intrigue cost him, in the distractions of war and travel — the Earl never ceased to cherish the passion for literature which was implanted in him in boyhood. His devotion to his old college, St. John's, is characteristic. When a new library was in course of construction there during the closing years of his life, Southampton collected books to the value of 360*l*. wherewith to furnish it. This 'monument of love,' as the College authorities described the benefaction, may still be seen on the shelves of the College library. The gift largely consisted of illuminated manuscripts — books of hours, legends of the saints, and mediæval chronicles. Southampton caused his son to be educated at St. John's, and his wife expressed to the tutors the hope that the boy would 'imitate' his father 'in his love to learning and to them.'

Southampton's collection of books.

Even the State papers and business correspondence in which Southampton's career is traced are enlivened by references to his literary interests. Especially refreshing are the active signs vouchsafed there of his sympathy with the great birth of English drama. It was with plays that he joined other noblemen in 1598 in entertaining his chief, Sir Robert Cecil, on the eve of the departure for Paris of that embassy in which Southampton served Cecil as a secretary. In July following Southampton contrived to enclose in an official despatch from Paris 'certain songs' which he was anxious that Sir Robert Sidney, a friend

References in his letters to poems and plays.

of literary tastes, should share his delight in reading. Twelve months later, while Southampton was in Ireland, a letter to him from the Countess attested that current literature was an every-day topic of their private talk. 'All the news I can send you,' she wrote to her husband, 'that I think will make you merry, is that I read in a letter from London that Sir John Falstaff is, by his mistress Dame Pintpot, made father of a goodly miller's thumb — a boy that's all head and very little body; but this is a secret.'[1] This cryptic sentence proves on the part of both Earl and Countess familiarity with Falstaff's adventures in Shakespeare's 'Henry IV,' where the fat knight apostrophised Mrs. Quickly as 'good pint pot' (pt. i. ii. 4, 443). Who the acquaintances were about whom the Countess jested thus lightly does not appear, but that Sir John, the father of 'the boy that was all head and very little body,' was a playful allusion to Sir John's creator is by no means beyond the bounds of possibility. In the letters of Sir Toby Matthew, two of which were written very early in the seventeenth century (although first published in 1660), the sobriquet of Sir John Falstaff seems to have been bestowed on Shakespeare: 'As that excellent author Sir John Falstaff sayes, "what for your businesse, news, device, foolerie, and libertie, I never dealt better since I was a man."'[2]

When, after leaving Ireland, Southampton spent the autumn of 1599 in London, it was recorded that he and his friend Lord Rutland 'come not to Court' but 'pass away the time merely in going to plays every day.'[3] It seems that the fascina-

His love of the theatre. tion that the drama had for Southampton and his friends led them to exaggerate the influence that it was capable of exerting on the emotions of the multitude. Southampton and Essex in February 1601 requisitioned and paid for the revival of Shakespeare's 'Richard II' at the Globe Theatre on the day preceding that fixed for their insurrection, in the hope that the play-scene of the deposition of a king might excite the citizens of London to countenance their rebellious design.[4] Imprisonment sharpened Southampton's zest for the theatre.

---

[1] The original letter is at Hatfield. The whole is printed in Historical Manuscripts Commission, 3rd Rep. p. 145.

[2] The quotation is a confused reminiscence of Falstaff's remarks in 1 *Henry IV*. II. iv. The last nine words are an exact quotation of lines 190-1.

[3] *Sidney Papers*, ii. 132.   [4] See p. 175.

Within a year of his release from the Tower in 1603 he entertained Queen Anne of Denmark at his house in the Strand,
and Burbage and his fellow-players, one of whom was Shakespeare, were bidden to present the 'old' play of 'Love's Labour's
Lost,' whose 'wit and mirth' were calculated 'to please her
Majesty exceedingly.'

But these are merely accidental testimonies to Southampton's
literary predilections.   It is in literature itself, not in the prosaic
records of his political or domestic life, that the amplest proofs
survive of his devotion to letters.   From the hour that, as a
handsome and accomplished lad, he joined the Court and made

London his chief home, authors acknowledged his
appreciation of literary effort of almost every quality
and form.   He had in his Italian tutor Florio, whose
circle of acquaintance included all men of literary reputation, a
mentor who allowed no work of promise to escape his observation.   Every note in the scale of adulation was sounded in
Southampton's honour in contemporary prose and verse.   Soon
after the publication, in April 1593, of Shakespeare's 'Venus
and Adonis,' with its salutation of Southampton, a more youthful apprentice to the poet's craft, Barnabe Barnes,
confided to a published sonnet of unrestrained
fervour his conviction that Southampton's eyes —
'those heavenly lamps' — were the only sources of true poetic
inspiration.   The sonnet, which is superscribed 'to the Right
Noble and Virtuous Lord, Henry, Earl of Southampton,' runs :

*Poetic adu-
lation.*

*Barnabe
Barnes's
sonnet,
1593.*

> Receive, sweet Lord, with thy thrice sacred hand
>   (Which sacred Muses make their instrument)
>   These worthless leaves, which I to thee present,
> (Sprung from a rude and unmanurèd land)
> That with your countenance graced, they may withstand
>   Hundred-eyed Envy's rough encounterment,
>   Whose patronage can give encouragement
> To scorn back-wounding Zoilus his band.
> Vouchsafe, right virtuous Lord, with gracious eyes —
> Those heavenly lamps which give the Muses light,
> Which give and take in course that holy fire —
> To view my Muse with your judicial sight :
> Whom, when time shall have taught, by flight, to rise
> Shall to thy virtues, of much worth, aspire.

Next year a writer of greater power, Tom Nash, betrayed little less enthusiasm when dedicating to the Earl his masterly essay in romance, 'The Life of Jack Wilton.' He describes Southampton, who was then scarcely of age, as 'a dear lover and cherisher as well of the lovers of poets as of the poets themselves.' 'A new brain,' he exclaims, 'a new wit, a new style, a new soul, will I get me, to canonise your name to posterity, if in this my first attempt I am not taxed of presumption.'[1] Although 'Jack Wilton' was the first book Nash formally dedicated to Southampton, it is probable that Nash had made an earlier bid for the earl's patronage. In a digression at the close of his 'Pierce Pennilesse' he grows eloquent in praise of one whom he entitles 'the matchless image of honour and magnificent rewarder of vertue, Jove's eagle-borne Ganimede, thrice noble Amintas.' In a sonnet addressed to 'this renowed lord,' who 'draws all hearts to his love,' Nash expresses regret that the great poet, Edmund Spenser, had omitted to celebrate 'so special a pillar of nobility' in the series of adulatory sonnets prefixed to the 'Faerie Queen'; and in the last lines of his sonnet Nash suggests that Spenser suppressed the nobleman's name

Because few words might not comprise thy fame.[2]

[1] See Nash's *Works*, ed. Grosart, v. 6. The whole passage runs: 'How wel or ill I haue done in it I am ignorant: (the eye that sees round about it selfe sees not into it selfe): only your Honours applauding encouragement hath power to make me arrogant. Incomprehensible is the height of your spirit both in heroicall resolution and matters of conceit. Vnrepriuebly perisheth that booke whatsoeuer to wast paper, which on the diamond rocke of your judgement disasterly chanceth to be shipwrackt. A dere louer and cherisher you are, as well of the louers of Poets, as of Poets them selues. Amongst their sacred number I dare not ascribe my selfe, though now and then I speak English: that smal braine I haue, to no further vse I conuert saue to be kinde to my frends, and fatall to my enemies. A new brain, a new wit, a new stile, a new soule will I get mee to canonize your name to posteritie, if in this my first attempt I am not taxed of presumption. Of your gracious fauor I despaire not, for I am not altogether Fames out-cast. . . . Your Lordship is the large spreading branch of renown, from whence these my idle leaues seeke to deriue their whole nourishing.'

[2] The complimentary title of 'Amyntas,' which was naturalised in English literature by Abraham Fraunce's two renderings of Tasso's *Aminta* — one direct from the Italian and the other from the Latin version of Thomas Watson — was apparently bestowed by Spenser on the Earl of Derby in his *Colin Clouts come Home again* (1595); and some critics assume that Nash referred in *Pierce Pennilesse* to that nobleman rather than to Southampton. But Nash's comparison of his paragon to Ganymede suggests extreme youth, and Southampton was nineteen in 1592,

Southampton was beyond doubt the nobleman in question.
It is certain, too, that the Earl of Southampton was among
the young men for whom Nash, in hope of gain, as he admitted,
penned 'amorous villanellos and qui passas.' One of the least
reputable of these efforts of Nash survives in an obscene love-
poem entitled 'The Choosing of Valentines,' which may be
dated in 1595. This was not only dedicated to Southampton
in a prefatory sonnet, but in an epilogue, again in the form of a
sonnet, Nash addressed his young patron as his 'friend.'[1]

while Derby was thirty-three. 'Amyntas,' as a complimentary designation, was
widely used by the poets, and was not applied exclusively to any one patron of
letters. It was bestowed on the poet Watson Ƅy Richard Barnfield and by other
of Watson's panegyrists.

[1] Two manuscript copies of the poem, which has not been printed, are extant
— one among the Rawlinson poetical manuscripts in the Bodleian Library, and the
other among the manuscripts in the Inner Temple Library (No. 538). Mr. John S.
Farmer has kindly sent me transcripts of the opening and concluding dedicatory
sonnets. The first, which is inscribed ' to the right honourable the Lord S[outhamp-
ton],' runs:

> Pardon, sweete flower of matchles poetrye,
>   And fairest bud the red rose euer bare,
> Although my muse, devorst from deeper care,
>   Presents thee with a wanton Elegie.
>
> Ne blame my verse of loose unchastitye
>   For painting forth the things that hidden are,
> Since all men act what I in speeche declare,
>   Onlie induced with varietie.
>
> Complaints and praises, every one can write,
>   And passion out their pangs in statlie rimes;
> But of loues pleasures none did euer write,
>   That have succeeded in theis latter times.
>
> Accept of it, deare Lord, in gentle parte,
> And better lines ere long shall honor thee.

The poem follows in about three hundred lines, and the manuscript ends with a
second sonnet addressed by Nash to his patron :

> Thus hath my penne presum'd to please my friend.
>   Oh mightst thou lykewise please Apollo's eye.
> No, Honor brookes no such impietie,
>   Yet Ovid's wanton muse did not offend.
>
> He is the fountaine whence my streames do flowe—
>   Forgive me if I speak as I was taught;
> Alike to women, utter all I knowe,
>   As longing to unlade so bad a fraught.
>
> My mynde once purg'd of such lascivious witt,
>   With purifide words and hallowed verse,
> Thy praises in large volumes shall rehearse.
>   That better maie thy grauer view befitt.
>
> Meanwhile ytt rests, you smile at what I write
> Or for attempting banish me your sight.
>   THO. NASH.

Meanwhile, in 1595, the versatile Gervase Markham inscribed to Southampton in a sonnet, his patriotic poem on Sir Richard Grenville's glorious fight off the Azores. Markham was not content to acknowledge with Barnes the inspiriting force of his patron's eyes, but with blasphemous temerity asserted that the sweetness of his lips, which stilled the music of the spheres, delighted the ear of Almighty God. Markham's sonnet runs somewhat haltingly thus:

Mark-
ham's son-
net, 1595.

> Thou glorious laurel of the Muses' hill,
>   Whose eyes doth crown the most victorious pen,
> Bright lamp of virtue, in whose sacred skill,
>   Lives all the bliss of ear-enchanting men,
> From graver subjects of thy grave assays,
>   Bend thy courageous thoughts unto these lines —
> The grave from whence my humble Muse doth raise
> True honour's spirit in her rough designs —
> And when the stubborn stroke of my harsh song
> Shall seasonless glide through Almighty ears
> Vouchsafe to sweet it with thy blessèd tongue
> Whose well-tuned sound stills music in the spheres;
>   So shall my tragic lays be blest by thee
>   And from thy lips suck their eternity.

Subsequently Florio, in associating the Earl's name with his great Italian-English dictionary — the 'World of Words' — more soberly defined the Earl's place in the republic of letters when he wrote: 'As to me and many more the glorious and gracious sunshine of your honour hath infused light and life.'

Florio's
address,
1598.

The most notable contribution to this chorus of praise is to be found, as I have already shown, in Shakespeare's 'Sonnets.' The same note of eulogy was sounded by men of letters until Southampton's death. When he was released from prison on James I's accession in April 1603, his praises in poets' mouths were especially abundant. Not only was that grateful incident celebrated by Shakespeare in what is probably the latest of his sonnets (No. cvii.), but Samuel Daniel and John Davies of Hereford offered the Earl congratulation in more

The con-
gratula-
tions of the
poets in
1603.

prolonged strains.   Daniel addressed to Southampton many
lines like these :

> The world had never taken so full note
>   Of what thou art, hadst thou not been undone :
> And only thy affliction hath begot
>   More fame than thy best fortunes could have won ;
> For ever by adversity are wrought
>   The greatest works of admiration ;
> And all the fair examples of renown
> Out of distress and misery are grown . . .
> Only the best-compos'd and worthiest hearts
> God sets to act the hard'st and constant'st parts.[1]

Davies was more jubilant :

> Now wisest men with mirth do seem stark mad,
> And cannot choose — their hearts are all so glad.
> Then let's be merry in our God and King,
> That made us merry, being ill bestead.
> Southampton, up thy cap to Heaven fling,
> And on the viol there sweet praises sing,
> For he is come that grace to all doth bring.[2]

Many like praises, some of later date, by Henry Locke (or
Lok), George Chapman, Joshua Sylvester, Richard Braithwaite,
George Wither, Sir John Beaumont, and others could be
quoted.   Beaumont, on Southampton's death, wrote an elegy
which panegyrises him in the varied capacities of warrior,
councillor, courtier, father, and husband.   But it is as a literary
patron that Beaumont insists that he chiefly deserves remembrance :

> I keep that glory last which is the best,
> The love of learning which he oft expressed
> In conversation, and respect to those
> Who had a name in arts, in verse or prose.

---

[1] Daniel's *Certaine Epistles*, 1603; see Daniel's *Works*, ed. Grosart, i. 216 seq.

[2] See Preface to Davies's *Microcosmos*, 1603 (Davies's *Works*, ed. Grosart, i 14).
At the end of Davies's *Microcosmos* there is also a congratulatory sonnet addressed
to Southampton on his liberation (*ib*. p. 96), beginning:

> Welcome to shore, unhappy-happy Lord,
> From the deep seas of danger and distress.
> There like thou wast to be thrown overboard
> In every storm of discontentedness.

To the same effect are some twenty poems which were published in 1624, just after Southampton's death, in a volume entitled 'Teares of the Isle of Wight, shed on the Tombe
of their most noble valorous and loving Captaine and
Governour, the right honorable Henrie, Earl of Southampton.' The keynote is struck in the opening stanza of the
first poem by one Francis Beale:

Elegies on
Southamp-
ton.

> Ye famous poets of the southern isle,
> Strain forth the raptures of your tragic muse,
> And with your Laureate pens come and compile
> The praises due to this great Lord: peruse
>   His globe of worth, and eke his virtues brave,
>   Like learned Maroes at Mecænas's grave.

V

*THE TRUE HISTORY OF THOMAS THORPE
AND 'MR. W. H.'*

IN 1598 Francis Meres enumerated among Shakespeare's best
known works his 'sugar'd sonnets among his private friends.'
None of Shakespeare's sonnets are known to have been in
print when Meres wrote, but they were doubtless in circulation
in manuscript.   In 1599 two of them were printed for the first
The publi-   time by the piratical publisher, William Jaggard, in
cation of   the opening pages of the first edition of 'The
the sonnets   Passionate Pilgrim.'   On January 3, 1599–1600,
in 1609.   Eleazar Edgar, a publisher of small account, obtained
a license for the publication of a work bearing the title, 'A
Booke called Amours by J. D., with certein other Sonnetes by
W. S.'   No book answering this description is extant.   In
any case it is doubtful if Edgar's venture concerned Shakespeare's 'Sonnets.'   It is more probable that his 'W. S.' was
William Smith, who had published a collection of sonnets
entitled 'Chloris' in 1596.[1]   On May 20, 1609, a license for the
publication of Shakespeare's 'Sonnets' was granted by the
Stationers' Company to a publisher named Thomas Thorpe,
and shortly afterwards the complete collection as they have
reached us was published by Thorpe for the first time.   To

---

[1] 'Amours of J. D.' were doubtless sonnets by Sir John Davies, of which only a
few have reached us.   There is no ground for J. P. Collier's suggestion that J. D.
was a misprint for M. D., *i.e.* Michael Drayton, who gave the first edition of his
sonnets in 1594 the title of *Amours*.   That word was in France the common
designation of collections of sonnets (cf. Drayton's *Poems*, ed. Collier, Roxburghe
Club, p. xxv).

he volume Thorpe prefixed a dedication in the following
erms :

TO THE ONLIE BEGETTER OF
THESE INSUING SONNETS
MR. W. H., ALL HAPPINESSE
AND THAT ETERNITIE
PROMISED
BY
OUR EVER-LIVING POET
WISHETH
THE WELL-WISHING
ADVENTURER IN
SETTING
FORTH
T. T.

The words are fantastically arranged. In ordinary gram-
matical order they would run : ' The well-wishing adventurer
n setting forth [*i.e.* the publisher] T[homas] T[horpe] wisheth
Mr. W. H., the only begetter of these ensuing sonnets, all
happiness and that eternity promised by our ever-living poet.'

Few books of the sixteenth or seventeenth century were
ushered into the world without a dedication. In most cases it was
the work of the author, but numerous volumes, besides Shakespeare's ' Sonnets,' are extant in which the publisher (and
not the author) fills the *rôle* of dedicator. The cause of the
substitution is not far to seek. The signing of the dedication
was an assertion of full and responsible ownership in the pub-
ication, and the publisher in Shakespeare's lifetime was the
full and responsible owner of a publication quite as often as the
author. The modern conception of copyright had not yet been
evolved. Whoever in the sixteenth or early seventeenth century
was in actual possession of a manuscript was for practical
purposes its full and responsible owner. Literary work largely
circulated in manuscript.[1] Scriveners made a precarious livelihood by multiplying written copies, and an enterprising publisher had many opportunities of becoming the owner of a
popular book without the author's sanction or knowledge.
When a volume in the reigns of Elizabeth or James I was
published independently of the author, the publisher exercised

[1] See note to p. 88, *supra*.

unchallenged all the owner's rights, not the least valued o
Publishers'
dedica-
tions. which was that of choosing the patron of the enter
prise, and of penning the dedicatory complimen
above his signature. Occasionally circumstances
might speciously justify the publisher's appearance in the guis
of a dedicator. In the case of a posthumous book it sometime
happened that the author's friends renounced ownership o
neglected to assert it. In other instances, the absence of ar
author from London while his work was passing through the
press might throw on the publisher the task of supplying the
dedication without exposing him to any charge of sharp practice
But as a rule one of only two inferences is possible when a pub
lisher's name figured at the foot of a dedicatory epistle: either
the author was ignorant of the publisher's design, or he had re
fused to countenance it, and was openly defied. In the case o
Shakespeare's 'Sonnets' it may safely be assumed that Shake
speare received no notice of Thorpe's intention of publishing
the work, and that it was owing to the author's ignorance o
the design that the dedication was composed and signed by the
'well-wishing adventurer in setting forth.'

But whether author or publisher chose the patron of his
wares, the choice was determined by much the same considera-
tions. Self-interest was the principle underlying transactions
between literary patron and *protégé*. Publisher, like author
commonly chose as patron a man or woman of wealth anc
social influence who might be expected to acknowledge the
compliment either by pecuniary reward or by friendly advertise-
ment of the volume in their own social circle. At times the
publisher, slightly extending the field of choice, selected a
personal friend or mercantile acquaintance who had rendered
him some service in trade or private life, and was likely to
appreciate such general expressions of good will as were
the accepted topic of dedications. Nothing that was fantastic
or mysterious entered into the Elizabethan or the Jacobean
publishers' shrewd schemes of business, and it may be asserted
with confidence that it was under the everyday prosaic conditions
of current literary traffic that the publisher Thorpe selected
'Mr. W. H.' as the patron of the original edition of Shake-
speare's 'Sonnets.'

A study of Thorpe's character and career clears the point
doubt. Thorpe has been described as a native of Warwickshire, Shakespeare's county, and a man eminent in his
profession. He was neither of these things. He
is a native of Barnet in Middlesex, where his father kept an
n, and he himself through thirty years' experience of the book
ade held his own with difficulty in its humblest ranks. He
joyed the customary preliminary training.[1] At midsummer
84 he was apprenticed for nine years to a reputable printer
d stationer, Richard Watkins.[2] Nearly ten years later he
ok up the freedom of the Stationers' Company, and was
ereby qualified to set up as a publisher on his own account.[3]
e was not destitute of a taste for literature; he knew scraps
Latin, and recognised a good manuscript when he saw one.
ut the ranks of London publishers were overcrowded, and
ch accomplishments as Thorpe possessed were poor com-
ensation for a lack of capital or of family connections among
ose already established in the trade.[4] For many years he
ntented himself with an obscure situation as assistant or clerk
a stationer more favourably placed.

It was as the self-appointed procurer and owner of an un-
inted manuscript—a recognised *rôle* for novices to fill in the book
ade of the period — that Thorpe made his first distinguishable
pearance on the stage of literary history. In 1600 there
l into his hands in an unexplained manner a written copy of
Marlowe's unprinted translation of the first book of
'Lucan.' Thorpe confided his good fortune to Edward
Blount, then a stationer's assistant like himself, but
with better prospects. Blount had already achieved
a modest success in the same capacity of procurer
picker-up of neglected 'copy.'[5] In 1598 he became proprietor
Marlowe's unfinished and unpublished 'Hero and Leander,'
d found among better-equipped friends in the trade both

---

[1] The details of his career are drawn from Mr. Arber's *Transcript of the
gisters of the Stationers' Company.*
[2] Arber, ii. 124.   [3] *Ib.* ii. 713.
[4] A younger brother, Richard, was apprenticed to a stationer, Martin Ensor, for
en years from August 24, 1596, but he disappeared before gaining the freedom of
Company, either dying young or seeking another occupation (cf. Arber's
anscript, ii. 213).
[5] Cf. *Bibliographica*, i. 474-98, where I have given an account of Blount's pro-
ional career in a paper called 'An Elizabethan Bookseller.'

a printer and a publisher for his treasure-trove. Blou
good-naturedly interested himself in Thorpe's 'find,' and
was through Blount's good offices that Peter Short underto
to print Thorpe's manuscript of Marlowe's 'Lucan,' a
Walter Burre agreed to sell it at his shop in St. Pau
Churchyard. As owner of the manuscript Thorpe exerted t
right of choosing a patron for the venture and of supplying t
His dedica- dedicatory epistle. The patron of his choice w
tory ad-   his friend Blount, and he made the dedication t
dress to   vehicle of his gratitude for the assistance he had j
Edward
Blount in   received. The style of the dedication was somewl
1600.   bombastic, but Thorpe showed a literary sense wh
he designated Marlowe 'that pure elemental wit,' and a go
deal of dry humour in offering to 'his kind and true frien
Blount 'some few instructions' whereby he might acco
modate himself to the unaccustomed *rôle* of patron.[1] For t
conventional type of patron Thorpe disavowed respect.
preferred to place himself under the protection of a friend
the trade whose good will had already stood him in good ste
and was capable of benefiting him hereafter.

This venture laid the foundation of Thorpe's fortunes. Thr
years later he was able to place his own name on the title-pa
of two humbler literary prizes — each an insignificant pamph
on current events.[2] Thenceforth for a dozen years his na
reappeared annually on one, two, or three volumes. After 16
his operations were few and far between, and they ceas
altogether in 1624. He seems to have ended his days in pover
and he has been identified with the Thomas Thorpe who w
granted an almsroom in the hospital of Ewelme, Oxfordshi
December 3, 1635.[3]

[1] Thorpe gives a sarcastic description of a typical patron, and amply attests
purely commercial relations ordinarily subsisting between dedicator and dedica
'When I bring you the book,' he advises Blount, 'take physic and keep state.
sign me a time by your man to come again. . . . Censure scornfully enough
somewhat like a traveller. Commend nothing lest you discredit your (that wh
you would seem to have) judgment. . . . One special virtue in our patrons of th
days I have promised myself you shall fit excellently, which is to give nothi
Finally Thorpe, changing his tone, challenges his patron's love 'both in this an
hope, many more succeeding offices.'
[2] One gave an account of the East India Company's fleet ; the other repo
a speech delivered by Richard Martin, M.P., to James I at Stamford Hill du
the royal progress to London.
[3] Calendar of State Papers, Domestic Series, 1635, p. 527.

Thorpe was associated with the publication of twenty-nine volumes in all,[1] including Marlowe's 'Lucan'; but in almost all his operations his personal energies were confined, as in his initial enterprise, to procuring the manuscript. For a short period in 1608 he occupied a shop, The Tiger's Head, in St. Paul's Churchyard, and the fact was duly announced on the title-pages of three publications which he issued in that year.[2] But his other undertakings were described on their title-pages as printed for him by one stationer and sold for him by another; and when any address found mention at all, it was the shopkeeper's address, and not his own. He never enjoyed in permanence the profits or dignity of printing his 'copy' at a press of his own, or selling books on premises of his own, and he can claim the distinction of having pursued in this homeless fashion the well-defined profession of procurer of manuscripts for a longer period than any other known member of the Stationers' Company. Though many others began their career in that capacity, all except Thorpe, so far as they can be traced, either developed into printers or booksellers, or, failing in that, betook themselves to other trades.

Very few of his wares does Thorpe appear to have procured direct from the authors. It is true that between 1605 and 1611 there were issued under his auspices some eight volumes of genuine literary value, including, besides Shakespeare's Sonnets,' three plays by Chapman,[3] four works of Ben Jonson,

character his business.

---

[1] Two bore his name on the title-page in 1603; one in 1604; two in 1605; two in 1606; two in 1607; three in 1608; one in 1609 (*i.e.* the *Sonnets*); three in 1610 (i.e. *Histrio-mastrix, or the Playwright*, as well as Healey's translations); two in 1611; one in 1612; three in 1613; two in 1614; two in 1616; one in 1618; and finally one in 1624. The last was a new edition of George Chapman's *Conspiracie and Tragedie of Charles Duke of Byron*, which Thorpe first published in 1608.

[2] They were *Wits A.B.C. or a centurie of Epigrams* (anon.), by R. West of Magdalen College, Oxford (a copy is in the Bodleian Library); Chapman's *Byron*, and Jonson's *Masques of Blackness and Beauty*.

[3] Chapman and Jonson were very voluminous authors, and their works were sought after by almost all the publishers of London, many of whom were successful in launching one or two with or without the author's sanction. Thorpe seems to have taken particular care with Jonson's books, but none of Jonson's works fell into Thorpe's hands before 1605 or after 1608, a minute fraction of Jonson's literary life. It is significant that the author's dedication — the one certain mark of publication with the author's sanction — appears in only one of the three plays by Chapman that Thorpe issued. viz. in *Byron*. One or two copies of Thorpe's impression of *All Fools* have a dedication by the author, but it is absent from most of them. No

and Coryat's 'Odcombian Banquet.' But the taint of mysteriou origin attached to most of his literary properties. He doubtle owed them to the exchange of a few pence or shillings with scrivener's hireling; and the transaction was not one of whic the author had cognisance.

It is quite plain that no negotiation with the author precede the formation of Thorpe's resolve to publish for the first tim Shakespeare's 'Sonnets' in 1609. Had Shakespeare associate himself with the enterprise, the world would fortunately ha been spared Thorpe's dedication to 'Mr. W. H.' 'T. T.' place would have been filled by 'W. S.' The whole transactio was in Thorpe's vein. Shakespeare's 'Sonnets' had bee

Shake-
speare's
sufferings
at publish-
ers' hands.

already circulating in manuscript for eleven years only two had as yet been printed, and those we issued by the pirate publisher, William Jaggard, i the fraudulently christened volume 'The Passiona Pilgrim, by William Shakespeare,' in 1599. Shakespeare, e cept in the case of his two narrative poems, showed utter i difference to all questions touching the publication of h works. Of the sixteen plays of his that were published in h lifetime, not one was printed with his sanction. He made n audible protest when seven contemptible dramas in which h had no hand were published with his name or initials on th title-page while his fame was at its height. With only on publisher of his time, Richard Field, his fellow-townsman, wh was responsible for the issue of 'Venus' and 'Lucrece,' is likely that he came into personal relations, and there is nothin to show that he maintained relations with Field after the pul lication of 'Lucrece' in 1594.

In fitting accord with the circumstance that the publicatio of the 'Sonnets' was a tradesman's venture which ignored th author's feelings and rights, Thorpe in both the entry of th book in the 'Stationers' Registers' and on its title-pag brusquely designated it 'Shakespeares Sonnets,' instead c following the more urbane collocation of words invariabl adopted by living authors, viz. 'Sonnets by William Shake speare.'

known copy of Thorpe's edition of Chapman's *Gentleman Usher* has any dedic tion.

In framing the dedication Thorpe followed established precedent. Initials run riot over Elizabethan and Jacobean books. Printers and publishers, authors and contributors of prefatory commendations, were all in the habit of masking themselves behind such symbols. Patrons figured under initials in dedications somewhat less frequently than other sharers in the book's production. But the conditions determining the employment of initials in that relation were well defined. The employment of initials in a dedication was a recognised mark of a close friendship or intimacy between patron and dedicator. It was a sign that the patron's fame was limited to a small circle, and that the revelation of his full name was not a matter of interest to a wide public. Such are the dominant notes of almost all the extant dedications in which the patron is addressed by his initials. In 1598 Samuel Rowlands addressed the dedication of his 'Betraying of Christ' to his 'deare affected *friend* Maister H. W., gentleman.' An edition of Robert Southwell's 'Short Rule of Life' which appeared in the same year bore a dedication addressed 'to my deare affected *friend* M. [*i.e.* Mr.] D. S., gentleman.' The poet Richard Barnfield also in the same year dedicated the opening sonnet in his 'Poems in Divers Humours' to his '*friend* Maister R. L.' In 1617 Dunstan Gale dedicated a poem, 'Pyramus and Thisbe,' to the 'worshipfull his verie *friend* D. [*i.e.* Dr.] B. H.' [1]

There was nothing exceptional in the words of greeting which Thorpe addressed to his patron 'Mr. W. H.' They followed a widely adopted formula. Dedications of the time usually consisted of two distinct parts. There was a dedicatory epistle, which might touch at any length, in either verse or prose, on the subject of the book and the writer's relations with

The use of initials in dedications of Elizabethan and Jacob an books.

[1] Many other instances of initials figuring in dedications under slightly different circumstances will occur to bibliographers, but all, on examination, point to the existence of a close intimacy between dedicator and dedicatee. R. S.'s [*i e.* possibly Richard Stafford's] 'Epistle dedicatorie' before his *Heraclitus* (Oxford, 1609) was inscribed 'to his much honoured father S. F. S.' *An Apologie for Women, or an Opposition to Mr. D. G. his assertion . . . by W. H. of Ex. in Ox.* (Oxford, 1609), was dedicated to 'the honourable and right vertuous ladie, the Ladie M. H.' This volume, published in the same year as Shakespeare's *Sonnets*, offers a pertinent example of the generous freedom with which initials were scattered over the preliminary pages of books of the day.

his patron.   But there was usually, in addition, a preliminary
salutation confined to such a single sentence as Thorpe dis-
Frequency
of wishes
for 'happi-
ness' and
'eternity' in
dedicatory
greetings. played on the first page of his edition of Shakespeare's sonnets.   In that preliminary sentence the
dedicator habitually 'wisheth' his patron one or
more of such blessings as health, long life, happiness,
and eternity.   'Al perseverance with soules happiness' Thomas Powell 'wisheth' the Countess of Kildare on
the first page of his 'Passionate Poet' in 1601.   'All happi-
nes' is the greeting of Thomas Watson, the sonnetteer, to his
patron, the Earl of Oxford, on the threshold of Watson's 'Passionate Century of Love.'   There is hardly a book published by
Robert Greene between 1580 and 1592 that does not open with
an adjuration before the dedicatory epistle in the form : 'To
—— —— Robert Greene wisheth increase of honour with the
full fruition of perfect felicity.'

Thorpe in Shakespeare's sonnets left the salutation to stand
alone, and omitted the supplement of a dedicatory epistle;
but this, too, was not unusual.   There exists an abundance
of contemporary examples of the dedicatory salutation without
the sequel of the dedicatory epistle.   Edmund Spenser's
dedication of the 'Faerie Queen' to Elizabeth consists
solely of the salutation in the form of an assurance that the
writer 'consecrates these his labours to live with the eternitie of her fame.'   Michael Drayton in both his 'Idea,
The Shepheard's Garland' (1593), and in his 'Poemes Lyrick
and Pastorall' (1609), confined his address to his patron to a
single sentence of salutation.[1]   Richard Braithwaite in 1611
exclusively saluted the patron of his 'Golden Fleece' with 'the
continuance of God's temporall blessings in this life, with the
crowne of immortalitie in the world to come;' while in like
manner he greeted the patron of his 'Sonnets and Madrigals'
in the same year with 'the prosperitie of times successe in this
life, with the reward of eternitie in the world to come.'   It is
'happiness' and 'eternity,' or an equivalent paraphrase, that had
the widest vogue among the good wishes with which the dedi-

[1] In the volume of 1593 the words run: ' To the noble and valorous gentleman
Master Robert Dudley, enriched with all vertues of the minde and worthy of al
honorable desert.   Your most affectionate and devoted Michael Drayton.'

cator in the early years of the seventeenth century besought
his patron's favour on the first page of his book. But
Thorpe was too self-assertive to be a slavish imitator.
His addiction to bombast and his elementary appreciation of
literature recommended to him the practice of incorporating in
his dedicatory salutation some high-sounding embellishments
of the accepted formula suggested by his author's writing.[1] In
his dedication of the 'Sonnets' to 'Mr. W. H.' he grafted on
the common formula a reference to the immortality which
Shakespeare, after the habit of contemporary sonnetteers,
promised the hero of his sonnets in the pages that succeeded.
With characteristic magniloquence, Thorpe added the decora-
tive and supererogatory phrase, 'promised by our ever-living
poet,' to the conventional dedicatory wish for his patron's 'all
happiness' and 'eternitie.'[2]

Thorpe, as far as is known, penned only one dedication
before that to Shakespeare's 'Sonnets.' His dedicatory
experience was previously limited to the inscription of Marlowe's
'Lucan' in 1600 to Blount, his friend in the trade. Three
Five dedi- dedications by Thorpe survive of a date subsequent
cations by to the issue of the 'Sonnets.' One of these is
Thorpe.   dedicated to John Florio, and the other two to the
Earl of Pembroke.[3] But these three dedications all prefaced

---

[1] In 1610, in dedicating *St. Augustine, Of the Citie of God* to the Earl of
Pembroke, Thorpe awkwardly describes the subject-matter as 'a desired citie sure
in heaven,' and assigns to 'St. Augustine and his commentator Vives' a 'savour of
the secular.' In the same year, in dedicating *Epictetus's Manuall* to Florio, he
bombastically pronounces the book to be 'the hand to philosophy; the instrument of
instruments; as Nature greatest in the least; as Homer's *Ilias* in a nutshell; in
lesse compasse more cunning.' For other examples of Thorpe's pretentious, half-
educated, and ungrammatical style, see p. 403, *n.* 2.

[2] The suggestion is often made that the only parallel to Thorpe's salutation of
happiness is met with in George Wither's *Abuses Whipt and Stript* (London, 1613).
There the dedicatory epistle is prefaced by the ironical salutation ' To himselfe
G. W. wisheth all happinesse.' It is further asserted that Wither had probably
Thorpe's dedication to 'Mr. W. H.' in view when he wrote that satirical sentence.
It will now be recognised that Wither aimed very gently at no identifiable book,
but at a feature common to scores of books. Since his *Abuses* was printed by
George Eld and sold by Francis Burton—the printer and publisher concerned
in 1606 in the publication of 'W. H.'s' Southwell manuscript—there is a
bare chance that Wither had in mind 'W. H.'s' greeting of Mathew Saunders,
but fifty recently published volumes would have supplied him with similar hints

[3] Thorpe dedicated to Florio *Epictetus his Manuall, and Cebes his Table, out*

volumes of translations by one John Healey, whose manuscripts
had become Thorpe's prey after the author had emigrated to
Virginia, where he died shortly after landing. Thorpe chose, he
tells us, Florio and the Earl of Pembroke as patrons of Healey's
unprinted manuscripts because they had been patrons of
Healey before his expatriation and death. There is evidence to
prove that in choosing a patron for the 'Sonnets,' and penning
a dedication for the second time, he pursued the exact procedure
that he had followed — deliberately and for reasons that he fully
stated — in his first and only preceding dedicatory venture. He
chose his patron from the circle of his trade associates, and
it must have been because his patron was a personal friend
that he addressed him by his initials, ' W. H.'

Shakespeare's ' Sonnets ' is not the only volume of the period
in the introductory pages of which the initials ' W. H.' play a

'W. H.'
signs dedi-
cation of
Southwell's
poems in
1606.

prominent part. In 1606 one who concealed himself under the same letters performed for ' A Foure-
fould Meditation ' (a collection of pious poems which
the Jesuit Robert Southwell left in manuscript at his
death) the identical service that Thorpe performed
for Marlowe's ' Lucan ' in 1600, and for Shakespeare's ' Sonnets '
in 1609. In 1606 Southwell's manuscript fell into the hands
of this ' W. H.,' and he published it through the agency of the
printer, George Eld, and of an insignificant bookseller, Francis
Burton.[1] ' W. H.,' in his capacity of owner, supplied the dedication with his own pen under his initials. Of the Jesuit's newly
recovered poems ' W. H.' wrote, ' Long have they lien hidden
in obscuritie, and haply had never seene the light, had not a
meere accident conveyed them to my hands. But, having
seriously perused them, loath I was that any who are religiously
affected, should be deprived of so great a comfort, as the due

of Greek originall by Io. Healey, 1610. He dedicated to the Earl of Pembroke
St. Augustine, Of the Citie of God. . . . *Englished by I. H.,* 1610, and a second
edition of Healey's *Epictetus,* 1616.

[1] Southwell's *Foure-fould Meditation* of 1606 is a book of excessive rarity, only
one complete printed copy having been met with in our time. A fragment of the
only other printed copy known is now in the British Museum. The work was
reprinted in 1895, chiefly from an early copy in manuscript, by Mr. Charles
Edmonds, the accomplished bibliographer, who in a letter to the *Athenæum* on
November 1, 1873, suggested for the first time the identity of ' W. H.,' the dedicator
of Southwell's poem, with Thorpe's ' Mr. W. H.'

consideration thereof may bring unto them.' 'W. H.' chose as patron of his venture one Mathew Saunders, Esq., and to the dedicatory epistle prefixed a conventional salutation wishing Saunders long life and prosperity. The greeting was printed in large and bold type thus:

To the Right Worſhipfull and *Vertuous Gentleman*, *Mathew* Saunders, Eſquire

W. H. wiſheth, with long life, a proſperous achieuement of his good deſires.

There follows in small type, regularly printed across the page, a dedicatory letter — the frequent sequel of the dedicatory salutation — in which the writer, 'W. H.,' commends the religious temper of 'these meditations' and deprecates the coldness and sterility of his own 'conceits.' The dedicator signs himself at the bottom of the page 'Your Worships unfained affectionate, W. H.'[1]

The two books — Southwell's 'Foure-fould Meditations' of 1606, and Shakespeare's 'Sonnets' of 1609 — have more in common than the appearance on the preliminary pages of the initials 'W. H.' in a prominent place, and of the common form of dedicatory salutation. Both volumes, it was announced on the title-pages, came from the same press — the press of George Eld. Eld for many years co-operated with Thorpe in business. In 1605 he printed for Thorpe Ben Jonson's 'Sejanus,' and in each of the years 1607, 1608, 1609, and 1610 at least one of his ventures was publicly declared to be a specimen of Eld's

[1] A manuscript volume at Oscott College contains a contemporary copy of those poems by Southwell which 'unfained affectionate W. H.' first gave to the printing press. The owner of the Oscott volume, Peter Mowle or Moulde (as he indifferently spells his name), entered on the first page of the manuscript in his own handwriting an 'epistel dedicatorie' which he confined to the conventional greeting of happiness here and hereafter. The words ran: 'To the right worshipfull Mr. Thomas Knevett Esquire, Peter Mowle wisheth the perpetuytie of true felysitie, the health of bodie and soule with continwance of worshipp in this worlde, And after Death the participation of Heavenlie happiness dewringe all worldes for ever.'

2 D

typography. Many of Thorpe's books came forth without any mention of the printer; but Eld's name figures more frequently upon them than that of any other printer. Between 1605 and 1609 it is likely that Eld printed all Thorpe's ' copy ' as matter of course and that he was in constant relations with him.

There is little doubt that the ' W. H.' of the Southwell volume was Mr. William Hall, who, when he procured that manuscript for publication, was an humble auxiliary in the publishing army. Hall flits rapidly across the stage of literary history. He served an apprenticeship to the printer and stationer John Allde from 1577 to 1584, and was admitted to the freedom of the Stationers' Company in the latter year. For the long period of twenty-two years after his release from his indentures he was connected with the trade in a dependent capacity, doubtless as assistant to a master-stationer. When in 1606 the manuscript of Southwell's poems was conveyed to his hands and he adopted the recognised *rôle* of procurer of their publication, he had not set up in business for himself. It was only later in the same year (1606) that he obtained the license of the Stationers' Company to inaugurate a press in his own name, and two years passed before he began business. In 1608 he obtained for publication a theological manuscript which appeared next year with his name on the title-page for the first time. This volume constituted the earliest credential of his independence. It entitled him to the prefix ' Mr.' in all social relations. Between 1609 and 1614 he printed some twenty volumes, most of them sermons and almost all devotional in tone. The most important of his secular undertaking was Guillim's far-famed ' Display of Heraldrie,' a folio issued in 1610. In 1612 Hall printed an account of the conviction and execution of a noted pickpocket, John Selman, who had been arrested while professionally engaged in the Royal Chapel at Whitehall. On the title-page Hall gave his own name by his initials only. The book was described in bold type as ' printed by W. H.' and as on sale at the shop of Thomas Archer in St. Paul's Churchyard. Hall was a careful printer with a healthy dread of misprints, but his business dwindled after 1613, and, soon disposing of it to one John Beale, he disappeared into private life.

'W. H.' and Mr. William Hall.

'W. H.' are no uncommon initials, and there is more interest attaching to the discovery of 'Mr. W. H.'s' position in life and his function in relation to the scheme of the publication of the 'Sonnets' than in establishing his full name. But there is every probability that William Hall, the 'W. H.' of the Southwell dedication, was one and the same person with the 'Mr. W. H.' of Thorpe's dedication of the 'Sonnets.' No other inhabitant of London was habitually known to mask himself under those letters. William Hall was the only man bearing those initials who there is reason to suppose was on familiar terms with Thorpe.[1] Both were engaged at much the same period in London in the same occupation of procuring manuscripts for publication; both inscribed their literary treasure-trove in the common formula to patrons for whom they claimed no high rank or distinction, and both engaged the same printer to print their most valuable prize.

No condition of the problem of the identity of Thorpe's friend 'Mr. W. H.' seems ignored by the adoption of the interpretation that he was the future master-printer William Hall. The objection that 'Mr. W. H.' could not have been Thorpe's friend in trade, because while wishing him all happiness and eternity Thorpe dubs him 'the only begetter of these ensuing sonnets,' is not formidable. Thorpe rarely used words with much exactness.[2]

'The onlie begetter' means 'only procurer.'

---

[1] A bookseller (not a printer), William Holmes, who was in business for himself between 1590 and 1615, was the only other member of the Stationers' Company bearing at the required dates the initials of 'W. H.' But he was ordinarily known by his full name, and there is no indication that he had either professional or private relations with Thorpe.

[2] Most of his dedications are penned in a loose diction of pretentious bombast which it is difficult to interpret exactly. When dedicating in 1610 — the year after the issue of the Sonnets — Healey's Epictetus his Manuall 'to a true fauover of forward spirits, Maister John Florio,' Thorpe writes of Epictetus's work: 'In all languages, ages, by all persons high prized, imbraced, yea inbosomed. It filles not the hand with leaues, but fills ye head with lessons: nor would bee held in hand but had by harte to boote. He is more senceless than a stocke that hath no good sence of this stoick.' In the same year, when dedicating Healey's translation of St. Augustine's Citie of God to the Earl of Pembroke, Thorpe clumsily refers to Pembroke's patronage of Healey's earlier efforts in translation thus: 'He that against detraction beyond expectation, then found your sweete patronage in a matter of small moment without distrust or disturbance, in this work of more weight, as he approoued his more abilitie, so would not but expect your Honours more acceptance.'

It is obvious that he did not employ 'begetter' in the ordinary sense. 'Begetter,' when literally interpreted as applied to a literary work, means father, author, producer, and it cannot be seriously urged that Thorpe intended to describe 'Mr. W. H.' as the author of the 'Sonnets.' 'Begetter' has been used in the figurative sense of inspirer, and it is often assumed that by 'only begetter' Thorpe meant 'sole inspirer,' and that by the use of those words he intended to hint at the close relations subsisting between 'W. H.' and Shakespeare in the dramatist's early life ; but that interpretation presents numberless difficulties. It was contrary to Thorpe's aims in business to invest a dedication with any cryptic significance and thus mystify his customers. Moreover, his career and the circumstances under which he became the publisher of the sonnets confute the assumption that he was in such relations with Shakespeare or with Shakespeare's associates as would give him any knowledge of Shakespeare's early career that was not public property. All that Thorpe — the struggling pirate-publisher, 'the well-wishing adventurer in setting forth' wares mysteriously come by — knew or probably cared to know of Shakespeare was that he was the most popular and honoured of the literary producers of the day. When Thorpe had the luck to acquire surreptitiously an unprinted manuscript by 'our ever-living poet,' it was not in the great man's circle of friends or patrons, to which hitherto he had had no access, that he was likely to seek his own patron. Elementary considerations of prudence impelled him to publish his treasure-trove with all expedition, and not disclose his design prematurely to one who might possibly take steps to hinder its fulfilment. But that Thorpe had no 'inspirer' of the 'Sonnets' in his mind when he addressed himself to 'Mr. W. H.' is finally proved by the circumstance that the only identifiable male 'inspirer' of the poems was the Earl of Southampton, to whom the initials 'W. H.' do not apply.

Of the figurative meanings set in Elizabethan English on the word 'begetter,' that of 'inspirer' is by no means the only one or the most common. 'Beget' was not infrequently employed in the attenuated sense of 'get,' 'procure,' or 'obtain,' a sense which is easily deducible from the original one of 'bring into being.' Hamlet, when addressing the players, bids them

in the very whirlwind of passion acquire and beget a tem-
perance that may give it smoothness.' 'I have some cousins
german at Court,' wrote Dekker in 1602, in his ' Satiro-Mastix,'
[that] shall beget you the reversion of the Master of the King's
Revels.' 'Mr. W. H.,' whom Thorpe described as 'the only
begetter of these ensuing sonnets,' was in all probability the
acquirer or procurer of the manuscript, who, figuratively speaking, brought the book into being either by first placing the
manuscript in Thorpe's hands or by pointing out the means
by which a copy might be acquired. To assign such significance to the word 'begetter' was entirely in Thorpe's vein.[1]
Thorpe described his *rôle* in the piratical enterprise of the
'Sonnets' as that of 'the well-wishing adventurer in setting
forth,' *i.e.* the hopeful speculator in the scheme. 'Mr. W. H.'
doubtless played the almost equally important part — one as
well known then as now in commercial operations — of the
'vender' of the property to be exploited.

[1] This is the sense allotted to the word in the great Variorum edition of 1821 by
Malone's disciple, James Boswell the younger, who, like his master, was a bibliographical expert of the highest authority. The fact that the eighteenth-century
commentators — men like Malone and Steevens — who were thoroughly well versed in
the literary history of the sixteenth century, should have failed to recognise any connection between ' Mr. W. H.' and Shakespeare's personal history is in itself a very
strong argument against the interpretation foisted on the dedication during the
present century by writers who have no pretensions to be reckoned the equals of
Malone and Steevens as literary archæologists.

VI

'*MR. WILLIAM HERBERT*'

FOR fully sixty years it has been very generally assumed that Shakespeare addressed the bulk of his sonnets to the young Earl of Pembroke. This theory owes its origin to a speciously lucky guess which was first disclosed to the public in 1832, and won for a time almost universal acceptance.[1] Thorpe's form of address was held to justify the mistaken inference that, whoever 'Mr. W. H.' may have been, he and no other was the hero of the alleged story of the poems; and the cornerstone of the Pembroke theory was the assumption that the letters 'Mr. W. H.' in the dedication did duty for the words 'Mr. William Herbert,' by which name the (third) Earl of Pembroke was represented as having been known in youth. The

Origin of the notion that Mr. W. H. stands for 'Mr. William Herbert.'

---

[1] James Boaden, a journalist and the biographer of Kemble and Mrs. Siddons, was the first to suggest the Pembroke theory in a letter to the *Gentleman's Magazine* in 1832. A few months later Mr. James Heywood Bright wrote to the magazine claiming to have reached the same conclusion as early as 1819, although he had not published it. Boaden re-stated the Pembroke theory in a volume on *Shakespeare's Sonnets* which he published in 1837. C. Armitage Brown adopted it in 1838 in his *Shakespeare's Autobiographical Poems*. The Rev. Joseph Hunter, who accepted the theory without qualification, significantly pointed out in his *New Illustrations of Shakespeare* in 1845 (ii. 346) that it had not occurred to any of the writers in the great Variorum editions of Shakespeare, nor to critics so acute in matters of literary history as Malone or George Chalmers. The theory is treated as proved fact in many recent literary manuals. Of its supporters at the date of writing the most ardent is Mr. Thomas Tyler, who published an edition of the sonnets in 1890, and there further advanced a claim to identify the 'dark lady' of the sonnets with Mary Fitton, a lady of the Court and the Earl of Pembroke's mistress. Mr. Tyler has endeavoured to substantiate both the Pembroke and the Fitton theories, by merely repeating his original arguments, in a pamphlet which appeared in April of this year under the title of *The Herbert-Fitton Theory: a Reply* [*i.e.* to criticisms of the theories by Lady Newdegate and by myself]. The Pembroke theory, whose adherents have dwindled of late, will henceforth be relegated, I trust, to the category of popular delusions.

originators of the theory claimed to discover in the Earl of
Pembroke the only young man of rank and wealth to whom the
initials 'W. H.' applied at the needful dates. In thus interpreting the initials, the Pembroke theorists made a blunder
that proves on examination to be fatal to their whole contention.

The nobleman under consideration succeeded to the earldom of Pembroke on his father's death on January 19, 1601

The Earl of (N. S.), when he was twenty years and nine months
Pembroke old, and from that date it is unquestioned that he was
known only always known by his lawful title. But it has been
as Lord overlooked that the designation 'Mr. William Her-
Herbert in
outh. bert,' for which the initials 'Mr. W. H.' have been long
held to stand, could never in the mind of Thomas Thorpe or
any other contemporary have denominated the Earl at any
moment of his career. When he came into the world on
April 9, 1580, his father had been (the second) Earl of Pembroke for ten years, and he, as the eldest son, was from the
hour of his birth known in all relations of life — even in the
baptismal entry in the parish register — by the title of Lord
Herbert, and by no other. During the lifetime of his father
and his own minority several references were made to him in
the extant correspondence of friends of varying degrees of
intimacy. He is called by them, without exception, 'my Lord
Herbert,' 'the Lord Herbert,' or 'Lord Herbert.'[1] It is true
that as the eldest son of an earl he held the title by courtesy,
but for all practical purposes it was as well recognised in common speech as if he had been a peer in his own right. No one
nowadays would address in current parlance, or even entertain
the conception of, Viscount Cranborne, the heir of the present
Prime Minister, as 'Mr. J. C.' or 'Mr. James Cecil.' It is just
as legitimate to assert that it would have occurred to an Elizabethan — least of all to a personal acquaintance or to a publisher

[1] Cf. *Sydney Papers*, ed. Collins, i. 353. 'My Lord (of Pembroke) himself with
my Lord Harbert (are) come up to see the Queen' (Rowland Whyte to Sir Robert
Sydney, October 8, 1591), and again p. 361 (November 16, 1595); and p. 372
December 5, 1595). John Chamberlain wrote to Sir Dudley Carleton on August 1,
1599, 'young Lord Harbert, Sir Henrie Carie, and Sir William Woodhouse, are all
in election at Court, who shall set the best legge foremost.' *Chamberlain's Letters*
Camden Soc.), p. 57.

who stood toward his patron in the relation of a person:
dependent — to describe 'young Lord Herbert,' of Elizabeth
reign, as 'Mr. William Herbert.' A lawyer, who in the way o
business might have to mention the young lord's name in
legal document, would have entered it as 'William Herbe
commonly called Lord Herbert.' The appellation 'Mr.' w:
not used loosely then as now, but indicated a precise soci:
grade. Thorpe's employment of the prefix 'Mr.' without qual
fication is in itself fatal to the pretension that any lord, wheth
by right or courtesy, was intended.[1]

Proof is at hand to establish that Thorpe was under n
misapprehension as to the proper appellation of the Earl o
Pembroke, and was incapable of venturing on th
meaningless misnomer of 'Mr. W. H.' Insignificar
publisher though he was, and sceptical as he was o
the merits of noble patrons, he was not proof again
the temptation, when an opportunity was directly offered him, o
adorning the prefatory pages of a publication with the nam
of a nobleman who enjoyed the high official station, the litera:
culture, and social influence of the third Earl of Pembrok·
In 1610 — a year after he published the ' Sonnets ' — there cam
into his hands the manuscripts by John Healey, that humb·
literary aspirant who had a few months before emigrated t
Virginia, and had, it would seem, died there. Healey, befo·
leaving England, had secured through the good offices of Joh·
Florio (a man of influence in both fashionable and literary circles
the patronage of the Earl of Pembroke for a translation o
Bishop Hall's fanciful satire, 'Mundus alter et idem.' Callin

(margin note: Thorpe's mode of addressing the Earl of Pembroke.)

---

[1] Thomas Sackville, the author of the *Induction* to *The Mirror for Magistrate*
and other poetical pieces, and part author of *Gorboduc*, was born plain ' Thom
Sackville,' and was ordinarily addressed in youth as ' Mr. Sackville.' He wrote :
his literary work while he bore that and no other designation. He subsequent
abandoned literature for politics, and was knighted and created Lord Buckhur:
Very late in life, in 1604, — at the age of sixty-eight, — he became Earl of Dorset.
few of his youthful effusions, which bore his early signature, ' M. [*i.e.* Mr.] Sackvill·
were reprinted with that signature unaltered in an encyclopædic antholog·
England's Parnassus, which was published, wholly independently of him, in 16c
after he had become Baron Buckhurst. About the same date he was similar
designated Thomas or Mr. Sackville in a reprint, unauthorised by him, of F
Induction to *The Mirror for Magistrates*, which was in the original text ascribe
with perfect correctness, to Thomas or Mr. Sackville. There is clearly no sort
parallel (as has been urged) between such an explicable, and not unwarrantab·
metachronism and the misnaming of the Earl of Pembroke ' Mr. W. H.' As mig
be anticipated, persistent research affords no parallel for the latter irregularity.

is book 'The Discoverie of a New World,' Healey had prefixed
o it, in 1609, an epistle inscribed in garish terms of flattery to
he 'Truest mirrour of truest honor, William Earl of Pembroke.' [1]
When Thorpe subsequently made up his mind to publish, on
is own account, other translations by the same hand, he found
t desirable to seek the same patron. Accordingly, in 1610, he
refixed in his own name, to an edition of Healey's translation
f St. Augustine's 'Citie of God,' a dedicatory address 'to the
onorablest patron of the Muses and good mindes, Lord William,
Earle of Pembroke, Knight of the Honourable Order (of the
Garter), &c.' In involved sentences Thorpe tells the 'right
gracious and gracefule Lord' how the author left the work at
death to be a 'testimonie of gratitude, observance, and heart's
onor to your honour.' 'Wherefore,' he explains, 'his legacie,
aide at your Honour's feete, is rather here delivered to your
Honour's humbly thrise-kissed hands by his poore delegate.
Your Lordship's true devoted, Th. Th.'

Again, in 1616, when Thorpe procured the issue of a second
edition of another of Healey's translations, 'Epictetus Manuall.
Cebes Table. Theoprastus Characters,' he supplied more conspicuous evidence of the servility with which he deemed it
incumbent on him to approach a potent patron. As this address
by Thorpe to Pembroke is difficult of access, I give it *in
extenso*:

To the Right Honourable, William Earle of Pembroke, Lord
Chamberlaine to His Majestie, one of his most honorable
Privie Counsell, and Knight of the most noble order of the
Garter, &c.

'Right Honorable. — It may worthily seeme strange unto
your Lordship, out of what frenzy one of my meanenesse hath
presumed to commit this Sacriledge, in the straightnesse of
your Lordship's leisure, to present a peece, for matter and
model so unworthy, and in this scribbling age, wherein great
persons are so pestered dayly with Dedications. All I can
alledge in extenuation of so many incongruities, is the bequest
of a deceased Man; who (in his lifetime) having offered some

---

[1] An examination of a copy of the book in the Bodleian — none is in the British
Museum — shows that the dedication is signed J. H , and not, as Mr. Fleay infers,
by Thorpe. Thorpe had no concern in this volume.

translations of his unto your Lordship, ever wisht if *thes*
ensuing were published they might onely bee addressed unt
your Lordship, as the last Testimony of his dutifull affection (t
use his own termes) *The true and reall upholder of Learne*
endeavors. This, therefore, beeing left unto mee, as a Legaci
unto your Lordship (pardon ,my presumption, great Lord, fror
so meane a man to so great a person) I could not without som
impiety present it to any other; such a sad priviledge have th
bequests of the *dead*, and so obligatory they are, more than th
requests of the *living*. In the hope of this honourable accept
ance I will ever rest,

> 'Your lordship's humble devoted,
> 'T. Th.'

With such obeisances did publishers then habitually cree
into the presence of the nobility. In fact, the law whic
rigorously maintained the privileges of peers left them n
option. The alleged erroneous form of address in the dedic
tion of Shakespeare's 'Sonnets' — 'Mr. W. H.' for Lord Herbe
or the Earl of Pembroke — would have amounted to the offenc
of defamation. And for that misdemeanour the Star Chambe
always acting in protecting the dignity of peers, would hav
promptly called Thorpe to account.[1]

Of the Earl of Pembroke, and of his brother the Earl
Montgomery, it was stated a few years later, 'from just obse
vation,' on very pertinent authority, that 'no men came nea
their lordships [in their capacity of literary patrons], but with
kind of religious address.' These words figure in the prefator
epistle which two actor-friends of Shakespeare addressed to th
two Earls in the posthumously issued First Folio of th
dramatist's works. Thorpe's 'kind of religious address'
seeking Lord Pembroke's patronage for Healey's books wa
somewhat more unctuous than was customary or needful. B
of erring conspicuously in an opposite direction he may, witho
misgiving, be pronounced innocent.

---

[1] On January 27, 1607–8, one Sir Henry Colte was indicted for slander in the St
Chamber for addressing a peer, Lord Morley, as 'goodman Morley.' A technic
defect — the omission of the precise date of the commission of the alleged offence —
the bill of indictment led to a dismissal of the cause. See *Les Reportes del Cas*
in Camera Stellata, 1593 to 1609, edited from the manuscript of Henry Hawarde
W. P. Baildon, F.S.A (privately printed for Alfred Morrison), p. 348.

VII

SHAKESPEARE AND THE EARL OF PEMBROKE

WITH the disposal of the allegation that 'Mr. W. H.' represented the Earl of Pembroke's youthful name, the whole theory of that Earl's identity with Shakespeare's friend collapses. Outside Thorpe's dedicatory words, only two scraps of evidence with any title to consideration have been adduced to show that Shakespeare was at any time or in any way associated with Pembroke.

In the late autumn of 1603 James I and his Court were installed at the Earl of Pembroke's house at Wilton for a period of two months, owing to the prevalence of the plague in London. By order of the officers of the royal household, the King's company of players, of which Shakespeare was a member, gave a performance before the King at Wilton House on December 2. The actors travelled from Mortlake for the purpose, and were paid in the ordinary manner by the treasurer of the royal household out of the public funds. There is no positive evidence that Shakespeare attended at Wilton with the company, but assuming, as is probable, that he did, the Earl of Pembroke can be held no more responsible for his presence than for his repeated presence under the same conditions at Whitehall. The visit of the King's players to Wilton in 1603 has no bearing on the Earl of Pembroke's alleged relations with Shakespeare.[1]

(marginal note: Shakespeare with the acting company at Wilton in 1603.*)*

[1] See pp. 231-2, *supra*. A tradition has lately sprung up in Wilton to the effect that a letter once existed there in which the Countess of Pembroke bade her son the Earl while he was in attendance on James I at Salisbury to bring the King to Wilton to witness a performance of *As You Like It*. The Countess is said to have added, 'We have the man Shakespeare with us.' No tangible evidence of the existence of the letter is forthcoming and its tenor stamps it, if it exists, as an ignorant invention. The circumstances under which both King and players visited Wilton in 1603 are completely misrepresented. The Court temporarily occupied Wilton

The second instance of the association in the seventeenth
century of Shakespeare's name with Pembroke's tells wholly
against the conjectured intimacy. Seven years
after the dramatist's death, two of his friends and
fellow-actors prepared the collective edition of
his plays known as the First Folio, and they dedicated the
volume, in the conventional language of eulogy, 'To the most
noble and incomparable paire of brethren, William Earl of
Pembroke, &c., Lord Chamberlaine to the King's most excellent Majesty, and Philip, Earl of Montgomery, &c., Gentleman
of His Majesties Bedchamber. Both Knights of the most
Noble Order of the Garter and our singular good Lords.'

*The dedi-
cation of
the First
Folio.*

The choice of such patrons, whom, as the dedication inti-
mated, 'no one came near but with a kind of religious address,'
proves no private sort of friendship between them and the dead
author. To the two Earls in partnership nearly every work of
any literary pretension was dedicated at the period. Moreover,
the third Earl of Pembroke was Lord Chamberlain in 1623, and
exercised supreme authority in theatrical affairs. That his
patronage should be sought for a collective edition of the works
of the acknowledged master of the contemporary stage was a
matter of course. It is only surprising that the editors should
have yielded to the passing vogue of soliciting the patronage of
the Lord Chamberlain's brother in conjunction with the Lord
Chamberlain.

The sole sentence in the editor's dedication that can be held

House, and Shakespeare and his comrades were ordered by the officers of the royal
household to give a performance there in the same way as they would have been
summoned to play before the King had he been at Whitehall. It is hardly necessary
to add that the Countess of Pembroke's mode of referring to literary men is well
known; she treated them on terms of equality, and could not in any aberration of
mind or temper have referred to Shakespeare as 'the man Shakespeare.' Similarly,
the present Earl of Pembroke purchased of a London picture-dealer last year what
purported to be a portrait of the third Earl of Pembroke, and on the back was pasted
a paper, that was represented to date from the seventeenth century, containing some
lines from Shakespeare's Sonnet lxxxi. (9–14), subscribed with the words 'Shakespeare unto the Earl of Pembroke, 1603.' The ink and handwriting are quite modern,
and hardly make pretence to be of old date in the eyes of any one accustomed to
study manuscripts. On May 5 of this year some persons interested in the matter, including myself, examined the portrait and the inscription, on the kind invitation of
the present Earl, and the inscription was unanimously declared by palæographical
experts to be a clumsy forgery unworthy of serious notice.

to bear on the question of Shakespeare's alleged intimacy with Pembroke is their remark that both Earls had 'prosequuted,' *i.e.* favoured, the plays 'and their authour living.' But this assertion only justifies the inference that the brothers shared the enthusiastic esteem which James I and all the noblemen of his Court extended to Shakespeare and his plays in the dramatist's lifetime. Apart from his work as a dramatist, Shakespeare, in his capacity of one of 'the King's servants' or company of players, was personally known to all the officers of the royal household who collectively controlled theatrical representations at Court. Throughout James I's reign his plays were repeatedly performed in the royal presence, and when the dedicators of the First Folio, at the conclusion of their address to Lords Pembroke and Montgomery, describe the dramatist's works as 'these remaines of your *Servant* Shakespeare,' they make it quite plain that it was in the capacity of 'King's servant' or player that they knew him to have been the object of their noble patrons' favour.

The sonnets offer no internal indication that the Earl of Pembroke and Shakespeare ever saw one another. Nothing at all is deducible from the vague parallelisms that have been adduced between the Earl's character and position in life and those with which the poet credited the youth of the sonnets. It may be granted that both had a mother (Sonnet iii.), that both enjoyed wealth and rank, that both were regarded by admirers as cultivated, that both were self-indulgent in their relations with women, and that both in early manhood were indisposed to marry, owing to habits of gallantry. Of one alleged point of resemblance there is no evidence. The loveliness assigned to Shakespeare's youth was not, as far as we can learn, definitely set to Pembroke's account. Francis Davison, when dedicating his 'Poetical Rhapsody' to the Earl in 1602 in a very eulogistic sonnet, makes a cautiously qualified reference to the attractiveness of his person in the lines:

No suggestion in the sonnets of the youth's identity with Pembroke.

> [His] outward shape, though it most lovely be,
> Doth in fair robes a fairer soul attire.

The only portraits of him that survive represent him in middle age,[1] and seem to confute the suggestion that he was reckoned handsome at any time of life; at most they confirm Anthony Wood's description of him as in person 'rather majestic than elegant.' But the point is not one of moment, and the argument neither gains nor loses, if we allow that Pembroke may, at any rate in the sight of a poetical panegyrist, have at one period reflected, like Shakespeare's youth, 'the lovely April of his mother's prime.'

But when we have reckoned up the traits that can, on any showing, be admitted to be common to both Pembroke and Shakespeare's alleged friend, they all proved to be equally indistinctive. All could be matched without difficulty in a score of youthful noblemen and gentlemen of Elizabeth's Court. Direct external evidence of Shakespeare's friendly intercourse with one or other of Elizabeth's young courtiers must be produced before the sonnets' general references to the youth's beauty and grace can render the remotest assistance in establishing his identity.

Although it may be reckoned superfluous to adduce more arguments, negative or positive, against the theory that the Earl of Pembroke was a youthful friend of Shakespeare, it is worth noting that John Aubrey, the Wiltshire antiquary, and the biographer of most Englishmen of distinction of the sixteenth and seventeenth centuries, was zealously researching, from 1650 onwards, into the careers alike of Shakespeare and of various members of the Earl of Pembroke's family — one of the chief in Wiltshire. Aubrey rescued from oblivion many anecdotes — scandalous and otherwise — about both the third Earl of Pembroke and about Shakespeare. Of the former he wrote in his 'Natural History of Wiltshire' (ed. Britton, 1847), recalling the Earl's relations with Massinger and many other men of letters. Of Shakespeare, Aubrey narrated much lively gossip in his 'Lives of Eminent Persons.' But neither in his account of Pembroke nor in his account of Shakespeare does he give any hint that they were at any time or in any manner acquainted or associated with one another. Had close relations existed between them,

Aubrey's ignorance of any relation between Shakespeare and Pembroke.

----

[1] Cf. the engravings of Simon Pass, Stent, and Vandervoerst, after the portrait by Mytens.

t is impossible that all trace of it would have faded from the
traditions that were current in Aubrey's time and were embodied
n his writings.[1]

[1] It is unnecessary, after what has been said above (p. 123), to consider seriously
the suggestion that the ' dark lady ' of the sonnets was Mary Fitton, maid of honour
to Queen Elizabeth. This frolicsome lady, who was at one time Pembroke's
mistress and bore him a child, has been only introduced into a discussion of the
sonnets on the assumption that her lover, Pembroke, was the youth to whom the
sonnets were addressed. Lady Newdegate's recently published *Gossip from a
Muniment Room*, which furnishes for the first time a connected biography of
Pembroke's mistress, adequately disposes of any lingering hope that Shakespeare
may have commemorated her in his black-complexioned heroine. Lady Newdegate
states that two well-preserved portraits of Mary Fitton remain at Arbury, and that
they reveal a lady of fair complexion with brown hair and grey eyes. Family history
places the authenticity of the portraits beyond doubt, and the endeavour lately made
by Mr. Tyler, the chief champion of the hopeless Fitton theory, to dispute their
authenticity is satisfactorily met by Mr. C. O. Bridgeman in an appendix to the
second edition of Lady Newdegate's book. We also learn from Lady Newdegate's
volume that Miss Fitton, during her girlhood, was pestered by the attentions of a
middle-aged admirer, a married friend of the family, Sir William Knollys. It has
been lamely suggested by some of the supporters of the Pembroke theory that Sir
William Knollys was one of the persons named Will who are alleged to be noticed
as competitors with Shakespeare and the supposititious ' Will Herbert ' for ' the
dark lady's' favours in the sonnets (cxxxv., cxxxvi , and perhaps clxiii.). But that
is a shot wholly out of range. The wording of those sonnets, when it is thoroughly
tested, proves beyond reasonable doubt that the poet was the only lover named Will
who is represented as courting the disdainful lady of the sonnets, and that no reference whatever is made there to any other person of that Christian name.

VIII

THE 'WILL' SONNETS

NO one has had the hardihood to assert that the text of the sonnets gives internally any indication that the youth's name took the hapless form of 'William Herbert'; but many commentators argue that in three or four sonnets Shakespeare admits in so many words that the youth bore his own Christian name of Will, and even that the disdainful lady had among her admirers other gentlemen entitled in familiar intercourse to similar designation.   These are fantastic assumptions which rest on a misconception of Shakespeare's phraseology and of the character of the conceits of the sonnets, and are solely attributable to the fanatical anxiety of the supporters of the Pembroke theory to extort, at all hazards, some sort of evidence in their favour from Shakespeare's text.[1]

In two sonnets (cxxxv.–vi.) — the most artificial and 'conceited' in the collection — the poet plays somewhat enigmatically on his Christian name of 'Will,' and a similar pun has been doubtfully detected in Sonnets cxxxiv. and cxlvii.   The groundwork of the pleasantry is the identity in form of the proper name with the common noun 'will.' Elizabethan meanings of 'will.' This word connoted in Elizabethan English a generous variety of conceptions, of most of which it has long since been deprived.   Then, as now, it was employed in the general psychological sense of volition; but it was more often specifically applied to two limited manifestations of the volition.   It was the commonest of synonyms alike for 'self-will' or 'stubbornness' — in which sense it

---

[1] Professor Dowden (*Sonnets*, p. xxxv.) writes: ' It appears from the punning sonnets (cxxxv. and cxliii.) that the Christian name of Shakespeare's friend was the same as his own, *Will*,' and thence is deduced the argument that the friend could only be identical with one who, like William, Earl of Pembroke, bore that Christian name.

till survives in 'wilful' — and for 'lust' or 'sensual passion.'
t also did occasional duty for its own diminutive 'wish,' for
caprice,' for 'good-will,' and for 'free consent' (as nowadays in
willing' or 'willingly ').

Shakespeare constantly used 'will' in all these significa-
ions. Iago recognised its general psychological value when

Shake-
peare's
ses of the
vord.

he said, 'Our bodies are our gardens, to the which
our wills are gardeners.' The conduct of the 'will '
is discussed after the manner of philosophy in
Troilus and Cressida' (II. ii. 51–68). In another of Iago's
sentences, 'Love is merely a lust of the blood and a permission
of the will,' light is shed on the process by which the word came
to be specifically applied to sensual desire. The last is a
favourite sense with Shakespeare and his contemporaries.
Angelo and Isabella, in 'Measure for Measure,' are at one in
attributing their conflict to the former's 'will.' The self-indulgent Bertram, in 'All's Well,' 'fleshes his "will" in the spoil of
a gentlewoman's honour.' In 'Lear' (IV. vi. 279) Regan's
heartless plot to seduce her brother-in-law is assigned to 'the
undistinguished space' — the boundless range — 'of woman's
will.' Similarly, Sir Philip Sidney apostrophised lust as 'thou
web of will.' Thomas Lodge, in 'Phillis' (Sonnet xi.) warns
lovers of the ruin that menaces all who 'guide their course by
will.' Nicholas Breton's fantastic romance of 1599, entitled
'The Will of Wit, Wit's Will or Will's Wit, Chuse you
Whether,' is especially rich in like illustrations. Breton brings
into marked prominence the antithesis which was familiar in
his day between 'will' in its sensual meaning, and 'wit,' the
Elizabethan synonym for reason or cognition. 'A song between
Wit and Will' opens thus :

> *Wit :* What art thou, Will ?   *Will :* A babe of nature's brood.
> *Wit :* Who was thy sire ?   *Will :* Sweet Lust, as lovers say.
> *Wit :* Thy mother who ?   *Will :* Wild lusty wanton blood.
> *Wit :* When wast thou born ?   *Will :* In merry month of May.
> *Wit :* And where brought up ?   *Will :* In school of little skill.
> *Wit :* What learn'dst thou there ?   *Will :* Love is my lesson still.

Of the use of the word in the sense of stubbornness or self-will
Roger Ascham gives a good instance in his 'Schoolmaster,'

2 E

(1570), where he recommends that such a vice in children as 'will,' which he places in the category of lying, sloth, and disobedience, should be 'with sharp chastisement daily cut away.'[1] 'A woman will have her will' was, among Elizabethan wags, an exceptionally popular proverbial phrase, the point of which revolved about the equivocal meaning of the last word. The phrase supplied the title of 'a pleasant comedy,' by William Haughton, which — from 1597 onwards — held the stage for the unusually prolonged period of forty years. 'Women, because they cannot have their wills when they dye, they will have their wills while they live,' was a current witticism which the barrister Manningham deemed worthy of record in his 'Diary' in 1602.[2]

It was not only in the sonnets that Shakespeare — almost invariably with a glance at its sensual significance — rang the changes on this many-faced verbal token. In his earliest play, 'Love's Labour's Lost' (II. i. 97–101), after the princess has tauntingly assured the King of Navarre that he will break his vow to avoid women's society, the king replies, 'Not for the world, fair madam, by my *will*' (*i.e.* willingly). The princess retorts 'Why *will* (*i.e.* sensual desire) shall break it (*i.e.* the vow), *will* and nothing else.' In 'Much Ado,' when Benedick, anxious to marry Beatrice, is asked by the lady's father 'What's your will?' he playfully lingers on the word in his answer. As for his 'will,' his 'will' is that the father's 'good-will may stand with his' and Beatrice's 'will' — in other words that the father may consent to their union. Slender and Anne Page vary the tame sport when the former misinterprets the young lady's 'What is your will?' into an inquiry into the testamentary disposition of his property. To what depth of vapidity Shakespeare and contemporary punsters could sink is nowhere better illustrated than in the favour they bestowed on efforts to extract amusement from the parities and disparities of form and meaning subsisting between the words 'will' and 'wish,' the latter being in vernacular use

Shake-speare's puns on the word.

---

[1] Ed. Mayor, p. 35.

[2] Manningham's *Diary*, p. 92; cf. Barnabe Barnes's *Odes Pastoral*, sestine 2:

> But women will have their own wills,
> Alas, why then should I complain?

as a diminutive of the former. Twice in the 'Two Gentlemen of Verona' (i. iii. 63 and iv. ii. 96) Shakespeare almost strives to invest with the flavour of epigram the unpretending announcement that one interlocutor's 'wish' is in harmony with another interlocutor's 'will.'

It is in this vein of pleasantry — 'will' and 'wish' are identically contrasted in Sonnet cxxxv. — that Shakespeare, to the confusion of modern readers, makes play with the word 'will' in the sonnets, and especially in the two sonnets (cxxxv.–vi.) which alone speciously justify the delusion that the lady is courted by two, or more than two, lovers of the name of Will.

One of the chief arguments advanced in favour of this interpretation is that the word 'will' in these sonnets is frequently italicised in the original edition. But this has little or no bearing on the argument. The corrector of the

Arbitrary and irregular use of italics by Elizabethan and Jacobean printers.

press recognised that Sonnets cxxxv. and cxxxvi. largely turned upon a simple pun between the writer's name of 'Will' and the lady's 'will.' That fact, and no other, he indicated very roughly by occasionally italicising the crucial word. Typography at the time followed no firmly fixed rules, and, although 'will' figures in a more or less punning sense nineteen times in these sonnets, the printer only bestowed on the word the distinction of italics in ten instances, and those were selected arbitrarily. The italics indicate the obvious equivoque, and indicate it imperfectly. That is the utmost that can be laid to their credit. They give no hint of the far more complicated punning that is alleged by those who believe that 'Will' is used now as the name of the writer, and now as that of one or more of the rival suitors. In each of the two remaining sonnets that have been forced into the service of the theory, Nos. cxxxiv. and cxliii., 'will' occurs once only; it alone is italicised in the second sonnet in the original edition, and there in my opinion arbitrarily and without just cause.[1]

---

[1] Besides punning words, printers of poetry in the sixteenth and seventeenth centuries made an effort to italicise proper names, unfamiliar words, and words deemed worthy of special emphasis. But they did not strictly adhere to these rules, and, while they often failed to italicise the words that deserved italicisation, they freely

The general intention of the complex conceits of Sonnets
cxxxv. and cxxxvi. becomes obvious when we bear in mind

The con-
ceits of Son-
nets cxxxv.-
vi. inter-
preted.
that in them Shakespeare exploits to the uttermost
the verbal coincidences which are inherent in the
Elizabethan word 'will.' 'Will' is the Christian
name of the enslaved writer; 'will' is the sentiment
with which the lady inspires her worshippers; and 'will'
designates stubbornness as well as sensual desire. These two
characteristics, according to the poet's reiterated testimony, are
the distinguishing marks of the lady's disposition. He often
dwells elsewhere on her 'proud heart' or 'foul pride,' and her
sensuality or 'foul faults.' These are her 'wills,' and they
make up her being. In crediting the lady with such a
constitution Shakespeare was not recording any definite observation or experience of his own, but he followed, as was
his custom, the conventional descriptions of the disdainful
mistress common to all contemporary collections of sonnets.
Barnabe asks the lady celebrated in his sonnets, from whose
'proud disdainfulness' he suffered,

> Why dost thou my delights delay,
> And with thy cross unkindness kills (*sic*)
> Mine heart, bound martyr to thy wills?

Barnes answers his question in the next lines:

> But women will have their own wills,
> Since what she lists her heart fulfils.[1]

Similar passages abound in Elizabethan sonnets, but
certain verbal similarities give good ground for regarding
Shakespeare's 'will' sonnets as deliberate adaptations — doubtless with satiric purpose — of Barnes's stereotyped reflections
on women's obduracy. The form and the constant repetition of
the word 'will' in these two sonnets of Shakespeare also seem
to imitate derisively the same rival's Sonnets lxxii. and lxxiii.
in which Barnes puts the words 'grace' and 'graces' through

italicised others that did not merit it. Capital initial letters were employed with like
irregularity. Mr. Wyndham in his careful note on the typography of the quarto of
1609 (pp. 259 seq.) suggests that Elizabethan printers were not erratic in their
uses of italics or capital letters, but an examination of a very large number of
Elizabethan and Jacobean books has brought me to an exactly opposite conclusion.

[1] Barnes's *Parthenophil* in Arber's *Garner*, v. 440.

much the same evolutions as Shakespeare puts the words 'will'
and 'wills' in the Sonnets cxxxv. and cxxxvi.[1]

Shakespeare's 'Sonnet' cxxxv. runs:

> Whoever hath her wish, thou hast thy Will,
> And will to boot, and will in over-plus;
> More than enough am I that vex thee still,
> To thy sweet will making addition thus.
> Wilt thou, whose will is large and spacious,[2]
> Not once vouchsafe to hide my will in thine?
> Shall will in others seem right gracious,
> And in my will no fair acceptance shine?
> The sea, all water, yet receives rain still,
> And in abundance addeth to his store;
> So thou, being rich in will, add to thy will,
> One will of mine, to make thy large will more.
>
>   Let no unkind no fair beseechers kill;
>   Think all but one, and me in that one — Will.

In the opening words, 'Whoever hath her wish,' the poet
prepares the reader for the punning encounter by a slight
variation on the current catch-phrase 'A woman will
have her will.' At the next moment we are in the
thick of the wordy fray. The lady has not only her
lover named Will, but untold stores of 'will'— in the sense alike
of stubbornness and of lust — to which it seems supererogatory
to make addition.[3] To the lady's 'over-plus' of 'will' is
punningly attributed her defiance of the 'will' of her suitor
Will to enjoy her favours. At the same time 'will' in others

*Sonnet
cxxxv.*

---

[1] After quibbling in Sonnet lxxii. on the resemblance between the *graces* of
his cruel mistress's face and the *Graces* of classical mythology, Barnes develops the
topic in the next sonnet after this manner (the italics are my own):

> Why did rich Nature *graces* grant to thee,
> Since thou art such a niggard of thy *grace!*
> O how can *graces* in thy body be?
> Where neither they nor pity find a place! . . .
> Grant me some *grace!* For thou with *grace* art wealthy
> And kindly may'st afford some *gracious* thing.

[2] Cf. *Lear*, IV. vi. 279, ' O undistinguish'd space of woman's will'; *i.e.* ' O boundless range of woman's lust.'

[3] Professor Dowden says 'will to boot' is a reference to the Christian name of
Shakespeare's friend, ' William [? Mr. W. H.] ' (*Sonnets*, p. 236); but in my view the
poet, in the second line of the sonnet, only seeks emphasis by repetition in accord-

proves to her 'right gracious,'[1] although in him it is unaccept-
able. All this, the poet hazily argues, should be otherwise; for
as the sea, although rich in water, does not refuse the falling
rain, but freely adds it to its abundant store, so she, 'rich in
will,' should accept her lover Will's 'will' and 'make her large
will more.' The poet sums up his ambition in the final couplet:

> Let no unkind no fair beseechers kill;
> Think all but one, and me in that one — Will.

This is as much as to say, 'Let not my mistress in her unkind-
ness kill any of her fair-spoken adorers. Rather let her think
all who beseech her favours incorporate in one alone of her
lovers — and that one the writer whose name of "Will" is a
synonym for the passions that dominate her.' The thought is
wiredrawn to inanity, but the words make it perfectly clear that
the poet was the only one of the lady's lovers — to the definite
exclusion of all others — whose name justified the quibbing
pretence of identity with the 'will' which controls her being.

The same equivocating conceit of the poet Will's title to
identity with the lady's 'will' in all senses is pursued in Sonnet
cxxxvi. The sonnet opens:

> If thy soul check thee that I come so near,
> Swear to thy blind soul that I was thy will,[2]
> And will thy soul knows is admitted there.

Here Shakespeare adapts to his punning purpose the familiar
Sonnet   philosophic commonplace respecting the soul's domi-
cxxxvi.   nation by 'will' or volition, which was more clearly

---

ance with no uncommon practice of his. The line 'And will to boot, and will in
over-plus,' is paralleled in its general form and intention in such lines of other
sonnets as

> Kind is my love to-day, to-morrow kind (cv. 5).
> Beyond all date, even to eternity (cxxii. 4).
> Who art as black as hell, as dark as night (cxlvii. 14).

In all these instances the second half of the line merely repeats the first half with a
slight intensification.

[1] Cf. Barnes's Sonnet lxxiii. :

> All her looks *gracious*, yet no *grace* do bring
> To me, poor wretch! Yet be the *Graces* there.

[2] Shakespeare refers to the blindness, the ' sightless view ' of the soul, in Sonnet
xxvii., and apostrophises the soul as the ' centre of his sinful earth ' in Sonnet cxlvi.

pressed by his contemporary, Sir John Davies, in the philo-
phic poem, 'Nosce Teipsum':

> Will holds the royal sceptre in the soul,
> And on the passions of the heart doth reign.

Whether Shakespeare's lines be considered with their context
r without it, the tenor of their thought and language positively
refutes the commentators' notion that the 'will' admitted to the
.dy's soul is a rival lover named Will. The succeeding lines
n:

> Thus far for love, my love-suit, sweet, fulfil.[1]
> Will will fulfil the treasure of thy love;
> Ay, fill it full with wills, and my will one.
> In things of great receipt with ease we prove
> Among a number one is reckon'd none:
> Then in the number let me pass untold,
> Though in thy stores' account, I one must be;
> For nothing hold me, so it please thee hold
> That nothing me, a something sweet to thee.

Here the poet Will continues to claim, in punning right of
his Christian name, a place, however small and inconspicuous,
mong the 'wills,' the varied forms of will (*i.e.* lust, stubbornness, and willingness to accept others' attentions), which are the
constituent elements of the lady's being. The plural 'wills' is
wice used in identical sense by Barnabe Barnes in the lines
lready quoted:

> Mine heart, bound martyr to thy *wills*,
> But women will have their own *wills*.

Impulsively Shakespeare brings his fantastic pretension to
a somewhat more practical issue in the concluding apostrophe:

> Make but my name thy love, and love that still,
> And then thou lovest me — for my name is Will.[2]

---

[1] The use of the word 'fulfil' in this and the next line should be compared with
Barnes's introduction of the word in a like context in the passage given above :

> Since what she lists her heart *fulfils*.

[2] Mr. Tyler paraphrases these lines thus: 'You love your other admirer named
'Will." Love the name alone, and then you love me, for my name is Will,' p. 297.
Professor Dowden, hardly more illuminating, says the lines mean: ' Love only my
name (something less than loving myself), and then thou lovest me, for my name is
Will, and I myself am all will, *i.e.* all desire.'

That is equivalent to saying ' Make " will " ' (*i.e.* that which
yourself) 'your love, and then you love me, because Will is n
name.' The couplet proves even more convincingly than th
one which clinches the preceding sonnet that none of the riva
whom the poet sought to displace in the lady's affections cou
by any chance have been, like himself, called Will. The writ
could not appeal to a mistress to concentrate her love on h
name of Will, because it was the emphatic sign of identi
between her being and him, if that name were common to hi
and one or more rivals, and lacked exclusive reference to hir
self.

Loosely as Shakespeare's sonnets were constructed, th
couplet at the conclusion of each poem invariably summaris
the general intention of the preceding twelve lines. The co
cluding couplets of these two sonnets cxxxv.–vi., in whic
Shakespeare has been alleged to acknowledge a rival of h
own name in his suit for a lady's favour, are consequently th
touchstone by which the theory of 'more Wills than one ' mus
be tested. As we have just seen, the situation is summari
embodied in the first couplet thus :

> Let no unkind no fair beseechers kill;
> Think all but one, and me in that one — Will.

It is re-embodied in the second couplet thus :

> Make but my name thy love, and love that still,
> And then thou lovest me — for my name is Will.

The whole significance of both couplets resides in th
twice-repeated fact that one, and only one, of the lady's lover
is named Will, and that that one is the writer. To assume tha
the poet had a rival of his own name is to denude both couplet
of all point. 'Will,' we have learned from the earlier lines o
both sonnets, is the lady's ruling passion. Punning mock-logi
brings the poet in either sonnet to the ultimate conclusion tha
one of her lovers may, above all others, reasonably claim he
love on the ground that his name of Will is the name of he
ruling passion. Thus his pretension to her affections rest, h
punningly assures her, on a strictly logical basis.

Unreasonable as any other interpretation of these sonnets
(cxxxv.–vi.) seems to be, I believe it far more
fatuous to seek in the single and isolated use of the
word 'will' in each of the sonnets cxxxiv. and
ii. any confirmation of the theory of a rival suitor named
Il.

Sonnet cxxxiv. runs :

> So now I have confess'd that he is thine,
> And I myself am mortgaged to thy will.[1]
> Myself I'll forfeit, so that other mine
> Thou wilt restore, to be my comfort still.
> But thou wilt not, nor he will not be free,
> For thou art covetous and he is kind.
> He learn'd but surety-like to write for me,
> Under that bond that him as fast doth bind.
> The statute of thy beauty wilt thou take,
> Thou usurer, that putt'st forth all to use,
> And sue a friend came debtor for my sake ;
> So him I lose through my unkind abuse.
>> Him have I lost ; thou hast both him and me ;
>> He pays the whole, and yet am I not free.

Here the poet describes himself as 'mortgaged to the lady's
' (*i.e.* to her personality, in which 'will,' in the double sense
tubbornness and sensual passion, is the strongest element).
deplores that the lady has captivated not merely himself,
also his friend, who made vicarious advances to her.
Sonnet cxliii. runs :

> Lo, as a careful housewife runs to catch
> One of her feathered creatures broke away,
> Sets down her babe, and makes all swift despatch
> In pursuit of the thing she would have stay ;
> Whilst her neglected child holds her in chase,
> Cries to catch her whose busy care is bent
> To follow that which flies before her face,
> Not prizing her poor infant's discontent :

The word 'Will' is not here italicised in the original edition of Shakespeare's
ets, and there is no ground whatever for detecting in it any sort of pun. The
resembles Barnes's line quoted above:
> Mine heart bound martyr to thy wills.

So runn'st thou after that which flies from thee,
Whilst I, thy babe, chase thee afar behind;
But if thou catch thy hope turn back to me,
And play the mother's part, kiss me, be kind:
    So will I pray that thou mayst have thy will,[1]
    If thou turn back and my loud crying still.

In this sonnet — which presents a very clear-cut pict〔
although its moral is somewhat equivocal — the poet represe〔

Meaning of Sonnet cxliii. the lady as a country housewife and himself as 〔 babe; while an acquaintance, who attracts 〔 lady but is not attracted by her, is figured a〔 'feathered creature' in the housewife's poultry-yard. The f〔 takes to flight; the housewife sets down her infant and purs〔 'the thing.' The poet, believing apparently that he has li〔 to fear from the harmless creature, lightly makes play with 〔 current catch-phrase ('a woman will have her will'), 〔 amiably wishes his mistress success in her chase, on condit〔 that, having recaptured the truant bird, she turn back and t〔 him, her babe, with kindness. In praying that the lady ' r〔 have her will' the poet is clearly appropriating the current cat〔 phrase, and no pun on a man's name of 'Will' can be fa〔 wrested from the context.

---

[1] Because 'will' by what is almost certainly a typographical accident is 〔 printed *Will* in the first edition of the sonnets, Professor Dowden is inclined to ac〔 a reference to the supposititious friend Will, and to believe the poet to pray tha〔 lady may have her Will, *i.e.* the friend 'Will [? W. H.].' This interpretation se〔 to introduce a needless complication.

IX

THE VOGUE OF THE ELIZABETHAN
SONNET, 1591–1597

THE sonnetteering vogue, as I have already pointed out,[1] reached its full height between 1591 and 1597, and when at its briskest in 1594 it drew Shakespeare into its current. An enumeration of volumes containing sonnet-sequences or detached sonnets that were in circulation during the period best illustrates the overwhelming force of the sonnetteering rage of those years, and, with that end in view, I give here a bibliographical account, with a few critical notes of the chief efforts of Shakespeare's rival sonnetteers.[2]

The earliest collections of sonnets to be published in England were those by the Earl of Surrey and Sir Thomas Wyatt, which first appeared in the publisher Tottel's poetical miscellany called 'Songes and Sonnetes' in 1557. This volume included sixteen sonnets by Surrey and twenty by Wyatt. Many of them were translated directly from Petrarch, and most of them treated conventionally of the torments of an unrequited love. Surrey included, however, three sonnets on the death of his friend

(margin note:) Wyatt's and Surrey's Sonnets, published in 1557.

---

[1] See p 83, *supra*.

[2] The word 'sonnet' was often irregularly used for 'song' or 'poem.' 'A proper sonnet' in Clement Robinson's poetical anthology, *A Handefull of Pleasant Delites*, 1584, is a lyric in ten four-line alternatively rhymed stanzas. Neither Barnabe Googe's *Eglogs, Epyttaphes, and Sonnettes*, 1563, nor George Turbervile's *Epitaphes, Epigrams, Songs and Sonets*, 1567, contains a single fourteen-lined poem. The French word 'quatorzain' was the term almost as frequently applied as 'sonnet' to the fourteen-line stanza in regular sonnet form, which alone falls within my survey. Watson is congratulated on 'scaling the skies in lofty *quatorzains*' in verses before his *Passionate Centurie*, 1582; cf. 'crazed quatorzains' in Thomas Nash's preface to his edition of Sidney's *Astrophel and Stella*, 1591; and *Amours in Quatorzains* on the title-page of the first edition of Drayton's *Sonnets*, 1594.

Wyatt, and a fourth on the death of one Clere, a faith[
follower. Tottel's volume was seven times reprinted by 158
But no sustained endeavour was made to emulate the examp[
of Surrey and Wyatt till Thomas Watson about 1580 circulat[
in manuscript his 'Booke of Passionate Sonnetes,' which [
wrote for his patron, the Earl of Oxford. The volume w[
printed in 1582, and under the title of ''ΕΚΑΤΟΜΠΑΘΙ

Watson's 'Centurie of Love,' 1582. or Passionate Centurie of Loue. Divided into tw[
parts: whereof the first expresseth the Authou[
sufferance on Loue: the latter his long farewell [
Loue and all his tyrannie. Composed by Thomas Watson, an[
published at the request of certaine Gentlemen his very frendes[
Watson's work, which he called 'a toy,' is a curious literar[
mosaic. He supplied to each poem a prose commentary, [
which he not only admitted that every conceit was borrowe[
but quoted chapter and verse for its origin from classic[
literature or from the work of French or Italian sonnetteers[
Two regular quatorzains are prefixed, but to each of th[
'passions' there is appended a four-line stanza which give[
each poem eighteen instead of the regular fourteen line[
Watson's efforts were so well received, however, that he applie[
himself to the composition of a second series of sonnets in stric[
metre. This collection, entitled 'The Teares of Fancie,' only
circulated in manuscript in his lifetime.[2]

Meanwhile a greater poet, Sir Philip Sidney, who died in
1586, had written and circulated among his friends a more
ambitious collection of a hundred and eight sonnets.

Sidney's 'Astrophel and Stella,' 1591. Most of Sidney's sonnets were addressed by him under
the name of Astrophel to a beautiful woman poetically
designated Stella. Sidney had in real life courted
assiduously the favour of a married lady, Penelope, Lady Rich,
and a few of the sonnets are commonly held to reflect the heat
of passion which the genuine intrigue developed. But Petrarch,
Ronsard, and Desportes inspired the majority of Sidney's
efforts, and his addresses to abstractions like sleep, the moon, his
muse, grief, or lust are almost verbatim translations from the
French. Sidney's sonnets were first published surreptitiously,

[1] See p. 103, *supra*.

[2] All Watson's sonnets are reprinted by Mr. Arber in Watson's *Poems*, 1895.

nder the title of 'Astrophel and Stella,' by a publishing advent-
rer named Thomas Newman, and in his first issue Newman
added an appendix of 'sundry other rare sonnets by divers
noblemen and gentlemen.' Twenty-eight sonnets by Daniel
were printed in the appendix anonymously and without the
author's knowledge. Two other editions of Sidney's 'Astrophel
and Stella' without the appendix were issued in the same year.
Eight other of Sidney's sonnets, which still circulated only in
manuscript, were first printed anonymously in 1594 with the
sonnets of Henry Constable, and these were appended with
some additions to the authentic edition of Sidney's 'Arcadia'
and other works that appeared in 1598. Sidney enjoyed in the
decade that followed his death the reputation of a demi-god,
and the wide dissemination in print of his numerous sonnets in
1591 spurred nearly every living poet in England to emulate
his achievement.[1]

In order to facilitate a comparison of Shakespeare's sonnets
with those of his contemporaries it will be best to classify the
sonnetteering efforts that immediately succeeded Sidney's under
the three headings of (1) sonnets of more or less feigned love,
addressed to a more or less fictitious mistress; (2) sonnets of
adulation, addressed to patrons; and (3) sonnets invoking metaphysical abstractions or treating impersonally of religion or
philosophy.[2]

In February 1592 Samuel Daniel published a collection of
fifty-five sonnets, with a dedicatory sonnet addressed to his
patroness, Sidney's sister, the Countess of Pembroke. As in many French volumes, the collection
concluded with an 'ode.'[3] At every point Daniel

*1. Collected
sonnets of
feigned
love.*

---

[1] In a preface to Newman's first edition of *Astrophel and Stella* the editor, Thomas
Nash, in a burst of exultation over what he deemed the surpassing merits of Sidney's
sonnets, exclaimed: ' Put out your rushlights, you poets and rhymers! and bequeath
your crazed quatorzains to the chandlers! for lo, here he cometh that hath broken
your legs.' But the effect of Sidney's work was just the opposite to that which
Nash anticipated. It gave the sonnet in England a vogue that it never enjoyed
before or since.

[2] With collections of sonnets of the first kind are occasionally interspersed
sonnets of the second or third class, but I classify each sonnet-collection according
to its predominant characteristic.

[3] Daniel reprinted all but nine of the sonnets that had been unwarrantably
appended to Sidney's *Astrophel*. These nine he permanently dropped.

betrayed his indebtedness to French sonnetteers, even when
apologising for his inferiority to Petrarch (No. xxxviii.). His title

Daniel's   he borrowed from the collection of Maurice Sève, whose
'Delia,'   assemblage of dixains called 'Délie, objet de plus haute
1592.   vertu' (Lyon, 1544), was the pattern of all sonnet
sequences on love, and was a constant theme of commendation
among the later French sonnetteers. But it is to Desportes
that Daniel owes most, and his methods of handling his material may be judged by a comparison of his Sonnet xxvi. with
Sonnet lxiii. in Desportes's collection, 'Cleonice: Derniere
Amours,' which was issued at Paris in 1575.

Desportes's sonnet runs :

> Je verray par les ans vengeurs de mon martyre
>   Que l'or de vos cheveux argenté deviendra,
>   Que de vos deux soleils la splendeur s'esteindra,
> Et qu'il faudra qu'Amour tout confus s'en retire.
> La beauté qui si douce à present vous inspire,
>   Cedant aux lois du Temps ses faveurs reprendra,
>   L'hiver, de vostre teint les fleurettes perdra,
> Et ne laissera rien des thresors que i'admire.
> Cest orgueil desdaigneux qui vous fait ne m'aimer,
> En regret et chagrin se verra transformer,
> Avec le changement d'une image si belle :
>   Et peut estre qu'alors vous n'aurez desplaisir
>   De revivre en mes vers chauds d'amoureux desir,
> Ainsi que le Phenix au feu se renouvelle.

This is Daniel's version, which he sent forth as an original
production :

> I once may see, when years may wreck my wrong,
>   And golden hairs may change to silver wire ;
>   And those bright rays (that kindle all this fire)
> Shall fail in force, their power not so strong.
> Her beauty, now the burden of my song,
>   Whose glorious blaze the world's eye doth admire ;
>   Must yield her praise to tyrant Time's desire ;
> Then fades the flower, which fed her pride so long.
> When if she grieve to gaze her in her glass,
>   Which then presents her winter-withered hue :
> Go you my verse ! go tell her what she was !
>   For what she was, she best may find in you.
> Your fiery heat lets not her glory pass,
>   But Phœnix-like to make her live anew.

In Daniel's beautiful sonnet (xlix.) beginning,

> Care-charmer sleep, son of the sable night,
> Brother to Death, in silent darkness born,

he has borrowed much from De Baïf and Pierre de Brach, sonnet-teers with whom it was a convention to invocate 'O Sommeil chasse-soin.' But again he chiefly relies on Desportes, whose words he adapts with very slight variations. Sonnet lxxiii. of Desportes's 'Amours d'Hippolyte' opens thus:

> Sommeil, paisible fils de la Nuict solitaire . . .
> O frère de la Mort que tu m'es ennemi!

Daniel's sonnets were enthusiastically received. With some additions they were republished in 1594 with his narrative poem, 'The Complaint of Rosamund.' The volume was called 'Delia and Rosamund Augmented.' Spenser in his 'Colin Clout's come Home again,' lauded the 'well-tuned song' of Daniel's sonnets, and Shakespeare has some claim to be classed among Daniel's many sonnetteering disciples. The anonymous author of 'Zepheria' (1594) declared that the 'sweet tuned accents' of 'Delian sonnetry' rang throughout England; while Bartholomew Griffin, in his 'Fidessa' (1596), openly plagiarised Daniel, invoking in his Sonnet xv. 'Care-charmer sleep, brother of quiet death.'

Fame of Daniel's sonnets.

In September of the same year (1592) that saw the first complete version of Daniel's 'Delia,' Henry Constable published 'Diana: the Praises of his Mistres in certaine sweete Sonnets.' Like the title, the general tone was drawn from Desportes's 'Amours de Diane.' Twenty-one poems were included, all in the French vein. The collection was reissued, with very numerous additions, in 1594 under the title 'Diana; or, The excellent conceitful Sonnets of H. C. Augmented with divers Quatorzains of honourable and learned personages.' This volume is a typical venture of the book-sellers.[1] The printer, James Roberts, and the publisher, Richard Smith, supplied dedications respectively to the reader and to Queen Elizabeth's ladies-in-waiting. They had swept together

Constable's 'Diana,' 1592.

[1] It is reprinted in Arber's *Garner*, ii. 225-64.

sonnets in manuscript from all quarters, and presented their customers with a disordered miscellany of what they called 'orphan poems.' Besides the twenty sonnets by Constable, eight were claimed for Sir Philip Sidney, and the remaining forty-seven are by various hands which have not as yet been identified.

In 1593 the legion of sonnetteers received notable reinforcements. In May came out Barnabe Barnes's interesting volume, 'Parthenophil and Parthenope: Sonnets, Madrigals, Elegies, and Odes. To the right noble and virtuous gentleman, M. William Percy, Esq., his dearest friend.'[1] The contents of the volume and their arrangement closely resemble the sonnet-collections of Petrarch or the 'Amours' of Ronsard. There are a hundred and five sonnets altogether, interspersed with twenty-six madrigals, five sestines, twenty-one elegies, three 'canzons,' and twenty 'odes,' one in sonnet form. There is, moreover, included what purports to be a translation of 'Moschus' first eidillion describing love,' but what is clearly a rendering of a French poem by Amadis Jamin, entitled 'Amour Fuitif, du grec de Moschus,' in his 'Œuvres Poétiques,' Paris, 1579.[2] At the end of Barnes's volume there also figure six dedicatory sonnets. In Sonnet xcv. Barnes pays a compliment to Sir Philip Sidney, 'the Arcadian shepherd, Astrophel,' but he did not draw so largely on Sidney's work as on that of Ronsard, Desportes, De Baif, and Du Bellay. Legal metaphors abound in Barnes's poems, but amid many crudities he reaches a high level of beauty in Sonnet lxvi., which runs :

> Ah, sweet Content! where is thy mild abode?
> Is it with shepherds, and light-hearted swains,
> Which sing upon the downs, and pipe abroad,
> Tending their flocks and cattle on the plains?
> Ah, sweet Content! where dost thou safely rest?
> In Heaven, with Angels? which the praises sing
> Of Him that made, and rules at His behest,
> The minds and hearts of every living thing.

---

[1] Arber's *Garner*, v. 333–486.

[2] Ben Jonson developed the same conceit in his masque, *The Hue and Cry after Cupid*, 1608.

> Ah, sweet Content! where doth thine harbour hold?
> Is it in churches, with religious men,
> Which please the gods with prayers manifold;
> And in their studies meditate it then?
> Whether thou dost in Heaven or earth appear;
> Be where thou wilt! Thou wilt not harbour here![1]

In August 1593 there appeared a posthumous collection of sixty-one sonnets by Thomas Watson, entitled 'The Tears of Fancie, or Love Disdained.' They are throughout of the imitative type of his previously published 'Centurie of Love.' Many of them sound the same note as Shakespeare's sonnets to the 'dark lady.'

Watson's 'Tears of Fancie,' 1593.

In September 1593 followed Giles Fletcher's 'Licia, or Poems of Love in honour of the admirable and singular virtues of his Lady.' This collection of fifty-three sonnets is dedicated to the wife of Sir Richard Mollineux. Fletcher makes no concealment that his sonnets are literary exercises. 'For this kind of poetry,' he tells the reader, 'I did it to try my humour;' and on the title-page he notes that the work was written 'to the imitation of the best Latin poets and others.'[2]

Fletcher's 'Licia,' 1593.

The most notable contribution to the sonnet-literature of 1593 was Thomas Lodge's 'Phillis Honoured with Pastoral Sonnets, Elegies, and Amorous Delights.'[3] Besides forty sonnets, some of which exceed fourteen lines in length and others are shorter, there are included three elegies and an ode. Desportes is Lodge's chief master, but he had recourse to Ronsard and other French contemporaries. How servile he could be may be learnt from a comparison of his Sonnet xxxvi. with Desportes's sonnet from 'Les Amours de Diane,' livre II. sonnet iii.

Lodge's 'Phillis,' 1593.

Thomas Lodge's Sonnet xxxvi. runs thus:

> If so I seek the shades, I presently do see
> The god of love forsakes his bow and sit me by;
> If that I think to write, his Muses pliant be
> If so I plain my grief, the wanton boy will cry.

---

[1] Dekker's well-known song, 'Oh, sweet content,' in his play of 'Patient Grisselde' (1599), echoes this sonnet of Barnes.   [2] Arber's *Garner*, viii 413-52.

[3] There is a convenient reprint of Lodge's *Phillis* in *Elizabethan Sonnet-Cycles* b; Martha Foote Crow, 1896.

2 F

If I lament his pride, he doth increase my pain;
If tears my cheeks attaint, his cheeks are moist with moan;
If I disclose the wounds the which my heart hath slain,
He takes his fascia off, and wipes them dry anon.
    If so I walk the woods, the woods are his delight,
    If I myself torment, he bathes him in my blood;
    He will my soldier be if once I wend to fight,
    If seas delight, he steers my bark amidst the hood.
        In brief, the cruel god doth never from me go,
        But makes my lasting love eternal with my woe.

Desportes wrote in 'Les Amours de Diane,' book II. sonnet iii. :

Si ie me siés à l'ombre, aussi soudainement
    Amour, laissant son arc, s'assiet et se repose:
    Si ie pense à des vers, ie le voy qu'il compose:
    Si ie plains mes douleurs, il se plaint hautement.
Si ie me plais au mal, il accroist mon tourment:
    Si ie respan des pleurs, son visage il arrose:
    Si ie monstre la playe en ma poitrine enclose,
    Il défait son bandeau l'essuyant doucement.
Si ie vay par les bois, aux bois il m'accompagne:
    Si ie me suis cruel, dans mon sang il se bagne:
    Si ie vais à la guerre, il deuient mon soldart:
Si ie passe la mer, il conduit ma vacelle:
    Bref, iamais l'inhumain de moy ne se depart,
    Pour rendre mon amour et ma peine eternelle.

Three new volumes in 1594, together with the reissue of
Daniel's 'Delia' and of Constable's 'Diana' (in a piratical miscellany of sonnets from many pens), prove the steady growth
of the sonnetteering vogue. Michael Drayton in June produced his 'Ideas Mirrour, Amours in Quatorzains,' containing
Drayton's   fifty-one 'Amours' and a sonnet addressed to 'his
'Idea,' 1594. ever kind Mecænas, Anthony Cooke.' Drayton
acknowledged his devotion to 'divine Sir Philip,' but by his
choice of title, style, and phraseology the English sonnetteer
once more betrayed his indebtedness to Desportes and his
compeers. 'L'Idée' was the name of a collection of sonnets
by Claude de Pontoux in 1579. Many additions were made
by Drayton to the sonnets that he published in 1594, and
many were subtracted before 1619, when there appeared
the last edition that was prepared in Drayton's lifetime. A
comparison of the various editions (1594, 1599, 1605, and 1619)

shows that Drayton published a hundred sonnets, but the majority were apparently circulated by him in early life.[1]

William Percy, the 'dearest friend' of Barnabe Barnes, published in 1594, in emulation of Barnes, a collection of twenty
'Sonnets to the fairest Cœlia.'[2] He explains, in an
Percy's   address to the reader, that out of courtesy he had
'Cœlia,'   lent the sonnets to friends, who had secretly com-
1594.
mitted them to the press. Making a virtue of necessity, he had
accepted the situation, but begged the reader to treat them as
'toys and amorous devices.'

A collection of forty sonnets or 'canzons,' as the anonymous
author calls them, also appeared in 1594 with the title 'Zeph-
'Zepheria,'   eria.'[3] In some prefatory verses addressed 'Alli
1594.   veri figlioli delle Muse,' laudatory reference was made
to the sonnets of Petrarch, Daniel, and Sidney. Several of the
sonnets labour at conceits drawn from the technicalities of the
law, and Sir John Davies parodied these efforts in the eighth
of his 'gulling sonnets' beginning, 'My case is this, I love Zepheria bright.'

Four interesting ventures belong to 1595. In January
appended to Richard Barnfield's poem of 'Cynthia' a pane-
gyric on Queen Elizabeth, was a series of twenty sonnets
extolling the personal charms of a young man, in emulation of
Virgil's Eclogue ii., in which the shepherd Coridon addressed
Barnfield's   the shepherd-boy Alexis.[4] In Sonnet xx. the author
sonnets to   expressed regret that the task of celebrating his
Ganymede,
1595.   young friend's praises had not fallen to the more
capable hand of Spenser ('great Colin, chief of shepherds all')
or Drayton ('gentle Rowland, my professed friend'). Barnfield
at times imitated Shakespeare.

Almost at the same date as Barnfield's 'Cynthia' made its
appearance, there was published the more notable collection by
Spenser's   Edmund Spenser of eighty-eight sonnets, which in
'Amoretti,'   reference to their Italian origin he entitled 'Amo-
1595.   retti.'[5] Spenser had already translated many son-

---

[1] See p. 110, note.   [2] Arber's *Garner*, vi. 135-49.
[3] *Ib.* v. 61-86.
[4] Reprinted in Arber's *English Scholars' Library*, 1882.
[5] It was licensed for the press on November 19, 1594.

nets on philosophic topics of Petrarch and Joachim Du Bellay. Some of the 'Amoretti' were doubtless addressed by Spenser in 1593 to the lady who became his wife a year later. But the sentiment was largely ideal, and, as he says in Sonnet lxxxvii., he wrote, like Drayton, with his eyes fixed on 'Idæa.'

An unidentified 'E. C., Esq.,' produced also in 1595, under the title of 'Emaricdulfe,'[1] a collection of forty sonnets, echoing English and French models. In the dedication to his 'two very good friends, John Zouch and Edward Fitton Esquiers,' the author tells them that an ague confined him to his chamber, 'and to abandon idleness he completed an idle work that he had already begun at the command and service of a fair dame.'

Emaric-dulfe,' 1595.

To 1595 may best be referred the series of nine 'Gullinge sonnets,' or parodies, which Sir John Davies wrote and circulated in manuscript, in order to put to shame what he regarded as 'the bastard sonnets' in vogue. He addressed his collection to Sir Anthony Cooke, whom Drayton had already celebrated as the Mecænas of his sonnetteering efforts.[2] Davies seems to have aimed at Shakespeare as well as at insignificant rhymers like the author of 'Zepheria.'[3] No. viii. of Davies's 'gullinge sonnets,' which ridicules the legal metaphors of the sonnetteers, may be easily matched in the collections of Barnabe Barnes or of the author of 'Zepheria,' but Davies's phraseology suggests that he also was glancing at Shakespeare's legal sonnets lxxxvii. and cxxxiv. Davies's sonnet runs:

Sir John Davies's 'Gullinge Sonnets,' 1595.

> My case is this, I love Zepheria bright,
> Of her I hold my heart by fealty :
> Which I discharge to her perpetually,
> Yet she thereof will never me acquit[e].
> For, now supposing I withhold her right,
> She hath distrained my heart to satisfy
> The duty which I never did deny,
> And far away impounds it with despite.

---

[1] Reprinted for the Roxburghe Club in *A Lamport Garland*, 1881, edited by Mr. Charles Edmonds.

[2] Sir John Davies's *Complete Poems*, edited by Dr. Grosart, ii. 51–62.

[3] See p. 128, note.

> I labour therefore justly to repleave [*i.e.* recover]
> My heart which she unjustly doth impound.
> But quick conceit which now is Love's high shrieve
> Returns it as esloyned [*i.e.* absconded], not to be found.
> Then what the law affords I only crave,
> Her heart for mine, in wit her name to have (*sic*).

'R. L., gentleman,' probably Richard Linche, published in 1596 thirty-nine sonnets under the title 'Diella.'[1] The effort is thoroughly conventional. In an obsequious address by the publisher, Henry Olney, to Anne, wife of Sir Henry Glenham, Linche's sonnets are described as 'passionate,' and as 'conceived in the brain of a gallant gentleman.'

Linche's 'Diella,' 1596.

To the same year belongs Bartholomew Griffin's 'Fidessa,' sixty-two sonnets inscribed to 'William Essex, Esq.' Griffin designates his sonnets as 'the first fruits of a young beginner.' He is a shameless plagiarist. Daniel is his chief model, but he also imitated Sidney, Watson, Constable, and Drayton. Sonnet iii., beginning 'Venus and young Adonis sitting by her,' is almost identical with the fourth poem — a sonnet beginning 'Sweet Cytheræa, sitting by a brook' — in Jaggard's piratical miscellany, 'The Passionate Pilgrim,' which bore Shakespeare's name on the title-page.[2] Jaggard doubtless stole the poem from Griffin, although it may be in its essentials the property of some other poet. Three beautiful love-sonnets by Thomas Campion, which are found in the Harleian MS. 6910, are there dated 1596.[3]

Griffin's 'Fidessa,' 1596.

Thomas Campion, 1596.

William Smith was the author of 'Chloris,' a third collection of sonnets appearing in 1596.[4] The volume contains forty-eight sonnets of love of the ordinary type, with three adulating Spenser; of these, two open the volume and one concludes it. Smith says that his sonnets were 'the budding springs of his study.' In 1600 a license was issued by the Stationers' Company for the issue of 'Amours'

William Smith's 'Chloris,' 1596.

---

[1] Arber's *Garner*, vii. 185–208.

[2] *Ib.* v. 587–622.

[3] Cf. Brydges's *Excerpta Tudoriana*, 1814, i. 35–7. One was printed with some alterations in Rosseter's *Book of Ayres* (1610), and another in the *Third Book of Ayres* (1617?); see Campion's Works, ed. A. H. Bullen, pp. 15–16, 102.

[4] Arber's *Garner*, viii. 171–99.

by W. S. This no doubt refers to a second collection of sonnets by William Smith. The projected volume is not extant.[1]

In 1597 there came out a similar volume by Robert Tofte, entitled 'Laura, the Joys of a Traveller, or the Feast of Fancy.' The book is divided into three parts, each consisting of forty 'sonnets' in irregular metres. There is a prose dedication to Lucy, sister of Henry, ninth Earl of Northumberland. Tofte

Robert Tofte's 'Laura,' 1597. tells his patroness that most of his 'toys' 'were conceived in Italy.' As its name implies, his work is a pale reflection of Petrarch. A postscript by a friend — 'R. B.' — complains that a publisher had intermingled with Tofte's genuine efforts 'more than thirty sonnets not his.' But the style is throughout so uniformly tame that it is not possible to distinguish the work of a second hand.

To the same era belongs Sir William Alexander's 'Aurora,' a collection of a hundred and six sonnets, with a few songs

Sir William Alexander's 'Aurora.' and elegies interspersed on French patterns. Sir William describes the work as 'the first fancies of his youth,' and formally inscribes it to Agnes, Countess of Argyle. It was not published till 1604.[2]

Sir Fulke Greville, afterwards Lord Brooke, the intimate friend of Sir Philip Sidney, was author of a like collection of

Sir Fulke Greville's 'Cælica.' sonnets called 'Cælica.' The poems number a hundred and nine, but few are in strict sonnet metre. Only a small proportion profess to be addressed to the poet's fictitious mistress, Cælica. Many celebrate the

---

[1] See p. 390 and note.

[2] Practically to the same category as these collections of sonnets belong the voluminous laments of lovers, in six, eight, or ten lined stanzas, which, though not in strict sonnet form, closely resemble in temper the sonnet-sequences. Such are *Willobie's Avisa*, 1594; *Alcilia: Philoparthen's Loving Folly*, by J. C., 1595; *Arbor of Amorous Deuices*, 1597 (containing two regular sonnets) by Nicholas Breton; *Alba, the Months Minde of a Melancholy Lover*, by Robert Tofte, 1598; *Daiphantus, or the Passions of Love*, by Anthony Scoloker, 1604; Breton's *The Passionate Shepheard, or The Shepheardes Loue: set downe in passions to his Shepheardesse Aglaia: with many excellent conceited poems and pleasant sonnets fit for young heads to passe away idle houres*, 1604 (none of the 'Sonets' are in sonnet metre; and John Reynolds's *Dolarnys Primerose . . . wherein is expressed the liuely passions of Zeale and Loue*, 1606. Though George Wither's similar productions—his exquisitely fanciful *Fidelia* (1617) and his *Faire-Virtue, the Mistresse of Phil'Arete* (1622) — were published at a later period, they were probably designed in the opening years of the seventeenth century.

charms of another beauty named Myra, and others invoke
Queen Elizabeth under her poetic name of Cynthia (cf. Sonnet
xvii.). There are also many addresses to Cupid and meditations on more or less metaphysical themes, but the tone is never
very serious. Greville doubtless wrote the majority of his
' Sonnets' during the period under survey, though they were not
published until their author's works appeared in folio for the first
time in 1633, five years after his death.

With Tofte's volume in 1597 the publication of collections
of love-sonnets practically ceased.   Only two collections on

Estimate of
number of
love-son-
nets issued
between
1591 and
1597.

a voluminous scale seem to have been written in the
early years of the seventeenth century. About 1607
William Drummond of Hawthornden penned a series
of sixty-eight interspersed with songs, madrigals,
and sextains, nearly all of which were translated or
adapted from modern Italian sonnetteers.[1]   About

1610 John Davies of Hereford published his ' Wittes Pilgrimage . . . through a world of Amorous Sonnets.' Of more than
two hundred separate poems in this volume, only the hundred
and four sonnets in the opening section make any claim to
answer the description on the title-page, and the majority of
those are metaphysical meditations on love which are not
addressed to any definite person. Some years later William
Browne penned a sequence of fourteen love-sonnets entitled
' Cælia' and a few detached sonnets of the same type.[2] The
date of the production of Drummond's, Davies's, and Browne's
sonnets excludes them from the present field of view. Omitting
them, we find that between 1591 and 1597 there had been
printed nearly twelve hundred sonnets of the amorous kind.
If to these we add Shakespeare's poems, and make allowance for others which, only circulating in manuscript, have
not reached us, it is seen that more than two hundred love-
sonnets were produced in each of the six years under survey.
France and Italy directed their literary energies in like direction during nearly the whole of the century, but at no other

[1] They were first printed in 1656, seven years after the author's death, in *Poems
by that famous wit, William Drummond*, London, fol. The volume was edited by
Edward Phillips, Milton's nephew. The best modern edition is that edited by Mr.
W. C. Ward in the ' Muses' Library ' (1894).

[2] Cf. William Browne's *Poems* in ' Muses' Library ' (1894), ii. 217 seq.

period and in no other country did the love-sonnet dominate literature to greater extent than in England between 1591 and 1597.

Of sonnets to patrons between 1591 and 1597, of which detached specimens may be found in nearly every published book of the period, the chief collections were:

A long series of sonnets prefixed to 'Poetical Exercises of a Vacant Hour' by King James VI of Scotland, 1591; twenty three sonnets in Gabriel Harvey's 'Four Letters and certain Sonnets touching Robert Greene' (1592) including Edmund Spenser's fine sonnet of compliment addressed to Harvey; a series of sonnets to noble patronesses by Constable circulated in manuscript about 1592 (first printed in 'Harleian Miscellany,' 1813, ix. 491); six adulatory sonnets appended by Barnabe Barnes to his 'Parthenophil' in May 1593; four sonnets to 'Sir Philip Sidney's soul,' prefixed to the first edition of Sidney's 'Apologie for Poetrie' (1595); seventeen sonnets which were originally prefixed to the first edition of Spenser's 'Faerie Queene,' bk. i.–iii. in 1590, and were reprinted in the edition of 1596;[1] sixty sonnets to peers, peeresses, and officers of state, appended to Henry Locke's (or Lok's) 'Ecclesiasticus' (1597); forty sonnets by Joshua Sylvester addressed to Henry IV of France 'upon the late miraculous peace in Fraunce' (1599); Sir John Davies's series of twenty-six octosyllabic sonnets, which he entitled 'Hymnes of Astræa,' all extravagantly eulogising Queen Elizabeth (1599).

II. Sonnets to patrons, 1591–7.

The collected sonnets on religion and philosophy that appeared in the period 1591–7 include sixteen 'Spirituall Sonnettes to the honour of God and Hys Saynts,' written by Constable about 1593, and circulated only in manuscript; these were first printed from a manuscript in the Harleian collection (5993) by Thomas Parke in 'Helicona,' 1815, vol. ii. In 1595 Barnabe Barnes published

III. Sonnets on philosophy and religion.

---

[1] Chapman imitated Spenser by appending fourteen like sonnets to his translation of Homer in 1610; they were increased in later issues to twenty-two. Very numerous sonnets to patrons were appended by John Davies of Hereford to his *Microcosmos* (1603) and to his *Scourge of Folly* (1611). 'Divers sonnets, epistles, &c' addressed to patrons by Joshua Sylvester between 1590 and his death in 1618 were collected in the 1641 edition of his *Du Bartas his divine weekes and workes*.

a 'Divine Centurie of Spirituall Sonnets,' and, in dedicating the collection to Toby Matthew, bishop of Durham, mentions that they were written a year before, while travelling in France. They are closely modelled on the two series of 'Sonnets Spirituels' which the Abbé Jacques de Billy published in Paris in 1573 and 1578 respectively. A long series of 'Sonnets Spirituels' written by Anne de Marquets, a sister of the Dominican Order, who died at Poissy in 1598, was first published in Paris in 1605. In 1594 George Chapman published ten sonnets in praise of philosophy, which he entitled 'A Coronet for his Mistress Philosophy.' In the opening poem he states that his aim was to dissuade poets from singing in sonnets 'Love's Sensual Empery.' In 1597 Henry Locke (or Lok) appended to his verse-rendering of Ecclesiastes [1] a collection of 'Sundrie Sonets of Christian Passions, with other Affectionate Sonets of a Feeling Conscience.' Lok had in 1593 obtained a license to publish 'a hundred Sonnets on Meditation, Humiliation, and Prayer,' but that work is not extant. In the volume of 1597 his sonnets on religious or philosophical themes number no fewer than three hundred and twenty-eight.[2]

Thus in the total of sonnets published between 1591 and 1597 must be included at least five hundred sonnets addressed to patrons, and as many on philosophy and religion. The aggregate far exceeds two thousand.

---

[1] Remy Belleau in 1566 brought out a similar poetical version of the Book of Ecclesiastes entitled *Vanité*.

[2] There are forty-eight sonnets on the Trinity and similar topics appended to Davies's *Wittes Pilgrimage* (1610 ?).

X

BIBLIOGRAPHICAL NOTE ON THE SONNET IN FRANCE, 1550–1600

In the earlier years of the sixteenth century Melin de Saint-Gelais (1487–1558) and Clement Marot (1496–1544) made a few scattered efforts at sonnetteering in France; and Maurice Sève laid down the lines of all sonnet-sequences on themes of love in his dixains entitled 'Délie' (1544). But it was Ronsard (1524–85), in the second half of the century, who first gave the sonnet a pronounced vogue in France. The sonnet was handled with the utmost assiduity not only by Ronsard, but by all the literary comrades whom he gathered round him, and on whom he bestowed the title of 'La Pléiade.' The leading aim that united Ronsard and his friends was the re-formation of the French language and literature on classical models. But they assimilated and naturalised in France not only much that was admirable in Latin and Greek poetry,[1] but all that was best in the recent Italian literature.[2] Although they were learned poets, Ronsard

*Ronsard
(1524–85)
and ' La
Pléiade.'*

---

[1] Graphic illustrations of the attitude of Ronsard and his friends to a Greek poet like Anacreon appear in *Anacréon et les Poèmes anacréontiques Texte grec avec les Traductions et Imitations des Poètes du XVI⁰ siècle*, par A. Delboulle (Havre, 1891). A translation of Anacreon by Remy Belleau appeared in 1556. Cf. Ste.-Beuve's essay, ' Anacréon au XVI⁰ siècle,' in his *Tableau de la Poèsie française au XVI⁰ siècle* (1893), pp. 432–47. In the same connection *Recueil des plus beaux Epigrammes grecs, mis en vers françois*, par Pierre Tamisier (edit. 1617), is of interest.

[2] Italy was the original home of the sonnet, and it was as popular a poetic form with Italian writers of the sixteenth century as with those of the three preceding centuries. The Italian poets whose sonnets, after those of Petrarch, were best known in England and France in the later years of the sixteenth century were Serafino dell' Aquila (1466–1500), Jacopo Sannazzaro (1458–1530), Agnolo Firenzuola (1497–1547), Cardinal Bembo (1470–1547), Gaspara Stampa (1524–53), Pietro Aretino

and the majority of his associates had a natural lyric vein, which gave their poetry the charms of freshness and spontaneity. The true members of 'La Pléiade,' according to Ronsard's own statement, were, besides himself, Joachim du Bellay (1524–60); Estienne Jodelle (1532–73); Remy Belleau (1528–77); Jean Daurat-Dinemandy, usually known as Daurat or Dorat (1508–88), Ronsard's classical teacher in early life; Jean-Antoine de Baïf (1532–89); and Ponthus de Thyard (1521–1605). Other of Ronsard's literary allies are often loosely reckoned among the 'Pléiade.' These writers include Jean de la Péruse (1529–54), Olivier de Magny (1530–59), Amadis Jamyn (1538?–85), Jean Passerat (1534–1602), Philippe Desportes (1546–1606), Estienne Pasquier (1529–1615), Scévole de Sainte-Marthe (1536–1623), and Jean Bertaut (1552–1611). These subordinate members of the 'Pléiade' were no less devoted than the original members to sonnetteering. Of those in this second rank, Desportes was most popular in France as well as in England. Although many of Desportes's sonnets are graceful in thought and melodious in rhythm, most of them abound in overstrained conceits. Not only was Desportes a more slavish imitator of Petrarch than the members of the 'Pléiade,' but he encouraged numerous disciples to practice 'Petrarchism,' as the imitation of Petrarch was called, beyond healthful limits. Under the influence of Desportes the French sonnet became, during the latest years of the sixteenth century, little more than an empty and fantastic echo of the Italian.

Desportes
(1546–1606).

The following statistics will enable the reader to realise how closely the sonnetteering movement in France adumbrated that

---

(1492–1557), Bernardo Tasso (1493–1568), Luigi Tansillo (1510–68), Gabriello Fiamma (*d.* 1585), Torquato Tasso (1544–95), Luigi Groto (*fl.* 1570), Giovanni Battista Guarini (1537–1612), and Giovanni Battista Marino (1565–1625) (cf. Tiraboschi's *Storia della Letteratura Italiana*, 1770–82; Dr. Garnett's *History of Italian Literature*, 1897; and Symonds's *Renaissance in Italy*, edit. 1898, vols. iv. and vi.). The notes to Watson's *Passionate Centurie of Love*, published in 1582 (see p. 103, note 1, *supra*); to Davison's *Poetical Rhapsody*, edited by Mr. A. H. Bullen in 1891, and to the *Poems of Drummond of Hawthornden*, edited by Mr. W. C. Ward in 1894, give many illustrations of English sonnetteers' indebtedness to Serafino, Groto, Marino, Guarini, Tasso, and other Italian sonnetteers of the sixteenth century.

in England. The collective edition in 1584 of the works of Ronsard, the master of the ' Pléiade,' contains more than nine hundred separate sonnets arranged under such titles as ' Amours de Cassandre,' 'Amours de Marie,' 'Amours pour Astrée,' 'Amours pour Hélène'; besides 'Amours Divers' and 'Sonnets Divers,' complimentary addresses to friends and patrons. Du Bellay's 'Olive,' a collection of love sonnets, first published in 1549, reached a total of a hundred and fifty. 'Les Regrets,' Du Bellay's sonnets on general topics, some of which Edmund Spenser first translated into English, numbered in the edition of 1565 a hundred and eighty-three. De Baif published two long series of sonnets, entitled respectively ' Les Amours de Meline' (1552) and 'Les Amours de Francine' (1555). Amadis Jamyn was responsible for ' Les Amours d'Oriane,' ' Les Amours de Callirée,' and ' Les Amours d'Artemis ' (1575). Desportes's ' Premières Œuvres ' (1575), a very popular book in England, included more than three hundred sonnets — a hundred and fifty being addressed to Diane, eighty-six to Hippolyte, and ninety-one to Cleonice. Belleau brought out a volume of ' Amours ' in 1576 ; and Ponthus de Thyard produced in 1587 his ' Erreurs Amoureuses,' sonnets addressed to Pasithée.

Chief collections of French sonnets published between 1550 and 1584.

Among other collections of sonnets published by less known writers of the period, and arranged here according to date of first publication, were those of Guillaume des Autels, 'Amoureux Repos' (1553); Olivier de Magny, 'Amours, Soupirs,' &c. (1553, 1559); Louise Labé, ' Œuvres ' (1555); Jacques Tahureau, 'Odes, Sonnets,' &c. (1554, 1574) ; Claude de Billet, 'Amalthée,' a hundred and twenty-eight love sonnets (1561); Vauquelin de la Fresnaye, 'Foresteries' (1555 et annis seq.); Jacques Grévin, 'Olympe' (1561); Nicolas Ellain, 'Sonnets' (1561) ; Scévole de Sainte-Marthe, ' Œuvres Françaises ' (1569, 1579) ; Estienne de la Boétie, ' Œuvres ' (1572), and twenty-nine sonnets published with Montaigne's 'Essais' (1580) ; Jean et Jacques de la Taille, ' Œuvres ' (1573); Jacques de Billy, 'Sonnets Spirituels' (first series 1573, second series 1578); Estienne Jodelle, ' Œuvres Poétiques ' (1574); Claude de Pon-

Minor collections of French sonnets published between 1553 and 1605.

toux, 'Sonnets de L'Idée' (1579); Les Dames des Roches, 'Œuvres' (1579, 1584); Pierre de Brach, 'Amours d'Aymée' (*circa* 1580); Gilles Durant, 'Poésies' — sonnets to Charlotte and Camille (1587, 1594); Jean Passerat, 'Vers . . . d'Amours' (1597); and Anne de Marquet, who died in 1588, 'Sonnets Spirituels' (1605).[1]

---

[1] There are modern reprints of most of these books, but not of all. There is a good reprint of Ronsard's works, edited by M. P. Blanchemain, in *La Bibliothèque Elzévirienne*, 8 vols. 1867; the *Étude sur la Vie de Ronsard*, in the eighth volume, is useful. The works of Remy Belleau are issued in the same series. The writings of the seven original members of 'La Pléiade' are reprinted in *La Pléiade Française*, edited by Marty-Laveaux, 16 vols., 1866-93. Maurice Sève's *Délie* was reissued at Lyon in 1862. Pierre de Brach's poems were carefully edited by Reinhold Dezeimeris (2 vols Paris, 1862). A complete edition of Desportes's works, edited by Alfred Michiels, appeared in 1863. Prosper Blanchemain edited a reissue of the works of Louise Labé in 1875. The works of Jean de la Taille, of Amadis Jamyn, and of Guillaume des Autels are reprinted in *Trésor des Vieux Poètes Français* (1877 et annis seq.). See Ste.-Beuve's *Tableau Historique et Critique de la Poesie Français du XVIe Siècle* (Paris, 1893); Henry Francis Cary's *Early French Poets* (London, 1846); Becq de Fouquières's *Œuvres choisies des Poètes Français du XVIe Siècle contemporains avec Ronsard* (1880), and the same editor's selections from De Baif, Du Bellay, and Ronsard; Darmesteter et Hatzfeld's *Le Seizième Siècle en France — Tableau de la Littérature et de la Langue* (6th edit , 1897); and Petit de Julleville's *Histoire de la Langue et de la Littérature Française* (1897, iii. 136-260).

INDEX

The Theatre and builds the Globe Theatre, 37, 200; performs, with Shakespeare and Kemp, before Queen Elizabeth at Greenwich Palace, 43; his impersonation of the King in *Richard III*, 63; litigation of his heirs respecting the Globe and the Blackfriars theatres, 200; his income, 203, 219; creates the title-part in *Hamlet*, 222, 231; his reputation made in leading parts of the poet's tragedies, 264, 265; anecdote of the poet and, 265; the poet's bequest to, 276

Burgersdijk, Dr. L. A. J., translation in Dutch by, 352

Burghley, Lord, 375, 376, 378

Burton, Francis, bookseller, 399 *n* 2, 400

Butter, Nathaniel, 180, 241

C., E.,' sonnet by, resemblance in Shakespeare's treatment of the ravages of lust with this subject in, 153 *n* 1; his collection of sonnets, ' Emaricdulfe,' 436

Caliban, the character of, 253, 257, 258, and *notes*

Cambridge, *Hamlet* acted at, 224

Cambridge edition of Shakespeare, 324

Camden, William, 191

Campbell, Lord, on the poet's legal acquirements, 364

Campion, Thomas, on Barnes's verse, 133; his sonnet to Lord Walden, 140; sonnets in Harleian MS., 437 and *n* 3

Capell, Edward, reprint of *Edward III* in his ' Prolusions,' 71, 224; his edition of Shakespeare, 319; his works on the poet, 320

Cardenio, the lost play of, 258, 259

Carter, Rev. Thomas, on the alleged Puritan sympathies of Shakespeare's father, 10 *n*

Casteliones y Montisis, Lope de Vega's, 55 *n* 1

Castille, Constable of, entertainments in his honour at Whitehall, 233, 234

Castle, William, parish clerk of Stratford, 34

Catherine II (of Russia), adaptation of the *Merry Wives* and *King John* by, 352, 353

Cawood, Gabriel, publisher of ' Mary Magdalene's Funeral Tears,' 88 *n*

Cecil, Sir Robert, an allusion to the Earl of Southampton by, 143; his relations with Southampton, 379, 381, 382

' Centurie of Spiritual Sonnets, A,' Barnes's, 132

Cervantes, his ' Don Quixote' the foundation of lost play of *Cardenio*, 258; death of, 272 *n* 1

Chamberlain, the Lord, his company of players. *See* Hunsdon, first Lord and second Lord

Chamberlain, John, 149, 261 *n*

Chapman, George, plays on Biron's career by, 51 *n*; his *An Humorous Day's Mirth*, 51 *n*; his *Blind Beggar of Alexandria*, 51 *n*; his censure of sonnetteering, 106; the question of his rivalry with Shakespeare for Southampton's favour, 134, 135 *n*, 183; his translation of the ' Iliad,' 227; his sonnets to patrons, 388, 440 *n*; sonnets in praise of philosophy, 441

Charlecote Park, probably the scene of the poaching episode, 27, 28

Charles I, the poet's plays the ' closet companions' of his ' solitudes,' 329; his copy of the Second Folio, 312

Charles II, his copy of the Second Folio, 312

Châteaubriand, 349

Chaucer, the story of ' Lucrece ' in his ' Legend of Good Women,' 76; hints in his ' Knight's Tale,' for *Midsummer Night's Dream*, 162; the plot of *Troilus and Cressida* taken from his ' Troilus and Cresseid,' 227; plot of *The Two Noble Kinsmen* drawn from his ' Knight's Tale ' of Palamon and Arcite, 260

Chenier, Marie Joseph, sides with Voltaire in the Shakespearean controversy, 349

Chester, Robert, his ' Love's Martyr,' 183, 184 *n*

Chettle, Henry, the publisher, his

2 H

A NEW AND COMPLETE

CONCORDANCE

OR

Verbal Index to Words, Phrases, and Passages in the Dramatic Works of William Shakespeare, with a Supplementary Concordance to the Poems

BY

JOHN BARTLETT, A.M.

Fellow of the American Academy of Arts and Sciences
Author of "Familiar Quotations," etc.

1 volume. Medium Quarto. 1900 pp. $7.50 net.

" This *monumental concordance* of Shakespeare's plays and poems has not far from two thousand pages in the clearest of typography. . . . *No words of praise are too high* for the zeal and discrimination which have produced *this superb book* of reference." — *The Literary World.*

" A work without which no lover of Shakespeare can be content." — *The New York Times.*

" Mr. BARTLETT, whose 'Familiar Quotations' is by so much the best compilation of its kind ever made that it is not likely to be superseded, except by future expansion on its own lines, has here completed *another monumental work*, which is done once and for all. There have been concordances of Shakespeare before; *there will never be any need for another.*" — *The Philadelphia Times.*

" Like the other works which Professor BARTLETT has produced, the new concordance is *the best of its kind*, the compiler having adopted a plan which makes it more comprehensive than any other similar treatment of Shakespeare." — *The Cleveland Leader.*

" Mr. BARTLETT's great volume supplies absolute completeness and furnishes a Concordance to Shakespeare's Works that is *invaluable*, and that may perhaps never be improved upon. . . . Its accuracy is indisputable. . . . The finish of such a stupendous work as this is an event in the world of literature. That it should be so well done is a tribute to the painstaking patience and the skill and knowledge of Mr. BARTLETT, to whom all literature is known, and to whom the world is indebted for its best indexes. . . . The Concordance from a mechanical standpoint is perfect. The publishers have produced a really great piece of book-making The Concordance *should find room on the shelves of every private library in the country*, and no student or reader of Shakespeare, casual or constant, will fail to flank his volumes of the master's work with this concordance." — *The Cincinnati Commercial Gazette.*

" The work *merits large praise.* Although the type is fine it is clear. . . . The simplicity of its arrangement greatly facilitates the use of the work, and it certainly meets every need of which a reasonable student of Shakespeare can be conscious, and *it must practically monopolize the ground.* No less complete concordance of course can compete with it; and, as it covers the whole ground satisfactorily, and as no additions or alterations are likely to be made in Shakespeare's text, it is one of the few works which seem likely to remain unrivalled in the very nature of the case. It is something for which to be grateful that it is the work of a competent scholar like Mr. BARTLETT." — *The Congregationalist.*

THE MACMILLAN COMPANY

66 FIFTH AVENUE, NEW YORK